From Early Child Development to Human Development

Investing in Our Children's Future

Editor

Mary Eming Young

Education Sector

Human Development Network

THE WORLD BANK

Washington, D.C.

Proceedings of a World Bank Conference
on Investing in Our Children's Future

Washington, D.C., April 10–11, 2000

Library of Congress Cataloging-in-Publication Data *has been applied for.*

Contents

Foreword v

Acknowledgments ix

Chapter 1   Introduction and Overview 1
Mary Eming Young

I.   The Benefits of Investing in Young Children

Chapter 2   Early Child Development and
the Brain—the Base for Health, Learning,
and Behavior Throughout Life 23
J. Fraser Mustard

Chapter 3   From Child Development to
Human Development 63
Jacques van der Gaag

II.   Measuring the Early Opportunity Gap

Chapter 4   Standards of Care: Investments
to Improve Children's Educational Outcomes
in Latin America 81
J. Douglas Willms

Chapter 5   Ensuring a Fair Start for All
Children: The Case of Brazil 123
Mary Eming Young

III.   Evaluating the Effectiveness of Early Childhood Programs

Chapter 6   Investing in Effective Childcare
and Education: Lessons from Research 145
John M. Love, Peter Z. Schochet, and
Alicia L. Meckstroth

Chapter 7   Mapping and Documenting
            Effective Programming 195
            Judith L. Evans

Chapter 8   Effective Early Childhood Programs:
            The U.S. Head Start Experience 219
            Louisa B. Tarullo

Chapter 9   Elements of Quality in Home Visiting
            Programs: Three Jamaican Models 233
            Kerida Scott-McDonald

IV.   The Private Sector's Influence on the Public Sector

Chapter 10   Role of the Private Sector in Early
             Child Development 257
             Robert G. Myers

Chapter 11   Communities Can Make a Difference:
             Five Cases Across Continents 293
             Simone Kirpal

V.   Investing in the Future: Action and Policy

Chapter 12   Narrowing the Gap for
             Poor Children 363
             Enrique V. Iglesias and Donna E. Shalala

Chapter 13   The Political Challenge:
             Commitment and Cooperation 375
             *Eduardo A. Doryan, Kul C. Gautam, and
             William H. Foege*

Authors 393
Index 397

Foreword

A child's early years are critically important, for they provide the foundation for the rest of life, as an adolescent and as an adult. Children who are well nurtured can live well and create better societies for all. Yes, children are our future and by investing in them at their earliest ages we invest in everyone's human and economic development.

In April 2000, the World Bank hosted a global conference which addressed the benefits and challenges of investing in early child development (ECD). This landmark conference brought together the world's leading experts, academicians, practitioners, and policymakers to focus on various aspects of ECD. They represented nongovernmental organizations and other private-sector groups, government agencies, and multilateral and bilateral organizations. This volume contains the proceedings of the conference. With its publication, the World Bank hopes to encourage countries to adopt policies that target early child development, especially for children and families living in poverty, and to spark other groups and organizations to invest in ECD programs.

The reasons for focusing on children are more than traditional and still pertinent humanitarian concerns for those least able to look after themselves. New insights from neuroscience and the behavioral and social sciences underscore the importance of giving children a better chance in life. Nurturing them in their early years is vital for attacking the worst effects of poverty and may be an effective way to break the relentless, vicious cycle of poverty that, too often, crosses generations. Children who live in poverty cannot go to school, do not learn to read, will have difficulty finding a job, and will have little hope for their, and their children's, future. Poverty diminishes people's spiritual resources, peace of mind, dignity, and freedom to live fully. And, unfortunately, poverty is like a bad gene—it is inherited.

Studies repeatedly show that children who are born in poverty, live in unsanitary conditions, experience little mental stimulation or nurturing, and have poor nutrition in their first years are far more likely than richer children to grow up stunted in both body and mind. Science tells us that early child development is critical and marks a child for life. The development of a young child's brain affects physical and mental health, capacity to learn, and behavior throughout childhood and adult life. The wiring and sculpting of billions of neurons in the early years establish the base for developing competence and coping skills later. For nations, the first few years of a child's life have a multiplier effect. Young children who are well nurtured tend to do better in school and are more likely to develop the skills they will need to compete in a global economy. Investing in young children is an essential investment in human and economic development.

During the past generation, we have seen greater progress than at any other time in history. Life expectancy has increased more during the past 40 years than during the past 4,000 years. In today's world, the communications revolution holds out the promise of universal access to knowledge. In this world, 5.7 billion people participate and compete in a market economy, compared with 2.9 billion only 20 years ago. Yet, 100 million more people are living in poverty today than 10 years ago, and many of these are children.

- Most children born into poverty are malnourished and neglected and, hence, cannot attain their potential even before they enter primary school.
- 125 million primary-school aged children are not in school, and most are girls.
- Another 150 million children start primary school but drop out before they have completed 4 years of education.
- Almost one-half of the children in the least developed countries of the world do not have access to primary education.
- Nearly 1 billion people, or one-sixth of the world's population, are illiterate, and most are women.
- In the next 25 years, the world's population is expected to increase by 2 billion people, and most of this increase will be in developing countries where poor families are already struggling.

These statistics are discouraging, but they also indicate many opportunities for taking action. Early child development is one way to reverse the trends. ECD interventions and programs fundamentally offer all children a fair chance to compete and succeed in life. They help ensure that the competition is fair for all children by providing the equipment and training they need to get ahead. Even by age 6, children who are malnourished and have never had a book read to them face a playing field that is already unfair.

Education is a great equalizer if all children have an equal opportunity to take advantage of it. To reduce poverty and achieve universal access to primary education, organizations must come together in support of early child development. The World Bank has an important role to play, but the total effort is much larger than the World Bank's investment alone. A strategy of cooperation, interaction, and partnership among many organizations, governments, multinationals, private-sector institutions, and civil groups offers the best possibility for launching and sustaining broad action in early child development. Simply acknowledging that early child development is important or simply increasing resources for primary education are not sufficient. Specific goals, policies, and actions are needed to ensure that children can take full advantage of, and benefit fully from, the opportunities offered in primary school.

The message communicated at this conference is the same as that conveyed 4 years ago at the World Bank's first conference on early child development: "It is never too early to become involved but it can easily be too late." This message is even more urgent today because of the growing number of poor children and the accumulation of documented evidence showing that positive ECD interventions can make a difference. Across the globe, children offer us the promise of creating a better world, but we must act now to help them fulfill that promise.

Mamphela Ramphele
Managing Director,
The World Bank

Acknowledgments

This proceedings of the World Bank conference, "Investing in Our Children's Future," was only feasible with the support and contributions of many individuals. Thanks are first extended to the World Bank's senior management, starting with James D. Wolfensohn, President, and Eduardo A. Doryan, Vice President and Head, Human Development Network, for their support of children's issues and the early child development (ECD) program. Sincere thanks are given to Elaine Wolfensohn for her personal commitment and guidance at every stage in the planning of the conference and for her support of the Bank's ECD initiative. Special thanks are due to Ruth Kagia, Director, Education Sector, Human Development Network, for her support and guidance in planning and organizing the conference.

The conference brought together the world's leading experts, academicians, and practitioners from nongovernmental organizations and civil society, as well as policymakers from governments and multilateral and bilateral organizations. They focused on the benefits, effectiveness, and support of early child development—some of the same issues addressed at the World Bank's first conference on early child development and at the "Children First Forum" organized by the Task Force for Child Survival and Development, both of which were held at The Carter Presidential Center, Atlanta, Georgia, in April 1996. The issues may be the same, but are even more urgent today.

The conference benefited from the ongoing support of Bill Foege, Mark Rosenberg, John Gates, Conrad Ferrara, and Pamela Wuichet of the Collaborative Center for Child Wellbeing (formerly the Task Force for Child Survival and Development). The conference also benefited immensely from being embedded into the broader framework of the World Bank's Children's Week 2000, a week-long event organized in collaboration with the Child Labor and Street Children Teams of the Bank, which include Bona Kim, Zafiris Tzannatos, Catalina Villamizar, and Kate Schecter and are coordinated by Stephen Commins. In this framework, the conference participants had the opportunity to attend a series of events and workshops related to early child development, child labor, and street children. We also thank Vision, Strength and Artistic (VSA) Expression and their affiliates, for organizing and showcasing its programs and artists and for an exhibition of beautiful artwork created by disabled children from around the world, and Jennifer Dickson of Counterpart Canada, for facilitating the participation of Raffi, child advocate and singer, who premiered his song "It Takes a Village to Raise a Child" and shared his vision at the conference. Thank you, Raffi.

Thanks are also extended to the Multilateral Development Department, Royal Ministry of Foreign Affairs, Norway, and the Ministry of Foreign Affairs, the Netherlands, for partially funding preparation of the conference background papers. In addition, many thanks are due to the team that helped organize the conference: Simone R. Kirpal, Amber Surrency, Claudine Cobra, and Julie Wagshal in the Bank's Education Sector, Human Development Network, and Ruth Hubbell-McKey and Bethany Chirico of Ellsworth Associates. A special note of appreciation goes to Francis James Dobbs, Christopher M. Walsh, and Peter Knight for liaison with the media and guidance on the design of media messages. Special thanks also to Gaby Fujimoto-Gómez and Carolina Gomez, from the Organization of American States (OAS), for coordinating the participation of ECD practitioners from Latin America; to Helen Keith, Early Childhood Services Planning and Development, for coordinating with participants from the Caribbean and providing guidance to develop the SERVOL case study; and to Marito Garcia and Susan Opper in the World Bank's African Region, Venita Kaul and Ward Heneveld on the Bank's India country team, and Antonio Lim in the Bank's Europe and Central Asia Region, for supporting the participation of several delegates from the countries in their respective regions.

Thanks also to all 280 participants from forty-eight countries who made the conference happen and, in particular, to Joan Lombardi of the Bush Center in Child Development and Social Policy, Yale University, for guiding the planning of the conference and facilitating the invitation to Secretary Donna E. Shalala of the U.S. Department of Health and Human Services, and to Ricardo Morán of the Inter-American Development Bank (IDB) for facilitating the invitation to Enrique V. Iglesias, President, IDB, who were the conference keynote speakers. Thanks also to Marjorie Newman-Williams and Waheed Hassan of the United Nation's Children's Fund (UNICEF) for facilitating the participation of Kul C. Gautam, Deputy Executive Director, UNICEF. Special thanks to Robert Myers, Maris O'Rourke, and Heather Weiss, and to Margaret Marland, Minister for Children of Ontario, Canada, for their cooperation in chairing the conference sessions.

The conference featured presentations on the role of private initiatives in influencing public policy. The participants benefited from George Soros' shared insights on his philanthropic activities and support of ECD programs worldwide. In addition, field practitioners from the private sector and civil society shared their experiences with their programs. Thanks in particular to Peter Hesse, who described his 10-year program in Haiti; Sister Ruth Montrichard, who spoke of her 25 years of dedication to the SERVOL program in Trinidad; Elizabeth Lorant, who described her work with the Soros Foundation beginning in the 1980s; and Kathy Bartlett, who described the Aga Khan Foundation's Madrasa program in East Africa.

Special acknowledgments are due to key partners in the support of early child development: UNICEF; the United Nations Educational, Scientific, and Cultural Organization (UNESCO); the World Health Organization (WHO); the Pan American Health Organization (PAHO); the U.S. Agency for International Development (USAID); IDB; the Asian Development Bank; OAS; and nongovernmental organizations, including Bernard van Leer Foundation, Aga Khan

Foundation, Save the Children USA, Christian Children's Fund, World Organization for Early Child Education, Academy of Educational Development (AED), World Vision, and the Consultative Group on Early Child Care and Development.

Many, many thanks to Linda M. Richardson for the text editing; without her persistence, meticulous efforts, and superb skills, the timely preparation of this proceedings would not have been possible.

Chapter 1

Introduction and Overview

Mary Eming Young

Early child development (ECD) programs that comprehensively address children's basic needs—health, nutrition, and emotional and intellectual development—foster development of capable and productive adults. And, early interventions can alter the lifetime trajectories of children who are born poor or are deprived of the opportunities for growth and development available to those more fortunate.

These facts are well known today and are founded on evidence from the neurobiological, behavioral, and social sciences and the evaluation of model interventions and large, publicly funded programs. The short- and long-term benefits of ECD programs for children are enormous. By providing basic health care, adequate nutrition, and nurturing and stimulation in a caring environment, ECD interventions help ensure children's progress in primary school, continuation through secondary school, and successful entry into the work force.

The economic returns to investing in young children are high. But, there is an even more compelling reason for underscoring the importance of the early years: Early interventions help children escape poverty. Among the world's 6 billion people, 2.8 billion live on less than US$2 a day, and 1.2 billion live on less than $1 a day (World Bank 2000). Within every country, there is a massive imbalance between rich and poor.

Disparities in children's development mirror these economic disparities, and poverty is associated with poor social indicators, especially for poor children. Without the basic nutrition, health care, and stimulation needed to promote healthy growth, many poor children enter school not ready to learn. These children do poorly in class, repeat grades, and drop out at high rates. They are at a disadvantage when they enter the workplace, earning the lowest wages, and, as parents, pass their poverty on to their children. Giving children a better chance is not only vital for attacking the worst effects of poverty, but also may be an effective way of breaking the relentless, vicious cycle of poverty transmitted across generations.

Core aspects of poverty are targeted in the goals for international development recently set forth by the development community. The goals are: reducing by half the proportion of people living in extreme poverty by 2015; a two-thirds decline in infant and under-5 mortality, and a three-fourths decline in maternal mortality; universal primary education for all by 2015; gender equality in education by 2005; national strategies for sustainable development by 2005; and ensuring that the current loss of environmental resources is reversed globally and nationally by 2015.

The goals in poverty, health, and education are mutually reinforcing. Higher school enrollment, especially for girls, reduces poverty. Reductions in mortality, gained through better basic health care, increases enrollment and performance in school, which reduces poverty. As a great equalizer, education diminishes the differences between rich and poor—but only if all children have an equal chance to take advantage of education.

To meet the goal for universal primary education, poor children must be given a fair chance to benefit from school. In unequal societies that have high levels of poverty, a level playing field even at age 6, or by the time a child enters school, may already be unfair for poor children. By intervening early, ECD programs offer all children the possibility to fully benefit from school and to succeed in the marketplace. In this way, ECD interventions help reconcile countries' goals for equity and efficiency (Birdsall 1999).

Early Child Development: Scientific Evidence

The importance of early child development has been noted by economists, behavioral scientists, educators, neuroscientists, and biologists. Fogel, the 1993 Nobelist in economics, states that the quality of early child development has a significant effect on the quality of populations and influences health outcomes in adult life (Fogel 1999). In an analysis of factors contributing to inequality in health, conducted for the U.K. government, Acheson (1998) finds that, although remediable risk factors affecting health occur throughout life, childhood is a critical and vulnerable state in which poor socioeconomic circumstances have lasting effects. He notes that, because adverse outcomes (e.g., mental illness, short stature, obesity, delinquency, and unemployment) result from early adverse environments, policies that reduce early adverse influences may have multiple benefits for a child's entire life course and into the next generation.

During early childhood, patterns of behavior, competency, and learning are initiated and established; socioenvironmental factors begin to modify genetic inheritance; brain cells grow in abundance; and biological pathways for handling stress arise. Increasing evidence from various sources (Rutter, Giller, and Hagell 1998; Tremblay 1999) documents that early-life conditions "have a long reach" for behavior, particularly antisocial behavior, delinquency, and crime. Longitudinal studies clearly show that most seriously antisocial adolescents and adults exhibit behavioral problems during childhood and that the origin of these problems traces back to fetal development and infancy (Karr-Morse and Wiley 1997).

The early years also affect children's learning, particularly their literacy and mathematics skills. Beginning at birth, most children are immersed in the language and literacy of their immediate family. As infants respond to their parents and siblings, speech emerges naturally and, by 12–18 months, toddlers usually begin to establish a recognizable vocabulary, which grows exponentially over the next few years as language structures emerge and speech and language continue to develop. These infant and toddler years are critical for establishing the foundation for future literacy development (Willms 1999). In addition, recent research shows that children's early mathematical capabilities are considerably differentiated by social class during these early years, when the neurological circuitry that underpins these capabilities also develops the most rapidly (Case, Griffin, and Kelly 1999).

Commenting on gene–environment interactions, neuroscientists claim that individuals' "skills, abilities, dreams, and prejudices" result from their genetic history and the particular physical and social environmental stimuli to which they are exposed. They note that inadequate and inappropriate social and emotional experiences in the early environment can compromise higher-level neural systems that provide the information needed to bond, imitate, and generally respond in socially appropriate ways (Cynader and Frost 1999). Research shows that, during key developmental periods, the amount of gray matter in some brain areas can nearly double within as little as a year and that this process is followed by a drastic loss of tissue as unneeded cells are purged and the brain continues to organize itself. By the age of 3 years, the brains of children are 2.5 times more active than the brains of adults, and they remain this way throughout the first decade of life (Shore 1997). Extensive rewiring continues throughout childhood. Although growth spurts occur in the brain even beyond early childhood, the rule for brain development appears to be "use it or lose it" during the early critical periods (Giedd and others 1999).

Stress also plays a role in early brain development. Studies of the biological pathways involved in reactions to stress show that the stresses to which individuals are exposed early in life may modify their ability to moderate and control responses to stress later in life (Cynader and Frost 1999); that the quality of sensory stimulation in early life helps shape the brain's endocrine and immune pathways; and that adults who were poorly nurtured in early life tend to retain sustained levels of stress hormones long after situations that cause arousal. Studies also show that mothers' handling of young animals can "set the program" for responses of the hypothalamus-pituitary-adrenal pathway to stress throughout life and that the absence of maternal care produces abnormal stress reactions later in life (McCain and Mustard 1999).

Implications for ECD

Brain development in the early years affects physical and mental health, learning, and behavior throughout life. What, how, and how much children learn later in school largely depends on the social and emotional competence and cognitive skills they develop in the first few years of life. The development of a young child's brain depends on environmental stimulation, especially the quality of care and interaction the child receives. The quality of care received, including nutrition, health care, and stimulation, during the first few years can have a long-lasting effect on brain development. When these basic needs are met, children can gain improved critical thinking skills, self-confidence, problem-solving abilities, and capacity to cooperate with others. These skills will determine children's overall school performance and possibly alter their developmental trajectory (Ramey and Ramey 1998).

Solutions to meet the intellectual and social development needs of young children are available, but need to be adopted more broadly and intensively. The knowledge base to support large-scale investments in ECD interventions is more than sufficient. These investments will pave the way for improving individuals' health, mental and physical performance, and productivity and, in a major way, help minimize or even prevent a host of related economic and social problems, including juvenile delinquency, teenage pregnancy, and social violence.

Do ECD Interventions Work?

ECD programs and interventions can improve children's chances in the world. Young children who participate in early interventions that include nutrition, health care, and nurturing have lower rates of school dropout, higher school enrollment, and higher achievement from primary grades to adulthood. The examples of effective ECD interventions across the world's regions are many, and some have been evaluated to measure their efficacy. Some of the best known examples include the Perry Preschool Project, the North Carolina Abecedarian Project, the Infant Health and Development Program, and the Head Start and Early Head Start programs in the United States; the Integrated Child Development Service (ICDS) in India; and the Initial Education Project in Mexico.

Studies of these interventions illuminate the particular benefits of ECD. For example, children who participated in ICDS scored higher on intellectual aptitude tests and had superior school attendance, academic performance, and general behavior than children who did not participate (Chaturvedi and others 1987). ICDS is the largest ECD program in the world, serving 32 million children. In Brazil, poor children who attended 1 year of preschool stayed in primary school 0.4 years longer than children who did not attend preschool (Barros and Mendonça 1999). For each year of preschool, children had a 7–12 percent increase in potential lifetime income, with the larger increases gained by children from families whose parents had the least amount of schooling (Barros and Mendonça 1999). The Abecedarian Project showed that the likelihood of children being held back in the same grade during primary school declined by almost 50 percent when children attended ECD programs (Ramey and others 2000). Studies also show that children from families with the least education derive the greatest cognitive and social benefits, and the effect of early interventions appears to be long-lasting. Gains such as these are real and verifiable, and they prove beyond a doubt that early interventions work.

The Next Step

Science clearly identifies why and when ECD programs should be implemented. And, ECD researchers and practitioners have determined, in large part, what programs are effective and for which groups they are most needed. These considerations can all be further broadened and refined, but the critical questions now for the global community are how to implement ECD interventions effectively and how to take these programs to scale.

That is, how can governments utilize the knowledge gained from science to define policies that will benefit young children? How can existing scientific knowledge about early child development be translated into interventions that benefit large numbers of young children deprived of their most basic needs from birth and, even, in utero? Which public policies are needed (e.g., specifically for poor and otherwise disadvantaged children)? What are the elements of program effectiveness? How can programs be brought to scale? What are the lessons learned in implementing these programs? And how can public-private partnerships be encouraged?

The next step is to address these questions in global venues and to solicit continued, sustained investments in early child development for all nations. Continued efforts are needed to evaluate ECD programs and to promote, initiate, and implement effective ECD programs throughout the world and especially for impoverished children.

Investing in Our Children's Future

To stimulate discussion of the questions posed above and investments in early child development, the World Bank hosted an international conference, entitled "Investing in Our Children's Future," in Washington, D.C., on April 10–11, 2000. The conference participants reviewed the state of knowledge on the benefits and effectiveness of early interventions, addressed the role and influence of the private sector, emphasized the importance of narrowing the gap for poor children, and highlighted the potential political and economic gains from investing in ECD. This volume contains the proceedings of the conference. The chapters consist of papers developed for or subsequent to the conference.

The volume builds on and extends previous and similar efforts, including an earlier conference hosted by the Bank, entitled "Early

Child Development: Investing in the Future." This conference was held at The Carter Presidential Center, Atlanta, Georgia, in April 1996, and the proceedings were published (Young 1997). Both conferences engaged representatives of governments, nongovernmental organizations, foundations, academia, and multilateral and bilateral agencies in interactive discussions and presentations on the importance of investing in young children.

The present volume is organized into five parts: The Benefits of Investing in Young Children, Measuring the Early Opportunity Gap, Evaluating the Effectiveness of Early Childhood Programs, The Private Sector's Influence on the Public Sector, and Investing in the Future: Action and Policy. Twelve chapters are included. The authors describe current understanding and suggest areas for future study and action. The contributions reflect their extensive research and practical experience.

The Benefits of Investing in Young Children

Two chapters in part I summarize the individual and societal benefits of investing in young children. In "Early Child Development and the Brain: The Base for Health, Learning, and Behavior Throughout Life," J. Fraser Mustard conveys current research and research findings on brain development. He notes historical evidence which suggests that the relationship between economic growth and improved health since the beginning of the industrial revolution is linked to improved outcomes for children associated with increased prosperity. He then reviews basic research on biological pathways; animal studies of development and function, gene–environment interactions, and immune effects; and population-based human studies of socioenvironmental effects and educational experiences—all of which substantiate the importance of early childhood. Mustard describes the benefits of several intervention efforts and highlights the relevance of ECD programs for developed countries, such as Canada, as well as developing countries. He emphasizes that good ECD programs should be available for all population sectors and can improve the quality of society by reducing inequalities in health, competence, and coping skills.

In "From Child Development to Human Development," Jacques van der Gaag defines the linkage between early child development and human development. He provides a brief history of development economics, commenting on the interests of Nobel laureates in economics to illustrate the historical shift from developing planning models to investing in people. Van der Gaag then describes four critical pathways—education, health, social capital, and equality—linking early child development to human development, through economic growth. He summarizes in chart form the immediate and long-term benefits of ECD programs for children, adults, and society in each pathway, and he concludes that well-executed and well-targeted ECD programs are initiators of human development and investments in the future of a nation.

Measuring the Early Opportunity Gap

Two chapters in part II address the need to measure inequalities in early child development and to target ECD programs effectively. In "Standards of Care: Investments to Improve Children's Educational Outcomes in Latin America," J. Douglas Willms summarizes the findings of the Primer Estudio Internacional Comparativo (PEIC), the first international study of school outcomes in Latin America which utilized common tests and questionnaires across (13) countries. He describes the concept of socioeconomic gradients and reviews results which show that the gradients, school outcomes, and school achievement profiles vary widely among countries in the region and that the gradients are related to inequalities in society and children's developmental outcomes. Based on an analysis of the data, Willms presents a framework to help policymakers evaluate and monitor school outcomes. This framework includes a definition of "vulnerable" children and standards of care for superior schooling; accounts for sector (private or public) and urbanicity; and incorporates key considerations for low-income countries. Willms suggests that these countries could reduce the risk for children associated with low parental education by one-half if they achieved the standards set forth.

In "Ensuring a Fair Start for All Children: The Case of Brazil," Mary Eming Young offers a special analysis of Brazil as an example of the potential implications of ECD policies to reduce inequality. She begins by summarizing the improved outcomes for vulnerable children in several ECD interventions in the United States as evidence to support investments in comprehensive programs, to reduce poverty, build human capital, and strengthen overall development. Young then summarizes the results of a recent World Bank study conducted by the Institute of Applied Economic Research in Brazil. This study reinforces findings presented by Willms concerning inequalities of early education, and investments in this education, for children who are poor or reside in rural areas. The evaluation of the effects of preschool education in Brazil supports many other studies, which show that attendance in preschool correlates with increased schooling overall, reduced grade repetition, and future earning capacity. Importantly, the gains of preschool education for children of illiterate parents appear to be higher than for children of educated parents. Overall, the calculation for Brazil yields a 2:1 benefit-cost ratio. Further, 1 year of preschool attendance results in a 7–12 percent increase in future earnings.

Evaluating the Effectiveness of Early Childhood Programs

Four chapters in part III address the question: What constitutes quality? In "Investing in Effective Childcare and Education: Lessons from Research," John M. Love, Peter Z. Schochet, and Alicia L. Meckstroth review research on the ingredients of quality. They identify two important ingredients—classroom structure (e.g., child–staff ratio, supportive services, staff characteristics) and classroom dynamics (e.g., positive teacher and child behaviors, effective teacher–child interactions, stability and continuity). They also highlight eight supporting factors, which include teacher education, in-service training, experience, continuity, and compensation; experienced and trained supervisors and directors; community partnerships; and safe and appropriate physical space. Studies of center- and family-based childcare, which are summarized in a useful chart at the end of the chapter, indicate important modifying factors associated with positive outcomes. These factors include lower child–staff ratios, smaller group sizes, appropriate caregiving, developmentally appropriate practices, and caregiver responsiveness. Benefits associated with higher-quality childcare include improved language, enhanced social skills, reduced behavior problems, and increased cooperation. Based on this information, the authors highlight five types of investments as most important for enhancing children's early development: well-trained, motivated, and committed staff; safe, sanitary, and accessible facilities; child–staff ratios and group sizes that foster appropriate teacher–child interactions; consistent supervision; and staff development to ensure continuing and improving quality. They conclude by calling for additional quantitative studies of quality that utilize contemporaneous, longitudinal, and pre-post designs.

In "Mapping and Documenting Effective Programming," Judith L. Evans describes the Effectiveness Initiative (EI), a 5-year, qualitative study of ten ECD programs. The aim is to better understand why programs are effective for diverse participants, communities, and cultures. By examining the context of the ten programs in depth, the participants are "mapping" the dimensions of effectiveness and identifying patterns of effectiveness across settings. Evans describes the ten programs; the organization, assumptions, and status of EI; the qualitative research tools that are being used (e.g., structured questions, analogies, storytelling, interviews); and the qualitative research strategy adopted (i.e., embedded communications). She notes the advantages of qualitative research for discerning and describing differences, identifying patterns, gaining intuitive understanding, focusing on process, and validating programming decisions. Evans urges that qualitative reviews and evaluations be built into all ECD efforts to ensure that scarce resources are invested wisely in effective programs.

In the next chapter, Louisa B. Tarullo focuses on one U.S. program, Head Start. In "Effective Early Childhood Programs: The U.S. Head Start Experience," Tarullo describes the program's initiative of program performance measures, launched in 1995, and the Family and Child Experiences Survey (FACES), a central part of the initiative.

Data collected in the survey are being used to assess outcomes and refine the overall program. The conceptual framework for measuring program performance links process and outcome measures for Head Start children and families. Tarullo depicts the framework in pyramid form. The ultimate outcome measure is "child's social competence," and five objectives are identified to support this outcome. Multiple performance measures are defined for each objective. Tarullo also depicts the study design for FACES and reports key findings from the 1997–98 follow-up. The data show that Head Start can enhance children's growth and development; strengthen families as primary nurturers of children; provide high-quality educational, health, and nutritional services to children; and improve children's outcomes (e.g., higher vocabulary scores). These data have been used to document and communicate Head Start's effects to the legislature and public and to improve the program further. Tarullo notes that the data are important evidence of the value of investments in early child development.

In "Elements of Quality in Home Visiting Programs: Three Jamaican Models," Kerida Scott-McDonald notes the overwhelming disadvantages of neglect, abuse, and inappropriate care experienced by young children in poor Jamaican communities. She comments that, for the one in three children under age 4 who live in poverty in Jamaica, home-based early childhood programs offer perhaps the greatest hope of breaking the cycle of poverty. Scott-McDonald commends Jamaica for achieving 85 percent preschool coverage for all 4–5 year olds, but notes that day-care coverage for infants and children from birth to age 3 is only about 14 percent. She identifies and describes twelve elements of quality in three home visiting programs in Jamaica that are increasing poor families' access to ECD interventions and, ultimately, building social capital. Scott-McDonald also comments on issues and concerns that still need to be addressed in Jamaica. She concludes that the greatest overall challenge for the home visiting programs is to ensure full institutionalization. Scott-McDonald argues that formal programs are too expensive for poor families and may be culturally irrelevant or insensitive to families' needs. She emphasizes that public-private partnerships are needed to take the home-based programs to scale and to integrate them into the nation's delivery of social services.

The Private Sector's Influence on the Public Sector

In part IV, two chapters consider the private sector's involvement in early child development. In "Role of the Private Sector in Early Child Development," Robert G. Myers illuminates the important and significant role that the private sector can have in improving children's development. He clarifies the terminology used to refer to early child development, presents six arguments for societies to invest in ECD programs and the implications for the private sector, and defines and depicts the dimensions and components of the private sector as related to early childcare and education. The broad view of the private sector adopted by Myers includes small, medium, and large business organizations; the variety of social organizations (e.g., community groups, nongovernmental organizations and private voluntary organizations, churches, philanthropies), and private individuals. These components can, and do, provide or support various ECD services, training, and materials. Myers goes on to review the reasons given for advocating private versus public care and education (e.g., availability of resources, cost-effectiveness, accountability, quality, equity) and suggests ways for increasing private-sector involvement in early childhood activities. He notes that the opportunities for becoming involved are many, and he encourages two components, business organizations and adults without children, to become much more involved in early childcare and education.

In "Communities Can Make a Difference: Five Case Studies," Simone Kirpal highlights the role of communities in early child development. She presents five examples of ECD programs around the world that give priority to extensive involvement of the local community, to create ownership and assure successful, cost-effective, and sustainable programs. The cases exemplify how effective ECD programs can involve local communities to achieve sustainability and how private-public partnerships can enhance the potential for taking the programs to scale. The five cases are the Montessori Preschool Project in Haiti; the Mother-Child Day Care Center Services in Uganda; SERVOL in Trinidad and Tobago; the Aga Khan Foundation's efforts in Kenya, Uganda, and Zanzibar (the Madrasa Resource Centers) and in Pakistan (Improving Pre- and Primary Education); and the Step by Step program in Central and Eastern Europe, the Former Soviet Union, Haiti, Mongolia, and South Africa. In her introduction to the cases, Kirpal describes seven essential features of a successful ECD program. These include a child-centered approach, parental involvement and family support, community ownership, cultural and financial sustainability, training and capacity building, integration within a broader development framework, and private-public partnership. She notes that the goal of any community development program should be to enable a process that will be maintained after outside funders leave. Involving communities from the outset and adopting a partnership approach that emphasizes the full participation of parents, families, and community members are necessary to begin this process.

Investing in the Future: Action and Policy

The two chapters in part V move the discussion to another level, from reviewing the data available to taking action and making policy. In the first chapter, Enrique V. Iglesias and Donna E. Shalala plead for a focus on children who are most vulnerable—the poor and disadvantaged. Derived from their keynote addresses at the conference, "Narrowing the Gap for Poor Children" relates how poverty is transmitted between generations and the steps that can be taken to break the cycle. Iglesias and Shalala urge communities and government to work together and to combine their resources to intervene effectively. The U.S. Head Start and Early Head Start programs are cited as an example of programs that are providing important lessons about government-sponsored, community-based early child development. Iglesias and Shalala argue that even modest investments in programs that involve parents, schools, and local health organizations can have broad impact for society, by breaking the cycle of poverty and lessening related effects such as violence, criminal behavior, and mental illness. They list six lessons from the Head Start experience: The earlier intervention begins, the better; quality counts; quality early childhood education begins with teacher training; parents must be involved and accommodated; early childhood education must be integrated with other needs; and government should make early childhood education a national laboratory and catalyst for change. Iglesias and Shalala conclude that the most important reason for investing in programs such as Head Start or quality childcare is to "even up the odds" for poor children. They emphasize that the time has come to narrow the gap between what can be done and what is being done for poor children.

In the final chapter, Eduardo A. Doryan, Kul C. Gautam, and William H. Foege address "The Political Challenge: Commitment and Cooperation." Derived from their remarks on the political and policy aspects of early child development, made at the conference, this chapter considers the societal benefits and constraints to investing in ECD programs and the political challenge for doing so. The authors emphasize that society can be transformed through ECD efforts that help realize the human potential, assure and protect human rights, foster democracy, and reduce poverty. They note that political decisions favoring early child development may be thwarted by the immediate costs of ECD programs (in contrast with the long-term gains, well after politicians have left office) and difficulties in integrating ECD programs into other services provided by different government agencies or sectors. The distance and time between a decision and an effect are highlighted as two barriers to good decisionmaking. Doryan, Gautam, and Foege emphasize that, despite these constraints, government has an essential role to play in early child development and that policymakers must consider the power, position, and perception of all stakeholders when designing or implementing ECD programs. They cite six steps for effective government action and five "rules" for investing a nation's resources in early child development. They agree that the time to act is now, and they urge the building of a global coalition to capture the enthusiasm of communities, the commitment of political leaders, and the passion of donors for early child development.

Conclusion

ECD programs are fundamentally about providing all children, who are born unknowingly into the game of life, a fair chance to succeed. Even by age 3 or 6, so many children are faced with so many obstacles. The field of play for them is not level and, for a lifetime, they will struggle uphill. Despite malnutrition, disease, neglect, and abuse, they strive to live and want to learn. Is this fair? Cannot the world offer them more?

Most parents do their best to help their children have a fair chance in school and at work. But many parents themselves need help, for they are struggling too. Communities, governments, and societies can band together to give all children and families a fair chance—to provide the childcare and education programs needed for those without them, to provide assistance for families to benefit from them, and to make sure that all programs are of high quality and effective. As the world becomes more complex and the marketplace becomes even more global, nations need to ensure their survivability by looking after their children so that both can participate and compete effectively in the world economy.

How is equal opportunity created? In most countries, education is the great equalizer, but only if all children have equal opportunities to take advantage of education. Children who live in poverty in any country do not have equal access. If educational facilities are available, they are of lesser quality than in more affluent areas, and poor children often have to forego education to work and bring income into the family. Many poor children do not even have family support and are on the streets earning their own way at very early ages.

Market reforms make physical and human capital assets more valuable, which poor families all too often do not have. Governments must be called upon to supplement these conventional reforms with more aggressive policies and programs to augment the assets of the poor and to ensure that they too can exploit new market opportunities. Placing a premium on policies and programs targeting early childhood is an obvious first choice because these efforts engender a lifetime of improvement for the children and families benefiting from them. The poorer the families are, and the more unequal the society is, the greater need there is for governments to channel taxes and other public resources to ECD interventions that can stop the intergenerational transmission of poverty, which undermines the development of any nation (Birdsall 1999).

Each country in the world needs to invest in the future of its children, and the private sector must participate in this investment. Private businesses and organizations have important roles to play and can influence government to take the right steps. Targeted investments in early child development by private-public partnerships will help prepare all children to learn and succeed and to develop into healthier, more productive adults.

Continued evaluation of the effectiveness of ECD programs will provide the guidance needed for making good investments. The monitoring and evaluation of programs for their efficacy, efficiency, and benefit-cost furnishes critical information for making policy decisions about which types of programs to support and which communities or populations to target. As with any investment, financial costs will be weighed against potential benefits and feasibility of implementation. The challenge ahead is to fund ECD programs that can cost-effectively improve the lives of children and families at risk.

In his closing remarks at the conference, Foege specifically challenged the international community to deliberately plan a global coalition to fund ECD initiatives that would promote, measure, and improve children's well-being. This coalition could be assembled similar to the new Global Alliance for Vaccines and Immunization and would include, in each country, a focal responsibility for child development.

By placing children at the center of the global agenda to reduce poverty, we can "be the first generation to think both as nationals of our countries and as global citizens in an ever-shrinking and more connected planet"—an opportunity and a challenge for us recently noted by James D. Wolfensohn (2001). As he eloquently states, "Our children will inherit the world we create. The issues are urgent. The future for our children will be shaped by the decisions we make and the courage and leadership we show today."

References

Acheson, D. 1998. *Independent Inquiry into Inequalities in Health: Report.* London: The Stationery Office.

Barros, R.P. de, and R. Mendonça. 1999. *Costs and Benefits of Pre-school Education in Brazil.* Background study commissioned to IPEA by the World Bank. Rio de Janeiro: Institute of Applied Economic Research.

Birdsall, N. 1999. Investing in Children: The Role of the State in Unequal Societies. Remarks presented at a seminar on Breaking the Poverty Cycle: Investing in Early Childhood, Annual Meeting of the Boards of Governors of the Inter-American Development Bank and the Inter-American Investment Corporation, Paris, France, March 14, 1999. [www.iadb.org/sds/soc]

Case, R., S. Griffin, and W.M. Kelly. 1999. Socioeconomic Gradients in Mathematical Ability and Their Responsiveness to Intervention during Early Childhood. In D.P. Keating and C. Hertzman, eds., *Developmental Health and the Wealth of Nations.* New York: Guilford Press.

Chaturvedi, E., B.C. Srivastava, J.V. Singh, and M. Prasad. 1987. Impact of Six Years Exposure to ICDS Scheme on Psycho-social Development. *Indian Pediatrics* 24:153–60.

Cynader, M.S., and B.J. Frost. 1999. Mechanisms of Brain Development: Neuronal Sculpting by the Physical and Social Environment. In D.P. Keating and C. Hertzman, eds., *Developmental Health and the Wealth of Nations.* New York: Guilford Press.

Fogel, R.W. 1999. Catching Up With the Economy. *American Economic Review* 89(1):1–21.

Giedd, J.N., J. Blumenthal, N.D. Jeffries, F.X. Castellanos, H. Liu, and A. Zijdenbos. 1999. Brain Development during Childhood and Adolescence: A Longitudinal MRI Study. *Nature Neuroscience* 2(10):861–3.

Karr-Morse, R., and M.S. Wiley. 1997. *Ghosts from the Nursery: Tracing the Roots of Violence.* New York: Atlantic Monthly Press.

McCain, M.N., and J.F. Mustard. 1999. Early Years Study: Reversing the Real Brain Drain. Toronto: Publications Ontario.

Ramey, C.T., F.A. Campbell, M. Burchinal, M.L. Skinner, D.M. Gardner, and S. L. Ramey. 2000. Persistent Effects of Early Childhood Education on High-Risk Children and Their Mothers. *Applied Developmental Science* 4(1):2–14.

Ramey, C.T., and S.L. Ramey. 1998. Prevention of Intellectual Disabilities: Early Interventions to Improve Cognitive Development. *Preventive Medicine* 27:224–32.

Rutter, M., H. Giller, and A. Hagell. 1998. *Antisocial Behavior by Young People.* Cambridge: Cambridge University Press.

Shore, R. 1997. *Rethinking the Brain — New Insights into Early Development.* Families and Work Institute. New York, N.Y.

Tremblay, R.E. 1999. When Children's Social Development Fails. In D.P. Keating and C. Hertzman, eds., *Developmental Health and the Wealth of Nations.* New York: Guilford Press.

Willms, D. 1999. Quality and Inequality in Children's Literacy: The Effects of Families, Schools, and Communities. In D. P. Keating and C. Hertzman, eds., *Developmental Health and the Wealth of Nations.* New York: Guilford Press.

Wolfensohn, J.D. 2001. The Challenges of Globalization. The Role of the World Bank. Address to the Bundestag. Berlin, Germany, April 2, 2001.

World Bank. 2000. *World Development Report 2000/2001, Attacking Poverty.* New York: Oxford University Press.

Young, M.E., ed. 1997. *Early Child Development: Investing in our Children's Future.* International Congress Series 1137. Amsterdam: Elsevier Science B.V.

Part I

The Benefits of Investing in Young Children

Chapter 2

Early Child Development and the Brain—the Base for Health, Learning, and Behavior Throughout Life

J. Fraser Mustard

For most mammals that have been studied in detail, the conditions influencing physical development and behavior in the early stage of life have a significant effect on the later stages. Although the importance of the early years of life for the health and coping skills of many mammals has been recognized, the importance for human development and health is still controversial (Bruer 1999; Kagan 1998; Keating and Hertzman 1999). The emerging understanding of the influence of the social and physical environment (water quality, secure physical environment, good nutrition, and excellent nurturing) in the early years of human development on risks for physical and mental health problems and competence and coping skills in adult life has led to proposals that investments in mothers and children will reduce inequalities in development and health in adult life (Acheson 1998; Keating and Hertzman 1999; McCain and Mustard 1999).

This knowledge, coupled with the increasing evidence that the early period of child development affects cognition, learning, and behavior in the later stages of life (Keating and Hertzman 1999; McCain and Mustard 1999; Wickelgren 1999), is creating a broader consensus about the fundamental importance of the early years of development. Much of this evidence comes from research in the natural and social sciences involving historical studies, neuroscience, genetics, longitudinal studies of birth cohorts, population epidemiology, cross-sectional studies, and randomized trials of the effects of improved support for early child development on later stages of life.

One of the challenges is to combine the knowledge from the natural sciences and the social sciences. In his book *Consilience: The Unity of Knowledge,* Wilson (1998) sets out the difficulties of integrating knowledge about humans from the natural and social sciences when the interpretation involves the beliefs and values of a society and the different frameworks, beliefs, and cultures of intellectual disciplines. This chapter addresses early child development and health, competence, and coping skills in adult life from the perspective of various disciplines in the natural and social sciences. The sections present historical evidence, research findings from biological and animal studies and from epidemiological and longitudinal studies in humans, and a case example of a new early child development (ECD) initiative in Canada.

Historical Evidence

One of the striking changes in Western countries has been the effect of the industrial revolution on the prosperity and health of populations in these countries. Fogel (1994), McKeown (1976), and others (Steckel and Floud 1997) have tried to assess the cause of the remarkable decline in mortality following the start of the industrial revolution.

In his study of Great Britain, McKeown (1976) estimates that direct public health measures account for about 25 percent of the reduction in mortality rate, and he concludes, by exclusion, that improved health was largely related to improved nutrition resulting from the gradual increase in prosperity and food production and distribution. His conclusion is controversial (Szreter 2000). However, Fogel (2000), in a broader and deeper assessment of a number of Western countries, also concludes that better nutrition, largely resulting from the industrial revolution and improved prosperity, is the main factor causing the fall in mortality rates.

In his analysis, Fogel (2000) finds that life expectancy improved as the mean heights of populations increased. Because nutrition during early childhood (including in utero) has a major effect on adult height (Floud, Wachter, and Gregory 1990), Fogel concludes that the increase in life expectancy is related to improved conditions for early childhood. He speculates that conditions during early childhood affected the risks for health problems in adult life. Obviously, other changes besides improved nutrition, such as reduction in family size, affected early child development during this period. Reduced family size could have led to reduced risk of childhood infections and, possibly, better nurturing of young children by parents (Reves 1985).

This historical evidence shows a relationship between economic growth and improved health that is not due to health care and is only partially explained by conventional public health measures. The relationship, however, is linked to the improved outcomes for children associated with more prosperous societies.

Being an economic historian, Fogel also considers the effect of a healthier, more competent population on economic growth. He concludes that much of the economic growth in developed countries in association with the industrial revolution was a consequence of the better quality of the population. He estimates that the improved quality of the population may have accounted for as much as 50 percent of the economic growth in the United Kingdom following the start of the industrial revolution (Fogel 2000). This evidence indicates a relationship between technological innovation, economic prosperity, changes in the social environment and the health and well-being of populations and the effects of populations' improved health and well-being on economic growth. In his recent book, Fogel (2000) discusses the ways new knowledge and technological innovation are producing major economic and social changes in societies today and the potential effects of these changes on populations.

The historical evidence leaves two unresolved questions: How does early life affect human development and the risk for physical and mental health problems in adult life? And, what biological pathways are involved and how do the conditions of early child development affect these pathways?

Research Findings

Human and animal studies provide substantial evidence of the effects of nutrition and experience in the early years on brain development and competence, coping skills, behavior, and health later in life (Acheson 1998; Gunnar 1998; Hales 1997; Keating and Hertzman 1999; Lucas, Morley, and Cole 1998; McCain and Mustard 1999; McEwen 1998; Meaney and others 1996; Selye 1936, 1976; Suomi 1997). New knowledge about the development of the brain in early life and its effects on all aspects of body function, through pathways involving the endocrine systems, the immune system, and mental processes, is providing clues about other biological pathways (Francis and others 1999; Gunnar 1998; Keating and Hertzman 1999; McEwen 1998). The biological evidence supports the hypothesis that brain development in early childhood is a factor influencing health, learning, and behavior throughout the life cycle.

Biological Pathways

Biological studies provide intriguing evidence of the relationship between brain development and experiences in early childhood. Clues about this relationship are found in pertinent studies of the brain/hormone pathways, sensory pathways (e.g., the visual cortex), and stages of brain development in humans.

Brain/Hormone Pathways

Understanding of the hypothalamus-pituitary-adrenal gland (HPA) system and the autonomic nervous system and stress has grown exponentially since the work of Selye (1936). The development of these systems in early life and their effects on brain function and other important pathways in the endocrine and immune systems are now better understood through studies of psychoneuroendocrinology and psychoneuroimmunology. Basically, external or internal sensory stimuli to the brain can, through the HPA system, lead to increased production of corticosteroids (sterols) and activation of the autonomic nervous system. Sterol levels and their duration in the blood affect all body systems and organs, including the brain. The brain regulates sterol levels in the blood through a feedback system involving the hypothalamus. Regulation of the release of corticotropin-releasing hormone (CRH) from the hypothalamus not only affects the HPA pathway, but also the hippocampus and other pathways involved in the limbic system (McEwen and Seeman 1999). A critical question is: How is the regulation of the CRH pathway set?

The hippocampus and hypothalamus have steroid receptors that are important in a number of aspects of brain function influencing behavior, loss of cognitive function, memory loss with aging, substance abuse, and suicide (Gunnar 1998; Francis and others 1999; McEwen and Seeman 1999; Selye 1936). Studies in newborn rat pups indicate that external and internal stimuli during early life can set the sensitivity and regulation of the CRH-HPA system (Francis and others 1999; Gunnar 1998; McEwen 1998; Meaney and others 1996).

Some of the regulation appears to be mediated by the effects of stimuli, including sterols, in activating genetic components in the neurons in the hippocampus and hypothalamus that are part of the process for determining cell differentiation and function in early life. Sterols regulate gene expression by several pathways involving activation of specific genes and via regulation of RNA transcription. Understanding of the influence and sustained effects of variations in environmental conditions (experience) on the development of neural systems, at both the level of gene expression and synaptic development, is growing. Some investigators are exploring how changes at sites that regulate the transcription of genes may serve as a mechanism for long-term effects on neuron function.

Stimulation of the CRH-HPA pathway can occur through at least three routes: by endogenous factors from the circulation such as those associated with illness; by direct stimulation from visceral sensing systems (e.g., pain and blood pressure); and by stimulation of the hypothalamus through the brain's external sensing systems (e.g., vision, touch, sound, smell). The hippocampus is an important structure because of its involvement with the limbic hypothalmic pituitary adrenal cortical (LHPA) system and the prefrontal cortex (Dettling and others 2000; Francis and others 1999; McEwen and Seeman 1999). The hippocampus influences memory, learning, and behavior. Chronic high levels of sterols can cause loss of neurons in the hippocampus, with effects on memory and behavior (McEwen 1999; Sapolsky 1992, 1997). Animal studies impressively demonstrate that early experiences (stimulation) influence the development of these brain pathways and affect the response of these pathways to internal or external stimulation later in life.

McEwen and Schmeck (1994) summarize this dynamic interaction, the effects of early experiences, and the function of the CRH-HPA pathway as follows:

> "All this means that while the brain evokes hormones and their multitude of effects, the tide of hormone affects the brain too. The implications are profound; individual differences in experience are translated into differences in brain function, even brain structure; that is what makes the situation so complex, so difficult to resolve into such tidy simplicities as nature versus nurture. Early life experiences and the hormone exposures that are determined by the brain's reactions to those experiences provide cues that will change the way the brain responds to new experiences in the future" (McEwen and Schmeck 1994, p. 178).

Much of the evidence from both human and animal studies that now relates early experience to physical and mental health problems later in life points to the CRH-HPA pathway (Francis and others 1999; McEwen 1998, 1999; McEwen and Schmeck 1994; McEwen and Seeman 1999; Sapolsky 1997). The exceptional work of Barker and colleagues (Barker 1992, 1997; Phillips and others 1998) in relating birthweight and length of gestation to health in adult life shows the "long reach" of conditions in utero and early life to adult conditions such as coronary heart disease, high blood pressure, noninsulin-dependent diabetes, reduced immune function in later stages of life, and obesity. Experiments in a variety of animals confirm the link between intrauterine growth retardation and hypertension and metabolic disorders.

Recently, Barker's group (Phillips and others 1998) found that plasma sterol levels in 64-year-old men were inversely related to their birthweight. The higher plasma sterol levels found in men with a low birthweight in relation to gestational age were significantly associated with higher blood pressure, plasma glucose levels, and insulin resistance. Barker's group concludes, as does Meaney's group from studies with rats, that the CRH-HPA axis can be programmed in utero (Phillips and others 1998; Smythe and others 1994).

Thus, the development and regulation of the CRH-HPA pathway in early life, resulting from external and internal stimuli received in utero and shortly after birth, influence the regulation and function of this pathway throughout the life cycle. Because this pathway can affect memory, cognition, behavior, metabolic pathways, the immune system, and the cardiovascular system throughout life, the development of brain function in early life is very important. In addition, evidence indicates that the response of the autonomic nervous system, which is more difficult to study, is also influenced by conditions in early life, probably related, in part, to the development of the limbic HPA system (Francis and others 1999).

Sensory Pathways

Another set of brain pathways influenced by conditions in early life is the wiring and sculpting of the regions of the cortex that connect to the sensing systems (e.g., vision, touch, sound, smell). The neurons in the different sensing parts of the brain cortex that differentiate in response to signals received in early life influence how well individuals recognize the world around them and respond to inputs from the sensing organs. Groundbreaking research on vision (Cynader and Frost 2000; Hubel and Weisel 1962) shows a sensitive period during the early stages of development when vision neurons in the occipital cortex of the brain are most sensitive to the wiring and sculpting of neurons necessary for normal vision. As with the CRH-HPA system, during a sensitive period in early development, stimuli from the retina of the eye switch on the genetic machinery in the neurons in the occipital cortex to enable them to differentiate for their function in vision. In animal studies, if the sensitive period is missed, turning on the genetic mechanism is difficult.

Despite different interpretations of this work by nonspecialists, one neuroscientist (Cynader 2000) in the vision field recently clearly stated the implications of this research:

"Studies of the plasticity of the visual cortex during the critical period of postnatal development are particularly germane in light of recent controversies about the importance of early childhood experience in determining cortical competency in adults. These controversies—which have profound implications for early childhood education, parenting, and childcare—have been characterized more by polemics than by neuroscience research. The visual cortex represents the best model that we have for understanding how sensory stimulation of the early brain influences brain circuitry and function throughout life. Its study should increase our knowledge of the ways in which early sensory inputs determine the long-term capabilities of the brain" (Cynader 2000, pp. 1943–44).

The evidence from animal and human studies is consistent with the conclusion that the wiring and sculpting of the brain is most dynamic during the early years of life and is substantially affected by the quality of nurturing or stimuli received during this period of development. These effects are not "all or nothing," however, at least as indicated by the experimental results on vision. Still, the longer the period before signals from the eye reach the visual cortex in a young child, the poorer the individual's visual acuity will be in adult life (Cynader and Frost 2000). That is, this component of the brain will not function as well as it could if normal signals from the eye had passed to the visual cortex during the sensitive period for the wiring and sculpting of neurons.

The same relationship holds for other sensory pathways such as sound and touch (Cynader and Frost 2000; Hyman 1999). All of the research demonstrates that substantially improving the relevant wiring and sculpting for the sensing pathways is difficult later if the brain's sensing system does not develop during the optimum period.

Evidence is increasing for the interconnection of sensing pathways, such as vision, with other key centers in the brain (Rauschecker 1999). Although relatively less is known about the development of neural pathways to other parts of the brain that affect arousal, emotions, behavior, language, and mathematical skills, some neuroscientists speculate that the wiring and sculpting of these pathways develop in a similar way to the sensory systems (Cynader and Frost 2000; Hubel 1994; Le Doux 1999). Recent evidence about the "cross-modal exchange" of different sensing systems with each other and other parts of the brain provides a framework for understanding the lasting effects of the development of these pathways in early life.

Stages of Development

Recent noninvasive studies of human brain development demonstrate that some structures develop earlier than others and that brain development is most active in the early years of life. By the second decade, this activity declines to approximately the values in adult life (Chugani, Phelps, and Mazziotta 1987; Huttenlocher 1994). Findings suggest that some developments occur early (e.g., sensing pathways such as vision, sound, touch; cross-modal connections; CRH-HPA pathways), whereas other pathways develop later (e.g., literacy, mathematics) and are likely influenced by the earlier base (Case 1996; Cynader and Frost 2000; Hyman 1999). Some complex developments, such as behavior, emotion, and arousal, may be influenced at different stages. Fortunately, the hippocampus, a key structure for memory, remains plastic throughout life and can generate new neurons (Kandel 1999; Kempermann and Gage 1999). However, evidence from studies of the effect of experiences in early life on the development and regulation of the CRH-HPA pathway and cortisol levels indicates that a poor early environment can lead to poor regulation of cortisol, which can negatively affect the development, function, and regeneration of the hippocampus throughout life.

Researchers are currently pursuing strategies to influence gene expression at later stages of development to overcome, or at least partially overcome, the failure to establish appropriate gene expression in early stages of development (Cynader and Frost 2000; Smythe and others 1994).

Animal Studies

Much of the understanding of human physiology and disease and many of the technologies for diagnosis and treatment come from animal studies. Currently, scientists are experimenting with the transfer of animal tissue to humans to alleviate health problems, including some brain disorders. Because of cultural, philosophical, and other factors, many investigators resist attempts to apply knowledge from animal experiments to an understanding of brain function and development in humans. Some reservation about the relevance of animal studies to humans is sensible, but to ignore the core information is a mistake, partly because studies in animals can reveal how various organs of the body, such as the brain, develop and interact at cellular and organ levels throughout life. The pertinent research for early child development includes studies of development and function, gene–environment interactions, and immune effects.

Development and Function

In a number of studies with mice, rats, and monkeys (Black and others 1998; Coe 1999; Greenough, Volkman, and Juraska 1973; Meaney and others 1988), researchers have examined the effects of early life events on brain development and brain characteristics and function later in life. The evidence from these and other studies in animals shows that the circumstances of early life influence brain development and that this early development affects behavior, learning, health, and memory in later life.

Data from rats show a number of interesting observations relating developmental neurobiology to function. Rat pups given an enriched animal cage (toys to play with) and involved with their mother show clear benefits. In contrast to pups that are not given enriched housing, the animals, as adults, have more neurons and more neural connections (an outcome of brain wiring and sculpting) and perform better on tests of rat competence. Greenough and colleagues note that adult rats exposed to a similar, enriched environment also exhibit new neurons and increased neural connections (Black and others 1998). However, the changes occur faster and are greater in young rats.

Other studies show that rat pups that are licked intensively by their mothers in early life develop a regulatory control for their CRH-HPA axis that provides a more balanced response to stimuli (i.e., lower sterol levels and a faster return to lower baseline values) (Francis and others 1999; Meaney and others 1996, 1988). One of the striking features shown in these studies is that well-licked rat pups have better memories as they age. Also, the loss of hippocampus neurons was less in these rats as they aged, which is compatible with the observation that excess sterol levels can cause loss of neurons in the hippocampus (Sapolsky 1992, 1997). In sum, rat pups with much touch (licking from their mother) have a better regulated CRH-HPA pathway and retain better memory and cognitive function as they age.

In one interesting study in rats, Francis and others (1999) crossed foster pups from mothers that groomed and licked intensely with pups from mothers that had low licking and grooming behavior. The results showed that, regardless of the biological mother, pups placed with "good" mothers developed CRH-HPA pathways similar to rats from, and reared by, these mothers. The female pups from "poor" mothers, reared by "good" mothers, had the same biological and mothering characteristics as the mothers that reared them.

Gene–Environment Interactions

The early life and development of monkeys have been studied extensively. In one set of experiments (Suomi 1997, 2000), rhesus monkeys were grouped into genetically vulnerable and resistant strains. The genetically vulnerable strain was characterized as hyperreactors to stress or challenge. If not raised by a nurturing mother, these monkeys have an overstimulated CRH-HPA system with exaggerated cortisol responses and poor return to resting levels. These vulnerable animals, poorly nurtured when young, show avoidance of novel stimuli as well as anxious and depressive reactions to maternal separation. As adults, they show increased anxiety and depressive behavior, excessive alcohol consumption when given access to alcohol, impulse aggression and violent behavior, and high circulating sterol levels. The females tend to be poor mothers.

Researchers have studied in detail the biological pathways in these animals, which show high sterol levels in response to mild stress, high resting sterol levels, low brain serotonin levels, and a disrupted circadian rhythm for sterols. When offspring from "poor" mothers in the vulnerable strain are taken and reared by highly nurturing mothers (Suomi 1997, 2000), the high-risk infants become secure and precocious in their exploratory patterns. As adults, they rise to the top of the social hierarchy; have a robust immune response, a better regulated sterol pathway, and normal brain serotonin levels; and the females become very nurturing mothers.

Researchers have found a genetic characteristic related to serotonin metabolism in the vulnerable monkeys (Bennett and others 2000; Suomi 2000). If poorly nurtured, the animals with the short allele have excess sterol responses to stimuli and low brain serotonin levels; if well nurtured, the animals do not show these adverse responses (Suomi 2000). This finding exemplifies the effect of environment on gene expression.

Immune Effects

One of the important effects of the HPA system is on the immune system. Excess activity of the CRH-HPA system with increased sterol levels in early life can produce permanent and marked reductions in immune competence (Coe 1999; Suomi 2000). The effect of sterols on the immune system is complex; for example, a strong CRH-HPA response can be beneficial in bringing an acute illness under control. Studies also show that infant monkeys reared in a deprived environment exhibit changes in antibody function that can increase their risk of autoimmune disorders and conditions such as asthma.

Human Studies

Epidemiological randomized social experiments, longitudinal studies, and observational studies in populations indicate how early life experiences affect a child's health, learning, and behavior. This experience-dependent early development is influenced by nutrition, parenting capability, and other factors that support early child development. The studies clearly demonstrate the value and benefit of good ECD programs involving parents.

Environmental Effects

Population-based, epidemiological studies in developed countries document the social partitioning of health, learning, and behavior. The studies show a gradient relationship between measures of health, cognition, and behavior and socioeconomic status (SES) (Bennett and others 2000; Case, Griffin, and Kelly 1999; Hertzman 1999; Macintyre 1994; Marmot and others 1995; Power and Hertzman 1999; Willms 1999). Individuals at the bottom of the SES index (levels IV and V) have the lowest scores, and those at the top of the index have the highest scores. Several points are of interest.

First, the gradients for health, learning, and behavior in developed countries tend to be linear (i.e., there is no poverty threshold). Second, the gradient cannot be explained solely by genetics; the social environment clearly has an effect. Third, some countries have high performance and fairly flat gradients. Fourth, in developed countries, the greatest number of children in difficulty are in the large middle class. For example, Canadian data show that about 32 percent of children in poor families *and* more than 20 percent of children in affluent families do not develop well in the early years (McCain and Mustard 1999). The cause of these gradients, or social partitioning, of populations is not just family income.

Understanding the pathways for the social environment's effect on health, learning, and behavior is a challenge. The evidence from longitudinal studies supports brain development as being a contributing factor, which involves the establishment of pathways that influence learning, behavior, and physical and mental health throughout life. Power and Hertzman (1999) refer to this process as "biological embedding," a concept that relates the environment of early life to the switching on of genetic mechanisms responsible for differentiation of the specific function of neurons in different regions of the brain.

Longitudinal studies of cohorts of children from birth to adult life show similar effects of SES gradients for health, behavior, and learning (Case, Griffin, and Kelly 1999; Power and Matthews 1997; Power and Hertzman 1997, 1999; Power and others 1997; Tremblay 1999; Wadsworth 1991). Figure 1 depicts the gradients for academic achievement at age 23 in relation to social class at birth for children from the 1958 British birth cohort. Percentages

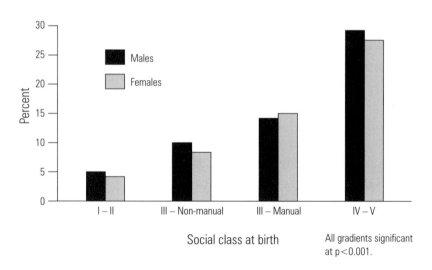

All gradients significant at $p < 0.001$.

Reprinted with permission of *The Lancet* from Power and Matthews (1997).

Figure 1. Social Class at Birth and Percent With Education Qualifications (O Level or Greater) at Age 23, 1958 British Birth Cohort

with education qualifications improve with each step upward in social class at birth.

The figure shows that the percentage of children with no educational qualifications (below 0 level in the British system) at age 23 is highest for children born in the lowest social classes (IV and V) of British society, compared with only 5 percent of children born in the highest social classes (I and II). The percentage with educational qualifications increases at each higher level of social class at birth for both males and females. The gradient is obviously influenced by individuals' circumstances at birth and their life courses to age 23.

Figure 2 shows the gradients for health at age 33 among the same cohort. In the figure, "psychological distress" (as assessed by the twenty-four-item malaise inventory of psychological and somatic symptoms) relates to future mental health problems, and "poor self-rated health" relates to chronic health problems in later life. The figure shows a gradient for health in relation to social class

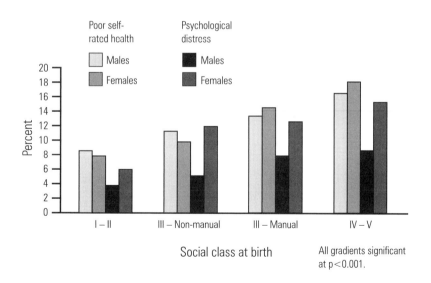

Reprinted with permission of *The Lancet* from Power and Matthews (1997).

Figure 2. Social Class at Birth and Health at Age 33, 1958 British Birth Cohort

at birth. The gradient for future mental health problems at age 33 is most striking for females. Some aspects of both gradients (future mental health and chronic health problems) may reflect the effect of early life environment on the development of the CRH-HPA pathway, as discussed earlier.

The data showing poor self-rated health in the early adult years as a predictor of chronic health problems later in life are compatible with Barker and colleagues' findings that many chronic health problems of individuals in adult life can be related to conditions during their mother's pregnancy and the early years of life (Barker 1992, 1997; Phillips and others 1998). The data also agree with the conclusion of Acheson's report (1998) on inequalities in health in the United Kingdom—that early child development affects physical and mental health problems in adult life.

The cohort data in figures 1 and 2 show that children in all social classes are subject to environmental factors that affect health, behavior, and learning in early life and that the proportion of children affected is greater in the lower social classes. These data, of course, do not take into account the effect of any events during life up to ages 23 and 33. Power, Hertzman, and colleagues have assessed such effects and concluded that a poor early start compounded by a poor life course has the greatest effect on health, behavior, and learning (Power and Hertzman 1997; Power and others 1997).

Early Experience and Development

Data from other longitudinal studies in other countries show a clear relationship between the early years and competence, coping skills, and health in later years. A Swedish study (Andersson 1992) of a sample of children born in 1975 from low- and middle-income urban households shows that children who attended good ECD centers, which involved parents, before age 1, had the best social skills and cognitive abilities at age 13. Male children entering the school system in Sweden with poor verbal skills tended to be functionally illiterate as teenagers, and a significant number of them ended up in the justice system (Stattin 1993).

Studies of children in the French Ecoles Maternelle program (Bergmann 1996) show that this program enhances performance in the school system for children from all social classes and that the earlier the children entered the preschool program, the better their outcome. A study in the United Kingdom (Osburn and Milbank 1987) shows that children in good half-day preschool programs had better cognitive development and academic achievement than children who were not in these programs and that children from disadvantaged backgrounds gained more than children from advantaged backgrounds.

A striking observation from the longitudinal studies is that female children who are reared in dysfunctional families without external support in the early years are at increased risk for behavior and mental health problems in later life (Maughan and McCarthy 1997; Rodgers, Power, and Hope 1997; Rutter, Giller, and Hagell 1998). Many male children reared in dysfunctional families show clear evidence of antisocial behavior when they enter the school system, and about one-third of them will be delinquent in their teens (Tremblay 1999). Females show an increased risk for mental health problems, such as depression, in adult life (Maughan and McCarthy 1997; Rodgers, Power, and Hope 1997). These findings hold true for children in all social classes, and the proportion having difficulties increases for those at lower SES levels.

Improving Early Child Development: The Effects

A number of studies in developed and developing countries have addressed the effects of programs for enhancing early child development on learning, behavior, and health later in life. Randomized trials of social interventions are far more difficult to conduct than randomized trials of medical drugs, and they tend to be small in size. The results of these studies, however, can be tested for consistency with the findings from biological and animal studies and from population-based epidemiological and longitudinal studies.

A few studies demonstrate the effects of enhancing early child development for poor populations. In *Jamaica*, Grantham-McGregor and others (1991, 1997) examined the effects of good nourishment and nurturing on the development of children stunted at birth, in comparison with a normal control group. The stunted children were randomized into four groups, receiving no enhanced nutrition and nurturing, improved nutrition, enhanced nurturing or stimulation, or improved nutrition and nurturing. After 2 years, the group given no support showed poor development; the groups given either improved nutrition or stimulation improved about equally and achieved about 50 percent of the development occurring in the control group; and the group given both nurturing and nutrition equaled the development of the control group. This study highlights the value of both nutrition and nurturing on early child development for infants who clearly were at a disadvantage at birth. The mothers of the stunted children in this study did not have a healthy pregnancy, and the children will carry some of the risks at birth identified by Barker (1992, 1997). The results from this study are compatible with those from animal and biological studies.

The *Carolina*, or *Abecedarian*, project demonstrates the effect of an ECD initiative in a poor African-American population in the United States (Campbell and Ramey 1994; Ramey 1990; Ramey and others 2000). The children, whose mothers had a low intelligence quotient (IQ), were randomized into two groups. One group was placed in an ECD program which involved parents and home visits throughout the years beginning shortly after birth and continuing until the children entered school. The other group, the control, did not participate. The program was an intensive ECD initiative having one qualified early childhood educator for every three infants and toddlers until age 3 and one for every six children over age 3.

The children participating in the ECD program showed gains in cognition (including IQ), educational performance, and improved behavior that were still evident at age 21, compared with the control group. The program's effect on IQ is of particular interest because of a recent review (Wickelgren 1999) which concludes that circumstances during the first years of life appear to affect IQ. The children in the Carolina program also showed significant gains in mathematics performance during their school years. At age 21, more than four times as many children who had been in the preschool program were enrolled in 4-year degree programs, compared with children who had been in the control group. Special programs for the control group when they entered the school system did not have a significant effect on their development—further highlighting the importance of the preschool program.

The well-known *High/Scope Study* (Berruta-Clement 1984; Schweinhart 1993) provides evidence from a randomized study of the effects of an ECD initiative in the United States on children from families in poor socioeconomic circumstances. The children entered the program at age 3 and continued until they entered the school system at age 6. This program began after the Abecedarian project and operated only during the school year. It involved parents, one early childhood educator for six children, and home visits. At ages 18 to 20, the children who had attended the preschool program showed better school performance and employment and fewer behavior problems, such as teenage pregnancies and criminal activities. Their assessment at age 27 showed some striking effects. Compared with the control group, fewer females in the intervention were in programs for "educable mental impairment," and the males in the intervention had far fewer criminal arrests. The results are compatible with (a) increasing evidence showing that females in poor early child development environments are at increased risk for mental health problems in adult life and (b) data showing that overcoming the disadvantages of poor brain development in the very early years is difficult later. The study did not show a sustained effect on IQ, perhaps because it enrolled children at age 3, after the very early years when IQ effects appear to be realized (Wickelgren 1999).

Mathematical ability is an example of a development occurring in the immediate preschool period. Programs designed to enhance basic cognitive ability in mathematics at ages 4 to 5 years have an effect (Case, Griffin, and Kelly 1999; Griffin, Case, and Siegler 1994). Case and colleagues examined whether performance in mathematics in school years could be improved through an initiative called *Right*

Start in the United States. The strategy used, "the cognitive weight of numbers," draws on multiple sensing pathways and, probably, is influenced by the cross-modal information exchange that the sensing pathways develop in early life. In the study, children in a poor socioeconomic neighborhood were randomized into an intervention group and a control group and compared with children in a middle-class school. At age 9, the children participating in the special preschool intervention program surpassed the children in the middle-class school, whereas the children in the control group performed less well than those in the middle-class school. Case speculates that individuals who miss this sensitive period of development may have difficulty with complex mathematics later in life.

Case's findings are compatible with the conclusions of Fuchs and Reklis (1994), who studied the effects of early child development on mathematics performance of students in various U.S. states. Fuchs and Reklis found that a state's mathematics performance in schools was high when children entered the school system with good early child development and low when early child development was low. They conclude that strong preschool programs are required to improve the mathematics performance of U.S. students overall. These results are compatible with the findings from the Abecedarian project and the concept that functions of the brain develop at different stages in the early years.

Studies of ECD programs in other parts of the world are beginning to show similar effects. A study in _India_ (Kaul and others 1991) also shows an effect of programs in the early years on subsequent ability in mathematics. A World Bank study (World Bank 2001) summarizes the results of ECD programs in _Brazil_ as follows: increased completion of primary school by one-third, lower grade repetition, and lower drop-out rates. These results and others from _Bolivia_ (Behrman, Cheng, and Todd 2000) further document that good ECD programs enhance outcomes in learning.

Observational Studies. Observational studies also show the benefits of good support in the early years of life. One of the most recent studies (Ames and others 1997) compares the outcome of children from

Romania adopted into Canadian British Columbia families shortly after birth with children adopted after spending many months or years in Romanian orphanages. The description of these orphanages indicates that they were poor environments for good early child development. The children adopted shortly after birth exhibit similar development as Canadian-born children in middle-class families, but many of those adopted after spending many months or years in Romanian orphanages have significant behavioral problems, poor attachment to caregivers, and lower IQs than those adopted early. From a detailed analysis of Romanian orphanage studies, O'Connor and others (2000) conclude that children who spent more time in the orphanages before adoption showed persistently poor outcomes.

Gunnar and colleagues studied the CRH-HPA axis in Romanian children adopted into British Columbia homes and found that those adopted late have higher sterol levels (Donzella and others 2000; Gunnar 1998; Gunnar and Donzella 1998). These sterol data agree with the results of animal studies showing that a poor nurturing environment in early life can lead to an overactive and poorly regulated CRH-HPA system and elevated sterol levels, with effects on cognition, memory, and behavior. In reviewing the stress-sterol pathway and early childhood, Gunnar concludes that caregivers and parents have a very powerful effect on the development of this pathway in early life through the quality of their nurturing. The data from both animal and human studies on the CRH-HPA axis and its development and effects are remarkably congruent.

A study of orphans from *Korea* (Lien, Meyer, and Winick 1977) adopted into American homes also shows an effect of the quality of the early years on development and performance in later life. All the children adopted into American families early after birth had higher IQ scores than children who had spent considerable time in Korean orphanages before adoption. Those who were well nourished when adopted had the highest scores—again emphasizing the importance of nutrition in the early years.

Despite the limitations of the orphanage studies and other possible explanations, all the findings are compatible with the results of animal studies. The human data indicate the importance of the early years in establishing the base for competence and coping skills throughout life.

Literacy

A major observation from many studies is the relationship between verbal skills at about age 5 and literacy in later life. SES gradients in literacy may, in part, reflect early child development. Willms (1999) who has been involved in studies of literacy in developed countries, conducted by the Organization for Economic Cooperation and Development (OECD) and Statistics Canada, emphasizes the importance of early childhood, as well as school systems, for literacy.

Recent OECD studies of three measures of literacy in OECD countries show that, for all the countries, level of literacy is a gradient when plotted against SES measures such as parents' level of education (OECD and Statistics Canada 2000; Willms 1999, *in this volume*). Some countries have a high performance and fairly flat gradient; other countries have a fairly steep gradient. Literacy in later life is related to verbal skills or language development in early life (McKeough 1992; Stattin 1993; Willms *in this volume*).

In the United States, population measures of verbal skills in early life show a fairly steep SES gradient (Brooks-Gunn, Duncan, and Britto 1999) compatible with the fairly steep literacy gradient found in the adult population (OECD and Statistics Canada 2000; Willms 1999). The greatest number of children not achieving their possible level of performance is in the middle class, a finding that strongly refutes the claim that few families in the middle class with young children do not have good early child development environments (Bruer 1999). Those who make this claim do not know or believe the findings from population-based, epidemiological studies.

The United States has a significant problem because more than 45 percent of the population functions at low literacy (on the OECD scale). Included at this low level are persons with very poor skills who, for example, may not be able to determine from information printed on a package the correct amount of medicine to give a child, can only read simple and clearly presented material, and can only perform tasks that are not too complex. Improving early child development is a serious challenge for U.S. society if it wishes to reduce the inequalities in literacy.

In developing countries, such as Chile, more than 85 percent of the population functions at levels 1 and 2 (on the OECD scale). To improve the socioeconomic circumstances of these countries, the World Bank and others must support efforts to improve literacy in written and cognitive performance and to encourage countries to invest in preschools [i.e., "tier 1,"] (McCain and Mustard 1999). Improving the literacy performance of populations will take at least 20 to 25 years if efforts are initiated now. Importantly, the tier 1 preschool initiatives must apply to all social classes (not only those in poverty) because of the evidence showing a gradient relationship between literacy and SES. Interestingly, one country (Cuba) that has invested for decades in mothers and children in the early years has a high literacy performance for all of its population regardless of social class (Willms *in this volume*).

A relevant observational study conducted for a number of U.S. states by the Stanford economist Fuchs (Fuchs and Reklis 1994) addressed the relationship between an index of early child development, readiness to learn at the time a child enters the school system, and the performance of children on a mathematics test at grade eight. The correlation was positive, with a correlation coefficient greater than +0.8. Math performance in the schools was clearly related to the level of early child development at the time the children entered the school system. Fuchs and Reklis (1994) conclude that investment in preschools for all children is at least equally important as investment in schools, to substantially improve mathematics outcomes in the United States. In addition to Case's research and the data from population epidemiological studies and the OECD, this evidence refutes the naive assumption that only a small number of children could benefit from good ECD programs (Bruer 1999).

The assessments of literacy in developed countries (OECD 2000) and Latin America yield some remarkable results (Willms *in this volume).* Some countries show high performance in test areas and fairly flat gradients, and others show much poorer performance across all social classes. The countries with high performance and fairly flat gradients tend to have high-quality preschool programs for children which involve parents. Perhaps because literacy is a measure of brain development and function and brain development affects health, the correlation between estimates of a country's literacy and life expectancy is strong (OECD 2000). This subject is covered more extensively in the chapter by Willms later in this volume.

Early Child Development in Developed Countries: The Case of Canada

Early child development is as important for developed countries as for developing countries. Canada is one example.

Assessing the Needs

In 1998, the Honorable Margaret McCain and the author were asked to chair a reference group and prepare a report on children's early years in the province of Ontario (McCain and Mustard 1999). The report was addressed to the Premier, the Minister for Children, and the government of Ontario. In preparing the report, the reference group received many anecdotal accounts of children in difficulty in the wealthiest province in Canada and indications that the problem was increasing, but the group could not confirm this information because the government of Ontario did not have a relevant database. Fortunately, the National Longitudinal Survey of Children and Youth (NLSCY) had generated key data on children and youth in Ontario and Canada, from which the reference group could undertake a population assessment of the quality of early child development in Ontario.

The survey included measures of verbal skills for children (an important predictor of future development) at ages 4 and 5 years for all social classes. Figure 3 shows a clear gradient for this measure when plotted against families' SES. Although the children in the poorest circumstances showed the poorest performance, 10 percent of the children from affluent families also did poorly. Also, the children in

Ontario did not perform as well on the literacy test, at every SES level, as did children in the rest of Canada. The largest number of children not doing well, in comparison with the rest of Canada, were in the middle class.

Verbal skill at ages 4 and 5 also is a predictor of subsequent behavioral and cognitive development. Not surprisingly, the literacy gradient for youth and young adults in Ontario was steeper than for Canada's three prairie provinces (Alberta, Saskatchewan, and Manitoba) and Quebec.

Figure 4 shows the gradient in literacy performance for the population in Canadian provinces by socioeconomic status (McCain and Mustard 1999). The provinces fall into two groups—those with high performance and shallow gradients (Quebec and the three prairie provinces) and those with relatively steep gradients. The SES scale is similar to that in figure 3.

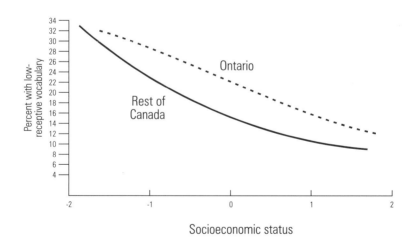

Based on the Peabody Picture Vocabulary Test. Socioeconomic status is a composite measure of family income and mothers' and fathers' occupations and incomes; poor are on left, affluent on right.

Figure 3. Socioeconomic Gradients of Children, Ages 4 and 5 Years, With Low-Receptive Vocabulary, Ontario and Canada, National Longitudinal Study of Children and Youth, 1994, Canada

An assessment of mathematics performance among Ontario's children reveals a similar gradient (McCain and Mustard 1999). Importantly, all these data indicate that a significant number of children from affluent families are not performing at desirable levels, while a higher portion of the children at the low end of the SES scale are also having difficulty.

Assessment of the development of Ontario's children in relation to family income shows that about 32 percent of the children in families at the bottom quartile of income, and more than 20 percent of the children in families at the top quartile of income, are not doing well. Complete analysis of the data shows that the greatest number of children in difficulty are in the middle class and that income is not the determining factor. Rather, the quality of parenting and caregiving is an important factor influencing the quality of a child's early development. Based on these findings, the study recommended to

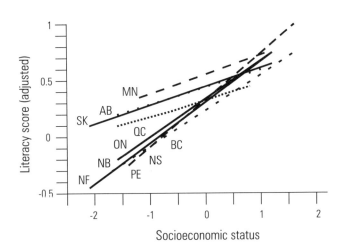

SK, Saskatchewan; AB, Alberta; MN, Manitoba; QC, Quebec; ON, Ontario; NB, New Brunswick; NF, Newfoundland; PE, Prince Edward Island; NS, Nova Scotia; BC, British Columbia.
Source: McCain and Mustard (1999).

Figure 4. Literacy and SES Gradients for Canadian Youth, by Province, 1994

the government of Ontario that good ECD and parenting programs beginning early in life should be available for all families with young children in Ontario, if the province is to have a more competent, high-quality population in the future.

The findings are additionally significant when related to the results of the literacy studies conducted by OECD and Statistics Canada (OECD 2000). The domains examined in these literacy studies are prose literacy, document literacy, and quantitative literacy. In Canada, more than 40 percent of the population functions at levels 1 and 2 (on the OECD scale) and about 22 percent at levels 4 and 5. In some developed countries, less than 25 percent are at levels 1 and 2 and more than 30 percent are at levels 4 and 5. To improve Canada's performance in the knowledge-based economy, Canada and Ontario must invest in good ECD programs. The data show that developed countries such as Canada, as well as developing countries, need to improve their populations' competence and coping skills for the future.

Recommendation: Early Child Development and Parenting Centers

The early-years study (McCain and Mustard 1999) recommended that the government of Ontario, in partnership with communities and involving the public and private sectors, establish early child development and parenting centers, to begin at conception and be sensitive to early child and brain development. Figure 5 depicts the framework for these centers.

The study specifically proposes that the centers begin support for families before a child is born, because of the importance of the in utero period; include five essential components, or core functions, for young children and their parents, from conception until entry into school (at age 6); and measure their success in improving outcomes for children. The early child development and parenting centers will be guided by the following principles:

1. Available, accessible, affordable, and optional early child development and parenting centers for all young children and families in Ontario, from conception to entry into grade one in

the school system (parents may choose to bring their children or not)

2. Centers that are both parent-oriented and child-oriented
3. ECD programs that are environments for children to engage in play-based, problem-solving learning with other children and adults
4. Responsive relationships between adults (early child development staff and parents) and children that increase the potential of play-based learning
5. Quality programs that teach family literacy and numeracy to parents and other caregivers from diverse cultural, ethnic, and linguistic backgrounds
6. Parenting programs that support parents and other caregivers in all aspects of early child development

Source of brain stimulation

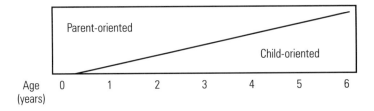

Components of Early Child Development and Parenting Centers:

- Parent support (including nonparental care arrangements) and education
- Play-based learning guided by early educators and parents
- Toy and resource libraries, family event
- Prenatal and postnatal supports
- Nutrition programs and information and referral services

Source: McCain and Mustard (1999).

Figure 5. Proposed Framework for Early Child Development and Parenting Centers for the Province of Ontario

7. Parent participation in ECD programs that enhance the child's early learning and optimal development in the home environment
8. Appropriate supports and expertise that are available to allow all children to participate fully, regardless of physical, developmental, language, learning, or behavior difficulties
9. Ability to provide special efforts that may be necessary to engage some families and children whose circumstances make it difficult for them to be involved in the centers
10. Centers, regardless of location, that are linked to the local primary school and with other institutions (e.g., libraries, recreation) and cultural activities in their communities
11. Centers that provide a flexible continuum of services to meet the needs of children and parents at home, work, and school
12. Monitoring of the effectiveness of the centers using a developmental readiness-to-learn measure of children when they enter the school system.

A measure of early development (Early Development Index), similar to that used by Fuchs and Reklis (1994), has been developed by the Canadian Institute for Advanced Research (CIAR), Human Development Program, the Founders' Network of CIAR, and McMaster University (Janus and Offord 2000). Use of this measure in assessments of thousands of children as they enter the school system shows that school performance is related directly to the quality of early child development. This sensitive outcome measure can be used to assess the effectiveness of community programs to improve early child development.

Ontario's government and the Minister for Children understand the importance of programs such as these for the community, and they appreciate the enormous importance of early child development. The minister's goal is to give the early years of human development the same importance as the later years (primary, secondary, and postsecondary education), and the government's plans, which are being introduced in Ontario, are community-based and involve both the private and the public sectors. The minister is implementing the recommendations of the early-years study (McCain and Mustard 1999).

Conclusion

All the studies noted herein demonstrate that good ECD programs should be available for all population sectors and that these initiatives will improve the overall quality of the population and reduce inequalities in health, competence, and coping skills. A key social consideration is that children who have a poor start are at increased risk of antisocial behavior, potentially resulting in increased crime and violence for society. High levels of social disruption impede development of competitive economies, whereas cohesive, stable societies with reasonable equity in competence and coping skills are best able to adapt to economic and social changes associated with exponential growth in knowledge and new technology.

The economic benefits of investing in early child development for society and individuals are very great. As economic historians have pointed out, improved health, competence, and coping skills were a significant factor in the economic growth of Western countries after the industrial revolution. Commenting on the value of early child development, van der Gaag concludes in the next chapter in this volume: "Well-executed and well-targeted ECD programs are initiators of [human development]. They stimulate improvements in education, health, social capital, and equality that have both immediate and long-term benefits for the children participating in the programs. Investments in ECD programs are in many ways investments in the future of a nation."

For the world regions to cope with the profound socioeconomic changes occurring, attention must be given to the competence and coping skills of all populations. Ontario has taken a major step in this direction with the establishment of early child development and parenting centers. The recommendations stimulating this action (McCain and Mustard 1999) were strongly influenced by the work of the World Bank and the conclusion in its recent volume on early child development (Young 1997):

"Because learning begins at birth, and even before, the starting point for involving families in ECD programs must be as early as possible.... Knowledge and understanding of ECD programs is no longer the constraint facing early child development. Rather, transforming this knowledge into action is the major limiting factor in implementing ECD programs and requires the combined support of governments, nongovernmental organizations, the private sector, and the media. The challenge to care for society's youngest members is not just a challenge for a single country or continent; it is a challenge for the entire world community" (p. 330).

References

Acheson, D. 1998. *Independent Inquiry into Inequalities in Health: Report.* London: The Stationery Office.

Ames, E. 1997. *The Development of Romanian Orphanage Children Adopted to Canada. Final Report.* Burnaby, B.C.: Simon Fraser University.

Andersson, B.-E. 1992. Effects of Day-Care on Cognitive and Socioemotional Competence of Thirteen-Year-Old Swedish School Children. *Child Development* 63:20–36.

Barker, D.J.P., ed. 1992. *Fetal and Infant Origins of Adult Disease.* London: British Medical Journal.

———. 1997. Fetal Nutrition and Cardiovascular Disease in Later Life. *British Medical Bulletin* 53(1):96–108.

Behrman, J.R., Y. Cheng, and P. Todd 2000. The Impact of the Bolivian Integrated 'PIDI' Preschool Program. World Bank Research Foundation Project on Evaluation of the Impact of Investments in Early Childhood Development on Nutrition and Cognitive Development. Washington, D.C.: World Bank.

Bennett, A.J, K.P. Lesch, A. Heils, J. Long, J. Lorenz, S.E. Shoaf, M. Champoux, S.J. Suomi, M.V. Linnoila, and J.D. Higley. 2000. Early

Experience and Serotonin Transporter Gene Variation Interact to Influence Primate CNS Function. *Molecular Psychiatry.*

Bergmann, B. 1996. *Saving Our Children from Poverty: What the United States Can Learn from France.* New York: Russell Sage Foundation.

Berruta-Clement, J.R. 1984. *Changed Lives: The Effects of the Perry Preschool Program on Youths Through Age 19.* Ypsilanti, Mich.: High/Scope Press.

Black, J.E., T.A. Jones, C.A. Nelson, and W.T. Greenough. 1998. Neuronal Plasticity and the Developing Brain. In N.E. Alessi, J.T. Coyle, S.I. Harrison, and S. Eth, eds., *Handbook of Child and Adolescent Psychiatry, Vol. 6: Basic Psychiatric Science and Treatment.* New York: John Wiley & Sons.

Brooks-Gunn, J., G.J. Duncan, and P.R. Britto. 1999. Are Socioeconomic Gradients for Children Similar to Those for Adults?: Achievement and Health of Children in the United States. In D. Keating and C. Hertzman, eds., *Developmental Health and the Wealth of Nations.* New York: Guilford Press.

Bruer, J.T. 1999. *The Myth of the First Three Years: A New Understanding of Early Brain Development and Lifelong Learning.* New York: Free Press.

Campbell, F.A., and C.T. Ramey. 1994. Effects of Early Intervention on Intellectual and Academic Achievement: A Follow-up Study of Children from Low-Income Families. *Child Development* 65:684–98.

Case, R. 1996. Mathematics Education for the Information Age. HDWP–29. Toronto: Canadian Institute for Advanced Research.

Case, R.S., S. Griffin, and W.M. Kelly. 1999. Socioeconomic Gradients in Mathematical Ability and Their Responsiveness to Intervention during Early Childhood. In D. Keating and C. Hertzman, eds., *Developmental Health and the Wealth of Nations.* New York: Guilford Press.

Chugani, H.T., M.E. Phelps, and J.C. Mazziotta. 1987. Positron Emission Tomography Study of Human Brain Functional Development. *Annals of Neurology* 22(4):487–97.

Coe, C.L. 1999. Psychosocial Factors and Psychoneuroimmunology Within a Lifespan Perspective. In D. Keating and C. Hertzman, eds., *Developmental Health and the Wealth of Nations*. New York: Guilford Press.

Cynader, M.S. 2000. Perspectives: Neuroscience. Strengthening Visual Connections. *Science* 287:1943–44.

Cynader, M.S., and B.J. Frost. 2000. Mechanisms of Brain Development: Neuronal Sculpting by the Physical and Social Environment. In D. Keating and C. Hertzman, eds., *Developmental Health and the Wealth of Nations*. New York: Guilford Press.

Dettling, A.C., S.W. Parker, S. Lane, A. Sebanc, and M.R. Gunnar. 2000. Quality of Care and Temperament Determine Changes in Cortisol Concentrations over the Day for Young Children in Childcare. *Psychoneuroendocrinology* 25:819–36.

Donzella, B., M.R. Gunnar, W.K. Krueger, and J. Alevin. 2000. Cortisol and Vagal Tone Responses to Competitive Challenge in Preschoolers: Associations With Temperament. *Developmental Psychobiology* 37:209–20.

Floud, R., K. Wachter, and A. Gregory. 1990. *Height, Health and History: Nutritional Status in the United Kingdom, 1750–1980*. Cambridge: Cambridge University Press.

Fogel, R.W. 1994. Economic Growth, Population Theory and Physiology: The Bearing of Long-term Processes on the Making of Economic Policy. National Bureau of Economic Research Working Paper No. W4638. Cambridge, Mass.

———. 2000. *The Fourth Great Awakening and the Future of Egalitarianism*. Chicago: University of Chicago Press.

Francis, D.D., F.A. Champagne, D. Liu, and M.J. Meaney. 1999. Maternal Care, Gene Expression, and the Development of Individual Differences in Stress Reactivity. In Socioeconomic Status and Health in Industrial Nations. *Annals of the New York Academy of Sciences* 896:66–84.

Fuchs, V., and D. Reklis. 1994. Mathematical Achievement in Eighth Grade: Interstate and Racial Differences. National Bureau of Economic Research Working Paper No. 4784. Cambridge, Mass.

Grantham-McGregor, S.M., C.A. Powell, S.P. Walker, and J.H. Himes. 1991. Nutritional Supplementation, Psychosocial Stimulation, and Mental Development of Stunted Children. *Lancet* 338(8758):1–5.

Grantham-McGregor, S.M., S.P.C. Walker, S.M. Chang, and C.A. Powell. 1997. Effects of Early Childhood Supplementation With and Without Stimulation on Later Development in Stunted Jamaican Children. *American Journal of Clinical Nutrition* 66:247–53.

Greenough, W.T., F.R. Volkmar, and J.M. Juraska. 1973. Effects of Rearing Complexity on Dendritic Branching in Frontolateral and Temporal Cortex of the Rat. *Experimental Neurology* 41:371–78.

Griffin, S., R. Case, and R. Siegler. 1994. Rightstart: Providing the Central Conceptual Prerequisites for First Formal Learning of Arithmetic to Students at Risk for School Failure. In K. McGilly, ed., *Classroom Lessons: Integrating Cognitive Theory and Classroom Practice.* Cambridge, Mass.: MIT Press.

Gunnar, M.R. 1998. Stress Physiology, Health and Behavioral Development. In A. Thornton, ed., *The Wellbeing of Children and Families: Research and Data Needs.* Institute for Social Research Report. Ann Arbor, Mich.: University of Michigan.

Gunnar, M.R., and B. Donzella. 1998. Social Regulation of the LHPA Axis in Early Human Development. Institute of Child Development. Minneapolis: University of Minnesota.

Hales, C.N. 1997. Non-Insulin-Dependent Diabetes Mellitus. *British Medical Bulletin* 53(1):109–22.

Hertzman, C. 1999. Population Health and Human Development. In D. Keating and C. Hertzman, eds., *Developmental Health and the Wealth of Nations.* New York: Guilford Press.

Hubel, H.D. 1994. Nature vs Nurture vs Knowledge. In B.S. McEwen and H. Schmeck, eds., *The Hostage Brain.* New York: Rockefeller University Press.

Hubel, H.D., and T.N. Weisel. 1962. Receptive Fields, Binocular Interaction and Functional Architecture in the Cat's Visual Cortex. *Physiology* 160:106–54.

Huttenlocher, P.R. 1994. Synaptogenesis in Human Cerebral Cortex. In G. Dawson and K.W. Fischer, eds., *Human Behavior and the Developing Brain*. New York: Guilford Press.

Hyman, S. 1999. Susceptibility and "Second Hits." In R. Conlan, ed., *States of Mind: New Discoveries About How Our Brains Make Us Who We Are*. New York: John Wiley & Sons.

Janus, M., and D. Offord. 2000. Readiness to Learn at School. *Isuma* 1(2):71–75.

Kagan, J. 1998. *Three Seductive Ideas*. Cambridge, Mass.: Harvard University Press.

Kandel, E. 1999. Of Learning, Memory, and Genetic Switches. In R. Conlan, ed., *States of Mind: New Discoveries About How Our Brains Make Us Who We Are*. New York: John Wiley & Sons.

Kaul, V. 1991. Starting Children Too Early on Number Work: A Mismatch of Developmental and Academic Priorities. Resources in Education. Research Report 143. ERIC Data Base. Urbana Champaigne: University of Illinois.

Keating, D.P., and C. Hertzman. 1999. *Developmental Health and the Wealth of Nations: Social, Biological, and Educational Dynamics*. New York: Guilford Press.

Kempermann, G., and F.H. Gage. 1999. New Nerve Cells for the Adult Brain. *Scientific American* 280:48–53.

Le Doux, J. 1999. The Power of Emotions. In R. Conlan, ed., *States of Mind: New Discoveries About How Our Brains Make Us Who We Are*. New York: John Wiley & Sons.

Lien, N.M., K.K. Meyer, and M. Winick. 1977. Early Malnutrition and "Late" Adoption: A Study of Their Effects on the Development of Korean Orphans Adopted into American Families. *American Journal of Clinical Nutrition* 30:1734–39.

Lucas, A., R. Morley, and T.J. Cole. 1998. Randomised Trial of Early Diet in Preterm Babies and Later Intelligence Quotient. *British Medical Journal* 317(7171):1481–87.

Macintyre, S. 1994. Understanding the Social Patterning of Health: The Role of the Social Sciences. *Journal of Public Health Medicine* 16(1):53–59.

Marmot, M., M. Bobak, and G.D. Smith. 1995. Explanations for Social Inequalities in Health. In B.C. Amick, S. Levine, A.R. Tarlov, and D.C. Walsh, eds., *Society and Health.* New York: Oxford University Press.

Maughan, B., and G. McCarthy. 1997. Childhood Adversities and Psychosocial Disorders. *British Medical Journal* 53(1):156–69.

McCain, M.N., and J.F. Mustard. 1999. *Early Years Study: Reversing the Real Brain Drain.* Toronto: Publications Ontario.

McEwen, B. 1999. Corticosteroids, the Aging Brain and Cognition. *Trends in Endocrinology and Metabolism* 10(3):92–96.

McEwen, B.S. 1998. Protective and Damaging Effects of Stress Mediators. *New England Journal of Medicine* 338(3):171–79.

McEwen, B.S., and H.M. Schmeck. 1994. *The Hostage Brain.* New York: Rockefeller University Press.

McEwen, B., and T. Seeman. 1999. Protective and Damaging Effects of Mediators of Stress. Elaborating and Testing the Concepts of Allostasis and Allostatic Load. In Socioeconomic Status and Health in Industrial Nations. *Annals of the New York Academy of Sciences* 896:30–47.

McKeough, A. 1992. Testing for the Presence of a Central Conceptual Structure. In R. Case, ed., *The Mind's Staircase: Exploring the Conceptual Underpinnings of Children's Thought and Knowledge.* Hillsdale, N.J.: Lawrence Erlbaum Associates.

McKeown, T. 1976. *The Modern Rise of Population.* New York: Academic Press.

Meaney, M.J., D.H. Aitken, C. van Berkel, S. Bhatnagar, and R.M. Sapolsky. 1988. Effect of Neonatal Handling on Age-Related Impairments Associated With the Hippocampus. *Science* 239:766–68.

Meaney, M.J., J. Diorio, D. Francis, J. Widdowson, P. LaPlante, C. Caldji, S. Sharma, J.R. Seckl, and P.M. Plotsky. 1996. Early Environmental Regulation of Forebrain Glucocorticoid Receptor Gene Expression: Implications for Adrenocortical Responses to Stress. *Developmental Neuroscience* 18:49–72.

O'Connor, T.G., M. Rutter, C. Beckett, L. Keaveney, J.M. Kreppner, and the English and Romanian Adoptees (ERA) Study Team. 2000. The Effects of Global Severe Privation on Cognitive Competence: Extension and Longitudinal Follow-up. *Child Development* 71: 376–90.

OECD (Organization for Economic Cooperation and Development), and Statistics Canada. 2000. *Literacy in the Information Age: Final Report of the International Adult Literacy Survey.* Paris: OECD. Canada: Minister of Industry.

Osburn, A.F., and J.E. Milbank. 1987. *The Effects of Early Education: A Report from the Child Health and Education Study.* Oxford: Clarendon Press.

Phillips, D.I.W., D.J.P. Barker, C.H.D. Fall, J.R. Seckl, C.B. Whorwood, P.J. Wood, and B.R. Walker. 1998. Elevated Plasma Cortisol Concentrations: A Link Between Low Birth Weight and the Insulin Resistance Syndrome? *Journal of Clinical Endocrinology and Metabolism* 83(3):757–60.

Power, C., and C. Hertzman. 1997. Social and Biological Pathways Linking Early Life and Adult Disease. *British Medical Bulletin* 53(1):210–21.

Power, C., and C. Hertzman. 1999. Health, Well-Being, and Coping Skills. In D. Keating and C. Hertzman, eds., *Developmental Health and the Wealth of Nations.* New York: Guilford Press.

Power, C., C. Hertzman, S. Matthews, and O. Manor. 1997. Social Differences in Health: Life-Cycle Effects Between Ages 23 and 33 in the 1958 British Birth Cohort. *American Journal of Public Health* 87(9):1499–1503.

Power, C., and S. Matthews. 1997. Origins of Health Inequalities in a National Population Sample. *Lancet* 350(9091):1584–89.

Ramey, C.T. 1990. *Early Intervention for High-Risk Children: The Carolina Early Intervention Program.* Binghamton, N.Y.: The Haworth Press.

Ramey, C.T., F.A. Campbell, M. Burchinal, M.L. Skinner, D.M. Gardner, and S.L. Ramey. 2000. Persistent Effects of Early

Intervention on High-Risk Children and Their Mothers. *Applied Developmental Science* 4:2–14.

Rauschecker, J.P. 1999. Making Brain Circuits Listen. *Science* 285:1686–87.

Reves, R. 1985. Declining Fertility in England and Wales as a Major Cause of the Twentieth Century Decline in Mortality. The Role of Changing Family Size and Age Structure in Infectious Disease Mortality in Infancy. *American Journal of Epidemiology* 122:112–26.

Rodgers, B., C. Power, and S. Hope. 1997. Parental Divorce and Adult Psychological Distress: Evidence from a National Birth Cohort: A Research Note. *Journal of Child Psychology and Psychiatry* 38(7): 867–72.

Rutter, M., H. Giller, and A. Hagell. 1998. *Antisocial Behavior by Young People.* Cambridge: Cambridge University Press.

Sapolsky, R.M. 1992. *Stress, the Aging Brain, and the Mechanisms of Neuron Death.* Cambridge, Mass.: MIT Press.

———. 1997. The Importance of a Well-Groomed Child. *Science* 277(5332):1620–21.

Schweinhart, L.J. 1993. *Significant Benefits: The High/Scope Perry Preschool Study Through Age 27.* Ypsilanti, Mich.: High/Scope Press.

Selye, H. 1936. *Nature* 138:22.

———. 1976. *The Stress of Life.* rev. ed. New York: McGraw-Hill.

Smythe, J.W., C.M. McCormick, J. Rochford, and M.J. Meaney. 1994. The Interaction Between Prenatal Stress and Neonatal Handling on Nociceptive Response Latencies in Male and Female Rats. *Physiology and Behavior* 55(5):971–74.

Stattin, H. 1993. Early Language and Intelligence Development and Their Relationship to Future Criminal Behavior. *Journal of Abnormal Psychology* 102(3):369–78.

Steckel, R.H., and R. Floud. 1997. *Health and Welfare during Industrialization.* Chicago: University of Chicago Press.

Suomi, S.J. 1997. Early Determinants of Behaviour: Evidence from Primate Studies. *British Medical Bulletin* 53(1):170–84.

————. 2000. A Biobehavioral Perspective on Developmental Psychopathology. In A.J. Sameroff, M. Lewis, and S.M. Miller, eds., *Handbook of Developmental Psychopathology.* New York: Kluwer Academic.

Szreter, S. 2000. The McKeown Thesis. *Journal of Health Services Research Policy* 5(2):119–20.

Tremblay, R.E. 1999. When Children's Social Development Fails. In D. Keating and C. Hertzman, eds., *Developmental Health and the Wealth of Nations.* New York: Guilford Press.

Wadsworth, M.E.J. 1991. *The Imprint of Time.* Oxford: Clarendon Press.

Wickelgren, I. 1999. Nurture Helps Mold Able Minds. *Science* 283:1832–34.

Willms, J.D. 1999. Quality and Inequality in Children's Literacy: The Effects of Families, Schools, and Communities. In D. Keating and C. Hertzman, eds., *Developmental Health and the Wealth of Nations.* New York: Guilford Press.

Wilson, E.O. 1998. *Consilience: The Unity of Knowledge.* New York: Alfred A. Knopf.

World Bank. 2001. *Brazil, Early Child Development: A Focus on the Impact of Preschools.* Washington, D.C.: World Bank, Human Development Network.

Young, M.E., ed. 1997. *Early Child Development: Investing in our Children's Future.* International Congress Series 1137. Amsterdam: Elsevier Science B.V.

Chapter 3

From Child Development to Human Development

Jacques van der Gaag

Early child development (ECD) and human development (HD) are closely linked. Early child development refers to the combination of physical, mental, and social development in the early years of life—those dimensions that are commonly addressed by integrated programs of ECD. These programs include interventions to improve the nutrition, health, cognitive development, and social interaction of children in the early years (Myers 1992; Young 1997).

Human development refers to similar dimensions—education, health (including nutrition), social development, and growth—but at the scale of a nation. The multidimensional framework for HD used in this chapter is a variant of one first proposed by the United Nations Development Programme in 1990. (In)equality is included in the discussion, but an even broader concept of HD would include additional dimensions such as human rights (Sen 1999).

Human development, broadly defined, is the overarching objective of most international and multinational development programs. Because HD is so closely linked to ECD, investing in ECD is the natural starting point for these programs and for the public policy that frames these programs.

Four critical "pathways" link ECD to HD. The first pathway runs through *education*. Interventions during the early years of a child have multiple benefits for subsequent investments in the child's education, ranging from on-time enrollment in elementary school to an increased probability of progressing to higher levels of education. The second pathway is through *health*. Like education, investments in health are an investment in human capital and have long-term benefits. The third pathway links the notion of improved social behavior (as a result of being enrolled in an ECD program) with the formation of *social capital*. This linkage is more speculative, but is suggested by some interesting research results. In the fourth pathway, ECD is linked to HD by the potential of ECD programs to address *inequality* in society. And, ultimately, education, health, social capital, and equality are linked to economic growth and, hence, to HD.

All these linkages are discussed in this chapter, which concludes with suggestions for further research to close some of the gaps in knowledge identified. To provide context, the chapter opens with a brief history of development economics.

Development Economics: A Brief History

The history of development economics is well described in the *Handbook of Development Economics*, volume 1 (Chenery and Srinivasan 1989), which is recommended for serious readers. A key point to note in this chapter is that early approaches to development, which were characterized by mathematical planning models, have been replaced gradually by development models which recognize that people are both the means and the ultimate cause of development. These more recent models underscore the importance of investing in (young) people as a central means to foster development.

The shift from planning models to people is illustrated by the salient contributions of four Nobel laureates in economics, all of whom were rewarded for their work on development. The first Nobel laureate in economics was Jan Tinbergen, who shared the prize in 1969 with Ragna Frisch. Tinbergen's influence on the field can still be felt around the world.

Tinbergen initially studied physics and, later, applied mathematical planning models to the economies of developing countries, mainly to determine optimal levels of investments. The planning, at least in concept, comprised three stages. First, at the macro level, a desired level of economic growth was chosen. Since labor was thought to be abundantly available, this desired growth rate determined the optimal level of overall investment. At the middle stage, the optimal distribution of this investment by region and by industry was determined, and, at the third stage, individual investments for projects were evaluated and allocated. Apart from the abundance of labor (to be recruited from rural areas), no people were included in these planning models.

It would be unfair to Tinbergen (who entered or, rather, invented the field of development economics because of concern for the living conditions of the world's poor) to suggest that people were forgotten in the development process. On the contrary, people were seen as an important production factor. Consequently, education was an important element in these models. Investments in education needed to be planned, as were investments in roads or in machines. Indeed, skilled labor (the result of such investments) could also be allocated by region or industry and, if needed, even imported.

Omitted from these early models, however, was the (economic) *behavior* of people. In 1979, the Nobel prize for economics was awarded to T.W. Schultz (and W.A. Lewis). Schultz's major contribution to the field was in showing that the behavior of people in developing countries is, like the people in developed countries, that of a rational *homo economicus*, reacting to incentives and opportunities. He stressed the importance of investing in human capital (skills and knowledge) to increase productivity (especially in agriculture) and entrepreneurship.

A third Nobel laureate (in 1993), R.W. Fogel, emphasized the importance of "people development" in yet another way. Taking a historical view, Fogel underscores the importance of the contribution of technological change to physiological improvements. He concludes that the "technophysio" evolution (as termed by him) accounts for about half of British economic growth over the past two centuries. He states: "Much of this gain was due to the improvement in human thermodynamic efficiency. The rate of converting human energy input into work output appears to have increased by about 50 percent since 1790" (Fogel 2000, pp.78–79). Fogel is also one of the few economists who have recognized the importance of long-term health effects from deprivation during early childhood.

A. Sen, who received the Nobel prize in 1998, also recognized the central role of investing in people. The resulting higher income, from higher productivity, reduces poverty and increases economic well-being. However, Sen also underscores better health, higher education levels, and improved nutrition as separate goals which, in addition to higher income, represent nonmonetary aspects of the quality of life (i.e., of "human development") that are valuable in and of themselves. In his latest book (Sen 1999), he extends this concept, to emphasize that individual freedom is the ultimate goal of economic life. In this treatise, Sen uses a very broad definition of freedom, which includes freedom from hunger, disease, ignorance, all forms of deprivation, poverty, as well as political and economic freedom and civil rights.

Linking ECD to HD: Four Pathways

Education

The first pathway, from ECD to HD, is through education. The importance of ECD for subsequent educational performance, and the role of education in economic and human development, are well known and supported by extensive scientific evidence accumulated from neurophysics, pediatrics, the medical sciences, child development, education, sociology, and economics. Ample evidence documents the importance of the early months and years in life for a child's physical, mental, and social development (Cynader and Frost 1999; McCain and Mustard 1999; Myers 1992; Young 1997). The rapid development of the brain during the early months and years is crucial, and newborns who receive proper care and stimulation will be readier to enter school on time and to learn.

Children participating in ECD programs receive psychosocial stimulation, nutritional supplementation, and health care, and their parents receive training in effective childcare. Children who have participated in these programs show higher intelligence quotients and improvements in practical reasoning, eye and hand coordination, hearing and speech, and reading readiness (Myers 1992). Grade repetition and dropout rates are lower, performance at school is higher, and the probability that a child will progress to higher levels of education increases (Barnett 1995; Barnett 1998; Grantham-McGregor and others 1997; Karoly and others 1998; Schweinhart and others 1993).

Over the long term, these children benefit from earlier schooling, better schooling, and more schooling, making them more productive and more "successful"as adults. Being well educated is the best predictor of "success" as an adult, regardless of how success is defined. The definition of success, as a better job and higher income in the marketplace or increased and improved production at home (e.g., childcare, nutritional practices, family health), can differ from case to case, but higher education is always associated with greater well-being, broadly defined (Haveman and Wolfe 1984; Psacharopoulos 1994).

The public benefits of education are also well known. For society, they include greater ability to adopt new technologies, better functioning of democratic processes, lower fertility rates, and lower crime rates (Carnoy 1992; Rutter, Giller, and Hagell 1998). As firmly established in the economic literature on development, education is also important for economic growth (Barro 1997).

The education pathway clearly demonstrates that the link between ECD and HD is straightforward, as abundantly documented by scientific evidence. Increased investments in ECD programs can be fully justified, and usually are, based on this evidence alone (van der Gaag and Tan 1998). Good education is a goal in itself and fosters economic prosperity. Yet, three additional pathways deserve at least the same attention as education.

Health

For many decades, the leading development agencies, including the World Health Organization, the United Nations Children's Fund (UNICEF), and the World Bank, have emphasized the importance of providing good nutrition, immunization, and other basic health care services for young children. The health benefits of these services are immediately evident (Bundy 1997; PAHO 1998; Stephenson and others 1993), and the cost-effectiveness of interventions to improve these services is well established (Horton 1999). Despite this knowledge, and shamefully, millions of children in developing countries still die before they have lived 1 year, and those who survive suffer from a myriad of easily preventable diseases.

ECD programs can make a dramatic difference. They are associated with decreased morbidity and mortality among children, fewer cases of malnutrition and stunting, improved personal hygiene and health care, and fewer instances of child abuse.

Less well known are the strong links between trauma in the early years of life (e.g., from malnutrition, even in utero, and infectious diseases) and an individual's health as an adult. Recent studies show that the links between health and nutrition in the early years of life and one's health status as an adult are much more numerous and stronger than previously known. The range of adult health outcomes now known to be associated with growth in utero and early life development, or lack of, includes blood pressure, respiratory function, and schizophrenia. Childhood social and educational factors also are strongly associated with physical and mental health outcomes in adult life (Wadsworth and Kuh 1997).

Scientific evidence of these links is also available in relation to the crucial period of brain development in utero and shortly after birth (Barker 1998; Ravelli 1999). Infant malnutrition has been associated with diabetes and reduced stature as an adult. Infection early in life has been related to the development of chronic bronchitis, acute appendicitis, asthma, Parkinson's disease, and multiple sclerosis in adulthood. And, low birthweight has been correlated with subsequent increased blood pressure, chronic pulmonary disease, cardiovascular disease, coronary heart disease, and stroke. Thus, although an investment in basic health and nutritional services for young children can be justified by immediate health and anthropometric outcomes for children, the linkage to their health status as adults heightens the importance of the interventions, which are standard components of integrated ECD programs.

The linkage to adults' health status is also significant for HD efforts. Evidence indicates that the association between adults' health status and economic well-being is at least as strong as the association between education and economic well-being (Hertzman 1999; Smith 1999). Adults with better health, higher life expectancy, and better weight and height measures tend to have higher productivity, less absenteeism from work, and higher incomes than their less fortunate counterparts.

However, the causality in the relationship between health status and economic well-being remains in question. Does good health lead to higher productivity (income) or does a higher income enable one to buy better health? Both relationships—health as cause and as effect—have been proven true. When possible to establish that good or poor health came first, a subsequent economic effect could be determined (e.g., the reduced earning power of adults stunted by malnutrition as a child) (Bundy 1997; Thomas and Strauss 1997). The converse, higher income leading to better health, also is well documented (Acheson 1998). Clearly, better health results in higher income in many instances, but additional research is needed to further unravel the dual relationship.

To establish a definitive link between health and the HD of a nation, the health-and-income nexus must be aggregated across individuals, for populations. Recent studies demonstrate this link. Like education, the health status of a population is related to the economic growth of that population (Barro 1997; Pritchett and Summers 1996; WHO 1998). Key examples in Africa are the economic (growth-reducing) effects of malaria and the epidemic of Acquired Immunodeficiency Syndrome (AIDS) (Bloom and Sachs 1998).

Surprisingly, most of the studies of health and economic growth are recent, and additional research is needed to understand more fully the many ways in which the health of a population, which is a good in itself, can influence the wealth of a nation. But, the fact that the link is very important is no longer debatable. Like education, the health pathway from ECD to HD is clear. If increasing the wealth of a nation is an overall objective, beginning with the health of a new-born is a logical first step.

Social Capital

The "social" benefits of ECD programs are less well defined than the health and education benefits. Still, they do exist. Many studies of the effects of ECD programs note the change in children's behavior (Kagitçibasi 1996; Karoly and others 1998). They are less aggressive and more cooperative, they behave better in groups, and they accept instructions (e.g., from parents) well. Overall the children have higher self-concepts and are more socially adjusted.

A few long-term (tracer) studies point to similar outcomes for the children's adult life: improved self-esteem, social competence, motivation, and acceptance of the culture's norms and values. In particular, evidence suggests that participation in ECD programs leads to reduced criminal behavior and less delinquency as an adult (Schweinhart and others 1993; Yoshikawa 1995; Zigler, Taussig, and Black 1992).

The link between improved social behavior and the formation and maintenance of "social capital" has yet to be established. Social capital includes many distinct social phenomena. At the macro level, it refers to informal institutional arrangements, trust, ethnic social networks, nonlegal market arrangements and other related phenomena (Coleman 1990; Putnam 1993). At the individual level, the term refers to a person's ability to draw upon social networks to better pursue his or her own interests, a phenomenon that usually involves reciprocal arrangements similar to the exchange of "IOU" slips when obtaining financial credit (Coleman 1988, 1990; Lin 1999).

Studies of the social benefits of ECD programs suggest that the benefits will continue later in life. As the brain needs to be wired properly for academic learning, so it needs to be prepared suitably for social learning. If studies can truly establish the link between the social benefits of ECD programs and improved skills of adults in creating and utilizing social capital, the link to HD can easily be made.

To do so only requires that the benefits to social capital at the individual level be aggregated to society as a whole. Although social capital is an ill-defined concept that refers to many different social phenomena, this linkage has already been established firmly in the sociology and economic literature (Narayan 1997; Woolcock 1999). Much empirical evidence has been acquired recently, and although it does not directly make the link between children and adults as suggested above, it is convincing and growing.

Interest in the link between culture, or values, and economic performance also is increasing. Recent studies suggest that "values" is an important concept for explaining differences in the growth of nations (Fukuyama 1995). If researchers determine that ECD programs can instill values that are reflected subsequently in adults' behavior, the link between ECD and HD through the pathway of social capital may be even greater than suggested here.

Equality

The fourth pathway, "equality," refers to a "level playing field." It is inextricably linked to the previous three pathways. Equality may refer to a level playing field in education, health, or social capital. And, like education, health, and social capital, equality is a good in itself and contributes to the economic performance of a nation. If ECD programs can be shown to contribute to achieving a more equal society, the link between ECD and HD, through the pathway of equality, can be easily established. In fact, ECD programs can contribute greatly to a leveling of the playing field if they are well targeted (Barros and Mendonça 1999). With a relatively small investment, ECD programs can decrease the disadvantage of poor children, compared with their more fortunate counterparts, in nutritional status, cognitive and social development, and health. The benefits of greater equality begin right after birth.

For adults, equality in education and health leads to equality of opportunity; better education and health lead to higher income. Significantly, data show that countries with a more equitable distribution of income are also more healthy (Deaton 1999; Hertzman 1999;

Wilkinson 1996). The evidence is undeniable, yet the reasons for the relationship are being debated. Nevertheless, the link between more equality of opportunity early in life and more equality in education, income, and health later in life appears to be strong, as does the aggregate link between greater equality in income and the health of society. And, again, the benefits begin with ECD.

Finally, numerous studies show that greater equality leads to higher sustainable growth (Aghion, Caroli, and García-Peñalosa 1999; Barro 1997). The link between ECD and HD, through the pathway of equality, is complex, but strong.

ECD: Benefits and Research Needs

Table 1 summarizes the benefits of ECD—better education, improved health, increased social capital, and greater equality. All of these outcomes are of value themselves, and the benefits are immediately tangible at the time of intervention (i.e., in a child's early years). ECD programs are most often justified by the immediate benefits to a child's social and cognitive development and health and nutritional status. Yet, as discussed above, these outcomes have positive, long-term consequences for the children as they mature into adults and for their nations as a whole. Except for the pathway of education, these long-term benefits are usually ignored by government officials and policymakers.

The link between ECD and HD through the pathway of education is clearly established and abundantly documented. New developments in health research, particularly those addressing the relationship between child health and adult health, also provide ample evidence of a link between ECD and HD. As additional research findings become available, the pathway of health is likely to become as significant to HD as is education. International organizations and governments may need to fundamentally rethink health care efforts worldwide and to direct a much larger share of health care budgets to the health care of children, especially in their early years. The aim will be not only to address children's immediate health problems, but also to reduce their future health risks as adults.

Table 1. ECD Benefits for Children, Adults, and Society: Summary

Benefits of ECD	Pathways linking ECD to HD			
	Education	Health	Social capital	Equality
For children (immediate)	Higher intelligence, improved practical reasoning, eye and hand coordination, hearing and speech; reading readiness; improved school performance; less grade repetition and dropout; increased schooling	Less morbidity, mortality, malnutrition, stunting, child abuse; better hygiene and health care	Higher self-concept; more socially adjusted; less aggressive; more cooperative; better behavior in groups; increased acceptance of instructions	Reduced disadvantages of poverty; improved nutritional status, cognitive and social development, and health
For adults (long-term)	Higher productivity; increased success (better jobs, higher incomes); improved childcare and family health; greater economic well-being	Improved height and weight; enhanced cognitive development; less infections and chronic diseases	Higher self-esteem; improved social competence, motivation, acceptance of norms and values; less delinquency and criminal behavior	Equality of opportunity, education, health, and income
For society	Greater social cohesion; less poverty and crime; lower fertility rates; increased adoption of new technologies; improved democratic processes; higher economic growth	Higher productivity; less absenteeism; higher incomes	Improved utilization of social capital; enhanced social values	Reduced poverty and crime; better societal health; increased social justice; higher sustainable economic growth

ECD, Early child development; HD, human development.

The pathway of social capital is currently less clear, but suggestive. The link between social behavior as a child and as an adult needs to be confirmed, and the link between social behavior and social capital is still weak. The literature on social capital is relatively young, but current evidence indicates that this pathway for ECD to HD will become as firmly established as the pathways of education and health.

The pathway of equality from ECD to HD is undeniable and, as noted, is linked to the other three pathways. The finding that income equality is related to the health of society is a recent and surprising one, which reinforces the importance of ECD and suggests far-reaching policy implications.

Education, health, social capital, and equality are all important contributors to economic growth. Together with economic growth, they constitute the mutually reinforcing elements of a comprehensive framework for HD, as depicted in figure 1. This framework could be expanded easily, for example, to include gender issues or poverty (as it relates to equality).

Well-executed and well-targeted ECD programs are initiators of HD. They stimulate improvements in education, health, social capital, and equality that have both immediate and long-term benefits

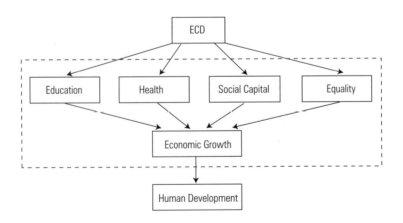

Figure 1. From Child Development to Human Development: A Comprehensive Framework

for the children participating in the programs. Investments in ECD programs are in many ways investments in the future of a nation.

Acknowledgment

The author thanks Wendy Janssens for excellent research assistance during the preparation of this chapter.

References

Acheson, D. 1998. *Independent Inquiry into Inequalities in Health: Report.* London: The Stationery Office.

Aghion, P., E. Caroli, and C. García-Peñalosa. 1999. "Inequality and Economic Growth: The Perspective of the New Growth Theories." *Journal of Economic Literature* 37 (December):1615–60.

Barker, D.J.P. 1998. *Mothers, Babies and Health in Later Life.* Edinburgh: Churchill Livingstone.

Barnett, W.S. 1995. Long-Term Effects of Early Childhood Programs on Cognitive and School Outcomes. *The Future of Children* 5(3):25–50.

———. 1998. Long-Term Cognitive and Academic Effects of Early Childhood Education on Children in Poverty. *Preventive Medicine* 27:204–07.

Barro, R.J. 1997. *Determinants of Economic Growth: A Cross-Country Empirical Study.* Cambridge, Mass.: MIT Press.

Barros, R.P. de, and R. Mendonça. 1999. *Costs and Benefits of Pre-School Education in Brazil.* Rio de Janeiro: Institute of Applied Economic Research.

Bloom, D.E., and J.D. Sachs. 1998. Geography, Demography, and Economic Growth in Africa, Harvard Institute for International Development. Brookings Papers on Economic Activity. Washington, D.C.: Brookings Institution.

Bundy, D.A.P. 1997. Health and Early Child Development. In M.E. Young, ed., *Early Child Development: Investing in our Children's Future.* Amsterdam: Elsevier Science B.V.

Carnoy, M. 1992. *The Case for Investing in Basic Education*. New York: United Nations Children's Fund.

Chenery, H., and T.N. Srinivasan. 1989. *Handbook of Development Economics, volume 1*. New York: North Holland.

Coleman, J. 1988. Social Capital in the Creation of Human Capital. *American Journal of Sociology* 94:S95–S120.

———. 1990. *Foundations of Social Theory*. Cambridge, Mass.: Harvard University Press.

Cynader, M.S., and B.J. Frost. 1999. Mechanisms of Brain Development: Neuronal Sculpting by the Physical and Social Environment. In D.P. Keating and C. Hertzman, eds., *Developmental Health and the Wealth of Nations: Social, Biological, and Educational Dynamics*. New York: The Guilford Press.

Deaton, A. 1999. Inequalities in Income and Inequalities in Health. National Bureau of Economic Research Working Paper No. W7141. New York.

Fogel, R.W. 2000. *The Fourth Great Awakening*. Chicago: University of Chicago Press.

Fukuyama, F. 1995. *Trust: The Social Virtues and the Creation of Prosperity*. New York: Free Press.

Grantham-McGregor, S.M., S.P. Walker, S.M. Chang, and C.A. Powell. 1997. Effects of Early Childhood Supplementation With and Without Stimulation on Later Development in Stunted Jamaican Children. *American Journal of Clinical Nutrition* 66:247–53.

Haveman, R.H., and B.L. Wolfe. 1984. Schooling and Economic Well-being: The Role of Nonmarket Effects. *Journal of Human Resources* 19(3):377–407.

Hertzman, C. 1999. Population Health and Human Development. In D.P. Keating and C. Hertzman, eds., *Developmental Health and the Wealth of Nations: Social, Biological, and Educational Dynamics*. New York: The Guilford Press.

Horton, S. 1999. Economics of Nutritional Investments (draft). In R.D. Semba and M.W. Bloem, eds., *Nutrition and Health in Developing Countries*. Totowa, N.J.: Humana Press.

Kagitçibasi, Ç. 1996. *Family and Human Development Across Cultures: A View from the Other Side*. Mahwah, N.J.: Lawrence Erlbaum Associates.

Karoly, L.A., P.W. Greenwood, S.S. Everingham, J. Hoube, M.R. Kilburu, C.P. Rydell, M. Sanders, and J. Chiesa. 1998. *Investing in Our Children: What We Know and Don't Know about the Costs and Benefits of Early Childhood Interventions*. Washington, D.C.:RAND.

Lin, N. 1999. *Inequality in Social Capital: Evidence from Urban China. Creation and Returns of Social Capital in Education and Labor Markets.* Center for Research in Experimental Economics and Political Decision Making/University of Amsterdam, Institute of Information and Computing Sciences (ICS)/University of Groningen and ICS/Utrecht University.

McCain, M.N., and J.F. Mustard. 1999. *Reversing the Real Brain Drain: Early Years Study, Final Report*. Toronto: Publications Ontario.

Myers, R.G. 1992. *The Twelve Who Survive*. London: Routledge.

Narayan, D. 1997. *Voices of the Poor: Poverty and Social Capital in Tanzania*. Washington, D.C.: World Bank.

PAHO (Pan American Health Organization), ed. 1998. *Nutrition, Health and Child Development: Research Advances and Policy Recommendations*. Scientific Publication No. 566. Washington, D.C.

Pritchett, L., and L.H. Summers. 1996. Wealthier Is Healthier. *Journal of Human Resources* 31(4):841–68.

Psacharopoulos, G. 1994. Returns to Investment in Education: A Global Update. *World Development* 22(9):1325–43.

Putnam, R. 1993. The Prosperous Community – Social Capital and Economic Growth. *The American Prospect* 356(spring):4–9.

Ravelli, A.C.J. 1999. Prenatal Exposure to the Dutch Famine and Glucose Tolerance and Obesity at Age 50. Thela Thesis. Amsterdam: University of Amsterdam.

Rutter, M., H. Giller, and A. Hagell. 1998. *Antisocial Behavior by Young People*. Cambridge: Cambridge University Press.

Schweinhart, L.J., H.V. Barnes, and D.P. Weikart (with W.S. Barnett and A.S. Epstein). 1993. *Significant Benefits: The High/Scope Perry Preschool Study Through Age 27*. Ypsilanti, Mich.: High/Scope Press.

Sen, A. 1999. *Development as Freedom.* New York: Alfred A. Knopf.

Smith, J.P. 1999. Healthy Bodies and Thick Wallets: The Dual Relation Between Health and Economic Status. *Journal of Economic Perspectives* 13(2):145–66.

Stephenson, L.S., M.C. Latham, E.J. Adams, S.N. Kinoti, and A. Pertet. 1993. Physical Fitness, Growth and Appetite of Kenyan Schoolboys With Hookworm, *Trichuris trichiura* and *Ascaris lumbricoides.* Infections Are Improved Four Months After a Single Dose of Albendazole. *Journal of Nutrition* 123:1036–46.

Thomas, D., and J. Strauss. 1997. Health and Wages: Evidence on Men and Women in Urban Brazil. *Journal of Econometrics* 77:159–85.

Van der Gaag, J., and J.-P. Tan. 1998. *The Benefits of Early Child Development Programs: An Economic Analysis.* Washington, D.C: World Bank, Human Development Network.

Wadsworth, M.E., and D. Kuh. 1997. Childhood Influences on Adult Health. *Paediatric and Perinatal Epidemiology* 11:2–20.

WHO (World Health Organization). 1998. Health, Health Policy, and Economic Outcomes. Health and Development Satellite, WHO Director-General, Transition Team. Geneva.

Wilkinson, R.G. 1996. *Unhealthy Societies: The Afflictions of Inequality.* London: Routledge.

Woolcock, M. 1999. Managing Risk, Shocks, and Opportunity in Developing Economies: The Role of Social Capital. Washington, D.C.: World Bank, Development Research Group.

Yoshikawa, H. 1995. Long-Term Effects of Early Childhood Programs on Social Outcomes and Delinquency. *The Future of Children* 5(3):51–75.

Young, M.E., ed. 1997. *Early Child Development: Investing in our Children's Future.* International Congress Series No. 1137. Amsterdam: Elsevier Science B.V.

Zigler, E., C. Taussig, and K. Black. 1992. Early Childhood Intervention: A Promising Preventative for Juvenile Delinquency. *American Psychologist* 47(8):997–1006.

Part II

Measuring the Early Opportunity Gap

Chapter 4

Standards of Care: Investments to Improve Children's Educational Outcomes in Latin America

J. Douglas Willms

At the 1990 World Conference on Education for All, held in Jomtien, Thailand, educators and policymakers recommended increased emphasis on care and stimulation during early childhood, improvements in the quality of education provided, and universal access to completion of primary education by the end of the millennium. During the 1980s, researchers showed that children in low-income countries have lower levels of literacy than children in high-income countries who receive similar amounts of schooling. Two plausible explanations for this finding are that children in poorer countries begin primary school without the developmental base to enable them to achieve their full potential and that the quality of schooling in low-income countries is lower than in high-income countries.

During the 1980s, research conducted in several countries provided compelling evidence that schools differ considerably in their outcomes, even after accounting for children's family backgrounds (Bryk, Lee, and Smith 1990; Gray 1989; Raudenbush and Willms 1991; Willms 1992). The results of large-scale studies of schooling in low-income countries demonstrated the importance of human and material resources (e.g., school infrastructure, class size, teachers' experience and qualifications, availability of instructional materials) for achieving better school outcomes (Fuller and Clarke 1994). Research by the World Bank showed that such factors have an even stronger relationship to academic achievement in low-income countries than to that in high-income countries (Heyneman and Loxley 1983).

In 1996, a consortium of thirteen Latin American countries conducted the Primer Estudio Internacional Comparativo (PEIC), the first international study of school outcomes in Latin America to utilize common tests and questionnaires across several countries. The PEIC study entailed (a) testing more than 50,000 pupils in grades 3 and 4 for language and mathematics skills and (b) administering questionnaires to pupils, parents, teachers, and school administrators. The data included considerable information on early childhood outcomes, including parents' home practices and whether the child attended day care. This comparative study is one of the first to assess the importance of these factors. The multinational study was funded by the Inter-American Development Bank; Convenio Andrés Bello; Ford Foundation; United Nations Educational, Scientific, and Cultural Organization (UNESCO); and the following participating countries: Argentina, Bolivia, Brazil, Colombia, Costa Rica, Chile, Cuba, Dominican Republic, Honduras, Mexico, Paraguay, Peru, and República Bolivariana de Venezuela.

Two substantive reports of the study have been published. The first report (UNESCO 1998) provides technical information on PEIC and descriptive analyses by country. The second report, entitled *Schooling Outcomes in Latin America*, was coauthored by Willms and Somers (2000) and prepared in consultation with the Laboratorio Latinoamericano de Evaluación de la Calidad de la Educación, which coordinated the study. The second report presents, for each country, detailed descriptions of the relationships between achievement outcomes and family socioeconomic status (SES), school sector (public, private), extent of urbanization (rural, urban, mega-city), material resources (e.g., class size, school infrastructure, teachers' qualifications), and school "culture" (e.g., parental involvement, teachers' attitudes, principals' autonomy, learning climate).

The present chapter summarizes some findings of the Willms and Somers (2000) report and extends the analysis to assess the relative importance of family and school factors. Four aims are to: (a) portray the relationship between school outcomes and SES, giving attention to urbanicity and sector; (b) estimate the magnitude of effects associated with risk factors relevant to childhood vulnerability in Latin America and discern the extent of these effects in mediating the relationship between school outcomes and SES; (c) suggest a framework for using findings from international studies to prescribe "standards of care" based on the most important predictors of early childhood outcomes; and (d) suggest ways to improve the capability for monitoring progress in early child development.

The chapter demonstrates how the suggested framework could be applied across the relevant countries using PEIC findings and indicates the achievement of standards within each country. Drawing from the Willms and Somers (2000) report, the chapter presents data on twelve countries, referred to herein as the "Region" (data for the thirteenth country, Costa Rica, were not available because of a specific coding problem, and data for Peru are included only for Regional estimates because country-specific results for this country are embargoed).

The chapter comprises five main sections, as follows: The Importance of Understanding Socioeconomic Gradients; School Outcomes in Latin America: Gradients and School Profiles; Standards of Care: A Suggested Framework; Childhood Vulnerability: Analysis and Findings; and Next Steps: Strengthening the Basis for Monitoring and Reform. A concluding section presents additional perspectives.

Several caveats should be noted. Any analysis of this sort and any attempt to set standards can be easily criticized. A framework that links processes to outcomes is necessarily limited by the data available and the difficulty of generalizing empirical findings which reflect local social, political, and economic realities. Collaborations with school districts and governments grappling with the use of data for monitoring have demonstrated that the main value of monitoring is to stimulate dialogue on desired outcomes of schooling and critical examination of current policies and practices. Accordingly, the overarching goal of the chapter is to generate dialogue about standards of care.

The Importance of Understanding Socioeconomic Gradients

Perhaps the most pervasive finding of research on human development is that children's developmental outcomes are related to the SES of their families. There is a "gradient": Children whose parents have lower levels of education and income and are working in less prestigious jobs are less likely to succeed academically, more prone to behavioral disorders, and more vulnerable to poor health than are children living in affluent families. Virtually every important social outcome seems to be related to SES. This relationship has become so firmly entrenched in understanding human development that the terms "children with delayed development," "children at risk," and "children living in poverty" are used synonymously. Because this relationship has become accepted as nearly universal, one may question whether further study of socioeconomic gradients is worthwhile.

Understanding socioeconomic gradients is essential for understanding factors that contribute to the success of society. A "socioeconomic gradient" describes the relationship between some developmental outcome and SES. Researchers of early child development are typically interested in outcomes describing children's cognitive, social, and behavioral development. These outcomes, such as achievement test scores, are usually measured on a continuous scale, but also can be measured dichotomously with indicators such as whether a child has a specific disease or behavior disorder or is particularly vulnerable.

SES refers to the relative position of a family or individual within a hierarchical social structure based on access to, or control over, wealth, prestige, and power (Dutton and Levine 1989; Mueller and

Parcel 1981). SES is usually operationalized as a composite measure comprising income, level of education, and occupational prestige. Gradients can be depicted as a line on a graph, with the developmental outcome on the vertical axis and an SES measure on the horizontal axis (see figure 1).

Implications of Socioeconomic Gradients

Gradients can be used to indicate the translation of investments in material, social, and cultural resources into skills and competencies over time (e.g., between decades). For a society, they depict overall outcomes (e.g., levels of literacy) as well as inequalities among social classes. These inequalities have several implications for society—for its social cohesion, health and well-being, and social policy.

Social Cohesion. Achieving equality of outcomes (i.e., "shallow gradients") is essential for achieving social cohesion. Ritzen's definition of social cohesion as "an inclusive civil society and responsive political institutions" (Ritzen 2000) is central to the World Bank's approach to policy and projects. Mounting evidence demonstrates that the economic success of societies depends on relationships among people within and among institutions, communities, and countries.

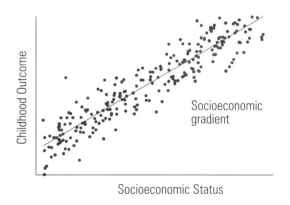

Figure 1. Socioeconomic Gradients, Defined

Researchers have used the term social capital to characterize the nature of relationships among people and the relationships' facilitation of collective action, social networks, and community norms and values (Coleman 1988). Research at the micro level has shown that the productivity of institutions and organizations depends on teamwork, communication, sharing of knowledge and ideas, and workers' embracing of organizations' aims. Research at the macro level has been focused on the nature of social support and collective action and their effect on people's trust and trustworthiness and sense of security and well-being. Currently, the concept of social capital is being incorporated into the new growth models of economic development.

Health and Well-Being. Inequalities in social outcomes appear to be a strong determinant of health and well-being. A number of studies show that health outcomes vary among neighborhoods, communities, health authorities, states and provinces, and countries, even after accounting for people's socioeconomic backgrounds. Two findings are especially relevant to socioeconomic gradients. First, gradients for mortality and health status are nonlinear: They are steep at low levels of income and become shallower at higher levels of income (Epelbaum 1999; House and others 1990; Mirowsky and Hu 1996; Wolfson and others 1999; Wolfson, Rowe, Gentleman, and Tomiak 1993). After people meet their basic needs for food, clothing, and housing, further increases in income seem to contribute only marginally to their health. Second, health is not only related to overall levels of income and wealth, but also to levels of income inequality in a society (Wilkinson 1992, 1996; Kaplan and others 1996; Wolfson and others 1999). The predominating explanations relate to people feeling relatively deprived or excluded.

Social Policy. Gradients can provide a focus for social policy, which is concerned mainly with achieving particular outcomes for society as a whole and, especially, for vulnerable groups. During the past few decades, governments have focused mainly on economic policies. Consequently, social policies have not changed at the same pace. Discussions about social policy have mainly concerned the functions of state governments, particularly provision of services (e.g., public education, health care, protective services) and redistribution of income by income transfers to targeted groups (Fellegi and Wolfson 1999). The roles of corporations, communities, and families in shaping social policy have received relatively little attention. Gradients are useful as a simple, straightforward device for shifting attention toward desired social outcomes and inequalities in outcomes. A simple display of gradients for a set of outcomes always begs the question, "Can we alter the gradients?"

Socioeconomic Gradients for Childhood Vulnerability

Socioeconomic gradients are pertinent to early childhood development and the vulnerability of children to society's inequalities. In PEIC and other studies, researchers have demonstrated the complex relationships and interactions between these gradients and children's vulnerability. Ten key questions for research have been elucidated by the Canadian Research Institute for Social Policy (Willms, forthcoming) and are summarized below.

1. *At what age do socioeconomic gradients for children's outcomes become evident?* Do gradients become stronger as children become older? For example, are gradients evident for the prevalence of children with low birthweight or for children's early developmental outcomes? Do gradients become stronger after children enter the formal school system?
2. *Are gradients stronger for some outcomes than for others?* For example, are gradients stronger for cognitive outcomes than for behavioral outcomes?
3. *Which SES components are related most strongly to children's social and cognitive outcomes?* Most recent research emphasizes the effects of poverty on children's outcome, but other factors (e.g., parents', and especially mothers', level of education) have a significant role. The relative importance of various SES components at different ages needs to be better understood.
4. *Are gradients linear or curvilinear?* A particular concern is whether gradients for children's developmental outcomes weaken above

a certain SES threshold and, if so, whether this threshold varies among communities. For example, the income threshold for health outcomes appears to be about $20,000: Below $20,000, the relationship between income and health is strong, and above $20,000, the relationship is weak (Epelbaum 1990; House and others 1990; Mirowsky and Hu 1996). Income gradients may be curvilinear as well as linear. In Canada, the income gradient for health outcomes is curvilinear, but the change in slope is more gradual, making it difficult to identify a threshold accurately (Boyle and Willms 1998; Wolfson and others 1993, 1999). Determining whether gradients are linear or curvilinear is particularly relevant to the development of policies for investing in early childhood by targeting resources to low-income families.

5. *What factors mediate the relationships between childhood outcomes and SES?* The term "mediating factors" describes the underlying processes for one variable influencing another (Baron and Kenny 1986) (e.g., income and achievement). For example, do parents in low-income families pursue a different approach to parenting which leads to poor developmental outcomes? If so, parenting styles could be a mediator of the socioeconomic gradient.

6. *Are there groups within society whose children are particularly vulnerable?* Special concerns are the outcomes for children in minority groups, single-parent families, and families with parents who were teenagers when they had their first child.

7. *Do children's outcomes vary by community?* In relation to children's development, "community" is defined as a group of citizens collectively concerned about the health and well-being of their children. Communities can be multiple and overlapping (e.g., neighborhoods, churches, municipalities, classrooms, schools, school districts). A concern is whether children's outcomes vary among communities regardless of family background.

8. *Do socioeconomic gradients vary among communities?* For example, are some communities particularly successful in abating

inequalities in children's outcomes? In many contexts, gradients vary among communities, and communities that have particularly steep or shallow gradients can be identified. For school outcomes, gradients tend to converge for children at higher SES levels (Willms 2000). This convergence has important implications for social policy for it suggests that children from relatively affluent family backgrounds tend to do well in any community, whereas children from less affluent backgrounds can have substantially different outcomes in different communities. Successful communities are able to bolster the social outcomes of their least-advantaged citizens.

9. *What are the effects of segregating children from lower socioeconomic backgrounds by, for example, residential segregation, private schooling, selective schooling, tracking or streaming, and ability grouping within classrooms or by other mechanisms that differentiate groups according to socioeconomic background?* This question is especially relevant to low-income countries because their school systems are highly segregated owing to disparities in income between rural and urban families and to private schooling. This "hypothesis of double jeopardy" implies that a child in a poor family is even more vulnerable when educated in a poor setting.

10. *If communities' gradients vary, what factors are associated with high outcome levels and shallow gradients?* If gradients for children's developmental outcomes vary among communities, can a community's achievement of superior or more equitably distributed outcomes be explained by community factors?

School Outcomes in Latin America: Gradients and School Profiles

The target population for PEIC was all children attending grades 3 and 4 in the thirteen participating countries. For each country, the sample included approximately 100 schools, with twenty grade 3 pupils and twenty grade 4 pupils in each school, for a total of 3,000–4,000 pupils. The data collected included achievement test scores in language (Spanish) and mathematics and questionnaires administered to each pupil, one of the pupil's parents, the teacher, principal, and school administrator. [See UNESCO (1998) and Willms and Somers (2000) for further details.] The findings for gradients and school profiles are depicted and summarized below.

Gradients

Figures 2–4 display the socioeconomic gradients, by country, for school outcomes (language scores, mathematics scores, and no grade repetition) in relation to parents' education. Parents' education (years of schooling) is averaged for a child's two parents (the full regression models included a variable for single- or two-parent families). The gradients are calculated based on ordinary least-squares relationships, and, because most countries had a significant nonlinear component, the square of parental education is included. The test scores for language and mathematics are scaled using the Rasch method to obtain a mean score of 250 for the Region, with a standard deviation of 50. No grade repetition is included as a measure of whether a child has repeated at least one grade before completing grade three.

In most analyses of schools' effectiveness, grade repetition is treated as a variable of school policy and is used in regression analyses as an independent variable to explain variation in academic test scores. In PEIC, grade repetition is treated as a dependent variable for three reasons: (a) progressing through school with one's same-age peers is an important school outcome strongly related to self-esteem, sense of belonging, and general well-being (Shepard 1989; Shepard and Smith 1989); (b) grade failure early is one of the best predictors of completing secondary school (Audas and Willms 2000; Rumberger 1995); and (c) reducing the rates of grade repetition is central to the long-term success of schooling in Latin America and is an outcome that can be improved easily through national and local policies. During the 1980s, a typical child in Latin America took 1.7 years to be promoted to the next grade (UNESCO-OREALC 1992).

To simplify the discussion and be consistent with the "standard" of a "no-fail" policy, a dichotomous variable is used in this chapter to indicate whether a child has repeated at least one grade. Willms and Somers (2000) used a "time to completion" measure to account for a child's grade repetition. However, neither measure accounts for children who leave school before completing a grade and then reenter the same grade the following year. A more detailed analysis of this

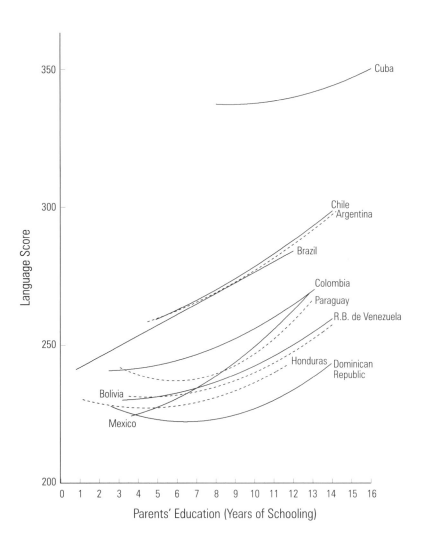

Figure 2. Socioeconomic Gradients for Language Scores, by Country

issue is under way for a few countries, beginning with Brazil, by re-constructing each child's educational history and applying a multi-level variant of event-history analysis.

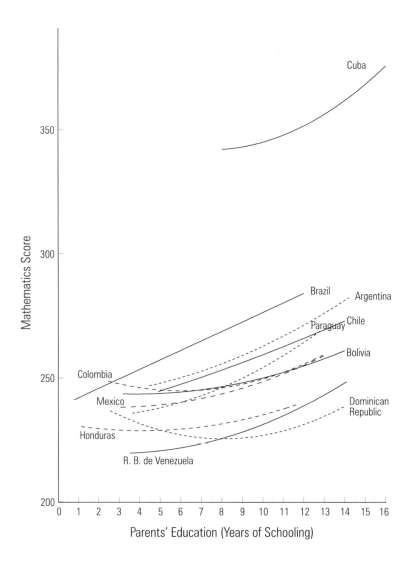

Figure 3. Socioeconomic Gradients for Mathematics Scores, by Country

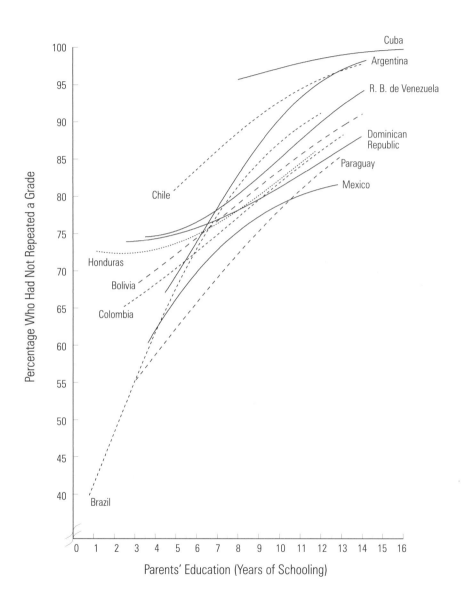

Figure 4. Socioeconomic Gradients for No Grade Repetition, by Country

The problem of grade repetition is acute in several Latin American countries. Some children report failing more than five times by the time they are in grade 3. However, the data for number of repetitions and children's age are inconsistent. It seems that, in many schools, pupils leave school during the academic year and return the following year in the same grade, a situation that many parents would not usually consider grade repetition.

Findings

Several important findings are evident from the analyses. (1) Countries vary dramatically in school outcomes and socioeconomic gradients. (2) The hypothesis of converging gradients does not hold; that is, the results for children of parents with high levels of education vary as much as those for children of parents with low levels of education. (3) The gradients in some countries are nonlinear, but levels of achievement increase at higher SES levels.

Previously, it seemed that "the success of a society, as gauged by these types of indicators, depends on the extent to which it is successful in reducing inequalities" (Willms 1999). The author's current working hypothesis is that (a) societies progress from relatively flat gradients with low levels of social outcomes to steep gradients with average levels of outcomes and, finally, to shallow gradients with high levels of social outcomes, and (b) this progression depends on how social and human capital are invested (Willms 2000).

Perhaps the most important point, however, is that the PEIC results for Cuba, similar to the results of the International Adult Literacy Study (IALS) for Sweden, demonstrate that high levels of social outcomes and equality of social outcomes can be achieved among low- and high-status groups. The nonlinear relationship, which is most evident among the lowest-scoring countries, suggests that a "premium" is associated with completing secondary school, a finding that is not inconsistent with the current working hypothesis. The elite of a country may attain a higher standard of achievement first, and lower socioeconomic groups may then slowly rise to meet these levels.

Moreover, the results for Cuba and Chile, which, by Latin American standards, have relatively low levels of grade repetition, demonstrate that high levels of achievement are possible without failing pupils. Brazil, which has a large percentage of children repeating grades, has achievement levels for language similar to those of Chile, and for mathematics, slightly higher. However, these results are based on grade cohorts, not age cohorts. The results for Brazil would be somewhat lower if, for example, the average scores of pupils ages 7 to 9 could be assessed in each country. This assessment will be one of the strengths of the Program of Indicators of Student Achievement (PISA) study, which targets all 15-year-olds in each country. If countries adopt a no-repetition policy or take measures to dramatically reduce repetition rates, many teachers will have to change their attitudes toward grade repetition and will need to be equipped with the necessary skills to teach in heterogeneous classrooms.

School Profiles

The analysis of school profiles offers additional detail on the variation in school outcomes within each country and for the Region. Figures 5–7 present these profiles for the Region. Hierarchical linear analysis yielded estimates of the average test scores for each school, with adjustment for measurement and sampling errors. The figures denote each school's sector (public or private), urbanicity (rural, urban, mega-city), and relative size. Similar plots for each country are given in the Willms and Somers (2000) report.

Findings

The school profiles show that schools in the Region vary widely in academic achievement even after accounting for parents' education. In the full report (Willms and Somers 2000), the variation among schools within each country was examined in relation to certain family background variables, which included parents' education, amount of time the parent was at home during work days, number of books in the home, and single- or two-parent family. Even with control for these variables, the schools' academic achievement levels varied

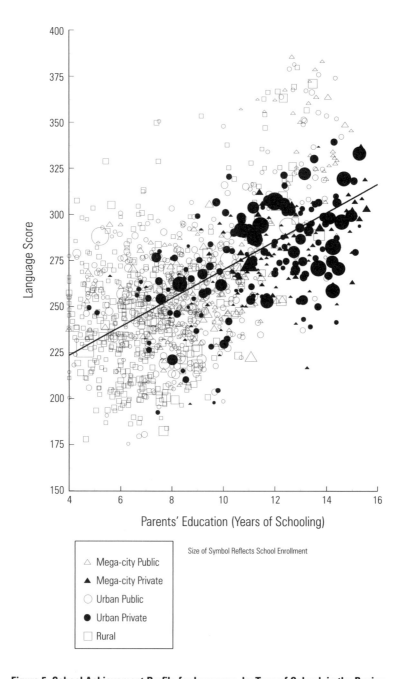

Figure 5. School Achievement Profile for Language, by Type of School, in the Region

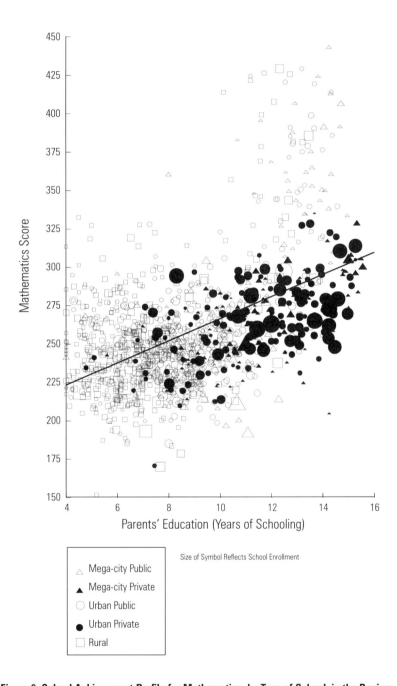

Figure 6. School Achievement Profile for Mathematics, by Type of School, in the Region

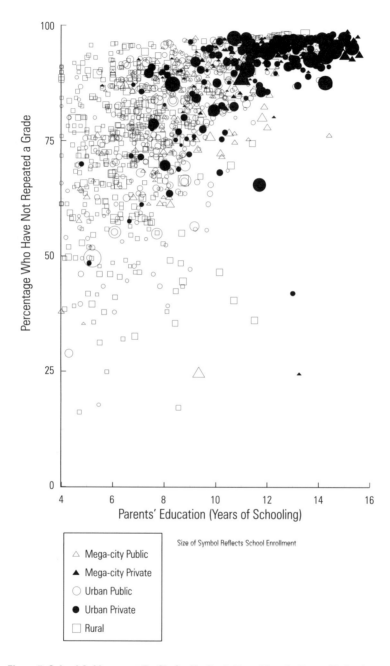

Figure 7. School Achievement Profile for No Grade Repetition, by Type of School, in the Region

substantially. At any SES level, the difference between the worst- and best-performing schools was about 1.5 standard deviations, which, for grades 3 and 4, amounts to about 1.5 years of schooling.

The PEIC data also included several factors pertaining to a child's early childhood experience (e.g., regular reading by parents to their child during preschool years, parental involvement in the child's schooling). As expected, these factors were related positively to school outcomes, a finding that has been substantiated by many other studies.

The data also included an item for child's attendance at day care, and the analysis showed small, but significant, effects associated with this variable. However, information was not collected on the nature or quality of day care or the period when the child attended day care. More detailed analyses of this variable within countries would likely indicate larger effects.

A principal aim of the study was to discern which schooling factors contributed to high educational achievement. Analysis revealed that a number of factors were positively associated with high test scores and the time pupils took to complete the first three grades of primary school. Significantly, the important factors included variables pertaining to school resources *and* to school policy and practice.

Standards of Care: A Suggested Framework

The above data can be analyzed further to yield suggested standards of care for evaluating and monitoring school outcomes currently and over time. Establishing standards for reform is not easy, however, and the data and analyses to substantiate standards and reforms must be scrutinized carefully. For policymakers, a main concern is the complexity of interpreting statistical data from analyses of regression coefficients and relative and attributable risks.

In the PEIC study, the multilevel regression results are complex and not easily translated into policies for reform. Generally, the interpretation of regression coefficients is fairly straightforward—they represent the effect on the outcome of a one-unit increase in the covariate when all other variables are held constant. For example, Willms and Somers (2000) estimate that the effect on language scores of teachers working another job is –11.2. That is, the language scores of children in schools where all teachers worked another job were 11.2 points less than those of children in schools where no teachers worked another job. However, the situation for PEIC and for similar studies is much more complex. Only about one-half of all pupils in the Region attended schools where no teachers worked another job, and less than 10 percent attended schools where all teachers worked another job; the remaining students (about 40 percent) attended schools where some teachers worked another job.

A related problem is that the effect may be important in *relative* terms, but not in *absolute* terms. For example, within a country, a minority group may have very low test scores, but the group comprises only 1 percent of the population. In regression analysis, the gap in test scores between minorities and nonminorities would be estimated as an unstandardized regression coefficient, and the difference would be expressed in the units of the test. The importance of the difference, in this instance, would be judged in "relative" terms.

However, the marginal contribution to R-squared (i.e., the proportion of the variance explained) would be quite small because the minority group comprises only 1 percent of the population. Even if the scores of all minority pupils could be immediately boosted up to the Regional mean, this overall mean would not change dramatically. The importance of the difference, in this instance, would be judged in "absolute" terms. This distinction is important for policymakers as they choose between targeted interventions to improve scores and outcomes of particular groups (e.g., pupils in rural schools in low-socioeconomic areas) and universal interventions to improve scores and outcomes of all pupils (see Offord and others 1997).

Relative risk and *attributable risk* are also commonly used by epidemiologists. In this case, "relative risk" denotes the ratio of the proportion of vulnerable individuals among those exposed to a risk factor to the proportion of vulnerable individuals among those *not* exposed to the risk factor. As a multiplier, relative risk indicates the potential increased likelihood of a child being vulnerable if the child changes from not being exposed to being exposed. "Attributable risk" expresses in percent the total occurrence of vulnerability that could be attributed to a particular risk factor.

To calculate these risks, the outcome variable must be dichotomous (i.e., vulnerable versus not vulnerable). For PEIC, the outcome variable is having low test scores versus not having low test scores, or repeating a grade versus not repeating a grade. The risk factors also must be dichotomous. For example, the PEIC risk factors include attending a school that has a poor library versus attending a school that has a good library, or attending a school that has low parental involvement versus attending a school that has high parental involvement.

The technique of assigning relative and attributable risk is used in the analysis summarized below to elucidate possible standards for reform. This technique is not as powerful as regression techniques, but the distinction between relative and absolute risk is more transparent.

An Outcome Standard for Children

The PEIC study defined a child as "vulnerable" if he or she had:

- A language test score below 221 in grade 3 or below 240 in grade 4 (these cutoff scores correspond approximately to the lowest one-third of scores), *or*
- A mathematics test score below 225 in grade 3 or below 239 in grade 4, *or*
- Repeated a grade during the first 3 years of elementary school.

This definition was based on several considerations. First, deciding on an outcome standard (cutoff score) for most achievement tests is arbitrary. In PEIC, one possibility was to use the results for Cuba as a standard for the Region. Another possibility was to use the mean or median test score as the standard and to denote those below the mean or median as vulnerable. Second, administrators in many countries voice concern about the "bottom third" of school-children. Third, experience shows that children who repeat a grade during the first few years of school are prone to leave school early.

Based on the definition used, the PEIC data show that more than one-half (50.5 percent) of all children in the Region are vulnerable in one of these respects (15.5 percent of children, for example, repeated a grade during the first 3 years). The dichotomous variable in PEIC for vulnerable versus not vulnerable thus pertains to about one-half of the population studied.

Standards for Superior Schooling

For the analysis, standards also were established for each relevant co-variate in the PEIC study. Table 1 notes the standards for the most important process variables identified by Willms and Somers (2000).

Pupils' Demographic and Early Childhood Characteristics

To gauge the relative importance of the above standards, the principal covariates in the analysis also were dichotomized. The following six characteristics were considered as demographic and early childhood variables.

Female. Of the children, 50.3 percent were girls and 49.7 percent were boys.

High Parental Education. Children "at risk" were those whose parents had 8 years or less of formal schooling. Of all children in the Region, 52.3 percent had parents with more than 8 years of schooling.

Two-Parent Family. Some 80 percent of the children in the Region lived in two-parent families.

Parents Read Frequently. Some 36.3 percent of all children in the Region lived in families where parents reported reading frequently to their child.

Table 1. Standards for Process Variables and the Percentage of Children in the Region Who Attended Schools That Met With the Standard

Process variable	Standard	Percentage of children in the region who attended schools that met with the standard
Small classes	Enrollments of 25 pupils or less	54.2
Adequate material resources	More than 6.574 (the Regional mean) instructional materials available in the school. (To determine the mean, school principals were asked whether they had certain materials from a list of twelve items.)	52.3
Adequate library	At least 1,000 books in the school library	32.1
Well-trained teachers	An average of more than 3.46 years (the Regional mean) of teacher training for all teachers in the sample	54.8
Teachers working only one job	All teachers in the school work only one job	52.5
Single-grade classrooms	No multigrade classrooms in the school	12.6
Pupils tested regularly	All teachers use tests regularly	17.8
No ability grouping	No grouping of pupils by ability	38.7
Positive learning environment	A learning climate higher than the Regional mean of 0.600. [The index comprises the mean of three variables: whether some pupils in the classroom disturbed others (no=1, yes=0), fights happened often (no=1, yes=0), and pupils in the class were good friends (yes=1, no=0). Responses were obtained from pupils' questionnaires, and a composite mean for discipline was aggregated by school.]	51.3
Strong parental involvement	Parental involvement higher than the Regional mean of 2.535. [The index comprises the mean of three variables: whether the parent participates in school-related activities (seldom=1, sometimes=2, always=3), knows his or her child's teacher (no=1, a little=2, a lot=3), and attends parent–teacher meetings (never or seldom=1, almost always=2, always=3). Responses were obtained from parents, and a composite mean for parental involvement was aggregated by school.]	53.8

Child Attended Day Care. Some 74 percent of all children in the Region attended some form of day care.

Parents Involved in Child's Schooling. Parents scoring 2.5 or higher on the parental involvement index were considered involved. Some 60.9 percent of the children in the Region lived in families where parents were involved in their schooling.

Childhood Vulnerability: Analysis and Findings

Using the established standards and the demographic and early childhood variables, the relative importance of each factor was assessed in a series of logistic regression models. The process variables (e.g., attending large classes instead of small classes) are considered risk factors.

Odds Ratios for Risk Factors

Table 2 presents the odds ratios derived from the logistic regression coefficients.

Sex and Family Background

This first set of variables presented in Table 2 includes sex, single-parent family, and low parental education. The results of the regression analysis indicate that the odds of being vulnerable for boys was 8 percent higher than for girls. Willms and Somers (2000) found that the differences associated with gender were relatively small: Girls averaged about 6 points higher on the language test, whereas boys averaged about 2 points higher on the mathematics test; and boys took slightly longer on average than girls to complete the first 3 years of schooling, but the difference was less than 1 month.

The odds of being vulnerable for a child in a single-parent family was about 26 percent higher than the odds of being vulnerable in a two-parent family. And, the most striking effect is associated with having parents with a low level of education. The odds ratio for this risk factor is 3.26, indicating that children whose parents had

Table 2. Odds Ratios for Childhood Vulnerability Associated With Sex and Family Background, Urbanicity (Rural, Urban, Mega-city), Sector (Public, Private), Early Child Development, School Resources, and School Policy and Practice

Variable	Regression model/coefficient				
	I	II	III	IV	V
Sex and family background					
Male	1.08	1.08	1.06	1.11	1.10
Single-parent family	1.26	1.27	1.25	1.24	1.26
Low parental education	3.37	2.91	2.58	2.32	2.14
Sector and urbanicity					
Rural		2.29	2.48	1.30	1.60
Urban public		1.57	1.76	1.33	1.58
Mega-city public		1.18	1.33	(1.03)	(1.07)
Urban private		2.23	1.31	1.25	1.31
Mega-city private (base)		(1.00)	(1.00)	(1.00)	(1.00)
Early child development					
No day care			1.39	1.15	1.11
Infrequently reads to child			1.79	1.60	1.50
Low parental involvement			1.39	1.32	1.16
School resources					
Large classes				1.62	1.54
Lacking classroom materials				1.72	1.68
Inadequate library				2.26	2.04
Low teacher training				(1.04)	(.94)
School policy and practice					
Teachers working in other jobs					1.16
Multigrade classes					1.39
Infrequent testing					1.14
Ability grouping					(1.06)
Poor classroom climate					1.68
Low parental involvement at school					1.56

( ) Not statistically significant.

primary school education or less were more than three times as likely to be vulnerable as children whose parents had at least some secondary schooling. This risk factor is by far the most important and outweighs the effects of gender and family structure.

Sector and Urbanicity

Figures 5–7 demonstrated that a marked "socioeconomic divide" is associated with school sector (public versus private) and urbanicity (rural, urban, mega-city). To relate this finding to childhood vulnerability, the analysis included designation of mega-city private schools as the baseline category, and odds ratios were determined to indicate children's risk associated with the other categories. The results suggest that the odds of being vulnerable in urban private schools or mega-city public schools is about 20 percent higher than in mega-city private schools. This substantial effect is almost as large as that associated with living in a single-parent family, but it pales in comparison with the effects associated with attending urban public or rural schools. Compared with a child in mega-city private schools, the odds of a child being vulnerable in urban public schools was more than 1.5 times and, for a child in rural schools, more than 2.25 times.

Notably, the effects associated with low parental education are mediated by sector and urbanicity. The odds ratio for a child with parents having low education decreased from 3.37 to 2.91 if the child attended a mega-city private school.

Early Child Development

The variables included in this analysis are no attendance at day care, infrequent parental reading to the child, and low parental involvement. The effects of all three factors are substantial, as indicated by the odds ratios of 1.39, 1.79, and 1.39, respectively. These effects are evident after controlling for the other variables. Again, the effects associated with low parental education are further mediated by effective early child development. The odds ratio for low parental education drops from 2.91 to 2.58 when the children attend day care and are read to by their parents and when their parent is involved in their schooling. These effects are especially striking because the factors were measured cursorily and do not account for the amount of time in day care, the quality of day care, or parenting style and parental involvement. These more specific variables would be appropriate to capture and could be obtained in similar studies.

School Resources

The next set of variables in Table 2 describes school resources. The only factor that is not statistically significant is teacher training. The other factors have odds ratios ranging from 1.62 to 2.26, which are surprisingly large, especially because these effects are attributable to resources after accounting for sex and family background and for sector and urbanicity. These variables mediated the effects of low parental education only slightly, from 2.58 to 2.32 for a child in a school with good resources. However, these variables explained the effects associated with sector and urbanicity (see "Effects by Sector and Urbanicity" below).

School Policy and Practice

This set of factors is influenced more directly by school administrators and teachers than are those pertaining to school resources. The odds ratio for ability grouping was not statistically significant, and the odds ratios for the other factors ranged from 1.14 to 1.68. The effects of a poor classroom climate and low parental involvement at school are particularly striking, with odds ratios of 1.68 and 1.56, respectively. All the variables in this set further mediated the risk associated with low parental education, reducing it to 2.14 for a child in a school with good policies and practices.

Relative and Attributable Risks

Table 3 displays the relative and attributable risks for the variables associated with sex and family background and school factors. Four variables would require large expenditures to improve the school system—to reduce class size, obtain more classroom materials, improve school libraries, and require that teachers be better trained. The *relative risk* associated with these variables is 1.50, 1.74, 2.29, and 1.12, respectively. The data indicate, for example, that children who attend schools with large classes (i.e., more than 25 pupils) are 1.5 times as likely to be vulnerable as those who attend schools that meet the standard. Similarly, children in schools without adequate classroom

Table 3. Relative and Attributable Risks for Childhood Vulnerability Associated With Sex and Family Background and School Factors

Variable	Relative risk (ratio)	Attributable risk (percent)
Sex and family background		
Male	1.05	2.6
Single-parent family	1.10	2.0
Low parental education	1.74	26.1
Early child development		
No day care	1.33	7.6
Infrequently reads to child	1.41	20.7
Low parental involvement	1.27	9.5
School resources		
Large classes	1.50	18.7
Lacking classroom materials	1.74	26.1
Inadequate library	2.29	46.5
Low teacher training	1.12	5.0
School policy and practice		
Teachers working in other jobs	1.23	10.1
Multigrade classes	1.22	2.8
Infrequent testing	1.11	8.6
Ability grouping	1.12	6.8
Poor classroom climate	1.49	19.5
Low parental involvement at school	1.53	20.0

materials are 1.74 times as likely to be vulnerable as those who attend schools with adequate classroom materials.

The *attributable risk* associated with large classes is 18.7 percent. This finding suggests that childhood vulnerability could be reduced by 18.7 percent if all children could attend small classes. The entire story, no doubt, is much more complex, for these analyses are based on simple bivariate cross-tabulations. For example, the most effective teachers may be in schools with small classes, or the schools with the most classroom materials may tend to be those with smaller classes.

Simply reducing class size may therefore not achieve the desired results. Also, the variables, as defined, may be "proxies" for other significant variables. For example, having an inadequate school library has an attributable risk of 46.5 percent. Yet, increasing the size of all school libraries will most likely not improve school outcomes accordingly. These results, nevertheless, indicate the relative and absolute importance of the variables selected.

The relative risks of the six factors pertaining to school policy and practice range from 1.11–1.12, for ability grouping and lack of testing, to 1.22–1.23, for multigrade classrooms and teachers working in other jobs, to 1.49–1.53, for poor classroom climate and low parental involvement at school. The attributable risks for the first four factors listed in the table range from less than 3 percent to slightly more than 10 percent, but the attributable risks associated with poor classroom climate and low parental involvement are considerable—about 20 percent.

Also worth noting is that the relative and attributable risks of being male or living in a single-parent family are very low. The relative risk of living in a family with parents having a low level of education is 1.74, and the attributable risk is 26.1 percent. These data suggest that if all children could live in families with parents educated beyond primary schooling, childhood vulnerability could be reduced by more than 25 percent. Achieving this is, of course, impossible in the near future. Curiously, however, these relative and attributable risks are the same as those associated with lack of classroom materials, a factor that is not impossible to correct.

The analysis also indicates that parents' actions (i.e., what they *do*) are extremely important. The relative risk associated with parents who read infrequently to their child is 1.41, and the risk for low parental involvement in the child's education is 1.27. These results suggest that childhood vulnerability could be reduced by more than 20 percent if all parents read regularly to their child, and by almost 10 percent if all parents were involved in their child's schooling. Children who did not attend day care were 1.33 times more likely to be vulnerable than those who did attend day care, and the attributable risk is quite low—less than 8 percent.

Effects by Sector and Urbanicity

The above analyses provide a framework for assessing the relative importance of the factors by sector and urbanicity. Table 4 presents the percentages of vulnerable children in each sector and urban category. Based on the criteria used, 65.2 percent of the children in rural schools were vulnerable. In the private sector, 29.0 percent were vulnerable in mega-city schools and 33.8 percent were vulnerable in urban schools. In the public (nonrural) sector, 39.9 percent of the children were vulnerable in mega-city schools, and 49.6 percent were vulnerable in urban schools. Similar to the findings for the entire Region, about one-half of all children in urban public schools were vulnerable.

The major question raised by this analysis is: "How would the sectors differ if all schools achieved the standards for school resources and school policy and practice?" To answer this question, the odds ratios were estimated for sector and urbanicity within a logistic regression model. Mega-city private schools served as the base for comparison (1.0). The odds ratios for the other schools are greater than 1.0 because children were considered more likely to be vulnerable if they were in one of these four categories. To assess the effects associated with the selected risk factors, the odds ratios were adjusted for family background, early child development, school resources, and school policy and practice, singly and in combination. Table 4 presents the results.

Table 4 shows that the odds of a child being vulnerable in a rural school are more than 4.5 times that in a mega-city private school. The odds ratios for a child in an urban public school is 2.41; in a mega-city public school, 1.62; and in an urban private school, 1.25.

Some of the disparities are attributable to a child's background. When adjusted for family background and early child development (FB/ECD), the odds ratios decrease considerably for a child in public school: from 4.57 to 2.48 in a rural school, 2.41 to 1.76 in an urban school, and 1.62 to 1.33 in a mega-city school. The odds ratio for a child in an urban private school increases slightly, from 1.25 to 1.31.

When controlling for school resources (SR) only, the odds ratios also decrease considerably for a child in public school: from 4.57 to 1.70 in a rural school, 2.41 to 1.54 in an urban school, and 1.62 to 1.11 in a mega-city school. The odds ratio for a child in an urban

Table 4. Odds Ratios of Childhood Vulnerability by Sector and Urbanicity, Controlling for Family Background, Early Child Development, School Resources, and School Policy and Practice

| | | Sector/urbanicity | | | |
| | | Public | | Private | |
Odds ratio/variable	Rural	Urban	Mega-City	Urban	Mega-City
Percentage of vulnerable children	65.2	49.6	39.9	33.8	29.0
Unadjusted	4.57	2.41	1.62	1.25	1.00
Adjusted for:					
Sex and family background and early child development (FB/ECD)	2.48	1.76	1.33	1.31	1.00
School resources (SR)	1.70	1.54	1.11	1.26	1.00
School policy and practice (SPP)	4.57	2.66	1.73	1.54	1.00
FB/ECD + SR	1.30	1.33	1.03	1.25	1.00
FB/ECD + SPP	3.16	2.14	1.52	1.52	1.00
FB/ECD, SR, + SPP	1.60	1.58	1.07	1.31	1.00

Note: The baseline for comparison is mega-city private schools.

private school remains the same. Comparison of these results with those for FB/ECD reveals an extremely important finding: The disparities *among* sectors and urbanicity are related more strongly to school resources than to a pupil's family background and early child development.

When controlling for school policy and practice (SPP) only, the odds ratios do not change appreciably by sector or urbanicity. This result demonstrates clearly that disparities among sectors and urbanicity are not attributable to school policy and practice, even though these factors are extremely important within sectors and rural or urban settings.

Even when accounting for family background and early child development, these two significant findings hold. Comparison of FB/ECD only with FB/ECD+SR reveals a large decrease in the odds ratios whereas comparison of FB/ECD only with FB/ECD+SPP reveals small decreases.

When controlling for family background and early child development, school resources, and school policy and practice, the odds ratios do not change as dramatically as when not controlling for school policy and practice. This finding suggests that some of the mediating effects of school resources on the differences among sectors and urbanicity are further mediated by school policy and practice. That is, maintaining a positive classroom climate and achieving high parental involvement at school are probably easier when class sizes are small, for example. In sum, the findings indicate that both school resources and school policy and practice are important determinants of school outcomes, but school resources (not school policy and practice) distinguish the results for rural schools versus nonrural schools.

Achieving High Standards in Latin America: Current Status

The analyses demonstrate the importance of achieving high standards for families and schools. Table 5 documents the percentage of children in each country of the Region who are in families and schools that meet these standards and the percentage of children who are *not* vulnerable (i.e., are above the threshold for vulnerability).

A particularly interesting finding revealed in the table is that Cuba scores high on virtually every measure—the exceptions are frequent testing and no ability grouping. This finding suggests that Cuba's very high test scores are not attributable solely to parents' higher level of education, but also are due to factors pertaining to early child development, school resources, and school policy and practice. When meeting with members of the Laboratorio, the Minister of Education for Cuba explained Cuba's remarkable success with school outcomes by first noting not the quality of Cuba's schools, but the fact that almost every child attends a center for early child development. Other factors, such as high levels of teacher training, were cited only secondarily.

Next Steps: Strengthening the Basis for Monitoring and Reform

The challenges in conducting international comparative studies of early child development are enormous, and these challenges are especially acute in low-income countries. In comparison with other

Table 5. Percentage of Children in Families and Schools That Meet the Standards Selected

Variable	Country/percent of children											
	AR	BO	BR	CH	CO	CU	HO	ME	PA	RD	VE	All
Family background												
Two-parent family	84	83	82	84	74	78	64	89	79	72	70	80
High parental education	59	50	23	67	47	89	18	49	36	44	61	52
Early child development												
Day care	87	70	78	70	67	94	59	84	50	67	86	75
Frequently reads to child	37	28	43	40	26	73	30	25	26	38	35	36
High parental involvement	51	48	65	66	69	84	57	53	62	49	70	61
School resources												
Small classes	84	80	57	33	36	88	2	—	29	11	27	54
Classroom materials	79	18	71	94	48	69	4	57	13	25	30	52
Adequate library	43	7	56	45	21	76	17	5	12	8	27	32
High teacher training	12	58	48	80	58	73	39	60	11	50	43	55
School policy and practice												
Teachers working one job	41	11	73	46	68	99	68	—	78	59	68	52
No multigrade classes	86	83	98	78	68	99	65	93	100	95	98	87
Frequent testing	41	53	31	86	24	39	57	72	27	14	45	46
No ability grouping	30	32	62	11	33	64	52	18	40	53	38	39
Good classroom climate	35	59	52	32	41	97	27	37	37	61	22	51
High parental involvement	29	10	56	73	76	98	32	33	55	26	87	54
Children *not* vulnerable	66	38	55	71	45	95	25	41	47	26	35	50

AR, Argentina; BO, Bolivia; BR, Brazil; CH, Chile; CO, Colombia; CU, Cuba; HO, Honduras; ME, Mexico; PA, Paraguay; RD, Dominican Republic; VE, R.B. de Venezuela.

national and international studies, PEIC stands out as a remarkable achievement. The study provides a strong basis for monitoring early child development. The findings indicate that one can accurately estimate socioeconomic gradients, discern the importance of school resources, and identify the effect of investments in early childhood by families and schools. Perhaps more than any other study, PEIC indicates that parents' and teachers' actions (i.e., what they *do* with their resources) can have an effect comparable to improving the level of resources. If countries achieved the standards set forth in this chapter, they would reduce the risk associated with low parental education by nearly one-half. Flattening the gradients is possible, and some countries have already achieved many of the standards proposed.

The framework for standards of care suggested in this chapter is founded on several key considerations for low-income countries. For these countries, the standards must: (a) be based on empirically derived findings about their effects on measurable outcomes; (b) be achievable through a coordinated effort by families, schools, and governments; (c) be inexpensive to measure regularly; and (d) provide a means for gauging societal improvements over time.

Additional studies in Latin America would benefit by including many of the measures developed in PEIC and suggested herein. The information gained from PEIC could be enhanced in several ways, as suggested below. The first suggestion would be costly to implement, but the others would be relatively inexpensive.

1. Develop a study comparable to PEIC, but with a target population of all 5-year-old children. A target population of even younger children is preferable, but reaching all 5-year-olds may be a sufficient challenge for the next study. This study would be conducted in conjunction with a study of all 9-year-old children. By repeating the monitoring effort every 4 years, one could assess the results for the 5-year-old cohort in the same schools when the majority of children are 9 years old.

2. Give preference to studies focused on age cohorts rather than grade cohorts. Although more complex administratively, a study of age cohorts would indicate the progression of children developmentally in school and control directly for any effects associated with grade repetition.

3. Track "communities," however defined. For example, if a study first sampled communities, defined geographically, and then sampled schools and pupils, outcomes and socioeconomic gradients for the community could be examined and the stability of the estimates could be discerned. By using multilevel models that extend PEIC's analyses and incorporating time as an element (Willms and Raudenbush 1989), powerful information could be obtained about the effects of policies and practices for early childhood. *Changes* in intercepts and gradients could be related to changes in policy and practice within local communities.

4. Integrate geography better into the analyses. In almost all research on schools' effectiveness, schools are treated as independent entities and not in relation to other schools in the community. Understanding of the roles of local communities could be improved dramatically if sufficient geographic data were available to display findings on country maps. Importantly, the effects of particular policies and practices could be documented "on the ground."

5. Integrate small-sample, quantitative and qualitative studies of early child development into large-scale monitoring efforts. For example, the Willms and Somers (2000) report indicates schools that are particularly successful or unsuccessful in achieving high standards, based on the number of pupils and level of resources. Ethnographic studies are needed to understand why these schools are successful. Small-scale studies could be piggybacked onto large-scale studies to determine, for example, the results of the lowest-performing schools 4 years after a concerted effort is made to enhance their standards of school policy and practice, as suggested in PEIC.

Two immediate opportunities for building on PEIC's findings are in Brazil and Pakistan. The World Bank recently contracted to provide technical assistance to Brazil's National Institute for Educational Research (INEP). Brazil already has a sophisticated system for monitoring schools, which includes a school census. Under the new contract, researchers could approach analysis of the monitoring data from a gradient perspective and give greater emphasis to standards of care, changes in community gradients over time, and geographic variations. INEP could then exploit historical records of achievement (e.g., over the past 10 years) to give educators and administrators findings based on more than a 1-year snapshot.

The opportunity in Pakistan entails an operational research approach to studying human development. The Aga Khan University (AKU) in Pakistan is developing an Institute of Human Development and has acknowledged the important role that this institute could play in research and training and in influencing policy formation in developing and Muslim countries. This research could demonstrate the importance of investments in human development in low-income countries. An immediate opportunity is the development of a study to examine the effects on children's development (ages 0 to 6) of a training program to improve parenting skills and increase parents' engagement in play and other literacy-related activities. This training program could be delivered through AKU's network of primary health care centers. Instruments and data collection procedures for conducting monitoring on a wide-scale basis for children during the early years could be developed as part of this research effort.

Conclusion

In recent years, low-income countries have increasingly participated in large-scale international studies such as the Third International Mathematics and Science Study (TIMSS) and the IALS, both conducted in 1994. During 2000, several low-income countries participated in PISA, a study of academic achievement among 15-year-olds conducted by the Organization for Economic Cooperation and

Development. This bold and important move by these governments could yield long-term benefits for their systems of schooling. Too often, however, the findings of large-scale studies have little internal effect. Too much emphasis may be placed on "horse-race" comparisons of average levels of achievement among countries, and few resources are usually available for data analyses within countries.

Systems to monitor internal effects are needed. They could provide information on changes in achievement levels over time, inequities of achievement between males and females or among pupils of different socioeconomic backgrounds, varying achievement levels among jurisdictions, and the relationship between the quality of schools and their material and human resources or policies and practices.

The PEIC study has provided invaluable information for analyzing children's educational outcomes within and between countries. The standards of care derived from such analysis provide the basis for investments to improve children's school outcomes in Latin America and to monitor early child development. One of the most prominent findings noted in the first report on PEIC (UNESCO 1998) was the remarkable success of Cuba: Its average test scores, for both reading and mathematics, were about 2 standard deviations above the mean for the Region. Two other important findings across the Region and in most countries were that (a) the average test scores of pupils residing in mega-cities (having more than 1 million people) were somewhat higher than those of pupils in smaller cities and markedly higher than those of rural pupils and (b) pupils in private schools tended to have higher scores than those in public schools (UNESCO 1998).

The second report (Willms and Somers 2000), on which this chapter is based, included among the outcomes a measure of the time needed for pupils to complete the first 3 years of primary schooling. Most Latin American countries still practice grade retention and, in some cases, pupils may repeat a grade two or three times before advancing to the next grade. The data show that achievement test scores and grade repetition were strongly related to children's family background, school sector, and extent of urbanization. However, even after accounting for the pupils' family backgrounds, the schools differed substantially in the academic achievement of pupils and the time pupils took to complete the first 3 years of primary school. Some, but not all, of this variation was attributable to school resources, especially the availability of classroom instructional materials, adequate school library, small classes, and well-trained teachers.

Further analysis showed that school policies and practices have substantial effect. Test scores were higher and grade repetition was less in schools which had teachers who did not hold other jobs, no multigrade classes, frequent testing of pupils, and no grouping of pupils by ability. Two of the most important factors affecting outcomes were the learning climate of the classroom and the extent of parents' involvement in children's schooling, at home and at school.

It is hoped that these findings will provoke focused discussions and dialogue about standards of care, as well as targeted investments to improve children's educational outcomes in Latin America and elsewhere. Additional studies that build on the framework suggested in this chapter would strengthen the basis for monitoring outcomes and reforms.

Notes

This chapter extends the research for a report entitled *Schooling Outcomes in Latin America*, which was prepared by the author and Marie-Andrée Somers for UNESCO in cooperation with the Laboratorio Latinoamericano de Evaluación de la Calidad de la Educación. Preparation of the report was supported by UNESCO, and this chapter, by the World Bank. The research was supported by the Canadian Institute for Advanced Research, which funds the New Brunswick/Canadian Imperial Bank of Commerce (NB/CIBC) Chair in Human Development at the University of New Brunswick, and by Human Resources Development Canada, Statistics Canada, and the U.S. Spencer Foundation. The opinions expressed in this chapter are solely the author's.

References

Audas, R., and J.D. Willms. 2000. *Engagement and Dropping Out of School: A Life Course Perspective*. Report prepared for Human Resources Development Canada. Ottawa.

Baron, R.M., and D.A. Kenny. 1986. The Moderator-Mediator Variable Distinction in Social Psychological Research: Conceptual, Strategic, and Statistical Considerations. *Journal of Personality and Social Psychology* 51:1173–82.

Boyle, M.H., and J.D. Willms. 1998. Place Effects for Areas Defined by Administrative Boundaries. *American Journal of Epidemiology* 149(6):577–85.

Bryk, A.S., V.E. Lee, and J.B. Smith. 1990. High School Organization and Its Effects on Teachers and Students: An Interpretative Summary of the Research. In W. H. Clune and J. F. Witte, eds., *Choice and Control in American Education. Volume 1: The Theory of Choice and Control in Education*. London: Falmer Press.

Coleman, J.S. 1988. Social Capital in the Creation of Human Capital. *American Journal of Sociology* 94 (supplement):S95–S120.

Dutton, D.B., and S. Levine. 1989. Overview, Methodological Critique, and Reformulation. In J. P. Bunker, D. S. Gomby, and B. H. Kehrer, eds., *Pathways to Health*. Menlo Park, Calif.: Henry J. Kaiser Family Foundation.

Epelbaum, M. 1990. Sociomonetary Patterns and Specifications. *Social Science Research* 19:322–47.

Fellegi, I., and M. Wolfson. 1999. Towards Systems of Social Statistics: Some Principles and Their Application in Statistics Canada. *Journal of Official Statistics* 15(3):373–93.

Fuller, B., and P. Clarke. 1994. Raising School Effects While Ignoring Culture? Local Conditions and the Influence of Classroom Tools, Rules, and Pedagogy. *Review of Educational Research* 64(1):119–157.

Gray, J. 1989. Multilevel Models: Issues and Problems Emerging from Their Recent Application in British Studies of School Effectiveness. In D. R. Bock, ed., *Multi-level Analyses of Educational Data*. Chicago: University of Chicago Press.

Heyneman, S.P., and W.A. Loxley. 1983. The Effect of Primary-School Quality on Academic Achievement across Twenty-nine High- and Low-Income Countries. *American Journal of Sociology* 88(6):1162–94.

House, J., R. Kessler, R. Herzog, R.P. Mero, A.M. Kinney, and M.J. Breslow. 1990. Age, Socioeconomic Status, and Health. *The Millbank Quarterly* 68:383–411.

Kaplan, G.A., E.R. Pamuk, J.W. Lynch, R.D. Cohen, and J.L. Balfour. 1996. Inequality in Income and Mortality in the United States: Analysis of Mortality and Potential Pathways. *British Medical Journal* 312:999–1003.

Mirowsky, J., and P. Hu. 1996. Physical Impairment and the Diminishing Effects of Income. *Social Forces* 74(3):1073–96.

Mueller, C.W., and T.L. Parcel. 1981. Measures of Socioeconomic Status: Alternatives and Recommendations. *Child Development* 52:13–30.

Offord, D.R., H.C. Kraemer, A.E. Kazdin, P.S. Jensen, and R. Harrington. 1997. *Lowering the Burden of Suffering from Child Psychiatric Disorder: Trade-offs among Clinical, Targeted and Universal Interventions.* Toronto: The Canadian Institute for Advanced Research.

Raudenbush, S.W., and J.D. Willms, eds. 1991. *Schools,Classrooms, and Pupils: International Studies of Schooling from the Multilevel Perspective.* New York: Academic Press.

Ritzen, J. 2000. *Social Cohesion, Public Policy, and Economic Growth: Implications for OECD Countries.* Report prepared for Organization for Economic Cooperation and Development and Human Resources Development Canada. Ottawa.

Rumberger, R. 1995. Dropping Out of Middle School: A Multilevel Analysis of Students and Schools. *American Educational Research Journal* 32(3):583–625.

Shepard, L.A. 1989. A Review of Research on Kindergarten Retention. In L.A. Shepard and M.L. Smith, eds., *Flunking Grades: Research and Policies on Retention.* London: Falmer Press.

Shepard, L.A., and M.L. Smith. 1989. Flunking Grades: A Recapitulation. In L.A. Shepard and M.L. Smith, eds., *Flunking Grades: Research and Policies on Retention.* London: Falmer Press.

UNESCO (United Nations Educational, Scientific, and Cultural Organization). 1998. *Primer Estudio Internacional Comparativo.* Santiago, Chile.

UNESCO-OREALC (Regional Office for Education in Latin America and the Caribbean). 1992. *Situación Educativa de America Latina y del Caribe (1980–1989).* Santiago, Chile.

Wilkinson, R.G. 1992. Income Distribution and Life Expectancy. *British Medical Journal* 304:165–8.

———. 1996. *Unhealthy Societies: The Afflictions of Inequality.* London: Routledge.

Willms, J.D. 1992. *Monitoring School Performance: A Guide for Educators.* Lewes, U.K.: Falmer Press.

———. 1999. *Inequalities in Literacy Skills among Youth in Canada and the United States.* International Adult Literacy Survey No. 6. Ottawa: Human Resources Development Canada and National Literacy Secretariat.

———. 2000. *Three Hypotheses about Community Effects Relevant to the Contribution of Human and Social Capital to Sustaining Economic Growth and Well-being.* Report prepared for Organization for Economic Cooperation and Development and Human Resources Development Canada. Fredericton, N.B.: Canadian Research Institute for Social Policy, University of New Brunswick.

———. Forthcoming. *Vulnerable Children in Canada.* Ottawa: Human Resources Development Canada.

Willms, J.D., and S.W. Raudenbush. 1989. A Longitudinal Hierarchical Linear Model for Estimating School Effects and Their Stability. *Journal of Educational Measurement* 26(3):209–32.

Willms, J.D., and M.-A. Somers. 2000. *Schooling Outcomes in Latin America.* Fredericton, N.B.: Canadian Research Institute for Social Policy, University of New Brunswick.

Wolfson, M., G. Kaplan, J. Lynch, N. Ross, E. Backlund, H. Gravelle, and R.G. Wilkinson. 1999. Relation between Income Inequality and Mortality: Empirical Demonstration. *British Medical Journal* 319:953–57.

Wolfson, M., G. Rowe, J.F. Gentleman, and M. Tomiak. 1993. Career Earnings and Death: A Longitudinal Analysis of Older Canadian Men. *Journal of Gerontology* 48(4):S167–79.

Chapter 5

Ensuring a Fair Start for All Children: The Case of Brazil

Mary Eming Young

Early childhood is a time of great vulnerability *and* opportunity. Rapid and dramatic changes in physical and mental development occur during the first 3 years of human life. These developmental changes are currently viewed as the principal "building blocks" of adult cognitive and emotional functioning. Research on the brain shows that early experiences can shape individuals' development (see the chapter by Mustard in this volume) and that early childhood offers a unique opportunity to change the life course of all children and, especially, those at risk.

Many and various interventions have been undertaken worldwide to take advantage of this opportunity, for the benefit of children, families, and society. The interventions focus on children, parents, and families and often involve entire communities. The early child development (ECD) programs enhance children's physical and intellectual growth during their early years through a range of services, which include childcare, preschool, home visits by trained professionals, health and nutrition support, and parental education. The programs may be based in homes or childcare centers.

Evaluation of these programs demonstrates clearly that early childhood interventions are effective in improving children's success in school and later life, especially for vulnerable, at-risk children who live in poverty or in low-income families. These children often are born with low birthweights—a corollary of poverty and stunted development—and often have illiterate parents or mothers with low education. The negative consequences for children of income poverty have been well documented. They span the life course, from birth (e.g., low birthweight) through toddlerhood and preschool years (e.g., poor social and emotional competence, reduced cognitive test scores) to adolescence (e.g., reduced completion of secondary school and low literacy, early childbearing). Interventions early in life are small investments that bring high returns for the physical, mental, and economic well-being of children and the adults they become.

This chapter addresses the return on investments in early child development, especially for poor children. The benefits of preschool interventions for these children are summarized from several well-known U.S. interventions, and data from Brazil are shared as a case example of the opportunities available and the possibilities for ensuring a fair start for all children in the twenty-first century.

Early Interventions for Vulnerable Children: U.S. Findings

For all countries, ECD programs can promote learning readiness, increase school enrollment, reduce grade repetition and drop out from school, and increase individuals' future earning capacity. Preschool education is an important component of early child development and results in children who are better prepared for primary school, who perform better in school overall, and who often benefit from improved health and nutrition. The benefits for vulnerable children are especially large and help redress the inequities of their birth.

Research shows that early interventions particularly improve poor children's performance and achievement in primary school (Karoly and others 1998). Most of the interventions in the United States reporting positive results for these children are center-based programs for children ages 3–5 years (and some for children ages 0–3). Two notable U.S. interventions which utilized a quasi-experimental design and targeted infants and young children beginning at birth are the

Abecedarian project in North Carolina and the Infant Health and Development Program at various sites across the country. The outcomes of these efforts are summarized briefly below.

Other types of early childhood interventions in other countries have also yielded positive results. Some effective alternatives (e.g., in Mexico, Turkey) emphasize education and enrichment of parents, especially mothers. The return on investment can be significant, as determined for the Perry Preschool Project, a third successful U.S. intervention for low-income children summarized below.

The Carolina Abecedarian Project

The Carolina Abecedarian project was a single-site, randomized controlled trial that enrolled 111 children at birth who were biologically healthy but who came from very poor and undereducated families. The criterion for admission was a score indicating extreme risk on a thirteen-item high-risk index (Ramey and Ramey 1998). For example, the mean maternal intelligence quotient (IQ) was 85; the mean maternal education was 10 years; and approximately three-fourths of the mothers were unmarried.

The families of the control group (n=54) received pediatric follow-up services, unlimited iron-fortified formula, social work services, and home visits. The intervention group (n=57) received the same services as the control group plus an early childhood education program, Partners for Learning, which was developed for the intervention and implemented in the participating child development centers. Partners for Learning is an education program focusing on the first 36 months of life (Sparling, Lewis, and Ramey 1995) and consists of "games" that are incorporated into a child's daily activities, which address social, emotional, and cognitive development and particularly emphasize language. The centers enrolled children after 6 weeks of age and maintained a low child-to-teacher ratio (3:1 for children age 1 year or less and 4:1 for children ages 1–3 years). Parents received home visits and attended parent group meetings.

The results have been reported widely (Campbell and Ramey 1994, 1995; Ramey and Ramey 1998; Ramey and others 2000). By 36 months, the mean IQ scores were 101 and 84, respectively, for the intervention and control groups. The positive effects of the early intervention were greater for children of lesser-educated mothers than for those of more-educated mothers.

Upon completion of the intervention at age 5, the children entered primary school. They were studied and tested again at ages 12 and 15, and a follow-up to determine long-term effects was conducted at age 21. The children who received the early intervention performed better than the control group throughout the 20 years (figure 1). At age 21, they had higher mental test scores and higher reading scores, more were still in school (40 percent versus 20 percent), and more were in college or had graduated from college (35 percent versus 14 percent). They were, on average, 2 years older when their first child was born (19.1 years versus 17.1 years), and they had a higher employment rate (65 percent versus 50 percent).

Infant Health and Development Program

The Infant Health and Development Program (IHDP) was a longitudinal, eight-site, randomized trial of the effectiveness of an ECD program and family support services for approximately 1,000 low-birthweight, premature infants from birth to age 3 (Berlin and others

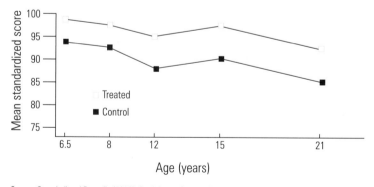

Source: Campbell and Pungello (1999), Frank Porter Graham Child Development Center, University of North Carolina, Chapel Hill.

Figure 1. Abecedarian Project, Cognitive Test Scores, Ages 6.5–21 Years

1998). The study is unique in structuring a randomly assigned comparison group. Eligible infants for the study had low birthweights (2,500 grams or less); were premature (37 weeks or less postconception); and were born between January 1985 and October 1985 in one of eight participating medical institutions. The eligible infants were stratified into two birthweight groups: lighter (< 2,001 grams) and heavier (2,001–2,500 grams) and then randomized into an intervention or comparison group. Two-thirds of the sample were in the lighter group and one-third was in the heavier group. One-third of the infants within each birthweight group was randomly assigned to the intervention group, and two-thirds were assigned to the comparison group.

Of the 1,302 eligible infants, 985 were randomized and were the principal sample. This sample came from racially and socioeconomically diverse families, which included African-American families (52 percent), European-American families (37 percent), and Hispanic-American families (11 percent). The families' incomes varied broadly.

The intervention began immediately after the infants were discharged from the hospital and continued until the children were 3 years old (corrected age). All infants received a pediatric follow-up, including a medical and developmental assessment, and were referred for other services as needed. In addition, the intervention group received (a) home visits on a weekly basis during the first year and then biweekly during the second and third years; (b) out-of-home education in child development centers beginning at 12 months and provided for 20 hours per week; and (c) parent group meetings at the child development centers every other month until the end of the program, to receive childrearing information and social support.

The IHDP demonstrated positive outcomes and, as in the Abecedarian project, the children of the poorest and least-educated mothers gained the most benefit (Berlin and others 1998; Duncan, Brooks-Gunn, and Klebanov 1994; IHDP 1990; McCarton and others 1997). Compared with the comparison group, the children in the intervention group had higher cognitive development scores and verbal scores at age 24 months and 36 months (figure 2). The positive effects were sustained through age 5 and age 8 (follow-ups). The children's socioemotional development also showed positive effects. They had fewer behavioral problems (based on the Richman-Graham Behavior Checklist) at ages 24 and 36 months. Mothers reported fewer symptoms of depression and were more likely to be employed by the time their children were 36 months old. During the 3 years of the intervention, the mothers averaged more months of employment than the mothers in the comparison group (Berlin and others 1998).

The Perry Preschool Project

The Perry Preschool Project targeted low-income children ages 3–5 years. At initial testing, the children selected ranged from 70 to 85 in intellectual performance. The sample of 123 children was randomly assigned to one of two groups: a program group (n=58) enrolled in the preschool program, or a no-program group (n=65) not enrolled in

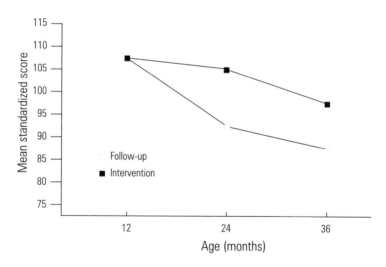

Source: Berlin and others (1998).

Figure 2. Infant Health and Development Program, Cognitive Development Over Time, Ages 12–36 Months

preschool. There were no differences in the children's or parents' abilities or disposition before the preschool program began. The program and no-program groups were matched in mean socioeconomic status, mean intellectual performance, and percentage of girls and boys. The intervention included a daily 2.5-hour classroom session every weekday and a weekly 90-minute home visit on weekday afternoons for 30 weeks per school year for 2 years. The teacher:student ratio was 1:6.

At age 27, the students who had attended the program had an employment rate twice as high, a high school completion rate one-third higher, 40 percent less crime, and 40 percent less teenage pregnancy than the students who had been in the no-program group (Schweinhart, Barnes, and Weikart 1993). Importantly, the Perry Preschool Project shows a strong return on investment. The estimated benefit to cost of this project is US$7 (in savings) to US$1 (cost). This return is impressive *and* it highlights the very dramatic differences that can be made with early interventions for disadvantaged children.

Indeed, much of the literature on international development concludes that a comprehensive program of early childhood services is a strong weapon against poverty, a builder of human capital, and one of the best investments a country can make in its overall development. Brazil is a case in point.

Brazil: A Case Example

Brazil is the ninth largest economy in the world, with a per capita gross national product of US$4,720. Although ranked as an upper-middle-income country, Brazil has a highly inequitable distribution of wealth resulting in a large gap between rich and poor.

Poverty is associated with poor social indicators, especially for children. Currently, in Brazil, 6.3 million children under age 6 are in families living in poverty. Children who are born poor, as correlated with their mother's education, have higher mortality rates, lower immunization rates, and higher rates of malnutrition. They also have lower access to early childhood services. These children tend to do poorly in school, repeat grades, and eventually drop out of school.

In 1998–99, the World Bank undertook a study to review the educational status of young children in Brazil and the policies and services targeted to preschool children. The findings of this study (World Bank 2001), summarized below, are important for all countries and relevant to their ECD efforts.

Early Childhood Services in Brazil

Public services for children younger than age 7 in Brazil consist of day-care centers (crèches), for children up to age 3, and preschools (prèescolas), for children ages 4–6. In 1999, the official age for entering primary school was 7; however, enrollment of 6-year-olds in primary school is considered optimal.

Since 1996, municipalities have been responsible for providing elementary and early childhood education, and Brazil's constitution requires that at least 25 percent of the budget be spent on maintaining and developing education. Public preschools are generally staffed by government employees, and they use a predetermined curriculum.

Private institutions (including for-profit, nonprofit, and government-subsidized organizations) play a substantial role in providing preschool and day-care services and account for almost 44 percent of the enrollments in formal programs. To meet the significant demand for preschools and day care, an array of nonformal ECD services are also offered by community-based, nongovernmental, and religious organizations in the public and private sectors. These nonformal, low-cost alternatives to formal public preschools are estimated to serve more than 1 million children through home visits, day-care centers, and training and literacy centers.

Preschool Enrollment

In 1997, approximately 27 percent of Brazil's 22 million children ages 0–6 years were enrolled in day-care and preschool programs. Approximately one-half attended public facilities, and one-half attended private facilities.

Data from Brazil's National Household Survey (IBGE 1997a) show that children in day care and preschool tend to be older and from richer and urban families. Approximately 61 percent of Brazil's children are enrolled in early childhood programs by age 6 (excluding primary school), compared with about 36 percent at age 4 and 55 percent at age 5. Enrollment for all children younger than age 3 averaged 6–8 percent across Brazil's regions, and only 1 percent of children under age 1 attended day care. Regionally, enrollment was highest in the Northeast and Southeast, averaging about 50 percent for children 4–6 years old. Enrollment in the Midwest, South, and North and in rural areas everywhere was low in comparison.

Early education in Brazil is clearly an issue of rich versus poor. The 1997 household data show that the average rate of enrollment for children ages 0–6 in the richest 10 percent of the population is 56 percent, or more than twice the rate (24 percent) for children from the poorest 40 percent. Also, three-fourths of all preschool children in Brazil attend urban schools, and more urban than rural children participate in early education (32 percent versus 21 percent) at ages 0–6. The gap is largest in the Southeast region, followed by the Midwest, South, and Northeast.

Expenditures for Early Childhood Education

In 1995, Brazil spent approximately US$1 billion in public funds on direct expenditures for early childhood education (Barros and Mendonça 1999; World Bank 2001). The expenditures ranged from US$37–$55 in the North and Northeast regions per child in preschool to US$173 in the South, US$324 in the Midwest, and more than US$660 in the Southeast. The state of São Paulo alone accounted for 75 percent of the nation's total spending on early childhood services. Total public spending for preschool in Brazil primarily reflects the ECD budget of a single wealthy state, although almost two-thirds of the country's poor live in a region (the Northeast) which, in 1995, received only 5 percent of these funds. Clearly, early childhood services means something far different for children in this region, and other poor or rural regions, than for children in São Paulo.

Despite its relative wealth, São Paulo also receives a disproportionate share of social assistance for children ages 0–6. The state accounts for only 6 percent of the poor children served by these programs, but receives almost 14 percent of the nation's total budget for these programs. In contrast, a poor state, such as Bahia, which has 17 percent of the poor children under age 7 served by social assistance programs, receives only 5 percent of the total budget for these programs (Barros and Mendonça 1999).

Is Brazil investing its educational resources appropriately and effectively? Three findings are significant (Barros and Mendonça 1999):

- Per-child spending at day-care and preschool levels is lower than at any other level of education. In 1995, total public expenditure for children ages 0–6 was approximately 17 times lower per student than the amount spent on tertiary education.
- Municipalities are responsible for about 90 percent of the direct expenses for preschool and day-care facilities, as well as elementary education, leaving few resources for ECD services. The effects are serious. For example, although malnutrition is most dangerous during early childhood, only 13 percent of the budget for school feeding is targeted to children ages 0–6.
- "Rich" children receive a disproportionate share of public expenditures. All Brazilian children, rich and poor, have the same constitutionally mandated access to preschool education; however, most public expenditures are disproportionately concentrated on educating nonpoor children.

Benefits and Costs

As part of the assessment of early childhood education in Brazil, the World Bank and the Institute of Applied Economic Research (IPEA) in Rio de Janeiro, Brazil, conducted an analysis to evaluate the effect of preschool education on children's nutrition, years of schooling, and future earning capacity, for different age cohorts. The study utilized data collected in 1996–97 for Brazil's survey of living standards (IBGE 1997b), which covered about 20,000 citizens between the ages of 25 and 64 in approximately 5,000 households in urban and rural areas in the Northeast and Southeast regions of Brazil. The principal findings are as follows (Barros and Mendonça 1999):

- Attendance in preschool has a positive and significant effect on the average years of schooling ultimately attained. One additional year of preschool correlates with about a half-year increase in the schooling ultimately attained, and the gain may be higher for children of illiterate parents.
- Preschooling also has a positive and statistically significant effect on the probability of completing a certain level of education by a specific age. The rates for grade repetition are reduced by 3–5 percentage points for each additional year of preschool. The reduction in grade-repetition rates is especially important in Brazil, where children average 1.4 years to complete a grade. Reduced repetition increases the efficiency of schooling and decreases the costs of schooling.
- Attendance in preschool has both direct and indirect positive effects on future earnings. For males, 1 year of preschool education directly results in a 2–6 percent increase in future earnings. Future income also is indirectly affected by increases in overall schooling. In general, 1 year of *primary* school is estimated to increase future income by approximately 11 percent (Barros and Mendonça 1999). [The economic literature on education estimates that 1 extra year of primary education increases someone's future productivity by 10–30 percent (van der Gaag and Tan 1998).] Because one additional year of *preschool* correlates with a half-year increase in schooling, it produces an indirect gain in future income of about 5 percent. The combined direct and indirect effects of 1 year of preschool are, thus, a minimum 7 percent increase in potential lifetime income—for children whose parents have only 4 years of education (figure 3). Importantly, the gains appear to be higher for children of illiterate parents. These children could gain a 12 percent increase in future earning capacity (figure 4).

This finding supports claims by other countries that the benefits of early childhood education are higher for children of low-income families than for children of middle- or high-income families. In the Brazil study, preschool education did not appear to significantly affect women's earnings, probably because of their informal participation in the workforce.

Based on these gains, the benefit:cost ratio of investing in preschool education is 2:1, demonstrating that each year of preschool education yields a high return on investment. The benefits outweigh the costs and compare favorably with most benefit:cost ratios for industrial and agricultural projects, which are less than 2:1 (van der Gaag and Tan 1998).

Returns to Investment

If education is considered an investment in human capital, the returns to this investment can be estimated. The benefit-cost analysis in the Brazil study shows a rate of return on preschool education of 7–12 percent. In other words, for each year of preschool education, participants can expect a 7–12 percent increase in future income. The

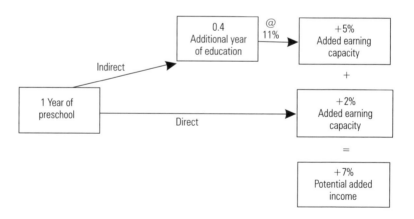

Source: Derived from Barros and Mendonça (1999).

Figure 3. Increase in Future Earning Capacity for Children Whose Parents Have 4 Years of Education

rate of return is 1.5 percent higher for the Southeast and tends to be higher among whites.

Willingness to Pay for Preschool

A calculation of the present value of the income derived from 1 year of attending preschool was compared with potential income without attending preschool. The calculation indicates that families would be willing to pay for preschool, especially those at higher-income levels. By charging fees for those who can afford to pay them, Brazil, and other countries, could extend preschool opportunities to more families and children at risk, thereby further enhancing the return on investment.

Policy Implications

The benefit-cost analysis conducted by IPEA and the World Bank suggests that early intervention in the schooling of 4–6 year olds can make a difference by improving their chances of attaining higher levels of education, reducing grade repetition, and earning a higher income in the future. The main effect of preschool appears to be

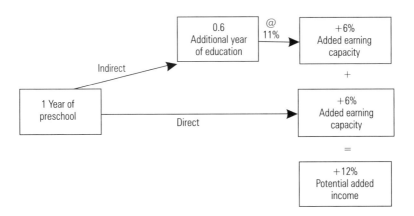

Source: Derived from Barros and Mendonça (1999).

Figure 4. Increase in Future Earning Capacity for Children Whose Parents Are Illiterate

better preparedness for further schooling. Investing in good-quality preschools can be expected to improve attainment and efficiency of higher levels of future schooling. Because public preschools in Brazil are accessible to both rich and poor, the indication of willingness to pay is especially important. The benefits of preschool education substantially outweigh the costs, which suggests that fees could be charged to families that can afford them. Preschool could then be subsidized or provided free to poor families that do not have access to this educational opportunity, but would benefit the most from it.

These findings are supported by similar studies in Brazil and elsewhere. They imply three major policy actions:

1. *Strengthen preschool financing to increase enrollment and efficiency.* The research demonstrates an impressive willingness to pay for preschooling. The actual fees being charged, however, undervalue the true demand. In Brazil's Northeast, for example, not-so-poor households are charged only a small fee per year. Instituting a better fee structure would be an important measure for improving the financing of preschools without having to depend on additional budgetary outlays.

2. *Increase access to preschool and early childcare for the poorest children.* Increasing access to preschool for these children should be a national priority in Brazil and elsewhere. Brazil's guarantee of free preschool for every child is commendable, but targeting this commitment to poor children will greatly enhance its effect. This targeted strategy could be enhanced further by expanding nonformal programs, as low-cost alternatives to standard public services, and exploring public-private partnerships in early child development.

3. *Combine preschool with other ECD services and support parents.* Combining preschool with other ECD services is recommended. Children ages 0–3, who are mostly cared for at home, need to be connected with primary health programs. Parents should be given information, support, and assistance for their efforts to provide emotional support and stimulation for their children.

Brazil is taking major strides to improve its ECD services. The National Plan for Education (1998–2008) sets forth ambitious goals and objectives for day care (ages 0–3) and preschool (ages 4–6) (figure 5).

Day Care (Ages 0–3)

Access Goal:

To expand day-care enrollments to at least a third of children 3 years or younger in the next 10 years.
- Expand the provision of day care at least 5 percent per year.
- Target poor children first.

Quality Goal:

To ensure that day-care programs provide a comprehensive package of health, nutrition, and education services to children (ages 0 to 3); are in formats flexible enough to meet families' needs; and have higher-quality staff.
[Specific objectives are set for 1, 2, 5, and 10 years.]

Information, Monitoring, Quality Control Goal:

To set national ECD standards and establish a municipal system for monitoring private, public, and community day-care centers.
[Specific objectives are set for 1, 3, and 5 years.]

Preschool (Ages 4–6)

Access Goal:

To achieve universal preschool enrollment.
In 1 year:
- Expand public preschool enrollments, focusing on poor children, by at least 5 percent per year.
- Replace the classe de alfabetização program for disadvantaged 7-year-olds with preschool for children under age 6 and regular primary school for children 7 and older.
In 5 years:
- Set universal preschool enrollment for 6-year-olds as a Basic Education requirement.
In 10 years:
- Increase the enrollment of 4–6 year olds from the current 40 percent to 66 percent.

Quality Goal:

[Specific objectives are cited for 1, 3, 5, and 10 years to set and enforce national standards for preschool infrastructures, educational curricula and services, and professional training.]

Information, Monitoring, Quality Control Goal:

To set national ECD standards for preschools.
[Specific objectives are set for 1, 3, and 5 years.]

Source: Fujimoto-Gómez (1999).

Figure 5. Brazil's National Education Plan, 1998–2008: Day Care (Ages 0–3) and Preschool (Ages 4–6)

As elsewhere in the world, such lofty goals must be matched by commitment to funding. In its overall National Education Plan, Brazil gives first priority to elementary education for children ages 7–14, followed by education of adults deprived of basic learning during childhood, and, then, early childhood services. Brazil's early childhood services program requires adequate public support. Chronic underfunding and failure to target available resources to help poor families continue to undermine the efficacy of these services in Brazil.

The first priority for any national ECD plan should be to ensure that poor children receive ECD services comparable with those provided for more-fortunate children. Partnering with the private sector can be an effective way for government to achieve its goals by leveraging its resources.

The Advance Brazil (Avança Brazil) Program is an example of the promise of such public-private partnerships. It is a multiyear plan (Plano Plurianual, PPA) of all governmental programs. *"Atençao à Criança"* is one of the Advance Brazil programs targeting early childhood, ages 0–6.

The *"Atenção à Criança"* Program

The *"Atençao à Criança"* Program for 2000–03 includes several key objectives to overcome poverty and social exclusion. An early childhood program is part of the framework. Overcoming poverty and exclusion in Brazil is a challenging task because Brazil has many inequities resulting from unequal income distribution and a long history of slavery. These inequities are compounded currently by budgetary crises, inability to respond to increasing social demands, and heightened unemployment and poverty resulting from globalization.

The *"Atençao à Criança"* Program is targeting the next decade as the "Decade for Overcoming Poverty." The program focuses on the family, including education of parents. One program, for children ages 0–6, has a 4-year budget of US$1 billion. The aim is to integrate all efforts toward the healthy growth and development of poor children, especially the poorest of the poor. The basic strategy is to provide universal access to prenatal care for poor women, universal registration (of birth) for all children, early childhood education (formal and nonformal), and services to families.

The educational programs include institutionalized day care and preschools, part- and full-time; noninstitutionalized home day care and "roving nurseries"; and alternative programs (e.g., by nongovernmental organizations) offering health, social development, education, nutrition, and family support. Services for families include nutritional, social, health, socioeducational, and income-generating support for parents and their children. The monetary resources for these activities are substantial, but have previously been provided piecemeal. The *"Atençao à Criança"* Program will integrate and direct all the resources for children who truly need care.

Additional efforts within the program target children ages 7–14, young adults ages 15–24, senior citizens over age 60, and people with disabilities. Schools, families, and communities are focal points in all these efforts. The strategy for implementing them involves decentralization, capacity building in the public sector, monitoring and evaluation, and "driving" for results.

This social agenda is based on the coordination of effort and a policy of inclusion. The savings to Brazil are sizeable. A child in preschool costs no more than US$100, but a child on the street costs US$200–$300, and a child in the penal system costs US$1,000 a month. The expenses of exclusion are high.

Importantly, the *"Atençao à Criança"* Program includes the Minister of Finance and managers and presidents of companies, which have a stake in investing in children. All expenditures will be measured to assess them adequately and to understand the gains that are made through inclusion, not exclusion. Investing *for* children is a very positive human and economic strategy, and the greatest effects are seen among the poor.

Source: W.E. Aduan, Federal Secretariat for Social Assistance, Brazil.

Conclusion

To achieve greater equality in society, supportive efforts are needed beginning with children just after birth. Quality interventions from early infancy are clearly important and their positive effects have been documented in well-controlled prospective studies and large-scale retrospective studies, such as the Brazil study highlighted in this chapter. Early childhood interventions significantly improve the educational attainment and success of poor children as they develop and mature. The needs are clear. Appropriate and cost-effective interventions are available. Governments can make a commitment to early child development and can coordinate targeted efforts to reach the poorest families and children. The opportunities are many for providing children early learning experiences that will increase their chances for later success and their society's overall productivity.

Note

The data presented in this chapter are derived from three documents: *Brazil, Early Childhood Development: A Focus on the Impact of Preschools* (World Bank 2001); "Costs and Benefits of Pre-School Education in Brazil," by R. Paes de Barros and R. Mendonça, Institute of Applied Economic Research, Rio de Janeiro, Brazil, November 1999; and "Boosting Poor Children's Chances," by Gaby Fujimoto-Gómez, Organization of American States, November 1999. The description of the *Atenção à Criança* Program is based on a presentation at the World Bank Conference on Investing in Our Children's Future, April 10–11, 2000, Washington, D.C., by Wanda Engel Aduan, Director, Federal Secretariat for Social Assistance and State Secretary for Social Assistance, Brazil.

References

Barros, R.P. de, and R. Mendonça. 1999. Costs and Benefits of Preschool Education in Brazil. Background study commissioned to

IPEA by the World Bank. Rio de Janeiro, Institute of Applied Economic Research.

Berlin, L.J., J. Brooks-Gunn, C. McCarton, and M.C. McCormick. 1998. The Effectiveness of Early Intervention: Examining Risk Factors and Pathways to Enhanced Development. *Preventive Medicine* 27:238–45.

Campbell, F.A., and E.P. Pungello. 1999. The Carolina Abecedarian Project. Website presentation on Long-Term Benefits of Intensive Early Education for Impoverished Children. Chapel Hill, N.C.: University of North Carolina, Frank Porter Graham Child Development Center. [www.fpg.unc.edu/~abc]

Campbell, F.A., and C.T. Ramey. 1994. Effects of Early Intervention on Intellectual and Academic Achievement: A Follow-up Study of Children from Low-Income Families. *Child Development* 65:684–98.

———. 1995. Cognitive and School Outcomes for High-Risk African-American Students at Middle Adolescence: Positive Effects of Early Intervention. *American Educational Research Journal* 32:743–72.

Duncan, G.J., J. Brooks-Gunn, and P.K. Klebanov. 1994. Economic Deprivation and Early Childhood Development. *Child Development* 65:296–318.

Fujimoto-Gómez, G. 1999. Boosting Poor Children's Chances. Background report commissioned to the Organization of American States. Washington, D.C.: World Bank, Human and Social Development Sector.

IBGE (Instituto Brasileiro de Geografia e Estatística) [Brazilian Statistical Institute]. 1997a. *Pesquisa National por Amostra de Domicílios* (PNAD) [National Household Survey]. Rio de Janeiro.

———. 1997b. *Pesquisa de Padrões de Vida* (PPV) [Living Standard Measurement Survey]. Rio de Janeiro.

IHDP (Infant Health and Development Program). 1990. Enhancing the Outcomes of Low-Birthweight, Premature Infants. *Journal of the American Medical Association* 263(22):3035–42.

Karoly, L., P.W. Greenwood, S.S. Everingham, J. Houbé, M.R. Kilburn, C.P. Rydell, M. Sanders, and J. Chiesa, eds. 1998. *Investing in Our*

Children: What We Know and Don't Know About the Costs and Benefits of Early Childhood Interventions. Santa Monica, Calif.:RAND.

McCarton, C.M., J. Brooks-Gunn, I.F. Wallace, C.R. Bauer, F.C. Bennett, J.C. Bernbaum, R.S. Broyles, P.H. Casey, M.C. McCormick, D.T. Scott, J. Tyson, J. Tonascia, and C.L. Meinert. 1997. Results at Age 8 Years of Early Intervention for Low-Birth-Weight Premature Infants: The Infant Health and Development Program. *Journal of the American Medical Association* 277(2):126–32.

Ramey, C.T., F.A. Campbell, M. Burchinal, M.L. Skinner, D.M. Gardner, and S.L. Ramey. 2000. Persistent Effects of Early Childhood Education on High-Risk Children and Their Mothers. *Applied Developmental Science* 4 (1):2–14.

Ramey, C.T., and S.L. Ramey. 1998. Prevention of Intellectual Disabilities: Early Intervention to Improve Cognitive Development. *Preventive Medicine* 27:224–32.

Schweinhart, L.J., H. Barnes, and D. Weikart. 1993. *Significant Benefits: The High/Scope Perry Preschool Study Through Age 27.* Monograph of the High/Scope Educational Research Foundation. No. 10. Ypsilanti, Mich.: High/Scope Educational Research Foundation.

Sparling, J., I. Lewis, and C.T. Ramey. 1995. *Partners for Learning: Birth to 36 Months.* Lewisville, N.C.: Kaplan Press.

van der Gaag, J., and J.P. Tan. 1998. *The Benefits of Early Child Development Programs: An Economic Analysis.* Washington, D.C.: World Bank, Human Development Network.

World Bank. 2001. *Brazil, Early Child Development: A Focus on the Impact of Preschools.* Washington, D.C.: World Bank, Human Development Network.

Part III

Evaluating the Effectiveness of Early Childhood Programs

Chapter 6

Investing in Effective Childcare and Education: Lessons from Research

John M. Love, Peter Z. Schochet, and Alicia L. Meckstroth

Childcare is becoming increasingly important in the United States and around the world as more and more parents are working and need care for their children. In addition, societies are increasingly interested in providing educational experiences and stimulation for all children to improve their chances of doing well in school and life. Often these experiences are provided in full-day settings referred to as childcare or in part-day programs such as preschool or prekindergarten. As more children are placed in these childcare and education settings, understanding how the children are faring has become critically important. Children's safety is only one issue; other concerns relate to children's learning and development—while they are safe and free from danger.

This chapter addresses four topics: the ingredients of quality childcare and education, the supports needed to achieve quality, relationships between quality and children's development and well-being, and investments to enhance children's development. The research and findings on these topics are described separately. Most of the research reviewed has been conducted in the United States, but the lessons learned may be relevant and pertinent to early child development (ECD) programs worldwide. Additional research is needed to appreciate the applicability of the findings in other national contexts and with differing levels of resources.

Ingredients of Quality Childcare and Education

The Research

Early research in childcare and the literature on preschool interventions provide a backdrop for understanding more recent studies of quality childcare and education. Quality is a concept typically used to describe features of program environments and children's experiences in these environments that are presumed to be beneficial to the children's well-being based on research and practice. Researchers have described empirical associations between features of childcare environments and aspects of children's growth and development. The wisdom of practice has been captured by the National Association for the Education of Young Children (NAEYC) in its descriptions of "developmentally appropriate practice" (Bredekamp 1987; NAEYC 1996). A number of authors have attempted to define and measure quality childcare (Ferrar 1996; Ferrar, Harms, and Cryer 1996; Ferrar, McGinnis, and Sprachman 1992; Harms 1992; Howes 1992; Layzer, Goodson, and Moss 1993; Love, Ryer, and Faddis 1992; Phillips 1987; Phillips and Howes 1987).

Two common features recur in these conceptualizations: a distinction between the dynamic (interactional) and static (structural) features of a classroom, and an acknowledgment that the larger program context (outside the classroom) is an important determinant of the quality of children's classroom experiences. Researchers have examined the variables representing both the classroom environment and the larger program context. A review of this research suggests that much progress has been made since Lamb and Sternberg (1990) concluded that early research on childcare focused too much "on the effects of daycare per se instead of recognizing that daycare has a myriad of incarnations and must always be viewed in the context of other events and experiences in the children's lives."

In the past 5 to 10 years, researchers have recognized the "myriad incarnations" of childcare by defining and measuring many quality variables, although they have not been as successful in understanding contextual variables. Tables 1 and 2 present an overview of studies that have measured variations in childcare quality *and* outcomes for children in center-based childcare (table 1) and in family childcare (table 2).

The Findings

Researchers define the quality of early childcare and education in many ways, yet all the definitions reflect two main dimensions, or types of ingredients that correspond to the conceptual features just described: (a) the structure of a program or classroom (i.e., the basic setup that does not change much from hour to hour or day to day), and (b) the dynamics of the program or classroom (i.e., the behavior and interactions of the adults and children which change constantly and are interdependent).

Classroom *structure* includes factors such as the size of the group and the ratio of number of children to adults, as well as the composition of the group and safety factors. A classroom of twenty children and two adults has a group size of twenty and a ratio of 10 to 1. This structure is different from a classroom that has thirty children and two adults. Different numbers of children at different ages also alters the composition: A classroom of twenty 4-year-olds presents a different environment than one with ten 4-year-olds, five 3-year-olds, and five 2-year-olds. Classroom structure also includes the physical environment, which should be arranged to assure the safety of children, with electrical outlets covered, cleaning supplies locked up out of reach of children, and facilities for adults to wash after diapering or toileting. Staff characteristics, including education and training, as well as the program director or supervisor and the support she or he provides, are also part of the structure.

Classroom *dynamics* includes four components: teacher's behavior, children's behavior, teacher–child interactions, and the stability and continuity of interactions. A teacher's behavior may be positive and/or negative. Positive behaviors include attentiveness, encouragement, engagement, sensitivity to children, and responsiveness to children's changing needs. Negative behaviors include harshness and detachment. Other behaviors may occur, but these particularly positive and negative behaviors are especially important for children, as shown by research, and they can be measured by observation and recording.

With respect to children's behavior, one might ask, "What are the indicators of quality? Aren't children just responding to the quality in the center or the home?" Of course, what children *do* while they are *in* a childcare setting at home or in a center is a good indicator of the quality of the environment. For example, a child's crying may indicate hunger or a wet diaper *or* a teacher speaking harshly to, or ignoring, the child.

Teacher–child interactions are a special dimension for consideration. Recognition of these interactions acknowledges that adults' behaviors affect children *and often* are a response to children's behaviors. In a quality childcare environment, teachers respond to children when the children talk and do things. Giving children interesting toys for play is not sufficient if a teacher does not respond when a child asks, "What is this?," or if a teacher does not offer encouragement when a child builds a tower of blocks.

Stability and continuity also are critical elements of classroom dynamics. Children need caregivers who are constant in their lives, and teachers need to be consistent in the ways they respond to children.

In sum, the important ingredients of quality childcare and education are:

- Classroom (and program) structure
  - Appropriate and effective group size, child–staff ratio, composition, safety
  - Supportive administration and services
  - Staff characteristics
- Classroom dynamics
  - Positive teacher behaviors (e.g., attentiveness, encouragement, engagement, sensitivity, responsiveness)

- Positive child behaviors (e.g., interaction with materials, cooperation, joy)
- Effective teacher–child interactions (e.g., teacher responsiveness, verbal interaction)
- Stability and continuity.

Supports Needed to Achieve Quality

The Research

Research emphasizes the importance of childcare staff as supports for achieving quality outcomes. These studies record a variety of staff characteristics in relation to children's outcomes. The variables include staff's level of formal education (Howes, Smith, and Galinsky 1995; Ruopp and others 1979); extent of experience in childcare (Kontos 1994; Ruopp and others 1979); specialized training in early childhood education and other certificates or credentials (Howes, Smith, and Galinsky 1995; Galinsky, Howes, and Kontos 1995); turnover and changes among teachers (Howes and Hamilton 1993); and experience of the center's director (Phillips, McCartney, and Scarr 1987).

Compared with research on the ingredients of quality, this research has been much less thorough and systematic in acknowledging that children's childcare experience occurs in the context of other events and experiences in their lives. Some studies include such variables in their analyses, as Belsky (1990) notes, but the research overall does not yet yield firm conclusions about the effects of childcare quality when controlling for other factors.

Some studies have examined variables describing child and family characteristics, such as family income (Studer 1992), mother's education (Kontos 1991, 1994), mother's employment (Kontos and others 1995), family structure (Kontos 1991; Schliecker, White, and Jacobs 1991), family socioeconomic status (Schliecker, White, and Jacobs 1991), child's membership in a racial or ethnic group (Helburn and others 1995), child's age when initially enrolled in out-of-home care

(Howes 1990; Kontos 1991), child's gender (Howes 1988; Howes and Olenik 1986; Howes and Stewart 1987), duration of child's day-care experience (Field 1991; Kontos 1991), child's temperament (Hestenes, Kontos, and Bryan 1993), family social support (Howes and Stewart 1987; Lamb and others 1988), and family stress (Howes and Stewart 1987). These variables reflect the major advances that have been made in the richness of childcare research during the past decade, but additional, systematic research is needed to relate these variables to children's childcare experiences.

The Findings

The research findings pertaining to staff characteristics point to eight factors that support quality childcare programs. These ingredients are:

- Teacher education, especially specialized training in early child-hood
- Inservice training beyond formal education
- Teacher experience with children
- Continuity of teaching staff—low turnover among the teaching staff
- Adequate staff compensation—wages that allow staff to be comfortable in their jobs and not worry about better-paying opportunities elsewhere
- A center director with experience and training who can supervise and support staff
- Community partnerships—linkages with other agencies that can provide health services and other supports
- Safe and appropriate physical space.

Relationship Between Quality and Children's Development and Well-Being

The relationship between childcare quality and children's development and well-being has been assessed in studies conducted in childcare centers and in family childcare settings. The findings indicate dimensions of quality related to positive childcare outcomes, outcomes associated with higher quality, and factors modifying the relationship between childcare quality and outcomes. Research on preschool interventions supports these findings.

Center-based Childcare: The Research

The twenty-eight studies listed in table 1 demonstrate associations between various measures of childcare-center quality and one or more child outcome measures. Synthesizing the findings of these studies is complicated, however, because the studies differ in (a) design (contemporaneous, longitudinal, and pre-post); (b) age of children (infant-toddler, preschool) during assessment and follow-up; (c) measures of childcare quality; (d) demographics of the sample; and (e) outcomes measured. In the table, the studies are grouped by type of design and listed alphabetically by author. The first nineteen studies used one-time, nonexperimental, contemporaneous designs. The next seven studies used longitudinal designs, most with a one-time follow-up assessment. The last two studies used pre-post designs, assessing the program quality and child outcomes at the beginning and the end of specified periods.

Center-based Childcare: The Findings

Dimensions of Quality Linked With Positive Outcomes

As suggested earlier, the ingredients of quality childcare typically are categorized into structural features, classroom dynamics, and staff characteristics. Hundreds of variables have been studied to elucidate these ingredients of quality.

The most commonly measured structural variable is child–staff ratio. Considerable evidence shows that lower ratios (that is, fewer children per adult) are associated with a wide range of positive developmental indicators. The research also suggests that such structural features are associated with children's well-being because they can provide the conditions that make possible more positive classroom dynamics. The National Day Care Study (Ruopp and others 1979) shows that children's social and cognitive development is enhanced in classrooms with a lower child–staff ratio and smaller group size. The Florida Child Care Quality Improvement Study (Howes, Smith, and Galinsky 1995) shows many significant improvements in children's intellectual and emotional development after Florida instituted stricter requirements for ratios in infant and toddler centers. When the ratio was more favorable, children engaged in more cognitively complex play with objects; showed higher levels of linguistic narrative and discourse skills; were more securely attached to their teachers; and showed less evidence of aggression, anxiety, and hyperactivity. Improved ratios resulted in significant changes in the program environments. Teachers became more warm, sensitive, and nurturing; showed greater responsiveness and encouragement; and were less negative in their disciplinary techniques.

Many studies using contemporaneous designs have shown strong correlations between structural measures (such as ratio) and program dynamics. When classrooms have lower ratios, the amount of adult interaction with children is greater (Layzer, Goodson, and Moss 1993), and teachers and children interact in more beneficial ways (Whitebook, Howes, and Phillips 1989). When classrooms score higher on structural dimensions such as safety and health, they are also rated as more developmentally appropriate (Love, Ryer, and Faddis 1992).

The Florida study is especially useful in helping to disentangle the effects of different dimensions of quality. By using a pre-post design, Howes, Smith, and Galinsky (1995) demonstrate that changing one structural variable—which is readily regulatable—leads to intertwined effects: overall (global) quality improves, teacher–child interactions improve, and children's well-being is enhanced along a number of dimensions. Howes and colleagues also note that the largest increases in some outcomes occur when classrooms add teachers with higher credentials *and* improve their child–staff ratios.

Other studies support the conclusion that ratio, in and of itself, is *not* the most important determinant of children's well-being. Dunn (1993) finds no significant relationship between ratio or group size and children's social and cognitive development. Using an experimental pre-post design, Love, Ryer, and Faddis (1992) find that changing ratios to *less* favorable conditions in California childcare centers does not significantly affect dynamic quality measures or selected aspects of children's behavior in the classroom.

Many studies have investigated the influence of a teacher's (or, more generally, caregiver's) qualifications on other indicators of program quality and child outcomes. The National Child Care Staffing Study (Whitebook, Howes, and Phillips 1989), the largest study to focus on staff characteristics, yields three pertinent conclusions: (a) teachers tend to provide higher-quality care and services to children, as measured through "appropriate and sensitive caregiving," when they have had more formal education, more early childhood training at the college level, and earn higher wages and benefits; (b) children are more competent in social and language development when they attend centers with lower staff turnover; and (c) higher-quality centers have higher staff wages, a better adult work environment, lower teacher turnover, and a more highly educated and trained staff.

In summary, studies are showing important relationships between a number of the dynamic variables describing childcare-center quality and measures of children's development or well-being. Variables such as appropriate caregiving, developmentally appropriate practices, and caregiver responsiveness describe caregiver–child interactions and the social environment in ways that directly affect children's daily experiences. A number of studies have failed to show strong relationships between structural features of a program or classroom. Those that do (e.g., the Florida study) demonstrate that structural/regulatable features do not operate in isolation but imply (and perhaps cause) positive changes in the classroom dynamics. Structural features seem to "set the stage," or provide the necessary conditions, for positive dynamics to occur. By themselves, variables such as lower ratios, smaller group sizes, and safer physical equipment and space do not improve language development or enhance the cognitive complexity of children's play. Nevertheless, they may be extremely important as conditions that permit caregivers to be more responsive and to create developmentally appropriate experiences for children.

Outcomes Associated With Higher Quality

Although most studies have focused on associations between quality measures and children's socioeconomic behavior and development, some studies have also measured children's cognitive development, particularly language development. A few longitudinal studies have assessed children's academic performance following their childcare experience. All of this research suggests that children are socially, emotionally, and cognitively better off when enrolled in higher-quality childcare centers.

When the quality of childcare is higher, peer interactions (including associative-cooperative levels of play) are "more optimal" (Field 1980); social development (including considerateness and sociability) is more positive (McCartney and others 1985; Phillips, McCartney, and Scarr 1987); affect is more positive (Howes 1990); and social skills (such as creativity, independence, extroversion, and interest in interacting with other children) are more advanced (Cost, Quality, and Child Outcomes Study Team 1995). Also, the complexity of play behaviors with peers relates positively to indicators of quality (Dunn 1993; File and Kontos 1993; Howes, Smith, and Galinsky 1995), and higher levels of social problem-solving skills are apparent in higher-quality centers (Holloway and Reichart-Erickson 1988).

When enrolled in higher-quality classrooms, children exhibit fewer or less serious behavior problems (Howes, Smith, and Galinsky 1995; Kontos 1991; Love, Ryer, and Faddis 1992) and better social adjustment, including less socially deviant behavior (Dunn 1993; Kontos 1991). Children also comply more with, and are less resistant to, adult requests (Howes and Olenick 1986; Peterson and Peterson 1986); are more cooperative, responsive, and innovative (Ruopp and others 1979); are more securely attached to their teachers (Howes, Phillips, and Whitebook 1992); and are both adult- and peer-oriented (Howes, Phillips, and Whitebook 1992).

Studies also have demonstrated the negative social manifestations associated with lower levels of quality. For example, lower quality childcare is associated with children's greater solitary play and aimless wandering (Vandell and Powers 1983); uninvolvement in classroom activities (Love, Ryer, and Faddis 1992); more intense "negative affects," such as frowning and crying accompanied by vocalizations and body movements (Hestenes, Kontos, and Bryan 1993); and less sustained verbal interactions (Peterson and Peterson 1986).

Self-control, or the self-regulation of behavior, is considered an important precursor to a successful school experience. The few studies that have measured this outcome show positive associations with program quality. For example, Howes and Olenick (1986) find that children in high-quality centers have higher levels of self-regulation than children in low-quality centers. Task orientation (another behavioral characteristic valued by elementary schools) also is greater among children attending higher-quality centers (McCarthy and others 1985; Phillips, McCartney, and Scarr 1987).

In addition, several studies show positive associations between receptive language and center quality (Cost, Quality, and Child Outcomes Study Team 1995; McCartney and others 1985; Schliecker, White, and Jacobs 1991; Studer 1992). Others show that children in higher-quality care settings perform better on tests of premath skills, such as counting and making comparisons (Cost, Quality, and Child Outcomes Study Team 1995) and verbal intelligence (McCartney 1984). At younger ages, children in settings with less verbal communication and less adult responsiveness show lower levels of language development (Melhuish and others 1990a).

Longitudinal studies following children into kindergarten, first grade, and beyond show that children from higher-quality childcare centers are less distractible, more task-oriented, and more considerate (Howes 1988, for kindergarten); have fewer behavioral problems (Howes 1988, for first grade); and are happier, less shy, and more socially competent and have friendlier interactions with peers (Vandell, Henderson, and Wilson 1988, for age 8). Studies following children in the preschool years, after their participation in center-based care as infants, show enduring associations with indicators of quality such as more positive and gregarious behavior with peers and less social withdrawal and aggression (Howes and Hamilton 1993) and greater personal maturity and social skills with peers and adults (Lamb and others 1988). Children who attended higher-quality childcare programs make better academic progress and are rated higher on school-related skills, such as class participation, in the first grade (Howes 1988) and, by the sixth grade, are assigned to a gifted program at a higher rate (Field 1991) and receive higher math grades (Field 1991).

Factors Modifying the Relationship Between Childcare Quality and Outcomes

Researchers are increasingly recognizing the importance of controlling for child and family background variables when analyzing relationships between quality indicators and child outcome measures (Cost, Quality, and Child Outcomes Study Team 1995; Phillips, McCartney, and Scarr 1987). The research in this area has not been sufficiently systematic to make broad generalizations about these interactions, and the findings may differ between settings because the studies focused on different factors, measures, and contexts. The divergent analysis strategies used (some inappropriately) further complicate generalizations across studies.

Several studies have examined differential effects depending on the age when children enter childcare. Howes (1990), for example, finds that teachers' socialization practices better predict children's outcomes when children enrolled as infants, but that families' socialization practices best predict outcomes for children who enrolled as toddlers. Kontos (1991), however, who studied 3–5 year olds, finds no differential effects.

Other studies have attempted to determine whether quality indicators operate differently for girls and boys. Howes and Olenick (1986) find different patterns of relationships among childcare, family, and child and parent behaviors. In particular, childcare quality predicts self-regulation and task persistence in toddler boys but not in girls, leading the authors to conclude that boys are more sensitive to the quality of care. Howes (1988) analyzed the combined effects of high quality and stable arrangements separately for boys and girls in the first grade and finds that academic skills are predicted by stability alone for girls, but that both stability and high quality predict academic skills for boys.

Family-based Childcare: The Research

Less research has focused on family-based childcare than on center-based care. The research on family-based care shows extremely wide differences in definitions and measurements of quality, geographic settings, and families' socioeconomic status and racial and ethnic compositions. Because family childcare more commonly serves infants and toddlers, the variation in ages is less than in center-based studies. Table 2 summarizes data from eight studies conducted between 1981 and 1995. A multisite study, Quality in Family Child Care and Relative Care (Galinsky and others 1994; Kontos and others 1995), has contributed significantly to the understanding of the relationship between the quality of family childcare and children's development.

Family-based Childcare: The Findings

Dimensions of Quality Linked With Positive Outcomes

Important elements of quality associated with positive outcomes in family childcare include global quality (Goelman and Pence 1988; Howes and Stewart 1987; Kontos 1994; Kontos and others 1995); stability of care (Howes and Stewart 1987); caregiver's training (Galinsky, Howes, and Kontos 1995); provider intentionality or professionalism and commitment to children (Kontos and others 1995); caregiver's behaviors and characteristics, such as sensitivity and responsiveness (Kontos and others 1995); and structural features such as group size (Howes and Rubenstein 1981; Kontos and others 1995). "Intentionality," identified by Kontos and others (1995), has not previously been articulated, but may be a key indicator of quality in family childcare (and perhaps center-based care). Kontos and colleagues argue that providers will give better-quality care if they are professionally prepared, seek opportunities to learn about childcare and child development, actively plan for children's experiences, and are actively involved in networks of other family childcare providers.

The Quality in Family Child Care and Relative Care study identifies the relationship between providers and parents as potentially crucial. Relatives are often assumed to be in the best position to provide needed childcare. However, in the study by Kontos and others (1995), the care provided by relatives (usually grandparents) was more likely to be rated as inadequate and the relatives were less sensitive and responsive in interacting with the target child. The authors note that, "when adults care for children under less than ideal circumstances (poverty, social isolation, not their chosen profession), the children are less likely to get the warmth and attention that parents rate as important attributes of quality childcare" (Kontos and others 1995, pp. 204–05).

Outcomes Associated With Higher Quality

As with the center-based studies, the outcomes measured in family daycare include cognitive and socioemotional development and focus especially on child–caregiver attachment. Goodman and Andrews (1981) find that adding a home-teaching educational program of 2 to 4 hours per week in a family day-care setting significantly improves children's receptive language, readiness skills, and basic concepts. Howes and Stewart (1987) show the importance of childcare quality on children's level of play with peers and objects, and Kontos and others (1995) measure children's object play as a reflection of their level of cognitive development. Children in regulated care were more frequently engaged in high-level object play than were children in care provided by relatives. Other studies show that higher-quality care results in improved development of social skills and personal maturity (Lamb and others 1988), less aimless wandering and more involvement in activities (Galinsky, Howes, and Kontos 1995), more vocalizations to peers (Howes and Rubenstein 1981), and enhanced sociability (Kontos 1994). Kontos and colleagues (1995) find few behavior problems in children in childcare provided by families and relatives.

The strength of a child's attachment with a caregiver has been an important outcome in studies of infants and toddlers. The security and trust that accompany secure attachments enable children to use available resources and materials better. Studies show a greater security of attachment when caregivers are sensitive and responsive (Kontos and others 1995) and when they have received specialized training (Galinsky, Howes, and Kontos 1995). The Quality in Family Child Care and Relative Care study shows no differences in security scores across different types of providers (Kontos and others 1995). Preliminary findings from another multisite childcare study (NICHD Early Child Care Research Network 1996) suggest that secure infant–mother attachment (at 15 months of age) results from a complex interaction of quality of childcare and quality of mother–infant interactions at home. A preliminary report of this study indicates that attachment may be adversely affected by poor-quality childcare (i.e., where caregivers are inattentive).

Research on language development shows that children benefit particularly in improved receptive vocabulary. Goelman and Pence (1987, 1988) and Goodman and Andrews (1981) find higher levels of language development among children attending higher-quality family childcare. However, Kontos and colleagues (1995) find that structural and process variables do not predict communicative competence (adaptive language); however, ratings by the providers may not have been a reliable method for assessing children's language. Kontos and colleagues also report that the percentage of children engaged in high-level peer play and object play is less than expected given the children's ages. They conclude that "children in family-based care are not experiencing caregiving environments likely to promote optimal development" (Kontos and others 1995, p. 163).

Factors Modifying the Relationship Between Childcare Quality and Outcomes

Several studies show differential effects of quality in relation to factors such as a family's socioeconomic status (Kontos 1994; Kontos and others 1995), maternal employment (Kontos and others 1995), and child's gender (Howes and Stewart 1987). These findings are too few, however, to warrant any firm conclusions about the most important factors moderating the relationship between family childcare and outcomes. The research does provide the foundation for future studies.

In sum, the research summarized in tables 1 and 2 shows that the quality dimensions most commonly associated with positive outcomes are:

- Lower child–staff ratios and smaller group sizes
- Appropriate caregiving
- Developmentally appropriate practices
- Caregiver responsiveness.

Child outcomes associated with higher-quality childcare are:

- Improved language
- Enhanced social skills
- Reduced behavior problems
- Increased cooperation.

Lower child–staff ratios and smaller group sizes are important *because* they make possible more-positive dynamics. When teachers have to interact with fewer children, they can better respond to individual children, pay attention to each child, give appropriate care, and create a developmentally appropriate classroom environment.

However, although structural features such as good ratios and group sizes make positive dynamics possible, they do not guarantee quality in teacher–child interactions. Staff have to know how to make the best of good conditions. Staff supports, such as appropriate training and effective supervision, are essential.

Investments in effective structures and supports yield positive dynamics and outcomes. Children have better vocabulary and communication skills, interact more positively with their peers *and* adults, and are less likely to be aggressive.

Preschool Interventions: Research on Quality

Much of the research and evaluation of preschool programs and interventions supports these findings and reinforces the importance of quality care and education in early childhood. Although childcare and preschool settings are generally distinguished by the nature and extent of services provided, the classroom dynamics are similar in both settings and, in many countries, childcare and education are combined in integrated service programs. The literature on preschool interventions, however, does not allow for comparable reviews of the correlates or effects of quality, because researchers have only recently begun to emphasize descriptions of quality dimensions in their studies. They have been more likely to contrast two or three treatment groups, or an intervention and a control group, rather than treating quality as a continuous variable for measuring child outcomes. The Perry Preschool study (Schweinhart, Barnes, and Weikart 1993), Abecedarian project (Campbell and Ramey 1994), and Syracuse Family Development Research Program (Lally, Mangione, and Honig 1987) are examples of these types of studies. Nevertheless, these studies can legitimately be interpreted as evidence of the benefits of enhanced program quality because the programs were designed as high-quality interventions. In each case, the children's outcomes were contrasted with the outcomes for children who attended lower-quality ECD programs or no ECD program.

In the literature on preschool education, quality is most often associated with the concept of developmentally appropriate practice. In a review of this literature, Bryant and colleagues (1994) identify several studies that illustrate the relationship between quality, defined as developmentally appropriate practice, and child outcomes. For example, the High/Scope study, conducted in the 1960s, shows that children who attend a developmentally appropriate, child-centered program are better adjusted socially than similar children who attend a teacher-directed program implementing a direct-instruction curriculum (Schweinhart, Weikart, and Larner 1986). In a study of children attending state preschool programs in North Carolina, Bryant, Peisner-Feinberg, and Clifford (1993) found that children's communication abilities at the end of preschool are positively associated with appropriate caregiving and that vocabulary development in kindergarten is positively associated with the quality of preschool. Burts and colleagues (Burts and others 1992; Hart and others 1995) show that children's attendance in developmentally appropriate kindergartens is associated with fewer stress behaviors. Also, Bryant and colleagues (1994) show that children who attend higher-quality Head Start classes have better cognitive, although not social, outcomes at the end of the Head Start year (see also the chapter by Tarullo in this volume).

Investments to Enhance Children's Development

The existing research demonstrates that the following five types of investment are most important for enhancing children's early development:

1. Well-trained staff who are motivated and committed to their work with children
2. Facilities that are safe and sanitary and accessible to parents
3. Ratios and group sizes that allow staff to interact appropriately with children
4. Supervision that maintains consistency
5. Staff development that ensures continuing and improving quality.

But, what if resources are scarce? What if a particular state or community cannot afford to find or build good facilities or find enough staff? The research conducted thus far is not sufficiently precise to indicate which elements of quality are most important. Investing in additional ongoing research is essential.

Ongoing Research and Evaluation

To develop and improve effective childcare programs, information about existing programs must be collected and evaluated continuously. Researchers have used a variety of statistical methods to assess the effects of childcare quality on children's well-being. These include nonexperimental designs (contemporaneous, longitudinal, and pre-post), to compare outcomes for children who attend classrooms or centers of different quality, and experimental studies, to compare outcomes for children who attend childcare classrooms randomly assigned to different quality-of-care conditions. All methods have a role to play in improving the understanding of important ingredients of quality in ECD programs.

Nonexperimental Designs

Most studies have relied on nonexperimental designs, for observing a sample of children attending a representative set of classrooms or centers in particular locales. These studies measured the quality of care provided, as well as developmental outcomes, and compared outcomes for children attending higher- and lower-quality centers. Different statistical methods were used for contemporaneous, longitudinal, and pre-post designs.

Studies employing a *contemporaneous design* measure childcare quality and outcomes at approximately the same time. They assess the contemporaneous effects of childcare quality on outcomes by computing correlation coefficients between the outcome and quality measures and determining the statistical significance of the correlation coefficients (see, for example, Howes, Phillips, and Whitebook 1992).

Studies employing a *longitudinal design* assess the long-term effects of childcare experiences of varying quality on children's outcomes. These studies obtain follow-up data for children who participate in good- and poor-quality childcare. The follow-up assessments are conducted at varying periods after the children's childcare experience. The statistical models estimated in the studies using a longitudinal design are similar to those estimated in studies using a contemporaneous design. Researchers usually begin their analyses by calculating the correlation coefficients between a center's quality and the outcome measures and then estimating regression models to control for child and family background variables.

Studies employing *pre-post* designs assess the effect of changes in center quality on children's well-being. These studies compare the outcomes of separate cross-sections of children before and after a change in center quality (pre-post cross-section designs), or compare the outcomes of longitudinal samples of children who do, or do not, experience a change in center quality (pre-post longitudinal designs). The most important study using a pre-post cross-section design is Howes, Smith, and Galinsky (1995), which assessed the effect of changes in Florida's requirements for childcare facilities' child–staff ratios on the quality of the children's development. The study by Howes and Hamilton (1993) is an example of a pre-post longitudinal design.

Experimental Designs

Experimental, or randomized, designs are the most rigorous methodology for estimating internally valid effects of a center's quality on children's well-being. With this design, classrooms in a sample of childcare centers are randomly assigned to different quality-of-care groups, and children requiring childcare are randomly assigned to the classrooms. Randomization ensures that there are no systematic observable or unobservable differences between children assigned to the different classrooms, except for the quality of care they receive, and that there are no systematic differences between the quality of teachers assigned to the different quality-of-care groups.

However, because parents or childcare staff may want to select specific teachers for certain children, randomly assigning children to classrooms is seldom feasible. Therefore, a more realistic design is to allocate children to specific classrooms (either by parents' or staff's choice, or randomly) and then randomly assign classrooms to different quality-of-care conditions. This design, however, may produce less-precise estimates of the effects of childcare quality for a sample size than when all children are also randomly assigned to classrooms, because there is a greater chance that the average characteristics of children will differ across classrooms. Hence, the standard errors of the estimated effects of childcare quality must take into account that a different allocation of classrooms to the quality-of-care groups could produce different results. Although not focusing on child outcomes, Love, Ryer, and Faddis (1992) conducted a study that illustrates some of the strengths and problems of using an experimental design to assess the effects of structural variables on classroom dynamics and children's behavior.

Randomized designs are, in theory, the most effective designs for obtaining reliable information on the effects of a policy intervention. Because these designs are often difficult to implement, however, they usually have practical limitations, and program staff are often unwilling to participate in randomized studies. Thus, many studies employing randomized designs use only program sites that agree to participate. The estimates of effect, based on experimental designs, must therefore be interpreted with caution.

Research Needs

The advantages and shortcomings of these nonexperimental and experimental methods are discussed in detail in Love, Schochet, and Meckstroth (1996). Because nonexperimental designs are more practical (less expensive and difficult than experimental designs), they are likely to prevail in future research. For future studies using nonexperimental methods to estimate the effects of a center's quality, two specific recommendations are as follows:

1. For studies employing contemporaneous or longitudinal designs, estimate models using established statistical methods that correct and test for systematic, unobservable differences between the characteristics of children who enroll in centers of different quality or in no centers.
2. Using pre-post designs, conduct additional studies to compare outcomes of a cross-section of children who attend childcare before a change in the center's quality with those of a separate cross-section of children who attend childcare after the change is made.

Conclusion

Extensive research over the past 20 years has found strong, positive relationships between a variety of quality measures and various dimensions of children's development and well-being. Most of the research reviewed in this chapter addresses programs in the United States, and circumstances in the developing world likely could alter the specifics of particular relationships. Nevertheless, the research suggests that investments in five areas may have the greatest benefit: (1) well-trained staff who are motivated and committed to their work with children, (2) facilities that are safe and sanitary and accessible to parents, (3) ratios and group sizes that allow staff to interact appropriately with children, (4) supervision that maintains consistency, and (5) staff development that ensures continuing and improving quality. Consistent investments in the structures and supports for early child development can yield tremendous payoffs by improving the well-being of children and their families and communities. Investments in research and evaluation will enable child development programs to continue to find ways to improve and increase their effectiveness.

Acknowledgments

This chapter draws on a review conducted with the support of the Rockefeller Foundation and published as Love, J.M., P.Z. Schochet, and A.L. Meckstroth, "Are They in Any Real Danger? What Research Does—and Doesn't—Tell Us About Child Care Quality and Children's Well-Being." *Child Care Research and Policy Papers: Lessons from Child Care Research Funded by the Rockefeller Foundation.* Princeton, N.J.: Mathematica Policy Research, Inc., May 1996.

References

Belsky, J. 1990. Parental and Nonparental Child Care and Children's Socioemotional Development: A Decade in Review. *Journal of Marriage and the Family* 52:885–903.

Bredekamp, S. 1987. *Developmentally Appropriate Practice in Early Childhood Programs Serving Children from Birth Through Age 8.* Washington, D.C.: National Association for the Education of Young Children.

Bryant, D.M., M. Burchinal, L.B. Lau, and J.J. Sparling. 1994. Family and Classroom Correlates of Head Start Children's Developmental Outcomes. *Early Childhood Research Quarterly* 9:289–309.

Bryant, D.M., E.S. Peisner-Feinberg, and R.M. Clifford. 1993. *Evaluation of Public Preschool Programs in North Carolina.* Chapel Hill, N.C.: Frank Porter Graham Child Development Center.

Burts, D.C., C.H. Hart, R. Charlesworth, P.O. Fleege, J. Mosely, and R.H. Thomasson. 1992. Observed Activities and Stress Behaviors of Children in Developmentally Appropriate and Inappropriate Kindergarten Classrooms. *Early Childhood Research Quarterly* 7:297–318.

Campbell, F.A., and C.T. Ramey. 1994. Effects of Early Intervention on Intellectual and Academic Achievement: A Follow-Up Study of Children from Low-Income Families. *Child Development* 65:684–98.

Cost, Quality, and Child Outcomes Study Team. 1995. Cost, Quality, and Child Outcomes in Child Care Centers: Public Report. Denver: University of Colorado at Denver, April.

Dunn, L. 1993. Proximal and Distal Features of Day Care Quality and Children's Development. *Early Childhood Research Quarterly* 8:167–92.

Ferrar, H.M. 1996. *Places for Growing: How to Improve Your Child Care Center.* Princeton, N.J.: Mathematica Policy Research, Inc.

Ferrar, H.M., T. Harms, and D. Cryer. 1996. *Places for Growing: How to Improve Your Family Child Care Home.* Princeton, N.J.: Mathematica Policy Research, Inc.

Ferrar, H.M., E. McGinnis, and S. Sprachman. 1992. The Expanded Child Care Options (ECCO) Approach to the Development of Enhanced-Quality Center-Based Child Care. Princeton, N.J.: Mathematica Policy Research, Inc., December.

Field, T. 1980. Preschool Play: Effects of Teacher:Child Ratios and Organization of Classroom Space. *Child Study Journal* 10(3):191–205.

———. 1991. Quality Infant Day-Care and Grade School Behavior and Performance. *Child Development* 62:863–70.

File, N., and S. Kontos. 1993. The Relationship of Program Quality to Children's Play in Integrated Early Intervention Settings. *Topics in Early Childhood Special Education* 13(1):1–18.

Galinsky, E., C. Howes, and S. Kontos. 1995. *The Family Child Care Training Study: Highlights of Findings.* New York, N.Y.: Families and Work Institute.

Galinsky, E., C. Howes, S. Kontos, and M. Shinn. 1994. *The Study of Children in Family Child Care and Relative Care: Highlights of Findings.* New York, N.Y.: Families and Work Institute.

Goelman, H., and A. Pence. 1987. Effects of Child Care, Family, and Individual Characteristics on Children's Language Development: The Victoria Day Care Research Project. In D. Phillips, ed., *Quality in Child Care: What Does Research Tell Us?* Washington, D.C.: National Association for the Education of Young Children.

———. 1988. Children in Three Types of Day Care: Daily Experiences, Quality of Care and Developmental Outcomes. *Early Childhood Development and Care* 33:67–76.

Goodman, N., and J. Andrews. 1981. Cognitive Development of Children in Family and Group Day Care. *American Journal of Orthopsychiatry* 51:271–384.

Harms, T. 1992. Preschool and Child Care Setting Characteristics. Paper prepared for the National Center for Education Statistics. Chapel Hill, N.C.: University of North Carolina, November.

Hart, C.H., D.C. Burts, M.A. Durland, R. Charlesworth, M. DeWolf, and P.O. Fleege. 1995. Stress Behaviors and Activity Type Participation of Preschoolers in More and Less Developmentally Appropriate Classrooms. In preparation.

Helburn, S., and others. 1995. Cost Quality and Child Outcomes in Child Care Centers: Executive Summary. Denver: University of Colorado at Denver, January.

Hestenes, L., S. Kontos, and Y. Bryan. 1993. Children's Emotional Expression in Child Care Centers Varying in Quality. *Early Childhood Research Quarterly* 8:295–307.

Holloway, S.D., and M. Reichhart-Erickson. 1988. The Relationship of Day Care Quality to Children's Free Play Behavior and Social Problem Solving Skills. *Early Childhood Research Quarterly* 3(1):39–53.

Howes, C. 1988. Relations Between Early Child Care and Schooling. *Developmental Psychology* 24(1):53–57.

———. 1990. Can the Age of Entry into Child Care and the Quality of Child Care Predict Adjustment in Kindergarten? *Developmental Psychology* 26(2):292–303.

———. 1992. Preschool Experiences. Paper prepared for the National Center for Education Statistics. Los Angeles: University of California at Los Angeles, September.

Howes, C., and C. Hamilton. 1993. The Changing Experience of Child Care: Changes in Teachers and in Teacher-Child Relationships and Children's Social Competence with Peers. *Early Childhood Research Quarterly* 8:15–32.

Howes, C., and M. Olenick. 1986. Family and Child Care Influences on Toddler's Compliance. *Child Development* 57:202–16.

Howes, C., D. Phillips, and M. Whitebook. 1992. Thresholds of Quality: Implications for the Social Development of Children in Center-based Child Care. *Child Development* 63:449–60.

Howes, C., and J. Rubenstein. 1981. Toddler Peer Behavior in Two Types of Day Care. *Infant Behavior and Development* 4:387–93.

Howes, C., E. Smith, and E. Galinsky. 1995. *The Florida Child Care Quality Improvement Study: Interim Report.* New York, N.Y.: Families and Work Institute.

Howes, C., and P. Stewart. 1987. Child's Play with Adults, Toys, and Peers: An Examination of Family and Child-Care Influences. *Developmental Psychology* 23(3):423–30.

Kontos, S. 1991. Child Care Quality, Family Background, and Children's Development. *Early Childhood Research Quarterly* 6:249–62.

———. 1994. The Ecology of Family Day Care. *Early Childhood Research Quarterly* 9:87–110.

Kontos, S., C. Howes, M. Shinn, and E. Galinsky. 1995. *Quality in Family Child Care and Relative Care.* New York, N.Y.: Teachers College Press.

Lally, J.R., P.L. Mangione, and A.S. Honig. 1987. Long-Range Impact of an Early Intervention with Low-Income Children and Their Families. San Francisco: Center for Child and Family Studies, Far West Laboratory for Educational Research and Development, September.

Lamb, M.E., C.P. Hwang, A. Broberg, and F.L. Bookstein. 1988. The Effects of Out-of-Home Care on the Development of Social Competence in Swedish Preschoolers: A Longitudinal Study. *Early Childhood Research Quarterly* 3:379–402.

Lamb, M.E., and K.J. Sternberg. 1990. Do We Really Know How Day Care Affects Children? *Journal of Applied Developmental Psychology* 11:351–79.

Layzer, J.I., B.D. Goodson, and M. Moss. 1993. *Observational Study of Early Childhood Programs, Final Report Volume 1: Life in Preschool.* Washington, D.C.: U.S. Department of Education.

Love, J.M., P. Ryer, and B. Faddis. 1992. *Caring Environments— Program Quality in California's Publicly Funded Child Development Programs: Report on the Legislatively Mandated 1990–91 Staff/Child Ratio Study.* Portsmouth, N.H.: RMC Research Corporation.

Love, J.M., P.Z. Schochet, and A.L. Meckstroth. 1996. Are They in Any Real Danger? What Research Does—and Doesn't—Tell Us About Child Care Quality and Children's Well-Being. *Child Care Research and Policy Papers: Lessons from Child Care Research Funded by the Rockefeller Foundation.* Princeton, N.J.: Mathematica Policy Research, Inc., May.

McCartney, K. 1984. Effect of Day Care Environment on Children's Language Development. *Developmental Psychology* 20(2):244–60.

McCartney, K., S. Scarr, D. Phillips, and S. Grajek. 1985. Day Care as Intervention: Comparisons of Varying Quality Programs. *Journal of Applied Developmental Psychology* 6:247–60.

Melhuish, E.C., E. Lloyd, S. Martin, and A. Mooney. 1990a. Type of Child Care at 18 Months—II. Relations with Cognitive and Language Development. *Journal of Child Psychology and Psychiatry* 31(6):861–70.

Melhuish, E.C., A. Mooney, S. Martin, and E. Lloyd. 1990b. Type of Child Care at 18 Months—I. Differences in Interactional Experience. *Journal of Child Psychology and Psychiatry* 31(6): 849–59.

NAEYC (National Association for the Education of Young Children). 1996. Developmentally Appropriate Practice in Early Childhood Programs Serving Children From Birth Through Age 8: A Position Statement of the National Association for the Education of Young Children. Washington, D.C.: Author, July.

NICHD (National Institute of Child Health and Human Development) Early Child Care Research Network. 1996. Infant Child Care and Attachment Security: Results of the NICHD Study of Early Child Care. Symposium presented at the meeting of the International Conference on Infant Studies, Providence, Rhode Island, April.

Peterson, C., and R. Peterson. 1986. Parent-Child Interaction and Day Care: Does Quality of Day Care Matter? *Journal of Applied Developmental Psychology* 7:1–15.

Phillips, D.A. 1987. Epilogue. In D.A. Phillips, ed., *Quality in Child Care: What Does Research Tell Us?* Washington, D.C.: National Association for the Education of Young Children.

Phillips, D.A., and C. Howes. 1987. Indicators of Quality in Child Care: Review of Research. In D.A. Phillips, ed., *Quality in Child Care: What Does Research Tell Us?* Washington, D.C.: National Association for the Education of Young Children.

Phillips, D., K. McCartney, and S. Scarr. 1987. Child-Care Quality and Children's Social Development. *Developmental Psychology* 23(4):537–43.

Ruopp, R.R., J. Travers, F. Glantz, and C. Coelen. 1979. *Children at the Center: Final Results of the National Day Care Study.* Cambridge, Mass.: Abt Books.

Schliecker, E., D.R. White, and E. Jacobs. 1991. The Role of Day Care Quality in the Prediction of Children's Vocabulary. *Canadian Journal of Behavioral Science* 23(1):12–24.

Schweinhart, L.J., H.V. Barnes, and D.P. Weikart. 1993. Significant Benefits: The High/Scope Perry Preschool Study Through Age 27. *Monographs of the High/Scope Educational Research Foundation,* no. 10. Ypsilanti, Mich.: High/Scope Educational Research Foundation.

Schweinhart, L.J., D.P. Weikart, and M.B. Larner. 1986. A Report on the High/Scope Preschool Comparison Study: Consequences of Three Preschool Curriculum Models Through Age 15. *Early Childhood Research Quarterly* 1:15–45.

Studer, M. 1992. Quality of Center Care and Preschool Cognitive Outcomes: Differences by Family Income. In P.A. Adler and P. Adler, eds., *Sociological Studies of Child Development,* vol 5. Greenwich, Conn.: JAI Press.

Vandell, D.L., V.K. Henderson, and K.S. Wilson. 1988. A Longitudinal Study of Children with Day-Care Experiences of Varying Quality. *Child Development* 59:1286–92.

Vandell, D., and C. Powers. 1983. Daycare Quality and Children's Free Play Activities. *American Journal of Orthopsychiatry* 53:293–300.

Whitebook, M., C. Howes, and D. Phillips. 1989. *Who Cares? Child Care Teachers and the Quality of Care in America: Final Report: National Child Care Staffing Study.* Berkeley, Calif.: Child Care Employee Project.

Table 1. Center-based Childcare Studies That Examine Quality of Care and Child Outcomes

Study (date)	Sample size/ages/demographics	Design and methodology	Outcomes measured	Relationships between quality and child outcomes
		Studies using contemporaneous designs		

Cost, Quality, and Child Outcomes Study Team (1995)	• 826 children (age 4)
	• 181 centers
	• 15% African American
	  68% white
	  6% Hispanic
	  4% Asian
	  63% of mothers have less than bachelor's degree
		• Contemporaneous design
		• Observational measures of classroom quality
		• Direct assessments, teacher ratings, and self-reports of child outcomes
			• Receptive language
			• Prereading skills
			• Premath skills
			• Self-perceptions of competence
			• Level of social play
			• Attitudes toward childcare
			• Social skills
				• Higher classroom quality index was associated with:
				  –Greater receptive language ability
				  –Higher premath skills
				  –More advanced social skills
				  –More positive self-perceptions
				• Effect of quality on receptive language was greater for minority children.

Dunn (1993)	• 60 children (ages 3 to 5)
	• 30 classrooms in 24 centers
	• 90% white
	  10% African American
	  Middle socioeconomic status
	  77% two-parent families
		• Contemporaneous design
		• Observational assessment, staff interviews, and questionnaires to measure classroom quality
		• Direct assessment, teacher ratings, and child achievement tests to measure child outcomes
			• Sociability
			• Social adjustment
			• Social play
			• Cognitive development and intelligence
			• Cognitive play
				• Children with married parents and those attending centers that offered less variety and more guidance (or more "total limits") were rated as better socially adjusted; children attending centers that provided more total limits had higher levels of complex social play.
				• Children attending classrooms with higher overall quality and whose caregivers had a child-related college major and less experience in the center scored higher on a test of intelligence.
				• Child–staff ratio and group size did not predict children's social and cognitive development.

continued

Table 1 (continued). Center-based Childcare Studies That Examine Quality of Care and Child Outcomes

Study (date)	Sample size/ages/ demographics	Design and methodology	Outcomes measured	Relationships between quality and child outcomes
Field (1980)	• 80 children (ages 3 to 4) • Four center-based preschool classrooms • 100% white • Middle socioeconomic status	• Contemporaneous design (observational and child data collection over a 9-month period) • Observational assessment of quality on two dimensions • Direct assessment of child outcomes	• Peer interactions • Play behaviors (fantasy play, associative-cooperative play)	• Children attending classrooms that had low teacher–child ratios and partitioned, special play areas exhibited more optimal behaviors (including interactions with peers, verbal interactions, fantasy play, and associative-cooperative play).
File and Kontos (1993)	• 28 children (ages 2.5 to 6) • 6 to 12 center classrooms (exact number not provided) • Demographic characteristics not provided 50% had mild or moderate cognitive and/or speech and language delays.	• Contemporaneous design (observational and child data collection over a 2-week period) • Observational assessment of quality • Direct assessment of child outcomes	• Cognitive play level (functional, constructive, and dramatic play) • Social play level (solitary, parallel, and interactive play)	• Positive teacher interactions with children, a characteristic indicative of high-quality classrooms, were related to a higher level of children's social play. Less teacher involvement in routine activities, less watching, less support of cognitive play, and more overall teacher uninvolvement were also related to higher levels of social play. • Children's experiences with their teachers were not related to their level of cognitive play.

Study (date)	Sample size/ages/ demographics	Design and methodology	Outcomes measured	Relationships between quality and child outcomes
Goelman and Pence (1987 and 1988)	• 105 children (approximately 3 to 4 years of age, ages not provided) • 53 centers • 52 family day-care providers • Predominantly white (Canadian) • Range of socioeconomic status represented • 50% two-parent families	• Contemporaneous design (observational and child data collection over a 1-year period) • Observational assessment and parent ratings of classroom quality • Direct assessment of child outcomes	• Language development • Peer interactions • Play activities (solitary, cooperative)	• Among children attending center-based care, quality of care did not predict language development scores. • Children in center-based care engaged in more high-quality "information activities" than children in family day care. However, for children in family childcare, the amount of information activities was not related to quality.
Hestenes, Kontos, and Bryan (1993)	• 60 children (ages 3 to 5) • 26 centers • 30 classrooms • Range of social classes represented • Race/ethnicity of children not provided	• Contemporaneous design (observational and child data collection on two separate occasions) • Observational assessment of classroom quality • Direct assessment of child outcomes	• Emotional expression (positive versus negative affect, intensity of affect, duration of affect) • Temperament (approach, adaptability, intensity, mood, and rhythm)	• Low levels of classroom engagement by teachers predicted more intense negative affect among children; children whose teachers showed high levels of classroom engagement displayed more intense positive affect, controlling for temperament and child demographics.

continued

Table 1 (continued). Center-based Childcare Studies That Examine Quality of Care and Child Outcomes

Study (date)	Sample size/ages/ demographics	Design and methodology	Outcomes measured	Relationships between quality and child outcomes
Holloway and Reichhart-Erickson (1988)	• 55 children (age 4) • 15 centers • 4% African American 94% white 2% Asian 91% two-parent families Predominantly middle socioeconomic status	• Contemporaneous design (observational and child data collection over a 3-week period) • Observational measures of classroom quality • Direct assessment of child outcomes	• Free-play activities • Social reasoning and problem solving • Peer interactions	• Children engaging in high-quality interactions with teachers and children attending centers with lower child-teacher ratios scored higher on a test of social reasoning skills. • In centers that were better able to accommodate groups of varying sizes, had smaller classes, and offered a variety of age-appropriate materials, children scored higher on a test of social reasoning skills. • In centers with a more spacious layout, children spent more time in focused, solitary play and less time observing. • Quality indicators were not significantly related to negative or positive social interactions with peers.
Howes and Olenick (1986)	• 89 children (ages 1.5 to 3) • Eight centers • 10% African American 70% white 13% Hispanic 7% Asian (based on race/ethnicity of father) 69% two-parent families	• Contemporaneous design • Observational assessment and caregiver reporting of classroom quality measures • Direct assessment (in home and center) and parent ratings of child outcomes	• Compliance • Resistance • Self-regulation	• Children attending high-quality centers were more compliant and less resistant and were more likely to self-regulate (or refrain from touching food and forbidden new toys). • Quality of care predicted self-regulation and resistant behavior among boys but not girls.

continued

Study (date)	Sample size/ages/ demographics	Design and methodology	Outcomes measured	Relationships between quality and child outcomes
Howes, Phillips, and Whitebook (1992)	• 414 children (ages 1 to 4.5) – 68 infants – 175 toddlers – 171 preschoolers • 233 center classrooms • Full range of social classes represented 21% African American 73% white	• Contemporaneous design • Observational assessment of quality • Direct assessment of children	• Attachment with teacher • Social orientation • Interaction with peers	• Children in classrooms rated higher on "appropriate caregiving" were more likely to be classified as secure (but not as avoidant or ambivalent). • Children in classrooms rated higher on "developmentally appropriate activities" were more likely to be both adult- and peer-oriented.
Howes and Rubenstein (1981)	• 40 children (ages 1.5 to under 2) • Eight centers 16 family day-care homes • 33% African American, Hispanic, or Asian 67% white Predominantly two-parent families Middle socioeconomic status	• Contemporaneous design • Observational assessment of classroom quality • Direct assessment and observer ratings of child outcomes	• Peer social behaviors • Peer social interaction • Structure of peer play	• The greater use of nonportable objects (indicative of a quality environment) in centers was positively related to the level of interactive play. • No overall differences in the frequency of socially directed peer behaviors were present between family day care and center care.

Table 1 (continued). Center-based Childcare Studies That Examine Quality of Care and Child Outcomes

Study (date)	Sample size/ages/demographics	Design and methodology	Outcomes measured	Relationships between quality and child outcomes
Kontos (1991)	• 100 children (ages 3 to 5) • 10 centers • Predominantly white • Range of socioeconomic status and urban/rural families represented • 57% two-parent (married) families	• Contemporaneous design (observations and child assessments collected over a 1-day period) • Observation and state licensing instruments used to assess quality • Caregiver ratings and child performance on standardized tests used to assess child outcomes	• Cognitive development • Language development • Social development	• Family background variables were significantly related to several measures of children's cognitive and language development. • Overall quality (a measure of a minimum level of quality) predicted better social adjustment scores and fewer behavior problems among children, controlling for family background and childcare experience. • Age of entry into childcare and duration of the childcare experience were not significant predictors of child development outcomes.
Love, Ryer, and Faddis (1992)	• Ages 3 to 5 (94% 3–4 year olds) • 112 center classrooms • 62 agencies • 37% African American • 19% white • 32% Hispanic • 13% Asian • 23% limited English proficient • Families eligible for childcare subsidy (average of only 1.4 children per agency paid full fee)	• Pre-post design; contemporaneous • Classrooms randomly assigned to change ratio after fall data collection • Contemporaneous assessment of classroom quality and child outcomes • Teacher ratings of behavior problems • Observer ratings of stress behaviors	• Behavior problems • Stress behaviors • Crying and fighting • Involvement in activities	• In classrooms that were more developmentally appropriate, children showed less stress and less crying and fighting. • In classrooms that were more developmentally inappropriate, children were more uninvolved in classroom activities and showed higher levels of stress. • When caregivers were attentive and encouraging, children showed less stress; when caregivers were more harsh, critical, and detached, children showed higher levels of stress. • In classrooms rated higher on scheduling, safety, and health, there was less crying and fighting.

Study (date)	Sample size/ages/demographics	Design and methodology	Outcomes measured	Relationships between quality and child outcomes
McCartney (1984)	• 166 children (ages 3 to 5) • Nine centers • 80% black Bermudians 20% white Bermudians • 84% spent most of work week in day care by age 2.	• Contemporaneous design (observational and child data collection over a 4-month period) • Observational measures of classroom quality • Direct assessment of child outcomes • Caregiver ratings of child outcomes	• Verbal intelligence • Verbal interaction with caregivers • Verbal interaction with peers • Language development	• Children attending centers with higher overall quality ratings were more likely to have greater verbal intelligence and language development, controlling for family background, age of entry in care, and number of hours in care. • Children who attended centers that allowed greater levels of child-initiated conversation, had many visitors, had less noise, and provided little free-play time scored higher on tests of language development.
McCartney, Scarr, Phillips, and Grajek (1985)	• 166 children (comparison group: 72 children) (ages 3 to 6) • Nine centers • 78% black Bermudians 22% white Bermudians Comparison group (100% black Bermudians)	• Contemporaneous, comparison group design (observations and child data collection over a 4-month period) • Observational assessment of classroom quality • Direct assessment of child performance on standardized tests; parent and caregiver ratings used to assess child outcomes	• Cognitive skills • Receptive language • Communication skills • Sociability • Considerateness • Dependency • Intelligence • Task orientation	• Low-income children attending a high-quality day-care intervention program had better language skills and were more considerate and sociable, compared with children attending other center programs of lower, but varying, quality. Findings hold when children attending the high-quality program are compared with a group with similar family backgrounds.
Peterson and Peterson (1986)	• 66 children (24 in home care) (ages 3 to 5) • Four centers • Predominantly white Predominantly middle socioeconomic status	• Contemporaneous design • Observational assessment of classroom quality • Direct assessment of child outcomes	• Parent-child interaction • Verbal communication • Compliance	• Children attending low-quality centers performed worse on sustained verbal interactions and compliance with task-oriented instructions than either children attending high-quality centers or children receiving maternal care in the home; no differences existed in these two outcomes for children receiving either high-quality center care or maternal care.

continued

Table 1 (continued). Center-based Childcare Studies That Examine Quality of Care and Child Outcomes

Study (date)	Sample size/ages/ demographics	Design and methodology	Outcomes measured	Relationships between quality and child outcomes
Phillips, McCartney, and Scarr (1987)	• 166 children (ages 3 to 5.5) • Nine centers • 78% black Bermudians 22% white Bermudians 68% from two-parent families 85% spent most of work week in day care by age 2.	• Contemporaneous design (observational and child data collection over a 4-month period) • Observational assessment and staff reporting of quality • Teacher and parent ratings of child outcomes	• Sociability • Considerateness • Dependence • Intelligence • Task orientation • Aggression • Hyperactivity • Anxiety	• Children in centers with higher overall quality were more socially developed in considerateness, sociability, intelligence, task orientation, and anxiety, controlling for age at entry, time in childcare, and family background. • Children having greater levels of verbal interaction with caregivers were more considerate, sociable, intelligent, and task-oriented. • In centers with directors who had greater levels of experience, children were less aggressive and anxious but also were less considerate and sociable.
Schliecker, White, and Jacobs (1991)	• 100 children (age 4) • 10 centers • Predominantly white Range of socioeconomic status represented 63% two-parent families	• Contemporaneous design (observational and child data collection over a 2-week period) • Observational assessment of classroom quality • Direct assessment of child outcomes	• Language development and comprehension	• Day-care quality (measured dichotomously) and socioeconomic status (a combined measure of income, occupation, education, and family structure) both significantly predicted vocabulary comprehension; day-care quality may be particularly important for single-parent, female-headed households.

continued

Study (date)	Sample size/ages/ demographics	Design and methodology	Outcomes measured	Relationships between quality and child outcomes
Studer (1992)	• 95 children in families currently using child-care center or nursery at time of the 1986 National Longitudinal Study of Youth (ages 3 to 4) • All two-parent families	• Contemporaneous design • Parental report of quality through survey responses • Direct assessment of child outcomes	• Receptive language	• Special training of caregiver, group size, and ratio were unrelated to receptive language ability. • Composite quality index was positively associated with receptive language ability only for low-income subsample. • Composite quality index was negatively related to receptive language ability for lower-middle-income group.
Vandell and Powers (1983)	• 55 children (ages 3 to 4) • Six centers • White • Middle socioeconomic status • Two-parent families • Attended day care an average of 2 years	• Contemporaneous design • Observational assessment of classroom quality • Direct assessment of behavior	• Interaction with peers • Interaction with adults • Vocalization with peers • Vocalization with adults • Solitary play • Unoccupied behaviors	• Children attending centers rated as high quality were more likely to have positive interactions and vocalizations with adults. • Children attending low-quality centers were more likely to engage in solitary play and aimless wandering. • No differences were found in peer-directed behaviors and interactions in centers of varying quality.

Table 1 (continued). Center-based Childcare Studies That Examine Quality of Care and Child Outcomes

Study (date)	Sample size/ages/ demographics	Design and methodology	Outcomes measured	Relationships between quality and child outcomes
		Studies using longitudinal designs		

Field (1991)	• 56 children. Average age 11.5 at follow-up. (Children began day care when less than 2 years old and continued for average of 2.7 years.)
	 • Six centers
	   Study 1: 28 children
	   Study 2: 56 children
	 • Heterogeneous sample by race/ethnicity (including African American, white, Hispanic; percentages not given) Middle socioeconomic status, highly educated families
		• Longitudinal design (parent reports of child's early care experience used as baseline data)
		 • Caregiver reporting of classroom quality measures
		 • Direct assessment and parent and teacher ratings of child outcomes
			• School grades
			 • Test scores
			 • Assignment to gifted program
			 • Work/study habits
			 • Leadership
			 • Emotional well-being
			 • Adult/child relations
			 • Peer relations, attractiveness, assertiveness, aggressivity, popularity
				• Children who had spent more time in high-quality day care were more likely to show more physical affection during peer interactions, to be assigned to the gifted program, and to receive higher math grades.

Study (date)	Sample size/ages/ demographics	Design and methodology	Outcomes measured	Relationships between quality and child outcomes
Howes (1990)	• 80 children (same children examined in Howes and Olenick 1986) (ages 3 to 7 primarily) • Began at ages 1.5 to 3 (see Howes and Olenick 1986) • Eight centers (estimate) 9% African American 74% white 13% Hispanic 1% Asian 76% two-parent families	• Longitudinal design • Observational assessment and caregiver reporting of classroom quality measures • Direct assessment and parent and teacher ratings of child outcomes	• Compliance, resistance • Self-regulation • Social adjustment/ peer interactions (social play, social pretend play, positive affect)	• Preschool children attending high-quality centers engaged in more social pretend activities, displayed more "positive affect" relative to angry and distressed behavior, and were rated by teachers as having sociable relations with peers. • Kindergarten children who entered lower-quality centers as infants were rated by teachers as more distractible, less task-oriented, and less considerate, compared with children who entered higher-quality centers as infants. • Among children enrolled as infants, childcare quality (measured through teacher socialization practices) best predicted child outcomes; among children enrolled as toddlers or preschoolers, family socialization practices best predicted child outcomes.
Howes (1988)	• 75 children enrolled in laboratory elementary school. • Childcare experience at age 4. Follow-up at first grade. • 12% African American 69% white 12% Hispanic 6% Asian Mothers' median education level: 14 years 70% two-parent families	• Longitudinal design • Observational measures of classroom quality • Teacher ratings of child outcomes	• Academic progress • School skills (independence, group skills, participation skills) • Behavior problems	• For girls, stable childcare arrangements predicted academic skills, controlling for family characteristics. • For boys, stable arrangements and high-quality care predicted academic skills, controlling for family characteristics. • For both boys and girls, high-quality care predicted enhanced school skills and low behavior problems.

continued

Table 1 (continued). Center-based Childcare Studies That Examine Quality of Care and Child Outcomes

Study (date)	Sample size/ages/ demographics	Design and methodology	Outcomes measured	Relationships between quality and child outcomes
Howes and Hamilton (1993)	• 72 children (48 at follow-up) (ages 1 to 2). Follow-up at ages 4 to 5. • 5 centers (and one large family day-care home) at start; 54 centers over course of study • 14% African American 61% white 25% Hispanic or Asian 67% middle socio-economic status	• Longitudinal design • Observational assessment of quality • Direct assessment of child outcomes	• Social competence with peers (complex play; prosocial, gregarious, aggressive, and withdrawn behaviors)	• Children having more changes in teachers were rated as lower in positive and gregarious behaviors and higher in social withdrawal and aggression. • Children who had secure teacher–child relationships (or teacher–child relationships that changed in a positive direction) had more positive, gregarious, and prosocial interactions with their peers and were less withdrawn and aggressive. • Changes in children's childcare center or setting were not related to children's social competence with peers.
Lamb, Hwang, Broberg, and Bookstein (1988)	• 140 children (ages 1 to 2). Follow-up at ages 2 to 4. • 53 centers 33 family day-care homes 54 maternal home care situations • 100% Swedish children Range of socioeconomic status represented 100% two-parent families Older mothers (average age = 31)	• Longitudinal design • Observational assessment of caregiver quality and home quality; parent ratings of social support • Direct assessment of child outcomes	• Personal maturity (independence, ego resiliency, and control) • Sociability • Adult–child interaction • Peer play • Activity level	• As measured at follow-up, children's sociability and personal maturity were not related to type of childcare. • The quality of care (regardless of type of provider) and family social support predicted personal maturity and social skills with familiar peers and unfamiliar adults.

Study (date)	Sample size/ages/ demographics	Design and methodology	Outcomes measured	Relationships between quality and child outcomes
Melhuish, Lloyd, Martin, and Mooney (1990a); Melhuish, Martin, Mooney, and Lloyd (1990b)	• 193 children (age 1.5). Assessments at 5 and 18 months. • Focus groups: —Home care—57 —Relative care—30 —Family day care—74 —Center care—32 • 100% British Range of socioeconomic and educational status	• Longitudinal design • Observational measures of child-care quality • Direct assessment, observer ratings, and parent reports of child outcomes	• Language development • Cognitive development	• Children in center-care settings that provided less verbal communication with and less responsiveness to children scored lower on a measure of language development.
Vandell, Henderson, and Wilson (1988)	• 20 children (age 4). Follow-up at age 8. • Six centers • White Middle socioeconomic status	• Longitudinal design • Observational assessment of classroom quality • Direct and videotaped assessment of children • Observer, parent, and peer ratings of behavior	• Interaction with peers • Interaction with adults • Solitary play • Unoccupied behaviors	• Children attending centers rated as high quality tended to have more friendly interactions with peers, were assessed as happier and more socially competent, and were less likely to be viewed as "shy"; results were relatively consistent at ages 4 and 8. • Having positive interactions with adults at age 4 was significantly correlated with ratings of empathy, social competence, and peer acceptance at age 8.

continued

Table 1 (continued). Center-based Childcare Studies That Examine Quality of Care and Child Outcomes

Study (date)	Sample size/ages/demographics	Design and methodology	Outcomes measured	Relationships between quality and child outcomes
		Studies using pre-post designs		
Howes, Smith, and Galinsky (1995)	• 880 children (ages 10 months to 5 years). (Different children examined during baseline and follow-up data collection; second follow-up completed in spring 1996) • 150 centers • Range of socioeconomic status and urban/rural families represented in the state of Florida (other demographic characteristics not reported)	• Pre-post design • Observational assessment of classroom and teacher quality • Direct assessment and observer ratings of child outcomes	• Peer play • Object play • Adaptive language proficiency • Behavior problems • Attachment to caregiver	• Changing child–teacher ratio requirements for infants from 6:1 to 4:1 and for toddlers from 8:1 to 6:1 resulted in more complex child play both with peers and objects, more secure attachment to caregivers, greater adaptive language proficiency, and fewer behavior problems (including aggression, anxiety, and hyperactivity). • Children in classrooms meeting professional standards for child–teacher ratios engaged in more elaborate peer play and had higher adaptive language scores, compared with children in classrooms with higher ratios. • Children in classrooms that improved by shifting to teachers with Child Development Associate (CDA) credentials or CDA equivalency had the largest increase in complexity of peer play and security of caregiver attachment. Children in classrooms with college-educated teachers who had early childhood training engaged in more complex peer play, had a more secure attachment with their caregiver, and had higher adaptive language scores.

Study (date)	Sample size/ages/ demographics	Design and methodology	Outcomes measured	Relationships between quality and child outcomes
Ruopp, Travers, Glantz, and Coelen (1979)	• 1,600 children (ages 3 to 5). (Infant/toddler substudy: ages 6 weeks to 3 years) • 49 centers in three cities in quasi-experiment; eight centers in one public school district in randomized experiment • Infant/toddler substudy: 74 groups of children and 54 centers • 65% African American 30% white Range of socioeconomic status, with low-income over-represented Less than 50% two-parent families	• Pre-post design (observational and child outcome data collection over a 1-year period) • Observational measures of classroom quality • Direct assessment of child outcomes • Randomized experiment and quasi-experiment • (Note: The findings for preschoolers are from the 49-center quasi-experiment and are generally supported by findings from the separate, randomized experiment.)	• Cognitive knowledge/school readiness • Receptive language ability • Adult–child interaction • Social behaviors (cooperation, innovation, apathy, distress) • Fine and gross motor skills	• Preschool children attending centers with smaller group sizes engaged in more adult–child social interaction, were more cooperative, responsive, and innovative, and made greater gains in receptive language ability; the effect of group size on receptive language ability was independent of child age, gender, race, family income, and other socioeconomic background characteristics. • Preschool children in centers that promoted reflective, innovative, and involved behavior showed greater gains in receptive language ability and cognitive knowledge. Children in centers where caregivers exhibited high levels of social and managerial interaction with children showed more rapid gains in receptive language ability. The effects of these center and caregiver characteristics on receptive language ability and cognitive knowledge were independent of child age, gender, race, family income, and other socioeconomic background characteristics. • Preschool children attending centers with teachers better trained or educated in child-related fields had more social interactions with teachers, were more cooperative, compliant, and involved, and had greater gains in cognitive knowledge; neither years of teacher experience nor level of formal education showed a consistent relationship to child outcomes.

continued

Table 1 (continued). Center-based Childcare Studies That Examine Quality of Care and Child Outcomes

Study (date)	Sample size/ages/ demographics	Design and methodology	Outcomes measured	Relationships between quality and child outcomes
Ruopp, Travers, Glantz, and Coelen (1979) (continued)				• Relationships between preschool child–caregiver ratios (5:1 to 10:1) and caregiver and child behavior were neither strong nor consistent; ratio was unrelated to gains in child test scores. • Toddlers attending centers with better child–staff ratios exhibited less overt distress; toddlers cared for by experienced staff exhibited more apathetic behavior; the degree of specialized staff training had no effect on child distress, child apathy, or exposure to potentially dangerous situations. • Infants attending centers with better child–staff ratios exhibited less overt distress, less apathetic behavior, and were exposed to fewer potentially dangerous situations; infants cared for by better educated but less experienced staff exhibited less apathy and were exposed to fewer potentially dangerous situations; infants cared for by staff with specialized training showed no significant behavioral differences.

Note: The table includes only findings that the authors report as statistically significant.

Source: Love, J.M., P.Z. Schochet, and A.L. Meckstroth. 1996. Are They in Any Real Danger? What Research Does—and Doesn't—Tell Us About Child Care Quality and Children's Well-Being. *Child Care Research and Policy Papers: Lessons from Child Care Research Funded by the Rockefeller Foundation.* Princeton, N.J.: Mathematica Policy Research, Inc.. May.

Table 2. Family-based Childcare Studies That Examine Quality of Care and Child Outcomes

Study (date)	Sample size/ages/ demographics	Design and methodology	Outcomes measured	Relationships between quality and child outcomes
		Studies using contemporaneous designs		
Goelman and Pence (1987 and 1988)	• 105 children (ages 3 to 4). Specific ages not provided. • 53 centers • 52 family day-care providers Predominantly white (Canadian) Range of socioeconomic status represented 50% two-parent families	• Contemporaneous design (observational and child data collection over a 1-year period) • Observational assessment and parent ratings of classroom quality • Direct assessment of child outcomes	• Language development • Peer interactions • Play activities (solitary, cooperative)	• Children attending high-quality family day-care homes had higher average scores for language development than children attending lower-quality family day-care homes. • Amount of "information activities" was not related to quality.
Goodman and Andrews (1981)	• 52 children (ages 2.5 to 4) • 32 family day-care providers (enhanced) • (Control group receiving nonenhanced family day care: 8 children) • (Comparison group receiving center-based care: 68 children, three centers) • 43% white 57% African American	• Contemporaneous design • An educational intervention was used to assess quality (the intervention varied in intensity among three treatment groups but in each case focused on the development of linguistic competence). • Direct assessment and observer ratings of child outcomes	• Cognitive performance • Verbal intelligence	• Children receiving an enhanced family day-care intervention showed greater improvement in cognitive performance on three standardized tests than did either control group children in family day-care settings or comparison group children in professionally run group day-care centers.

continued

Table 2 (continued). Family-based Childcare Studies That Examine Quality of Care and Child Outcomes

Study (date)	Sample size/ages/ demographics	Design and methodology	Outcomes measured	Relationships between quality and child outcomes
Howes and Rubenstein (1981)	• 40 children (20 in family day care) (18 to 24 months) • Eight centers 16 family day-care homes • 33% African American, Hispanic, or Asian 67% white Predominantly two-parent families Middle socioeconomic status	• Contemporaneous design • Observational assessment of class-room quality • Direct assessment and observer ratings of child outcomes	• Peer social behaviors • Peer social interaction • Structure of peer play	• Among family day-care homes, smaller group sizes and the presence of older peers in the group positively influenced children's vocalization to peers. • No overall significant differences in the frequency of socially directed peer behaviors were found between family day care and center care.
Howes and Stewart (1987)	• 55 children (ages 11 to 30 months) • 55 family day-care homes • Heterogeneous social classes and parent educational levels (including 18% low socioeconomic status) • 82% two-parent families	• Contemporaneous design • Observational assessment of family day-care quality • Direct assessment and observer ratings of child outcomes	• Play with peers • Play with objects • Play with adult care-givers	• A greater number of changes in the family day-care provider was associated with lower-level play with objects and peers. • For boys, earlier childcare entry and fewer changes in provider were also associated with higher-level play with objects. • Higher overall quality of care was related to higher levels of competent play with adults and with objects; for girls, the relationship was also significant for higher-level play with peers.

Study (date)	Sample size/ages/demographics	Design and methodology	Outcomes measured	Relationships between quality and child outcomes
Kontos (1994)	• 57 children (ages 2.5 to 4 years) • 30 family day-care providers • Middle socioeconomic status • 82% two-parent families	• Contemporaneous design • Observational assessment of family day-care quality • Direct assessment and teacher ratings of child outcomes	• Cognitive play • Intelligence quotient • Language interaction • Receptive vocabulary • Social play and sociability	• Children in family day-care homes that were rated at a higher level of overall quality were significantly less likely to engage in simple cognitive and social play, were rated as significantly more sociable, and scored higher in receptive vocabulary, controlling for maternal education, caregiver experience, and conditions of caregiving. • Children in higher-quality family day-care homes who had mothers with more education and caregivers with less experience were rated as significantly more sociable. • Children in higher-quality family day-care homes who had mothers with a higher level of education scored significantly higher in receptive vocabulary.
Kontos, Howes, Shinn, and Galinsky (1995); Galinsky, Howes, Kontos, and Shinn (1994)	• 226 children (ages 10 months to 5 years) • 226 family day-care providers • 42% white 23% African American 31% Hispanic Heterogeneous social classes and maternal educational levels • 81% two-parent families	• Contemporaneous design • Observational assessment of family day-care quality • Direct assessment, observer ratings, and caregiver ratings of child outcomes	• Peer play • Attachment security • Social adjustment/behavior problems • Object play • Use of language	• Children with sensitive and responsive caregivers were more likely to be securely attached to their caregivers. • Children who spent more time with their caregiver, were cared for in homes with more children per adult, and had caregivers who used more-responsive interactions engaged in a greater amount of play with objects; children with more-educated mothers and more-responsive caregivers engaged in more high-level object play. • Larger group sizes and child–staff ratios were related to more peer play.

continued

Table 2 (continued). Family-based Childcare Studies That Examine Quality of Care and Child Outcomes

Study (date)	Sample size/ages/ demographics	Design and methodology	Outcomes measured	Relationships between quality and child outcomes
Kontos, Howes, Shinn, and Galinsky (1995); Galinsky, Howes, Kontos, and Shinn (1994) (continued)				• Higher global quality was related to more object play, more high-level object play, and better child attachment security; however, higher global quality was related to less high-level peer play. • Neither family background characteristics nor childcare characteristics (structural or process quality) predicted children's language development or social adjustment. • Maternal working conditions and number of hours worked were unrelated to all aspects of children's development.
		Studies using pre-post designs		
Galinsky, Howes, and Kontos (1995)	• 130 children (ages 1 to 5, approximate; exact ages not given) • 130 family day-care providers • Geographic diversity (other sample demographics not provided)	• Pre-post design • Observational assessment of family day-care quality • Direct assessment and observer ratings of child outcomes	• Peer play • Attachment security • Object play	• Children with caregivers who had participated in a 16-hour training course behaved in a manner indicative of a secure attachment with their caregiver, were more engaged in activities (such as listening to stories), and spent less time wandering aimlessly, compared with children whose caregivers did not receive the special training course.

Study (date)	Sample size/ages/ demographics	Design and methodology	Outcomes measured	Relationships between quality and child outcomes
		Studies using longitudinal designs		
Lamb, Hwang, Broberg, and Bookstein (1988)	• 140 children (ages 1 to 2). Follow-up at ages 2 to 4. • 53 centers • 33 family day-care homes 54 maternal home care situations • 100% Swedish children Range of socioeconomic status represented 100% two-parent families Older mothers (average age = 31)	• Longitudinal design • Observational assessment of caregiver quality and home quality; parent ratings of social support • Direct assessment of child outcomes	• Personal maturity (independence, ego resiliency, and control) • Sociability • Adult-child interaction • Peer play • Activity level	• The quality of care (regardless of type of provider) and family social support predicted personal maturity and social skills with familiar peers and unfamiliar adults. • As measured at follow-up, there was no significant relationship between type of childcare and children's sociability or personal maturity.

Note: The table includes only findings that the authors report as statistically significant.

Source: Love, J.M., P.Z. Schochet, and A.L. Meckstroth. 1996. Are They in Any Real Danger? What Research Does—and Doesn't—Tell Us About Child Care Quality and Children's Well-Being. *Child Care Research and Policy Papers: Lessons from Child Care Research Funded by the Rockefeller Foundation.* Princeton, N.J.: Mathematica Policy Research, Inc., May.

Chapter 7

Mapping and Documenting Effective Programming

Judith L. Evans

Participants and professionals observing or engaged in early child-hood activities and programs tend to judge whether an activity or program is effective based on intuitive, overall impressions and, sometimes, mental checklists of "critical features." The signs of an effective early childhood program include a range of factors defined by professionals based on their individual experiences and goals, which may differ substantially. Figure 1 lists examples of the questions asked by early childhood professionals when evaluating the effectiveness of an early childhood program.

To examine in greater depth the effectiveness of early childhood programs, the Bernard van Leer Foundation launched the Effectiveness Initiative (EI) in January 1999 in partnership with the Consultative Group on Early Childhood Care and Development. The question being explored in this initiative is, "What makes early childhood programs effective, in a variety of contexts, for diverse participants and stakeholders—from children, to parents, to community members and policymakers?" The emphasis in this initiative is on the effectiveness of the process of early child development (ECD) programming, rather than specific outcomes of ECD programs. This chapter describes the key features of the initiative, including the participating programs, the organization and underlying assumptions, and the qualitative research tools and strategies used to collect and analyze program data.

For the Program

- Is the child central to what is going on? For example, when there are discussions about the program, is the focus on what is happening for children or on the facilities?
- What is the nature of child-adult interactions?
- Do the children stay "on task" when a stranger walks in?
- Is there a predictable structure to each day (timetable) that includes unstructured time and space?
- Are children and adults healthy and clean? What does "healthy and clean" mean, given the context?
- What is the nature of parent (mother and father) involvement in the program?
- Is there an acknowledgment of the value of individual differences and contributions?
- Are people able to adapt to new situations?
- Are the early childhood activities based on cultural characteristics? For example, are children allowed to look at adults directly? Are children allowed to ask questions of adults?
- What evidence is there for the kind of training that caregivers, teachers, parents, and supervisors have received?
- What kind of support (e.g., follow-up, advice) is provided to teachers, parents, and other participants by the organizers of the program?
- Is the program comprehensive? Does it address children's physical development (health and nutrition) and psychosocial development and the rights of children and families?
- Are there opportunities for children and adults to express themselves verbally and creatively?
- Does the curriculum include music and drama and other expressive opportunities?
- What use is made of storytelling?
- Is there fun, laughter, and joy ("a spring in the feet and a sparkle in the eye") of the children and caregivers?

For the Setting

- Is the environment conducive to learning? For example, is children's work displayed and are there materials and opportunities for exploration and problem solving?
- Is there a high level of activity and constructive noise?
- What is the child-to-adult ratio? Is it appropriate for the context? Does it vary based on the age of the children?
- What kinds of "coverage" does the program provide? Is it inclusive or exclusive in enrolling children with disabilities?
- Is there a monitoring and evaluation system in place?
- Is provision made for children's transition to primary school?
- Are people (of all ages) asking interesting questions for which they may not necessarily have a "right" answer"?
- Do people (of all ages) acknowledge they do not know all the answers, and are they willing to engage with others in seeking solutions?

Source: Brainstorming session, 1999 Meeting of the Consultative Group on Early Childhood Care and Development.

Figure 1. Early Childhood Programs: Possible Indicators of Effectiveness

The EI is an in-depth, 5-year exploration to better understand in what ways programs are effective for diverse participants, communities, and cultures. The initiative involves a qualitative study of programs that have been in place for at least 10 years and the development of methods and "maps" for examining other programs in the future. The goals are twofold:

- To gain deeper insight into the components of effective early childhood programs
- To stimulate interagency and international dialogue on effectiveness, beyond the present scant measures and indicators of program success.

The EI also is designed to test the use of qualitative research methods, which are relatively well developed in other disciplines, in international early childhood development. The initiative is not expected to yield a template for successful or ideal programs, but will "map" dimensions of effectiveness in specific programs and identify patterns of effectiveness across diverse settings.

Available data, published during the past 5 years by the Consultative Group on Early Childhood Care and Development, the World Bank, the Inter-American Development Bank, and other organizations, document the economic benefits of investments in early childhood. These data emphasize long-term economic outcomes benefiting individuals and industrialized societies, as measured by economic productivity. Although the ECD field has benefited greatly from the research generating these data, the findings should not constrain the continued search for effective early childhood programs. An economic emphasis narrows understanding of the full impact of effective early childhood programs on individual children, families, and communities. Also, current research findings emphasize preschool programs, and the potential benefits of home-based, parent support, and community development programs have not been explored in any depth.

One of the challenges for the EI is to create a set of methods and data that are broader than, but as persuasive as, current economic analyses of the benefits of early childhood programs. The aim is to understand the impact of a wide variety of early childhood strategies and to complement the quantitative research already conducted with qualitative research tools and methods.

Key questions for the EI are: What makes an early childhood program "work"? What aspects of a program are working? What can we learn from programs that feel "right" in some ways but wrong in other ways? How does a program change over time? Are effective programs always effective? Are programs effective for only one set of stakeholders, or are they meeting the needs of different sets of stakeholders? Are they effective in the same ways for the various stakeholders? Can a program that is failing to make a difference in one dimension nevertheless be effective in another?

The Effectiveness Initiative

The participants, organization, assumptions, and status of the EI are described below. A discussion of the tools and strategies being used follows.

Participants

The EI focuses on ten programs selected from more than forty programs funded by a variety of organizations, foundations, donor agencies, and government. The ten programs are geographically diverse and illustrate a variety of approaches to ECD. Each program appears to meet the definition of an effective ECD program, that is, a program that meets the developmental and cultural needs of young children and their families in ways that enable them to thrive. Figure 2 briefly describes the programs.

Organization

Organization of the EI has involved selection and preparation of research teams, framing of meaningful questions, and development of processes to enhance individuals' skills in listening, understanding, and interpreting people's experiences and situations.

1. *Madrasa Resource Center (MRC)* — Kenya

The Madrasa Project was created to provide a preschool experience for young children (ages 3–6 years) to help prepare them for school and provide basic religious teachings. The program has been expanded to Zanzibar and Uganda. The MRC, which is based in Mombasa, provides training and support. Uniquely, the program:
• Was developed by the Muslim community in response to its needs
• Combines traditional Koranic teachings and more secular education
• Prepares children to enroll and perform better in primary school
• Is experimenting with a unique financing system (community-based endowments)
• Provides a model for other Muslim countries.

2. *Assoçiação de Criança Familia e Desenvolvimento (CFD)* — Mozambique

Since 1995, CFD (the Association for the Child, Family, and Development) has focused on a variety of community-based activities, which include enabling almost 500 community network groups to systematize spontaneous ECD activities. Uniquely, the CFD program:
• Enlists community network groups as active development agents, which is crucial for the emerging Mozambique civil society
• Stimulates daily recreational activities for children based on culturally appropriate methods
• Restores traditional healing ceremonies to help children and families in psychosocial distress after Mozambique's civil war
• Shifted from Save the Children's Children and War Project to effectively support community initiatives within a broader mission and a longer-term perspective.

3. *Self-Employed Women's Association (SEWA)* — India

Since 1972, SEWA has been committed to the empowerment of women and the creation of autonomous unions organized for women who work in the informal sector. Since 1989, SEWA has been organizing and operating crèches (for children ages birth–3 years) for women working in the tobacco industry in rural
Kheda district and, more recently, in urban settings. Uniquely, the program:
• Was the first trade union in India to begin childcare services
• Was the first organization to address the needs of tobacco workers who had not been organized by the major central unions
• Was the first organization to systematically establish crèches and create a financing mechanism for them
• Works at the grassroots and policy level simultaneously.

4. *Association for the Advancement of the Ethiopian Family and Child (ALMAYA)* — Israel

ALMAYA originated in 1985 as the Community and Educational Project for Beta Israel, an ancient Jewish community in Ethiopia which emigrated to Israel. The project became an independent, nonprofit association in 1990. The National ALMAYA Resource, Dissemination, and Training Center supervises programs in approximately twenty-five towns throughout Israel,

continued

Figure 2. Programs Included in the Effectiveness Initiative

trains paraprofessionals and professionals, develops educational materials to enhance the community's Ethiopian heritage, and educates others about Beta-Israel's Ethiopian origins and life in Israel. Uniquely, the program:
• Exemplifies working with immigrant children and families in Israel
• Effectively responds to large waves of immigration
• Demonstrates how Ethiopian paraprofessionals can serve as agents of community change and role models, linking their community with the broader Israeli society
• Provides a model for paraprofessional training that incorporates cultural sensitivity and on-the-job and regular in-service training.

5. *Community-based Family Education (Mount Pinatubo)* — Philippines
This program was initiated with communities affected by the eruption of Mount Pinatubo. Based on an assessment of local culture, programs were developed with the community and include early childhood activities, parent education, and micro-enterprise projects. Income from the latter is shared equally by families, the cooperative, and the program. Uniquely, the program:
• Works effectively within the community to define the community's needs
• Exemplifies how to respond in an emergency situation
• Illustrates the synergies possible with an integrated, multipronged approach
• Illustrates how nongovernmental organizations can work with government and communities to achieve sustainable programs
• Provides an example of community-derived funding for an early childhood project.

6. *Proyecto de Mejoramiento Educativo, de Salud y del Ambiente (PROMESA)* — Colombia
This integrated community-based early childhood education program was designed initially as an alternative participatory approach to ECD that could serve as a model of integrated social development and as a research and development project. Beginning in 1978 with 100 families in four small farming and fishing villages on the coast of Colombia, the program now serves approximately 7,000 families along the coast and in the interior, and variations of the approach are being implemented elsewhere in Colombia and in other countries. Uniquely, the program:
• Relies on parents and community leaders as the main educational agents in the program
• Uses project staff as facilitators in development and links to other institutions
• Emphasizes interinstitutional coordination locally and regionally
• Emphasizes the children's program as the basis for integrated and sustainable social development
• Integrates evaluation, monitoring, and research.

7. *Programa No-formal de Educación Inicial (PRONOEI)* — Peru
This began as a nutrition program in the mid-1970s and evolved into a community-operated preschool. Later it became a model for nonformal education and was adopted by the Ministry of Education. Uniquely, the program:
• Was developed in collaboration with the community and at its request
• Adapted a proven curriculum model (the High/Scope curriculum)

continued

Figure 2 (continued). Programs Included in the Effectiveness Initiative

- Used resources from the community for implementation
- Used men from the community as teachers
- Has been evaluated several times
- Has been adopted officially as a national model program and is replicated in other parts of Latin America and elsewhere.

8. *Samenspel (Playing Together/Joint Action)* — Netherlands

Samenspel was established in 1989 as a small-scale project to test strategies for reaching immigrant
families (primarily from Morocco and Turkey) and to explore ways to encourage mothers with young children to participate in play afternoons. Training programs for teams of multi-ethnic play leaders developed gradually. Samenspel groups can be found at play-group and community centers and within self-help and immigrant organizations. Uniquely, the program:
- Provides an informal, low-key, and easily accessible mechanism for introducing immigrant women and children to the Dutch language and culture
- Emphasizes capacity-building based on experiential learning that draws from people's knowledge and experience
- Uses a flexible and adaptable approach for working with people from different contexts who have similar needs.

9. *Agueda Movement (Bela Vista)* — Portugal

The Agueda Movement began with creation of the Bela Vista preschool and is a conscious effort to provide for children who are socially marginalized. Outreach efforts to raise awareness led to community-based action and more inclusive activities to reduce duplication among Portugal's various social services and to increase access for children and families that are not being served. Uniquely, the program:
- Works within the infrastructure to make services more appropriate
- Raises awareness at community and national levels
- Develops additional services, as required, to meet identified needs
- Has a nonhierarchical organizational structure and decisionmaking process.

10. *Madres Guias (Guide Mothers)* — Honduras

This home- and center-based preschool program is designed to help children transition easily from home to preschool and then to primary school. The service providers, Guide Mothers, are local women trained to work with families in their homes and with children as they enter preschool. A radio program associated with the effort provides child development messages. Uniquely, the program:
- Has a well-developed curriculum and training process
- Plans to develop a training institute to train others in the country and elsewhere using their model
- Has a well-developed social support network for responding quickly to emergencies (e.g., the devastation by Hurricane Mitch).

Figure 2 (continued). Programs Included in the Effectiveness Initiative

Research Teams

For each of the ten programs, teams of four or more persons (generally, two local and two nonlocal) have been organized and consist of the program staff and local consultants, staff from other EI programs and the Bernard van Leer Foundation, experts in relevant disciplines (e.g., statistics, data analysis, and cost-benefit studies), and staff from international organizations funding ECD programs. These teams develop the initial site-specific questions and processes for engaging diverse stakeholders in "mapping" the details, evolution, and experiences of a program. The teams are supported by an advisory group of international early childhood professionals and foundation staff. They meet periodically to share their tools, methods, experiences, questions, concerns, and understanding.

Meaningful Questions

The framing of meaningful questions is key to generating understanding. Too often, development workers and/or funders ask questions that may limit people's responses, may not be salient, and may not reveal the real meaning of people's experiences. Getting beyond what we already know how to ask and hear is extremely difficult. In fact, Pearce (1971, p. 70) claims that, "We hear only the question to which we are capable of finding an answer." For the EI, the challenge is: Can some new questions be developed?

The EI is specifically exploring tools that help validate intuition (i.e., to better articulate or justify the sense that things are, or are not, working), which cannot be justified by a checklist or standardized instrument. By creating additional methods for observing and making sense of the contexts of programs, the EI can enhance the development workers' "toolkit" and help identify adequate language to validate "out-of-the-box" thinking.

New Processes

In addition to being able to ask new questions, listening better to better understand responses is an organizing feature of the EI. "Listening" does not denote a condescending, perfunctory, half-hearted effort of forming conclusions as information is presented. Rather, listening means finding ways to receive people's responses fully before trying to analyze, interpret, or categorize their meaning; it means "staying open" to hearing, seeing, and understanding.

The EI also emphasizes use of an appropriate lens for obtaining and viewing data. This lens combines an objective (observer or outsider's) perspective (the "etic" approach) and a subjective (actor or insider's) perspective (the "emic" approach) (Levi-Strauss 1966). The synthesis of these two approaches to listening will yield a fuller picture of effective programming than otherwise possible.

Assumptions

The EI staff bring explicit and implicit assumptions to the initiative based on their own practices and experiences. They have an agenda for action and strive to offer something to help others change (improve) their lives, and they hold certain beliefs about the nature of effectiveness. These beliefs, which have been incorporated into the EI, are as follows:

- *Effectiveness cannot be defined in terms of a universally agreed-upon truth.* No single dimension would make every early childhood program "effective." Truths are multiple, and disagreement about the components of an effective program is part of the process of understanding.
- *Effectiveness is not a static concept.* The effectiveness of an effort changes over time and with changing conditions.
- *Effectiveness cannot be placed on a linear scale* that ranks programs from most effective to least effective.
- *Effectiveness resides in an organization and varies within an organization.* Because some parts of an organization may be stronger than others, effectiveness is best represented as a profile.
- *Effectiveness takes time to identify and understand.* The essence of effective early childhood programming cannot be captured in a snapshot. Understanding effectiveness requires living with, and

experiencing, multiple, dynamic situations and time to recognize effectiveness in both process and outcomes.

- *Effectiveness is the result of experience* and is a composite of many experiences.

Current Status

The EI is well under way, and the energy, enthusiasm, and commitment of the EI participants is stimulating, directly and indirectly, a wide range of activities. The EI is already experiencing the benefits of synergy among the different programs, team members, and methods. Multiple team meetings have been held at each site, members of all teams have met in a series of workshops, and both regional meetings and international conferences have been convened. These meetings have provided opportunities to create a shared vision, probe serious questions collectively and publicly, formulate questions more thoughtfully, share strategies and questions in teams' working language (e.g., Spanish), present developments to audiences unfamiliar with the EI, and suggest possibilities for applying the process and results in other contexts.

Qualitative Research Tools: Meaning in Language

Qualitative research offers validated and tested tools that can be adapted for examining all the dimensions and complexity of ECD programs (Coffey and Atkinson 1996; Moustakas 1994). Utilizing data sources such as individual stories and anecdotes, interviews, field notes, recordings of natural interactions, documents, pictures, and other graphic representations, qualitative research can capture human experiences that are not approachable with quantitative methods (Geertz 1983).

The EI aims to develop various analytical tools to reveal a layered understanding, and different facets, of meaning. This research avoids a reductionist summing up of data, recognizes and explores complexity as much as possible, and views people as analyzers of meaning even as they create meaning. People live their lives embedded in language, so why do researchers turn to numbers to define truth?

Language is at the heart of meaning. As noted by Barritt and colleagues (1979), qualitative research seeks data dominated by language and cultural understanding, not numbers. Numbers are important, but they should not be the only points of reference. By focusing on language, the EI can highlight aspects of experience that might otherwise go unmarked. Barritt and colleagues (1979, ch. 6, p. 83) note that, "Analysis of language requires rhetorical skill, the attention to meaning, and the struggle to say it right; we cannot escape the tradition; we have to use it."

The EI offers an opportunity to validate an approach that allows people to tell their stories in their own language, without others' immediate classification, censorship, or interpretation. Collectively, the teams interpret the stories together and broaden the basis for analysis in the hope of truly hearing what is being told. This approach will provide insight into a community's values, beliefs, and practices and how to work within a culture to foster more equality—insights that are more difficult to obtain with other participatory techniques, such as Participatory Learning for Action (PLA). Robert Chambers' (1997) reflections on the development of the PLA methods, which he has successfully promoted, reveal that he has realized the limits of such open methodologies to "get at" meaning. Using open methodologies for gathering data is not sufficient, and meaning can only be understood by working more skillfully with data that are generated in various ways. When data are reduced, knowledge and understanding are compromised.

Most of the tools in the EI toolkit have been used previously by the EI participants and are being sharpened and used in different ways. The EI teams are expanding the use of questions, storytelling, and other narrative means and are learning and applying new methods of analysis and interpretation to better understand the effectiveness of early childhood programs. The tools being used include the development and organization of questions from different perspectives and the use of analogies to "map" program contexts, the gathering of stories about effective programs from groups of participants, and interviews with various stakeholders.

The Initial Questions

For the EI, an advisory committee of early childhood programmers, policymakers, and practitioners initially met to develop a set of questions about the nature of effective organizations. These questions, which were organized into different "cuts," or "maps," of a program's history, were shared during initial site visits to encourage the EI participants to reflect on their organization's history and the evolution of the program in the future. All programs adopted this initial set of questions, which consists of a set of overlapping "maps" for describing a project over time, beginning with the project's origin. The timeline and questions for each program relate to key events, change points, and crucial moments in the program's evolution. The specific dimensions of these "cuts" are as follows:

- *Influences.* This cut consists of a description of everything that has influenced the program over time (e.g., economic, political, and cultural effects and changes; participants' perception of changes). Two aims are to capture the effect of serendipity and personal choices on the program and to understand the effects of available financial and physical resources.
- *Attitudes and Values.* This cut is to identify and explore the underlying implicit and explicit assumptions of program participants (e.g., the values and beliefs about children's development and the way children learn, the value of intervening and the types of intervention thought to be appropriate). Attitudes and values affect the types of activities undertaken in a program.
- *Organizational Structure.* This cut involves creating an organizational chart and describing changes over time (e.g., in the program's leadership).
- *Organizational Culture.* This cut is to identify processes within the organization for addressing problems, overcoming obstacles, making decisions, recruiting, hiring and training staff, and other concerns. This cut also provides information on who participates in the program at different times and in different ways.

- *Linkages.* This cut charts the types of linkages formed with other organizations, individuals, donors, and government, as well as the organization's networks and its roles in these networks.
- *Outcomes.* This cut highlights the influences of the organization (e.g., on children and families, staff, community, other organizations) from the perspectives of various stakeholders and places the organization in a broader context (e.g., in relation to government policy).
- *Mapping the Future.* Speculative mapping is used to identify how key stakeholders envisage the future and the development of the program over time with respect to its underlying philosophy; assumptions, goals, and activities; organization; decision-making processes; linkages; and outcomes.

A River Analogy

The course of an ECD program can be compared to the life of a river, developing from a small spring or stream with a certain course or direction and influenced by many things as it flows from small beginnings into a lake or ocean. The depth and breadth of rivers, and projects, are determined by multiple contextual factors. Some flow in a predictable path, but most are diverted in some way from their natural course; at times, they are fed by tributaries and widen to cover more ground, and other times they shrink from drought; sometimes, dams impede their progress or cause them to flood and destroy fertile ground; some rivers flow into lakes and maintain their identity, while others flow into the ocean to become part of a broader sea, losing their uniqueness. Programs, too, progress in distinctive ways, and their courses and contours can be traced and mapped.

This type of analogy has been, and can be, used to spark creativity and help program teams tell and share their story with others. For the EI, the river analogy has helped participants visualize their projects; encouraged staff to share their experiences differently; stimulated lively discussions about key events, influences, and outcomes; and helped participants gain a deeper understanding about the dynamics of their program. Such discussions would not have arisen with the application of more standardized instruments, such as interviews and questionnaires.

Storytelling

Telling one's story is not always easy or natural, and it may be censored or "cut short" by others. Telling a program's story is compounded by two additional factors. First, the program implementers or beneficiaries do not necessarily know what outsiders want to know about their story, and, second, listeners may not hear the story as experienced by the teller. Outsiders' retelling of a program's story may not be recognizable to the program participants, and outsiders may not be able to identify aspects that make the program effective or are perceived by others as being effective. Eliciting the full richness of a story is a challenge for the EI and other initiatives.

Storytelling is used to access different sources, data, and ways of processing data. By gathering and analyzing stories, a better understanding can be gained of effective early childhood settings. The EI participants are asked to think of a moment in any ECD setting when they said, "This is really working." They are asked to describe this moment in writing in as much detail as possible. The stories are then shared among the group, and the group "codes" their meaning by identifying all words that have meaning and combining these later to identify themes. By analyzing and interpreting their stories in this way, the participants gain a better understanding of their shared concepts, attitudes, and practices and become aware of different views about the relevant features of a successful program. This storytelling method enables researchers to:

- Focus on the meaning of effectiveness in a particular ECD setting (i.e., understanding the participants' understanding of effective ECD programming)
- Generate a data set without requiring participants to agonize over writing long essays
- Give participants the tools to analyze their own stories

- Use stories to identify common and shared themes
- Use themes as a basis for more informed dialogue with those who are "living the experience."

Interviews

In the EI, program teams are conducting individual interviews with a wide variety of stakeholders (i.e., people at the site), who may include those currently involved in the program (parents, community members, staff, direct beneficiaries), past participants, local and national government officials, representatives of nongovernmental organizations, and funders. Summarizing data collected for PROMESA, figure 3 indicates some of the important themes and issues that may emerge about a program's effectiveness from these interviews. The successes and failures identified can then be explored further with the participants.

Individual interviews can enhance understanding of how organizations have evolved and their effects over time. Individuals have many stories to tell and will have unique and different perceptions of a program's evolution, for they have entered the program at different times and come from diverse backgrounds. Combining their stories with the perceptions and experiences of persons outside the program is another challenge in constructing a good, sound story of a program's effectiveness.

Qualitative Research Strategies: Embedded Communications

Each of the tools described above serves a specific function in gathering and analyzing data. Together, they offer a beginning, integrated set of activities to help determine effective ECD programming. The tools are not discrete activities, but are interwoven and form the toolkit for the EI. Creating the tools and instruments is part of the strategy to engage EI participants in qualitative research. Teams are developing and testing tools while also developing strategies for data analysis. Designing a communication strategy that helps to convey the EI process as well as outcomes is a related and essential effort. The

1. Continuity and stability in an organization (which may lead to solid performance and/or sedentarianism) vs. change and turnover (which might undercut actions or provide dynamism)
2. The importance of "tolerance of ambiguity" vs. an imposing structure
3. The personal growth and development of participants at various program levels, as both means and end
4. The process of recognizing one's capacities (at community and institutional levels)
5. The need to construct credibility with communities and funders and the process for doing so
6. Building and maintaining local confidence when operating at a distance
7. Forms of reinforcing internal and intrinsic motivation among program participants
8. The importance of a play approach to learning
9. The timing of separation by project "outsiders" and the effects of separation
10. Voluntarism vs. payment
11. Forms of integration and their implications for functioning; constructing a "transdisciplinary" view
12. Achieving sustainability; solving immediate problems vs. taking a longer view
13. Respecting local values and cultures and strengthening local customs while introducing new customs and values; defining the custodian of knowledge
14. The role of "connections" in the success of a program
15. Forms (and effects) of program dissemination
16. Building a workable system for registering and using program information which is not over-burdening
17. Discretion, tact, and diplomacy as styles of functioning internal to an organization and in relation to others outside
18. Organizations as families and the rule of families in organizations, particularly in relation to handling differences without "breaking apart"
19. The importance of different forms of communication
20. Converting adversity and crisis into opportunity and advantage
21. The place of (or need for) welfare aid ("asistencialismo") within a program that empha-sizes empowerment
22. The centrality of people within organizations vs. the centrality of organizations
23. Delegating responsibility
24. Strategies that allow communities and staff members to appropriate ("buy into") a particu-lar program philosophy
25. Combining disparate interests in joint actions for the common good; becoming "profes-sional" without succumbing to difficulties associated with professional organizations, forms of training, and organizational attitudes.

Source: Myers 1999.

Figure 3. Themes and Issues Emerging About PROMESA in Colombia

EI is enhancing the ability of all participants to engage openly in a review process that shares results as it proceeds.

Traditional social science research uses a linear communications model. Researchers (sometimes with funders) choose the research focus, determine the research questions, and design the research activities, which usually include data gathering, sorting, analyzing, and interpreting and the writing up of results. Each step of this process is accomplished separately in sequence. The goal of this traditional method is to maintain objectivity in the research, external to the person conducting the research. Information is gleaned as the research moves from one activity to the next, and participants (respondents) at one stage are usually excluded from the next stages. Rarely is information gathered, sorted, and reflected back to the respondents, giving them a chance to generate other questions, reshape the study, and dialogue with researchers about the nature of their experience and knowledge. They are not asked to help interpret their experience and are frequently not given the results of the research. Data technicians also are uninvolved after they have provided the data. Researchers analyze, write, and report the research results to an audience, which frequently does not include the groups with whom or for whom the research was conducted.

The qualitative research approach used in the EI requires a different communication model which may be termed *embedded* communication (Ilfeld 2000). Ideally, such research allows information to flow in all directions, through dialogue between diverse stakeholders and through collective design and implementation of the project. Three distinct, but interrelated, communication activities within this model are: (1) collecting and gathering raw data and information, (2) working with and analyzing the information and data, and (3) communicating the new understandings and knowledge to diverse audiences.

Each activity embodies all the steps in a traditional research design: framing questions; gathering data, sorting data, analyzing data, and interpreting data; and writing up or representing these data. The levels of activity represent increasing levels of refinement and polish, with level 1 focused on manipulating raw data and gathering information broadly, level 2 focused on shaping "first drafts" and first conclusions that are discussed with participants in a consultative process, and level 3 focused on shaping more formalized communications for audiences within and outside of the participants. The three levels can be viewed as a spiral, with each level influencing the others. For example, a decision to create a web site (level 3) may trigger a decision to collect new data and reexamine certain issues (level 1); and a sorting of information (level 2) from a series of interviews (level 1) may suggest a new direction for questioning (level 1), a new way to understand the experience (level 2), or the outline for a potential video (level 3). Figures 4 and 5 depict and describe the activities in this embedded communications model for qualitative research.

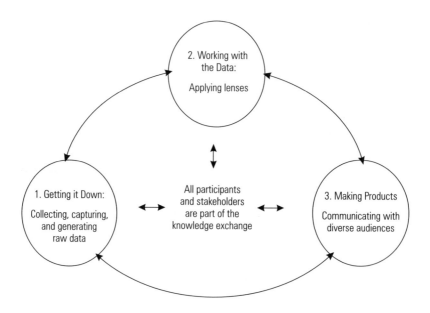

Figure 4. Embedded Communications Model for Qualitative Research

Ideally, all participants in a qualitative research activity are viewed as communicators. Mechanisms will be needed to capture each participant's and group's collective ideas, thoughts, experiences, and concerns. Participants should identify how they will record their thought processes. To record private thoughts and insights consistently across a group, the individuals can be asked to keep "books of

1. *Getting it Down:*	2. *Working with the Data:*	3. *Making Products:*
Collecting, capturing, and generating raw data	Applying lenses; sorting, analyzing, and framing knowledge	Formatting knowledge for communications with diverse audiences
Activities:	*Activities:*	*Activities:*
• Keep personal scrapbooks and journals—take notes, jot down thoughts and experiences regularly	• Sort materials, often using a particular focus or "lens" (e.g., all materials having to do with turning points, or all topics of interest to parents and parent educators)	• Write professional, scientific, popular nonfiction, and creative and dramatic descriptions
• Conduct meetings, discussions, and e-mail exchanges among participants	• Analyze themes and highlight key elements, concepts, and information	• Develop audiovisual materials (e.g., videos, photo documentaries, graphic illustrations, PowerPoint™ presentations, slide shows, plays, television and radio shows)
• Capture and write up specific experiences of ideas (focused documentation)	• Create a framework for organizing findings (usually suggested by the themes and insights that emerge)	• Develop meeting and workshop activities
• Generate understanding or insights through workshops, observations, site visits, etc.	• Shape documents and materials into a logical and intuitively meaningful order	• Conduct public and professional awareness and education campaigns using supportive materials (e.g., booklets and brochures, websites, CD-ROMs, media spots)
• Collect program data, including anecdotes and stories, quotes, statistics, interviews, etc.	• Embellish frameworks with details, examples, and illustrations taken from the raw data	
• Brainstorm and collectively problem-solve, recall, explore, and question		• Develop proposals and research designs for further work
• Review existing documentation and records to select those relevant to the effort		• Design program activities and plans for future program actions
• Record (photograph, videotape, and audiotape)		

Figure 5. The Embedded Communications Model: Description of Activities

shadows," or notebooks, where they jot notes, make sketches, paste quotations, and otherwise capture the "shadows" of ideas, thoughts, and experiences in one place. Group devices for collating information (see figure 6) could include "the wall" (a wall or bulletin board where people can place representations of the various kinds of knowledge they are gathering). Other group devices, such as an electronic

Site	What are we learning?	How did we learn it?	Questions raised/implications
Peru	Build bridges among the different actors; learn from and get children involved regardless of age; listen to all the voices; strengthen self-concept within Latin America; value our experience.	By doing it, sharing and building by using new methodologies, developing participatory tools and instruments, creating space for discussion and reflection, using the flexibility of the program.	How to ensure that what we are doing is also a relevant process for the program and its actors; how to promote changes within the program; how to safeguard the demands generated by the process; learn more about childrearing patterns and find ways to have them taken into account by policymakers.
Philippines	Learning to ask the right questions at the right time, and to simplify and modify information for program partners, need for more in-depth look at program.	Through daily recording, observing, regular meetings, focus group discussions, home visiting, interviewing.	Organize and analyze information; apply what we have learned from other teams and partners; documentation?; ultimate aim — self-sustaining communities that can address their own situation.

continued

Figure 6. Matrix of Learning at Program Sites: Questions and Issues

bulletin board, a shared filing system, a group Intranet site, or book-shelves and tables for arraying materials, also could be used.

Figure 6 presents a matrix used in the EI to collate information gathered within and between sites. These types of matrices are useful for identifying issues to address and sharing information and experiences.

Questions that we ask ourselves	Questions that we ask other programs	Experience that we like to share	Issues
How do we establish limits for data gathering; how can we get to know more about other teams' work, and learn from them; how to contribute to generate effectiveness within the program, even when the EI ends; what impact are we going to have on different stakeholders.	Charts from communities, work on profiles and attitudes, organizing data, good ideas for improving communications.	Return of information and capacity to build knowledge from experience; recognize the changes that experience generates.	Limits of data gathering, insights into other programs' strengths, the EI's way of exploration, impact on different stakeholders.
Interrelatedness of tools, capacity building, techniques, and strategies.	What did they learn from passing on leadership to locals; livelihood projects; advocacy; training and capacity building; migrants and displaced families; child-to-child exchanges; communications; workshops with everyone.	Share work in progress (specifically, training of government day-care workers) and how these maximize benefits; generate more information with communities; encourage advocacy to influence policymakers.	Application of the learning to strengthen our program; integration of program content and approach with tools and methods; form of documentation.

Figure 6 (continued). Matrix of Learning at Program Sites: Questions and Issues

In any group, each individual will offer different communications skills, interests, and aptitudes—as an articulator of ideas and thoughts, notetaker, interviewer, organizer of material, systems thinker, analyst, or tracker of details. Some individuals are more comfortable writing, whereas others prefer speaking, listening, photographing, taping, or devising actions. The group should embrace the contributions of all the individuals and enable them to participate fully in the documentation and communication effort.

The exchange of knowledge is both enriched and distilled by the codifying of it. A collating committee can sort through and track the information collected from individuals and the group. Codifying the knowledge improves the chances that knowledge will be exchanged effectively. For this reason, communications and documentation are integral parts of every activity and should be embedded throughout the qualitative research project.

Conclusion

The EI effort is pursuing the development and use of a variety of tools for gathering and processing data to achieve a better understanding of the observations made and to learn from the process. Whereas quantitative research begins with a blueprint of fixed and prescribed methods and procedures that are used with conformity across all sites, qualitative research consciously avoids having a normative blueprint and seeks to identify patterns and individual differences in case studies that would not become evident in research based on fixed assumptions. The qualitative research approach adopted for the EI enables researchers to obtain both information and insights on process.

The research outcomes may confirm intuitive understandings and validate programming decisions that are made based on these understandings. Beyond outcomes, however, the EI effort is equally or even more valuable because of the process undertaken. More than fifty people from around the world have embarked on a journey together and are actively engaged in a dialogue to generate questions and methodologies to address these questions which will contribute far beyond the EI. The cross-site exchanges, periodic meetings of all team members, and frequent sharing of information and activities foster joint ownership of qualitative research tools and strategies that can be used to assess ECD programs in a wide variety of early childhood settings. This type of ongoing evaluation is needed to support continued learning and improvement in ECD programming. Qualitative reviews and evaluation should be built into all programs as an important measure for ensuring that the scarce resources for ECD are invested wisely in effective programs. Overall, the EI promises to provide the ECD field a better understanding of the requirements for creating effective ECD programs in diverse settings and contexts, using diverse programming approaches.

Note

This chapter is adapted from "When ECD Works: Mapping the Contours of Effective Programming," by G. Salole and J. L. Evans in *Early Childhood Matters #93,* a publication of the Bernard van Leer Foundation, and the *Coordinators' Notebook #23*, a publication of the Consultative Group on Early Childhood Care and Development.

References

Barritt, L. S., A. J. Beekman, H. Bleeker, and K. Mulderij. 1979. Science Not Method. University of Michigan, Ann Arbor.

Chambers, R. 1997. *Whose Reality Counts? Putting the First Last.* London: Intermediate Technology Publications.

Coffey, A., and P. Atkinson. 1996. *Making Sense of Qualitative Data: Complementary Research Strategies.* London: Sage Publications.

Geertz, C. 1983. *Local Knowledge: Further Essays in Interpretive Anthropology.* New York: Basic Books.

Ilfeld, E.M. 2000. Embedded Research. Bernard van Leer Foundation, The Hague, Netherlands.

Levi-Strauss, C. 1966. *The Savage Mind.* London: Weidenfeld and Nicolson.

Moustakas, C. 1994. *Phenomenological Research Methods.* London: Sage Publications.

Myers, R. 1999. Effectiveness Initiative: An Evaluation of PROMESA: Report on a Visit to Colombia, August 27 to September 1, 1999. The Consultative Group on Early Childhood Care and Development. Tlalcoligia, Mexico.

Pearce, J.C. 1971. *The Crack in the Cosmic Egg.* New York: Washington Square Press.

Chapter 8

Effective Early Childhood Programs: The U.S. Head Start Experience

Louisa B. Tarullo

In 2000, the U.S. Head Start program marked its fifth year of development and implementation of program performance measures. As the United States' premier early childhood education program, Head Start is leading the way in developing and reporting on accountability of services, which Head Start provides each year to more than 800,000 children and their families. From the initial planning of this accountability system in 1995 to publication of the third progress report (Administration on Children, Youth, and Families 2001), Head Start has made dramatic progress in establishing outcome-oriented accountability. The system combines the best attributes of scientific research with program-level reporting and monitoring. It is based on consensus-driven criteria for program accountability.

This chapter describes Head Start's initiative of program performance measures and the Family and Child Experiences Survey, a central part of this initiative. Data collected in the survey are being used to assess Head Start's outcomes and to refine the overall program.

The Program Performance Measures Initiative

The Head Start Act (42 U.S.C. 9831 et seq. 1994) defines program performance measures as "methods and procedures for measuring, annually and over longer periods, the quality and effectiveness of programs operated by Head Start agencies" that will be used to identify strengths and weaknesses in the Head Start program—both nationally and by region—and to pinpoint areas requiring additional training and technical assistance. Specifically, the program performance measures were developed in accordance with the recommendations of the Advisory Committee on Head Start Quality and Expansion; the mandate of section 641A(b) of the Head Start Act, as reauthorized in 1994; and the Government Performance and Results Act (Public Law 103–62 of 1993).

In 1995, Head Start undertook a consensus-building process to develop the program performance measures. The process included discussions with staff and parents in the Head Start program; representatives of early childhood organizations; researchers; experts in education, child development, and early intervention; and officials in the Head Start bureau of the U.S. Department of Health and Human Services.

Conceptual Framework

In 1996–97, Head Start developed a conceptual framework for the program performance measures and revised and condensed the initial measures. The conceptual framework unifies and organizes the measures and shows the linkages between process and outcome measures for Head Start children and families (see figure 1).

The conceptual framework is based on the ultimate goal of Head Start: to promote the social competence of children. Social competence is defined as a child's every-day effectiveness in dealing with the present environment and later responsibilities in school and life. For a 5-year-old child who is ending preschool and entering primary school, an important life challenge and key test of social competence is school readiness (i.e., whether the child has acquired the skills, understandings, and behaviors that help ensure successful functioning in the new environment).

Head Start has adopted the "whole child" view of school readiness recommended by the Goal One Technical Planning Group of the U.S. National Education Goals Panel (Goal One Technical Planning Group 1991, 1993). In this view, school readiness is a multifaceted phenomenon comprising five developmental domains important to a child's readiness for school: physical well-being and motor development, social and emotional development, approaches to learning, language usage and emerging literacy, and cognition and general knowledge. Each domain is represented in the battery of measures used to assess the performance of Head Start programs. The performance measures account for the interrelatedness of cognitive, emotional, and social development; physical and mental health; and nutritional needs.

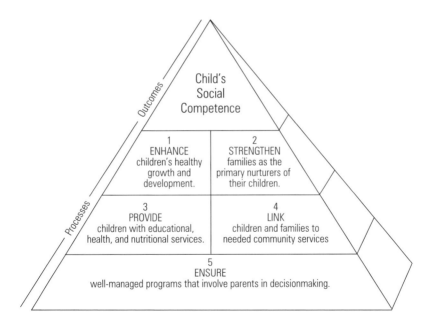

Figure 1. Head Start's Program Performance Measures: Conceptual Framework

A child's social competence is at the top of the conceptual frame-work, depicted as a pyramid. Five objectives support this outcome:

- Objective 1. Enhance children's healthy growth and development.
- Objective 2. Strengthen families as the primary nurturers of their children.
- Objective 3. Provide children with educational, health, and nutritional services.
- Objective 4. Link children and families to needed community services.
- Objective 5. Ensure well-managed programs that involve parents in decisionmaking.

Each objective is critical for helping children of low-income families attain their full potential. The objectives represent key cornerstones of the Head Start program. Objectives 1 and 2 represent outcomes or results that the program is designed to produce. Achieving both objectives is critical to the ultimate success of Head Start. Because parent involvement and family support are key tenets of Head Start, both child and family-oriented outcome measures are included. Objectives 3, 4, and 5 are on the lower tiers of the pyramid and contain key process measures for attaining objectives 1 and 2 and the ultimate goal of enhancing children's social competence. An important aspect of the pyramid is the strong empirical connection between the provision of quality services (process measures) and improvements in child development (outcome measures).

Program Performance Measures

Head Start has set forth twenty-four program performance measures grouped under the five program objectives (see figure 2).

For each program performance measure, performance indicators specify how the measure will be assessed. Figure 3 shows a section of Head Start's program performance measures matrix, which includes the objective, performance measure, performance indicator, data

OBJECTIVE 1: Enhance Children's Healthy Growth and Development.

1. Head Start children demonstrate improved emergent literacy, numeracy, and language skills.
2. Head Start children demonstrate improved general cognitive skills.
3. Head Start children demonstrate improved gross and fine motor skills.
4. Head Start children demonstrate improved positive attitudes toward learning.
5. Head Start children demonstrate improved social behavior and emotional well-being.
6. Head Start children demonstrate improved physical health.

OBJECTIVE 2: Strengthen Families as the Primary Nurturers of Their Children.

7. Head Start parents demonstrate improved parenting skills.
8. Head Start parents improve their self-concept and emotional well-being.
9. Head Start parents make progress toward their educational, literacy, and employment goals.

OBJECTIVE 3: Provide Children With Educational, Health, and Nutritional Services.

10. Head Start programs provide developmentally appropriate educational environments.
11. Head Start staff interact with children in a skilled and sensitive manner.
12. Head Start programs support and respect children's cultures.
13. Head Start assures children receive needed medical, dental, and mental health services.
14. Head Start children receive meals and snacks that meet their daily nutritional needs.
15. Head Start programs provide individualized services for children with disabilities.

OBJECTIVE 4: Link Children and Families to Needed Community Services.

16. Head Start parents link with social service agencies to obtain needed services.
17. Head Start parents link with educational agencies to obtain needed services.
18. Head Start parents link with health care services to obtain needed care.
19. Head Start parents secure childcare in order to work, go to school, or gain employment training.

OBJECTIVE 5: Ensure Well-Managed Programs that Involve Parents in Decisionmaking.

20. Head Start programs are well-managed.
21. Head Start parents are involved actively in decisions about program operations.
22. Head Start programs employ qualified staff.
23. Head Start programs support staff development and training.
24. Head Start programs comply with Head Start regulations.

Figure 2. Head Start's Program Performance Measures, by Objective

source, and 1997–98 data. The performance indicator for the first performance measure under objective 1, "Head Start children demonstrate improved emergent literacy, numeracy, and language skills," is
a change in the children's emergent literacy, as measured by assessments of the children.

A more process-oriented measure (not shown) for objective 3 (Provide children with educational, health, and nutritional services) is
"Head Start assures children receive needed medical, dental, and
mental health services." The performance indicator for this measure
is the number and percent of Head Start children who received needed medical services as reported by the program.

Progress on the indicators supporting each objective is being documented in periodic reports. Data are obtained from agency resources
such as Head Start's program information report (PIR), regional office
reports, and outcomes for classrooms, teachers, families, and children
reported in Head Start's Family and Child Experiences Survey.

OBJECTIVE 1: Enhance Children's Healthy Growth and Development

Performance measure	Performance indicator	Data source	1997–98 Data
1. Head Start (HS) children demonstrate improved emergent literacy, numeracy, and language skills.	HS children's emergent literacy.	Child Assessment (Woodcock-Johnson Letter-Wood Identification).	4-year-old HS children finishing the program had median standard scores of 89.8 (compared with the national mean of 100). HS children gained 1.6 points from fall to spring (no gain compared with norms).
		Woodcock-Johnson Dictation.	4-year-old HS children finishing the program had median standard scores of 88.1 (compared with the national mean of 100). In HS, children gained 1.5 points. In kindergarten, children gained 4.6 points.

Figure 3. Sample of Head Start's Program Performance Measures Matrix

Head Start's Family and Child Experiences Survey

Head Start's Family and Child Experiences Survey (FACES) is a central part of the program performance measures initiative. Through FACES, researchers are gathering comprehensive data on the cognitive, social, emotional, and physical development of children participating in Head Start; the characteristics, well-being, and accomplishments of families; the quality of Head Start classrooms; and the characteristics, needs, and opinions of teachers and other staff in Head Start.

The survey provides data on a nationally representative sample of Head Start programs, centers, classrooms, children, and parents. The sample is stratified by three variables: region of the country (northeast, midwest, south, or west); urbanicity (urban versus rural); and percentage of minority families in the program (50 percent or more versus less than 50 percent).

FACES includes six phases of data collection. The first phase (spring 1997) consisted of a field test of approximately 2,400 children and parents from a nationally stratified random sample of forty Head Start programs. The field test established the feasibility of large-scale interviewing of parents and assessment of children using selected instruments. The test also provided valuable information on the status of Head Start programs, children, and families.

The second and third phases (fall 1997 and spring 1998) consisted of data collection on a sample of 3,200 children and families in the same forty Head Start programs. The spring 1998 phase included assessments of children completing the Head Start program and of Head Start graduates completing kindergarten (a kindergarten field test). Data also were collected from interviews with parents and ratings by kindergarten teachers. The kindergarten cohort was subsequently followed into first grade.

The fourth phase (spring 1999) consisted of data collection in the forty Head Start programs and a follow-up of former Head Start children into kindergarten. The fifth phase (spring 2000) concluded the kindergarten follow-up of children who completed Head Start in spring 1999 and of first graders who completed Head Start in 1998. The sixth phase in spring 2001 completed the first-grade follow-up of children who completed Head Start in spring 1999. Continuing Head Start's commitment to ongoing assessments using performance measures, a new nationally representative cohort was selected for data collection beginning in fall 2000. Sampling 2,800 children and their families from forty-three new Head Start programs across the nation, FACES continues to examine child outcomes, program quality, and family well-being and achievements.

Figure 4 presents the study design of FACES. Through the six phases, researchers have been able to assess the effects of Head Start by comparing children and their parents before (pre-Head Start) and after (post-Head Start) exposure to the program. Because of the full cooperation of the Head Start programs studied and the diligent fieldwork conducted by the research teams, the completion rates for FACES are high, averaging more than 80 percent on all survey measures.

FACES: Findings

The FACES data collected during fall 1997 and spring 1998 offer important findings on the change in children's growth and development, the consistency of classroom quality, and the characteristics and accomplishments of Head Start families throughout the 1997–98 year. Follow-up into kindergarten reveals important information on Head Start graduates' performance in school. Key findings from 1997–98 are presented below.

Does Head Start Enhance Children's Healthy Growth and Development?

Participation in Head Start can enhance a child's growth and development. The data show the following:

- The typical child completing Head Start possessed the early literacy and numeracy knowledge and skills, as well as the social skills, that indicate a readiness to learn when the child reaches kindergarten and first grade.

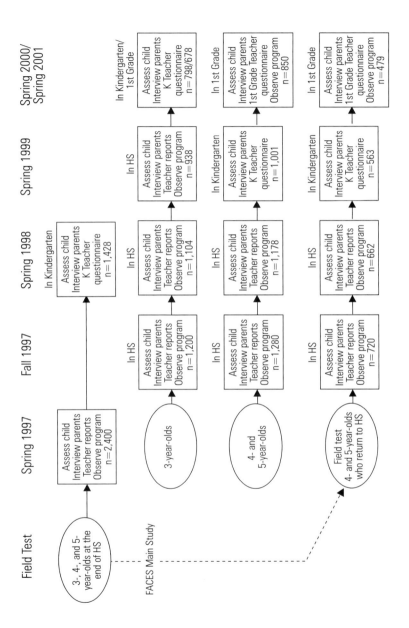

Figure 4. FACES Study Design: Samples and Data Collection

- Head Start children showed significant gains in vocabulary and writing skills and in social skills during the Head Start year. The children showed little progress, however, in letter recognition and book knowledge.
- During the year, the children's play became more complex, and they became more involved in interactive play with peers—an indicator of social development.
- Children who complete Head Start are "ready to learn," as shown by the extent of their learning by the end of kindergarten. By the end of kindergarten, Head Start graduates made substantial gains in word knowledge, letter recognition, math skills, writing skills, and phonemic awareness.

Does Head Start Strengthen Families as the Primary Nurturers of Their Children?

Participation in Head Start can strengthen families as primary nurturers. The data indicate the following:

- Primary caregivers (usually parents) were equally likely to be married or single. The typical caregiver was young (between 20 and 30 years of age), had at least a high school diploma or a graduate-equivalent degree (GED), and was employed. Despite the high proportion of caregivers in the workforce, 85 percent of the households participating in Head Start received supplemental sources of income.
- More than two-thirds of Head Start parents reported that they read to their children at least three to five times a week. Importantly, the frequency of parents' reading was linked to a child's vocabulary scores, and children who were read to more often showed greater word knowledge at the end of the year.
- Head Start parents cited significant accomplishments during the year. More primary caregivers were employed (an increase of 2 percent from fall to spring); 9 percent obtained a license, certificate, or degree; and fewer received welfare assistance (a decline of 3.5 percent from fall to spring).

- Head Start parents cited Head Start as an important source of support in rearing their child. They also reported a greater sense of control over their own lives at the end of Head Start than at the beginning.
- Fathers appeared to play an important and positive role in the lives of children. When the father was not present in the home, the resources available to the family, both socially and financially, were reduced. Families without fathers in the household were more likely to be exposed to violent crime or domestic violence.
- Most parents were active in their Head Start program, and approximately 80 percent had visited with Head Start staff in their home, attended a parent-teacher conference, and observed a classroom.
- More than 85 percent of parents were very satisfied with the services their child received to help the child grow and develop, prepare the child for kindergarten, and identify and provide other services for the child.

Does Head Start Provide Children With High-Quality Educational, Health, and Nutritional Services?

The quality of Head Start services is good. Key indicators include the following:

- The quality in Head Start classrooms has been consistently rated as good over three points of measurement by trained observers. In fall 1997, the average Early Childhood Environment Rating Scale (ECERS) score across Head Start's 518 classrooms was good. Nearly one-fifth of the classrooms were rated as very good or excellent, and no classroom was rated inadequate. These ratings compare favorably with those reported for other preschool and childcare programs.
- The average numbers for both class size and child:adult ratios were far better than those required by Head Start's program performance standards and the accreditation standards of the National Association for the Education of Young Children (NAEYC).

- Most Head Start teachers have good teaching qualifications. Nearly one-third of all teachers had a bachelor's or graduate degree, and teachers averaged nearly 12 years of teaching experience. The educational level of teachers correlated with the quality of classrooms; that is, the higher a teacher's educational level was, the better the classroom quality was.

What Is the Link Between Classroom Quality and Child Outcomes?

The observed quality of Head Start classrooms is linked to children's outcomes. The data show the following:

- Children in Head Start classrooms that had richer teacher–child interaction and more language learning opportunities had higher vocabulary scores. Also, children in classrooms that had lower child:adult ratios showed greater gains in vocabulary scores during the year.
- Children in classrooms rated higher for their learning environment materials spent more time in simple interactive play or pretend play and less time in noninteractive play.

Conclusion

The Head Start program performance measures initiative was launched in 1995. By 1999, Head Start had collected extensive information on its program's performance. Through FACES, Head Start has accumulated data on the change in children's performance during one or more years of participating in Head Start, the kindergarten progress of Head Start graduates, the quality and characteristics of Head Start programs, and the well-being and achievements of Head Start families. The data show that Head Start can enhance children's growth and development; strengthen families as primary nurturers of children; provide high-quality educational, health, and nutritional services to children; and improve children's outcomes.

The performance data have proved useful for documenting the accountability of Head Start externally and for improving the program internally. During Head Start's 1998 reauthorization, officials were able to report to the U.S. Congress on the quality of Head Start programs and the knowledge and skills of children who completed these programs. In addition, FACES data were presented to the Advisory Committee on Head Start Research and Evaluation, which was mandated and charged by the U.S. Congress to provide recommendations on the design of a study or studies to determine the national impact of Head Start. FACES data also have been disseminated widely within Head Start. The data are used in continuing efforts to improve Head Start and to refine training and technical assistance. Researchers have presented FACES findings at national conferences of researchers and practitioners, including Head Start's National Research Conference and meetings of the Society for Research in Child Development and the National Head Start Association. The data and findings reported are important evidence of the value of investments in early child development.

Notes

This chapter is derived from the third progress report on Head Start's program performance measures initiative. The full report, referenced below, can be accessed at the following website: http://www.acf.dhhs.gov/programs/core. The FACES study is being conducted by Westat, Inc., Abt Associates, Inc., Ellsworth Associates, Inc., and The CDM Group, Inc. It is directed by the Commissioner's Office of Research and Evaluation, Administration on Children, Youth, and Families, U.S. Department of Health and Human Services. The author represents a team of researchers who prepared this report, including: Nicholas Zill, Gary Resnick, Ruth Hubbell McKey, David Connell, Robert O'Brien, Mary Ann D'Elio, and Cheryl Clark.

References

Administration on Children, Youth, and Families. 2001. *Head Start FACES: Longitudinal Findings on Program Performance. Third Progress*

Report. Washington, D.C.: U.S. Department of Health and Human Services.

Goal One Technical Planning Group. 1991. The Goal One Technical Planning Subgroup Report on School Readiness. In National Education Goals Panel, ed., *Potential Strategies for Long-term Indicator Development: Reports of the Technical Planning Subgroups.* Report No. 91–0, pp. 1–18. Washington, D.C.: National Education Goals Panel.

———. 1993. Reconsidering Children's Early Development and Learning: Toward Shared Beliefs and Vocabulary. Draft Report to the National Education Goals Panel. Washington, D.C.: National Education Goals Panel.

Government Performance and Results Act (Public Law 103–62). 1993.

Head Start Act, Section 641A(b), 42 U.S.C. 9831 et seq. 1994.

Chapter 9

Elements of Quality in Home Visiting Programs: Three Jamaican Models

Kerida Scott-McDonald

Young children in poor Jamaican communities face overwhelming disadvantages of neglect, abuse, and inappropriate care owing to parents' lack of knowledge, time, and resources as well as high emotional stress. The children are placed further at risk because the traditional supports of extended families have weakened and affordable programs offering compensatory benefits to parents and children are not available or are of poor quality. The outcomes of these two factors, interacting cyclically over time, are dysfunctional families and new generations of children who become economically and developmentally deprived parents.

In Jamaica, approximately one in every three children under the age of 4 (i.e., approximately 70,000 children) lives in poverty. Home-based early childhood programs represent perhaps the greatest hope for breaking the cycle of poverty in this country. International research confirms that high-quality early childhood services can make a vast difference in the lives of children and that these services have the most significant effect on those who are economically deprived. Jamaica has achieved commendable preschool coverage, reaching 85 percent of all 4–5 year olds, but opportunities for infants and children from birth to age 3 are extremely limited. Day-care coverage for this age group is currently low (approximately 14 percent), and most programs are offered by private operators at rates far exceeding the capability of poor families.

The government, which is faced with a crippling burden of debt and competing demands from the social sector, cannot be expected to support wide-scale expansion of center-based childcare. Also, formal day-care services can be considered inappropriate and irrelevant in rural areas having the greatest incidence of poverty and where mothers are most often unemployed or earning their living in and around their homes.

Home visiting programs offer an important alternative in Jamaica for increasing the access of poor families to early childhood interventions and, ultimately, for building social capital. This chapter examines elements of quality that may be useful benchmarks in delivering such programs. Three home visiting models currently operating in Jamaica are reviewed to identify practices that appear to have contributed significantly to the success of the interventions. The three models offer the same basic ingredients of psychosocial stimulation for children as well as counseling, education, and parental support. The programs all serve children living in poverty, but each program serves distinctly different populations. The three programs are the:

- Roving Caregivers Program, which serves the needs of children of teenage mothers and families
- Community-Based Rehabilitation Program, which assists young children with disabilities
- Malnourished Children's Program, which addresses the nutritional and psychosocial needs of children admitted to the hospital for malnutrition.

Together, these programs address the three main principles underlying the Convention on the Rights of the Child (CRC)—survival, protection, and development. Any home visiting program considered for implementation on a national scale must give sufficient emphasis to each of these rights and goals for children. A brief overview of the three programs follows.

Overview

Roving Caregivers Program

The Roving Caregivers Program (RCP) is a core initiative implemented under the Community and Home-Based Learning component of the government of Jamaica/United Nations Children's Fund (UNICEF) Basic Education and Early Childhood Development Program. The objective of the initiative is to ensure development and expansion of effective and low-cost delivery of early childhood services to meet developmental needs of children ages birth to 3 years. RCP is a nonformal, multidimensional, integrated program of child development and parenting education. The basic ingredients include childcare, environmental education, referral information, personal development, skills training, and income generation.

RCP is implemented by the Rural Family Support Organization (RuFamSo) in two rural parishes in central Jamaica. These parishes were identified as the pilot region for implementation of the government's new policy on integration of early childhood education. RuFamSo, which has strong linkages with several development and international agencies, provides integrated services for families. Besides RCP, these services include the Teenage Mothers Project, Male Adolescent Program, Uplifting Adolescents Program, and Home-Based Nursery Program. All programs, including RCP, are a spinoff of the initial Teenage Mothers Project.

Initiated in 1992 as a joint effort with the Bernard van Leer Foundation, RCP is designed to assist high-risk families. Community child health clinics help target beneficiaries. RCP deploys a cadre of child development promoters to model stimulation activities in homes and to deliver parenting education messages. The caregivers (or rovers), who carry out their tasks on foot, are young secondary school graduates recruited from the communities in which they live. Rovers are selected based on the recommendations of their former school principals or guidance counselors. Depending on the proximity of the homes, interventions are organized for individuals and groups.

RCP has a strong training component. Rovers receive 1 week of preservice training and regular inservice training consisting of 1-day workshops every 2 weeks and 1-week courses every 3 months. The workshops are held to discuss issues and concerns related to visits, to review weekly plans, and to make play materials for stimulation activities. Home visits are monitored closely by project officers who conduct onsite supervisory visits every 2 weeks.

Within approximately 6 years, RCP has expanded from fifteen to twenty-five districts and currently benefits 3,500 children ages birth to 3 years and 700 homes in approximately sixty communities. In 1998, under a government poverty eradication initiative, the roving caregivers model was successfully tested in an urban setting, in eleven depressed inner-city communities for the benefit of 1,300 children.

Community-Based Rehabilitation Program

The Community-Based Rehabilitation Program is part of the Dedicated to the Development of the Disabled (3D) organization, which was established in 1985. 3D is committed to rehabilitation and integration of persons with disabilities into their communities by teaching and assisting caregivers to help persons with disabilities function at their highest potential. The community program offers a range of services, including early stimulation for children at risk of developing slowly, early identification of disabilities, assessment of abilities, development of individual home plans to enhance a child's abilities, group and individual parental counseling, psychoeducational assessments for school-aged children, and referrals to other agencies. The home-based program was initiated in one of Jamaica's fourteen parishes and now operates in four parishes, serving approximately 1,000 families. The children benefiting from the program are from birth to 6 years old who exhibit significantly slow or delayed development in one or more areas of self-help, speech and language, and motor or cognitive behavior.

Children are referred to 3D's community program by parents, doctors, nurses, day-care centers, social workers, and school teachers.

After referral, a complete assessment is conducted of the child using the Denver Developmental Screening Test. The child receives a complete medical examination and, after diagnosis, is placed in an intervention program administered by a child development aide. Based on the assessment, interviews with parents and community members, and observations in the home setting, the aide develops an individual child and home plan. When this groundwork is completed, the aide begins to guide parents in strategies for stimulation. Aides usually visit each child at least twice each month, beginning with weekly visits and then less frequently as the program progresses. Problems requiring an assessment by a specialist or a specific intervention are referred to other agencies. Each aide visits between twelve and twenty children each week and attends weekly case conferences with the project's supervisor to discuss child program and teaching methods. Initial training received by the aides is reinforced in continuous in-service training.

Malnourished Children's Program

The Malnourished Children's Program was established in 1994 by the Child Development Research Group of the Tropical Metabolism Research Unit (now renamed the Tropical Medicine Research Institute, TMRI) of the University Hospital of the West Indies to address early deficiencies of children hospitalized for malnutrition. Before initiation of this outreach program, hospital personnel observed that many children who recovered and were sent home from the TMRI had to be readmitted for the same condition after a short time. To address this problem, TMRI pioneered intervention strategies to reduce the high readmission rate by conducting follow-up home visits to monitor children discharged from the TMRI.

During each home visit, staff focus on stimulation, environmental factors potentially detrimental to the child's health, and the child's nutritional status and possible need for food supplementation. Parents of children admitted to the TMRI participate in an ongoing weekly program consisting of parenting education and a social welfare project. TMRI helps parents develop income-generating skills, begin self-help projects, and find jobs or shelter. TMRI also provides food packages, bedding, and clothing for needy, unemployed parents. The parents are required to attend at least twelve workshops and, on completion, are awarded a certificate of participation.

In addition to individual home visits, TMRI operates a community outreach program at three locations in poor communities within the Kingston metropolitan area, which has a high prevalence of malnutrition. This program includes regular psychosocial stimulation of children ages 3 and less, supported with a mobile toy-lending library. TMRI also has extended its parenting and child stimulation services to Jamaica's only exclusive hospital for children, through a weekly program at the nutrition clinic.

Home Visiting Programs: Elements of Quality

Twelve elements of quality can be noted in the practices of the three model programs described above. These elements, which have contributed significantly to the success of the programs, are:

1. Linkage of childcare supports with family supports
2. Recognition of women's multiple roles as mothers, homemakers, and income earners
3. Transfer of skills to the clients and households
4. Flexibility in service delivery
5. Acknowledgment of family configurations and building on existing networks for children
6. Sustainability of the program play materials
7. Strong referral systems and access support
8. High staff retention
9. Documentation
10. Strong feedback and monitoring mechanisms
11. Research orientation leading to action
12. Proactive measures to ensure sustainability and institutionalization.

The findings and impressions presented below for each element are based on interviews with program directors, staff members, and recipients as well as observations of meetings, training sessions, and other interventions. For analysis, the author assumed that the standards for program inputs were strongly related to the desired program outcomes, but made no attempt to establish direct connections between inputs and outcomes.

Linkage of Childcare Supports With Family Supports

All three programs described above are based on the primary principle that children cannot be assisted in isolation. The programs approach interventions on behalf of children from a holistic perspective, by providing support to families while giving direct supports to children.

As noted previously, RCP is a spinoff of the Teenage Mothers Project, which was established initially to address the problem of teen pregnancy (Jamaica's rate of teenage pregnancies is 108 per 1,000, the highest in the Caribbean). The project was expanded to include other services when it was realized that the problem of teen mothers could not be addressed in isolation. RCP, the home visiting program, was initiated to overcome the limited effects of intervening with only the teenage mother and her baby. A demonstration nursery provides day care for children while teenage mothers attend academic and skill-training classes, as well as counseling and self-esteem-building sessions. Sessions for fathers of the babies and for grandmothers (the mothers of the teenage girls) are also available. This multilayered strategy involves the entire family network, and the program has had an almost 100 percent success rate in preventing second pregnancies among the teenagers.

In the 3D program, both parents are required to participate in the intervention for their child with a disability. The roles of each family member are articulated in the home plan to encourage total support for the child. Also, in recognition of the importance of the wider community in influencing the development of the child, the aides work to build supportive relationships between families.

In the Malnourished Children's Program, staff strive to increase the economic stability of families by identifying employment opportunities and making job referrals for fathers. For each case, home visits facilitate ongoing identification of specific and interconnected social, environmental, and economic needs of children and their families.

Recognition of Women's Multiple Roles as Mothers, Homemakers, and Income Earners

A significant proportion of the households in Jamaica (45 percent) are headed by females. In addition, the participation of females in the labor force is low, amounting to only 10 percent of women, compared with 20 percent of males. Because of this double disadvantage, each program closely links childcare strategies to maternal care and support. In group parenting sessions, the following pertinent topics are addressed: referrals to antenatal clinics; promotion of breastfeeding, nutrition education, reproductive health, and environmental hygiene and safety; and training and support for income-generating activities.

In the 3D program, the sessions on reproductive health cover prenatal and genetic counseling. Parenting sessions include emphasis on time management, to help mothers cope with the additional demands of children with disabilities. The Malnourished Children's Program, which targets children whose survival and growth are particularly at risk, places significant emphasis on income-generation opportunities for mothers. Staff attempt to match the interests and abilities of each mother with marketable skills. The program sponsors mothers to take advantage of skill-training opportunities in areas such as childcare, geriatric care, dressmaking, and hairdressing. Mothers with very low literacy levels receive practical in-house training in areas such as setting tables, making beds, and relating to employers, to prepare them for domestic work. The program also provides tangible support to mothers who wish to buy and sell food or goods, buying these items in bulk and offering them to mothers at significantly reduced prices.

Transfer of Skills to Clients and Households

The three home visiting programs emphasize the empowerment of parents and the transfer of skills to their households through trained and monitored outreach workers. In RCP, parents are selected as parent group leaders for income-generating projects, thus building leadership skills, confidence, and self-esteem. Roving caregivers model stimulation activities for children with the expectation that parents will continue these activities between visits. Involving parents directly is a significant challenge initially because the rovers' visits are frequently viewed by parents or caregivers as opportunities to gain child supervision so that they can attend to household chores. However, the program emphasizes the guiding of parents in strategies for including stimulation-type activities in routine household tasks.

In the Malnourished Children's Program, parents are selected as play leaders for group stimulation sessions, and outreach workers observe and guide these activities. Parents also are asked to lead food-preparation demonstrations using cooking equipment traditionally found in their homes. In the 3D program, clients who demonstrate particular coping skills are selected and trained to become community rehabilitation workers. This strategy, which relies on the total transfer of skills, helps sustain and strengthen the gains of the overall program.

Flexibility in Service Delivery

A positive characteristic common to all the programs is flexibility in implementation. For example, RCP implemented stimulation activities initially in individual homes, but subsequently modified this approach for homes in close proximity (e.g., communal dwelling units consisting of several homes) to conduct activities in shared spaces within yards. This adaptation yielded an additional benefit because messages about child development reached many other adults in addition to those officially participating in the program. The children are grouped by age, and they benefit from social interaction during stimulation activities. When homes are more distant, RCP continues with individual home visits.

In the 3D program, homes are far apart and clients convene in health centers. In the Malnourished Children's Program, visits are conducted in high-density areas in suitable and available spaces (e.g., community centers, basic schools, under trees). Basic schools are community-operated and government-subsidized preschools catering to children ages 4–5 and providing a high level of coverage (approximately 95 percent) of the age cohort.

Maintaining flexibility in the organization of programs helps ensure that they are adapted to local conditions and meet the needs of staff and the circumstances of parents and communities. The programs also demonstrate flexibility in the type of assistance provided to families (i.e., the content of service delivery). All the programs acknowledge that families and children differ in their needs and stage of development and that the delivery of services and the types of support must be customized to accommodate these differences.

For example, the Malnourished Children's Program supports a variety of income-generating activities, based on the particular strengths or circumstances of the adults, rather than a predetermined group activity for all. In the 3D program, each home plan, which guides the interventions provided, is designed based on an assessment of that family's circumstances.

Acknowledgment of Family Configurations and Building on Existing Networks for Children

Child-shifting and alternate caregiving are commonplace in Jamaica. Rural-to-urban migration is common, and approximately 20,000 individuals emigrate from Jamaica each year. As a result, the variety of family configurations is myriad and the support networks for children are complex.

All three programs make a strong effort to identify primary and secondary caregivers and to work with these persons interchangeably. RCP regularly involves significant others in its stimulation and parent education activities. The 3D program's strategy incorporates a child-to-child approach, particularly when mothers work outside their homes and the intervention depends on the participation of siblings. In the Malnourished Children's Program, parents are asked to bring neighbors to the TMRI for training so that these individuals can sustain the children's activities when the parents are absent.

Sustainability of the Program Play Materials

The application of child development knowledge in a program's practices is a major determinant of quality for any early childhood intervention. For example, the fact that young children learn most effectively through experiential play is now firmly established. To grasp basic concepts and to develop sensory and motor systems, young children need a variety of concrete, hands-on materials.

However, providing a continuing and adequate supply of learning materials is a major challenge for early childhood programs in developing countries such as Jamaica. Although many early childhood activities can be done with items from the natural environment, some learning materials must be specially made. When there is no source of these materials locally, center-based programs must import items at great expense and then replenish them frequently as stocks dwindle or become worn.

A positive characteristic of all three home visiting programs is their emphasis on strategies for sustaining stimulation and other program materials. In RCP, outreach workers encourage use of household items and construction of stimulation materials. They spend part of their biweekly sessions making toys for upcoming visits, and parents are taught to make toys in parent group sessions. Still, maintaining a sufficient supply of materials for the number of households visited is difficult. In addition, some of the materials that are made are not durable, and the costs to replace them are high. Also, certain materials, to support children's manipulative skills, cannot be made easily by the rovers. To resolve this problem, RCP is establishing a small-scale production facility for materials development, linking the production of toys to the training of out-of-school youth in marketable skills.

The Malnourished Children's Program hires a person to make toys for the mobile toy-lending library. Students from a national technical and vocational training program and parents also help make toys. In a continuing collection drive, community-based factories and entrepreneurs are asked to donate "trashables" (e.g., cardboard, tins, cloth scraps, wood ends). In the 3D program, parents are taught to make toys as well as adaptive aids, which can be prohibitively costly for poor families.

Strong Referral Systems and Access Support

Another common strength of the programs is their use of available community and other resources and infrastructure to support optimal child development. Recognizing their respective advantages and limited capacities, they draw heavily on other services (e.g., child health clinics, the public health department, the Food-for-the-Poor organization, the women's crisis center, the Jamaica adult literacy program) to meet multiple needs of families. The programs enhance the awareness of clients about these services and provide practical support to facilitate access to them.

For example, the Malnourished Children's Program will pay for a multiparous woman to receive tubal ligation, if desired, at the family planning unit. The 3D organization will provide transportation for clients to access alternative services, and parent leaders will accompany clients on their first visit to these services. The organization also acts as a referee to enable clients to access benefits offered by credit unions or insurance programs.

Building on existing social systems is a key strategy for all three programs. Their experience demonstrates that information, by itself, is not sufficient and that active referrals are needed. Families living in poverty with children at risk need help to seek help.

High Staff Retention

Stability of staffing is another element of quality observed in the three home visiting programs. The administrators of these programs recognize that job satisfaction helps ensure staff stability which, in turn, is a prerequisite for staff growth and development. In RCP, outreach workers matriculate into the program directly from secondary schools and generally stay for approximately 3 years, leaving to explore new career opportunities. Their average 3-year tenure enables the program to benefit from their accumulated knowledge and experience, in the delivery of home visits and the modeling of program delivery for new recruits.

In the 3D program, outreach workers most often begin as beneficiaries and stay in the program for an average of 10 years. The fact that the employee's own children benefit from the program is a main incentive for staying. Other incentives include opportunities for professional and self-development, as well as guaranteed benefits of employment, such as health insurance.

Documentation

Each home visiting program strongly emphasizes documentation of processes and materials utilized in the program. This documentation is an effective strategy for ensuring continuity. In RCP, weekly activity guides are prepared to guide rovers in child stimulation and parenting education during home visits. These guides are placed in an activity "bank" that is drawn from and built on over time. In addition, a video documentary that describes the program has proven useful for training new caregivers and informing potential donors about the scope and nature of RCP.

The 3D program has established an entire documentation unit that includes cameras and video-editing facilities. This unit has documented the 3D training program in twelve videos with accompanying written material. Leaflets describing the program have been produced for distribution, and assessment tools have been developed to determine and record the children's developmental levels. The Malnourished Children's Program has published booklets to reinforce workshop topics and has compiled manuals on making toys.

To build on and strengthen the documentation of each of these programs, UNICEF is supporting development of a home-visiting manual. The hope is that this manual could be used as a national guide for home visiting early childhood programs.

Strong Feedback and Monitoring Mechanisms

Closely related to maintaining standards in any program is having a well-organized and meaningful system of feedback and monitoring. Such a system is well-established in each of the three programs and deserves to be highlighted as an important element of quality. In RCP, full-day feedback sessions are held every 2 weeks to review progress in the home visits, discuss strategies for overcoming emerging problems, and highlight and reinforce positive experiences. In addition, project officers accompany rovers at specific intervals to provide supervision and guidance onsite. The Malnourished Children's Program's monitoring component is similar except that feedback and planning sessions are held weekly and progress is recorded in a written logbook. In the 3D program, a case file is established for each child and the cases are reviewed weekly to discuss each child's progress. In addition, all staff are required to contribute to an evaluation meeting, held quarterly. Monitoring in this program is based on the "manpower model," which consists of a community-based rehabilitation coordinator who oversees the work of supervisors who, in turn, oversee community rehabilitation workers.

Research Orientation Leading to Action

All three home visiting programs are experimental or extensions and improvements of innovative programs that are testing new methods and materials for accomplishing their missions more effectively. Significantly, each program places heavy emphasis on research as part of its agenda. This research has helped to validate the programs and to justify further funding, as well as providing useful information for guiding practice. In two programs, the research is being used to substantiate the government's taking the programs to scale.

In RCP, the development of the children has been assessed using an internationally recognized instrument, and a tracer study was conducted on children in primary school 12 years after the RCP intervention. The effect of training on the knowledge of roving caregivers also has been evaluated.

Research conducted in the 3D program to validate an identification and assessment instrument (The Ten Question Screening Tool) has led to utilization of this tool by paraprofessionals in several developing countries. Recent research on community attitudes, which showed that neighbors are more likely to respond supportively if a family demonstrates strong acceptance of a child with a disability, stimulated revision of the program's strategies.

Internationally recognized research on the effects of food supplementation and stimulation (Grantham-McGregor and others 1991), conducted in the Malnourished Children's Program, supports the concept that psychosocial intervention can compensate for deficits associated with early malnutrition. Researchers in the program have conducted a longitudinal study of children from the program who are now 20 years old. More recently, research on the reasons for hospital readmission of children with malnutrition has led to a refining of program strategies, which has resulted in the end of readmissions for children participating in the program.

Proactive Measures to Ensure Sustainability and Institutionalization

Sustainability is a critical and most-sought-after component of intervention. A strong element of quality in the programs has been their proactive orientation toward securing sustainability and institutionalization. In particular, two of the three programs have assumed a role in mainstreaming their innovations. These programs planned strategically for various phases of their life cycle. From successful, small pilot projects operating on a trial-and-error basis, they moved through expansion and replication, during which services increased in scope and coverage. In this second phase, much networking was undertaken to increase the awareness of stakeholders about the programs' products and processes and to secure partnerships for sustainability.

For example, RCP established linkages with Jamaica's Social Development Commission, the national coordinating agency for community development and the government's poverty eradication program. RCP also asked the public health department to help with education and training of parents; various church groups to provide leadership; and other organizations and private entities to provide financial or in-kind contributions. In some cases, this networking was informal and one-to-one. In addition, RCP's advisory board held several consultation workshops with stakeholders and circulated the proceedings widely.

In a third phase, programs are attempting to transfer their models beyond the previous controlled conditions and to test their strategies in more realistic operating venues in existing programs and services. Through strong advocacy, RCP has secured government support to extend its coverage by using National Youth Service workers to implement the program in one of seventeen early childhood resource centers. Similarly, in one parish, the 3D program is conducting a pilot project utilizing government workers to deliver its services.

The Challenges Remaining

Figure 1 provides an overview of the three home visiting programs reviewed in this chapter. Although these programs exhibit twelve critical elements of quality for early childhood interventions, many questions, challenges, and concerns remain and need to be addressed thoughtfully. Key issues include:

- Avoiding a "hand-out mentality" which measures a program's worth by the food or other tangible benefits distributed
- Ensuring sustainability of food contributions
- Addressing the power and status of women and men
- Balancing the tension between promoting children's rights and respecting cultural beliefs and practices
- Ensuring provision of reinforcing public educational messages
- Devising strategies for increasing a program's coverage while maintaining quality.

Description	Roving Caregivers Program	3D Community-Based Rehabilitation Program	Malnourished Children's Program
		Program	
Implementing agency	Rural Family Support Organization (RuFamSo)	Dedicated to the Development of the Disabled (3D) Organization	Tropical Medicine Research Institute, University Hospital of the West Indies
Start Date	1995	1985	1994
Population	Poor families: 250 Homes 750 Children Children birth to 3 years	Families of children with disabilities (~1,000)	60 admitted per year Children 3 months to 3 years
Services	Psychosocial stimulation, counseling, parental education and supports, income generation Teenage Mothers Project Male Adolescent Program	Training of families to stimulate/teach life skills Early identification/ assessment of ability/disability Individual home plan Individual/group parent counseling Medical clinics	Psychosocial stimulation, counseling, parental education and supports Group stimulation and parent sessions in communities Mobile toy-lending library
Linkage of Childcare Supports With Family Supports			
	Demonstration nursery for children Academic and skill training classes for teen mothers	Both parents required to attend clinic Family roles defined to support child	Assistance with income generation and job referrals
Recognition of Women's Multiple Roles as Mothers, Homemakers, and Income Earners			
	Promotion of reproductive health and family planning Home hygiene and safety Training and support for income generation	Fertility management Prenatal and genetic counseling Time management	Matching mothers and skills Supporting mothers via sponsored attendance at other programs and in-house training
Transfer of Skills to Clients and Households			
	Parents selected as parent group leaders	Majority of community rehabilitation workers are parents	Parents selected as play leaders Parents lead food demonstrations
Flexibility in Service Delivery			
	Distant homes: one-to-one Close homes: group visit	Distant homes: clients convene in health centers	High-density areas: visits conducted in community centers, basic schools, and under trees

continued

Figure 1. Overview of Three Home Visiting Programs in Jamaica

	Program		
Description	**Roving Caregivers Program**	**3D Community-Based Rehabilitation Program**	**Malnourished Children's Program**
Acknowledgment of Family Configurations and Building on Existing Networks for Children			
	Involvement of grand-mothers	Involvement of siblings and schoolchildren Child-to-child	Working mothers bring in caregivers and neigh-bors for training
Sustainability of the Program Play Materials			
	Parents taught to make simple toys in parent group sessions Youths in Male Adolescent Program make toys	Parents taught to make and use adaptive aids	Person hired to make toys for mobile toy-lending library Parents and technical and vocational students help make toys Collection drive
Strong Referral Systems and Access Support			
	Child health clinics	Psychological assessments Housing trust National insurance program Food-for-the-Poor Credit union	Women's crisis center Jamaica adult literacy program Family planning unit
High Staff Retention			
	Rovers remain 3 years, on average	Community rehabilitation workers remain 10 years, on average Incentives and professional development opportunities	
Documentation			
	Weekly stimulation guides Video documentary Home-visiting manual	Documentation unit Training program docu-mented in twelve videos and written packages Leaflets and assessment tools	Booklets to reinforce workshop topics
Strong Feedback and Monitoring Mechanisms			
	Workshops biweekly Supervision onsite	Case file for each child Weekly case review Quarterly evaluation of child's progress "Manpower model"	Logbook Timetable for visiting discharged children Weekly feedback and planning sessions Supervision onsite

continued

Figure 1 (continued). Overview of Three Home Visiting Programs in Jamaica

	Program		
Description	**Roving Caregivers Program**	**3D Community-Based Rehabilitation Program**	**Malnourished Children's Program**
Research Orientation Leading to Action			
	Developmental assessments Tracer studies of children Evaluation of impact of training on rover's knowledge	Research to validate identification and assessment tool Research on community attitudes	Longitudinal studies Research to determine reasons for readmissions Mix of interventions for greatest effect
Proactive Measures to Ensure Sustainability and Institutionalization			
	Advocacy by advisory board Consultations with stakeholders	Pilot project in one parish to train government workers to deliver program	

Figure 1 (continued). Overview of Three Home Visiting Programs in Jamaica

The greatest overall challenge for the home visiting programs is to ensure full institutionalization. As part of its new policy on the integration of early childhood (day-care and preschool) services, the Jamaican government is grappling with whether and how it should take an early childhood home visiting program to scale. In light of the new policy, UNICEF is supporting an in-depth, strategic review of Jamaica's national early childhood program. This assessment includes a study of the feasibility of taking the home visiting model(s) to scale. UNICEF will be examining financial projections, targets and strategies, and existing structures, as well as the possibility of expanding the role of community health aides, deployed by the Ministry of Health, to include child development and early stimulation activities with health and nutrition services currently delivered to families.

To introduce a home visiting program on a national scale, regardless of the model or combination of models used, and to ensure that the economic returns on scarce resources are maximized, a well-structured system for targeting children, families, and communities needs to be developed. Information will be needed for determining the status of children, families, and communities in order to identify areas of greatest need and areas least likely to meet the needs without intervention. Clearly, general improvements in child survival, growth, and development depend on improvements in the home *and* in the community that shelters, nourishes, socializes, and protects a young child. Linking early childhood home visiting programs with more general community-based initiatives and social investments, which involve attention to community conditions and development of social infrastructure (e.g., supports for breastfeeding, nutrition, safe water, shelter) is critical.

Some might argue that social institutions in developing countries such as Jamaica do not have the capacity to incorporate such interventions, but accepting this notion would be fatalistic. High-quality programs for young children living in poverty have demonstrated, more than any other innovation, the ability to narrow the gap between rich and poor and to break the intergenerational cycle of poverty.

However, formal programs in childcare centers and professional interventions have proven to be too expensive for poor families and, in many cases, culturally irrelevant or insensitive to family needs. As signatories to the CRC, national governments are bound to the examination of alternative strategies for assisting families in childrearing. Article 18 of the CRC outlines the state's responsibility as follows: to "render appropriate assistance to parents/guardians for childrearing and develop institutions, facilities, and services for childcare." Home visiting programs such as those described in this chapter must be included among the social services provided for poor families. The link between early child development and poverty is well understood, and the maximum effectiveness and sustainability of efforts on behalf of children depend on direct parental involvement.

Conclusion

The home visiting programs reviewed in this chapter combine delivery of services to children, caregivers, and communities by providing stimulation and play activities, education and support of parents, promotion and organization of community involvement, and referral to agencies that offer educational, health care, economic, and other opportunities and support for children and adults. The approaches supporting early child development, particularly for children ages birth to 3 years, are comprehensive, holistic, and complementary. They incorporate, as noted, twelve essential elements of quality that should be part of any home visiting early childhood program.

The great challenge remaining for these three programs and concerned stakeholders is the mainstreaming of the programs within the nation's delivery of social services by the governmental sector, the nongovernmental sector, or a combination of both through creative partnerships. Because of competing social demands and limited resources, the home visiting programs will need to be examined carefully for their fit with the range of family needs and the intervention strategies, services, and personnel available.

References

Grantham-McGregor, S.M., C.A. Powell, S.P. Walker, and J.H. Himes. 1991. Nutritional Supplementation, Psychosocial Stimulation, and Mental Development of Stunted Children: The Jamaica Study. *Lancet* 338:1–5.

Part IV

The Private Sector's Influence on the Public Sector

Chapter 10

Role of the Private Sector in Early Child Development

Robert G. Myers

The private sector has an important and significant role to play in improving the development of young children. This chapter presents a framework for discussing the private sector's potential contributions and highlights specific ways for this sector to contribute. The chapter is organized into four sections: clarification of the concept of early child development (ECD) and reasons for supporting ECD; definitions of the private sector; review of the sometimes-conflicting reasons for advocating private versus public care and education; and suggested ways of increasing the involvement of the private sector, especially companies and individuals, in supporting early childhood activities. Key points are summarized in the conclusion.

Early Child Development

The concept of ECD includes terms such as early childhood, child development, childcare, and early education. Although often used in distinct ways, these terms, together, convey the essence of ECD. Appreciating the substance of ECD is important when considering the reasons for supporting ECD and the implications for private-sector involvement.

Definitions

In this chapter and volume, *early childhood* encompasses the period from conception until entry into school at about age 6 or 7. The period may be extended through ages 7 and 8 when designing ECD programs, to include the articulation between preschool programs and grades 1 or 2 of primary school. Early childhood is the period when the brain develops almost to its fullest and when humans learn to walk and talk, begin to establish moral foundations, gain self-confidence, and develop a general world view. This early period provides the foundation for later living and learning.

Child development is a multifaceted, integral, and continual process of change as children become able to handle ever-more-complex levels of moving, thinking, feeling, and relating to others. Physical, mental, social, and emotional development occurs as a child interacts with his or her surrounding environments—the family, community, and broader society.

Childcare consists of the actions taken by caregivers in the home or a nondomestic setting to ensure children's survival and to promote their growth and development. Good care responds to children's basic physical, mental, social, and emotional needs, determined biologically and by the cultural and socioeconomic context and environment. Too often, childcare is considered narrowly as custodial care that provides only protection and the fulfillment of biological needs, without regard for children's mental, social, and emotional development. Also, the needs of caregivers, as well as children, are important considerations when discussing forms of care. For example, sometimes, parents' needs take precedence over children's needs when choosing among childcare options.

Early education, or early learning, is the process of acquiring knowledge, skills, habits, and values through experience, experimentation, reflection, observation, and/or study and instruction during early childhood. Education is a crucial part of child development and involves a gradual unfolding of biologically determined characteristics. Unfortunately, early education is often associated narrowly with mental development occurring in preschool centers which, as their name implies, are designed to prepare children for success in school, giving little attention to broader developmental needs or care.

Although often labeled and organized separately, childcare and early education programs should offer the same basic program elements to help children develop their maximum potential. Childcare programs must meet parents' as well as children's needs, and therefore may have different hours of operation than early education programs; however, the basic attention given to the children should be the same. In the discussion below, the terms "early childcare and development," "early childhood education and care," and "ECD" are used interchangeably.

Why Support ECD Programs?

Common sense and scientific findings suggest that the early years of childhood are critical for formation of intelligence, personality, and social behavior and that a child who develops well during these years will have greater opportunities in life, be more productive, and, very likely, be a better citizen. The reasons why societies should want to invest in ECD have been elaborated elsewhere (e.g., Myers 1995). Some of these reasons may resonate more than others in particular groups and settings. Six arguments for ECD are, in brief:

1. *Human Rights.* Children have a right to live and develop to their full potential. The United Nations Children's Fund (UNICEF) and other international organizations supported by local human rights organizations have vigorously promoted this position, based on the near-universal signing of the Convention on the Rights of the Child, which includes the right to healthy development. However, some governments do not find this argument for supporting early childhood programs particularly compelling.

2. *Moral and Social Values.* Humanity transmits its values through children, beginning in infancy. This argument will be forceful for those who believe that core values are being lost and/or that

the particular values of their cultural group are not represented adequately in a homogeneous system of childcare and education supported by government.

3. *Economic Productivity.* Society benefits economically from improved early development by greater productivity in later life. This argument may be attractive to governments and businesses concerned about economic growth and competing in a world economy. However, as suggested later in this chapter, the general economic benefit and the chain of effects from early childhood through schooling to greater economic productivity may not convince private companies to invest in ECD (versus, for example, investing in secondary or technical education). Potentially more convincing for many employers is the notion that childcare programs may free up women to work and thereby increase the immediate availability of an important source of labor.

4. *Cost-Savings.* Investments in ECD are preventive and can reduce later needs for, and costs of, social welfare programs, remedial school programs, healthcare, and judicial and criminal services (Schweinhart and others 1993). This argument should be particularly attractive to governments, but may not be to private businesses or individuals because the immediate private (versus social) benefit to the firm or person may not be great or evident. Private decisions do not usually incorporate social externalities.

5. *Program Efficacy.* The efficacy of health, nutrition, education, and women's programs can be improved by combining these programs with ECD. Combined efforts result in enhanced interactive effects among health, nutrition, and early stimulation. From the perspective of industry and commerce, childcare programs may be good investments because workers (especially women) will lose less worktime due to child-related concerns.

6. *Social Equity.* Providing a "fair start" may help modify distressing socioeconomic and gender-related inequities. This argument will appeal particularly to governments and nongovernmental

organizations concerned with creating a more equitable society and to groups that have not had equal access to services. For industry, this argument may have to be linked to the notion of achieving greater social stability (a climate in which companies can operate with greater security) and to the altruistic values of company managers (which may also have an economic payoff because a company will be viewed as socially responsible).

Backed by scientific studies, this combination of social arguments should be compelling to governments and social organizations. However, the arguments may not be convincing to private firms or individuals because of the lack of a direct, private payoff. If governments do not act, the potential social benefits offered by ECD programs to the general population (e.g., crime reduction and related judicial costs) would be lost.

Implications for the Private Sector

Much discussion of private-sector involvement in education has been focused on higher and secondary education, with only some attention given to primary schools. Although parts of this broad discussion are pertinent to ECD, discussion of private-sector involvement in early childhood programs must differ for several reasons in addition to the obvious difference in children's ages. Four characteristics of ECD are particularly pertinent to discussion of private-sector involvement in this arena. These are the evolution of the field of early childhood education, the breadth and the selective nature of educational systems, and the "tension" between ECD and women's work.

Evolution of the Field

Early childhood education is at a different stage in financing, operation, and public-private control than other educational levels. Primary school education, for example, has become largely a public responsibility throughout the world, although this has not always been the case. Until the late nineteenth century in Europe, for example, religious organizations dominated in the provision of primary schooling, a trend that seems to be mirrored currently for early childcare and education in many countries.

In contrast, childcare and early education for healthy development of young children is essentially a private-sector responsibility, particularly in the developing world and especially for children under age 4. Mangenheim (1999) shows that the private-sector bias in early childcare and education also is characteristic of the United States.

In many parts of the developing world, care and education during a child's early years continue to be almost exclusively the responsibility of the family, with relatively little financial support from government. And, a large proportion of formal and informal childcare and early education programs are operated by nongovernmental, and often religious, organizations. In most countries, preschool education is not obligatory or universal, and governments therefore are not concerned legally with educational support at this level. This situation is similar to that for upper secondary and higher education, although the tradition of public involvement at these levels is much longer than for ECD.

There are, of course, important exceptions to the dominance of the private sector, broadly defined, in attending to young children. Preschool for children during the year immediately preceding entry into primary school has become obligatory in some countries. And, Latin America has a growing number of governmental educational programs for young children, reaching down to age 4 and sometimes age 3. In Europe, the public sector is deeply involved in supporting childcare and early education by a variety of strategies. In socialist countries, an intense governmental effort was made previously to fund and operate programs for young children, but much of this work has been undone with the shift of political and economic policies during the 1990s. In India, a very large number of children benefit from the public Integrated Child Development Service.

In countries where the private sector is already dominant in ECD and early education, "privatization" may not be the main issue. Instead, the task may be to identify ways that the private sector can help parents to educate their children, can improve existing childhood programs operated within the private sector, and can partner with government to improve access to, and quality of, ECD programs financed and administered by government. In some countries, the concern may be how to make early childhood programs more public and how to involve governments in a field they have been reluctant to enter.

Breadth

Most discussions of private-sector education have focused on children's participation in schools and what they learn there. However, early development and learning mostly occur outside schools in other educational and learning environments such as the family and community. Because development occurs as children interact with their environment(s), programs to improve early child development must encompass complementary strategies linked to the different environments that surround a child (Bronfenbrenner 1979). These strategies (Myers 1995) include:

- Attending to children in centers outside the home (creating an alternative environment for care and education)
- Educating and supporting parents, focusing on the home environment
- Supporting child-centered community development programs, focusing on changing the general conditions that affect child development in communities
- Strengthening the capacity of social institutions created to attend to children and families (in centers, homes, or communities)
- Advocating and legislating creation of a better policy and legal environment for programs.

The private sector can be involved in many more ways of improving early child development than by operating early childhood centers or providing resources to organizations that operate centers.

Selectivity

As children ascend in the educational system, they grow older and become a more select group socially and economically, particularly in the developing world. As they age, they also approach and then pass the legal age for entering the formal labor force. Through selection, the families of children who remain in the educational system are more likely to be able to pay for their child's education. Children from low-income families are more likely to be selected out of the system, and children who remain come from families with more re-sources. Also, children who remain are usually more able and more qualified than others for a position that will pay well after they complete school, making loans for education a feasible option.

From the perspective of the corporate sector, investing in these more-select children may make sense because companies will need a well-qualified workforce, especially in this time of globalization. These same conditions of selectivity, linked to age and labor-market availability, are less applicable to discussions of children during their first 5 or 6 years of life, even though many young children in the developing world work at a very early age.

Tension Between ECD and Women's Work

Early childhood programming is at the intersection of education and care, and it relates directly to a tension in allocating women's time between children's development and women's work. Although, in theory, this tension applies to both parents, most societies continue to assign women the almost exclusive role of caregiver, hence, the phrase "women's work." Because care is part of ECD, the discussion of ECD extends well beyond the boundaries of educational institutions and budgets to include other parts of public bureaucracies and home care by parents or others. Discussion of ECD programs also includes not only their effects on children's performance and productivity in school and later life and work, but also the family members' (especially mothers' and older sisters') earning and learning power as potential contributors to the labor force. This potential tradeoff between care and participation in the labor force recedes in importance as children mature and enter higher levels of education.

The Private Sector

Different meanings applied to the term "private sector" color and sometimes derail discussions of ECD. Failing to clarify the meaning of private sector can compromise discussions, because different organizations and individuals have different vested interests in the outcomes of early care and development, the types of resources they can offer, and their organizational ways.

Definitions

At a very general level, "private" connotes that which belongs to specific and separate individuals or groups, whereas "public" refers to goods and concerns held in common. Presently, "public" is usually equated with a government's statements and roles as representative of a people's common concerns. Hence, a contrast is often made between the private sector and the governmental sector. The tendency to equate "public" with "governmental," however, may contradict the original meaning of the word public. When a government truly represents a people's concerns, it may accurately be termed a "public" institution. However, in a dictatorship, the concerns of the government may or may not be public concerns and the people have no ownership or control of the government.

During the twentieth century, the role of governments in providing education increased rapidly, particularly at the elementary school level. Education (and schooling) came to be viewed as a public good that should be provided free of charge, often within the framework of a welfare state. During the past two decades, however, the welfare state has been challenged and initiatives to "privatize" social services, including education, have arisen.

Figure 1 presents the various dimensions of the private sector as related to early childcare and education. In many discussions, these dimensions are combined to represent the private sector, which is viewed as everything that is not governmental or everything "outside government" (van der Gaag 1995). The figure demonstrates that a broad definition which contrasts the private and governmental sectors encompasses organizations established explicitly to provide services and products that may or may not be educational. The private sector broadly includes profit and nonprofit institutions, religious and nonreligious institutions, nongovernmental organizations (NGOs), community groups, and private voluntary organizations (PVOs). Both organizations and individuals are included.

In some discussions, the definition of private sector as related to early childcare and education is limited to private care and education services provided directly by businesses or social groups (column 2, rows A and B). In others, the definition is focused on all activities (row A, columns 1 and 2) conducted for private profit by only the business community.

The distinction between organizations that are directly involved in care and education (column 2) and those that are not (column 1) helps clarify discussions about "privatization" versus "involving the

Dimension	Noncare/noneducation purposes and products (column 1)	Care/education products (services, training, materials) (column 2)
A. Business organizations		
Large organizations	Steel company, bank	Kindercare
Medium or small organizations	Shoe repair shop	Home daycare center
B. Social organizations		
Community groups	Local women's group	Women's group care center
NGOs/PVOs		
Churches	Religious group	Religious preschool
Philanthropies	General foundation	Childcare foundation
C. Private individuals	Adults without children	Mother in home, tutor

NGOs, Nongovernmental organizations; PVOs, private voluntary organizations.

Figure 1. Dimensions of the Private Sector as Related to Early Childcare and Education

private sector." Whereas privatization involves the shifting of owner-ship and operation (and sometimes financing) from governmental to nongovernmental organizations or individuals (that is, into column 2), "involving the private sector" suggests a broader search for ways to involve private institutions and individuals that are not already di-rectly involved in programs of care and education; emphasis is placed on column 1, but the concept pertains to all parts of the figure. In-volving the private sector may consist of finding ways to:

- Shift institutions and individuals from column 1 to column 2 as owners, operators, or caregivers (i.e., privatizing), or
- Capture resources from all parts of the private sector that could be used by public or private institutions for care and education to improve child development.

The advantages and disadvantages of privatization have been much debated and are not specifically addressed in this chapter. Rather, the focus is on the broader theme of "involving the private sector" in care and education.

Private-Sector Involvement: Statistics

Statistics on the involvement of the private sector in childcare and education mostly report enrollments of children in formal institu-tions owned and operated by business or social organizations (col-umn 2, rows A and B). The data include enrollments in for-profit and nonprofit educational institutions, religious and nonreligious institutions, and community groups and PVOs directly involved in education. The statistics omit the educational contributions of busi-ness or social organizations not established explicitly for education-al purposes, and they do not reflect individual or informal home care and education.

The statistical and administrative definition of private-sector in-volvement rarely, if ever, distinguishes explicitly among ownership, operation, or control of organizations and sources of financing. The dominating criterion almost always seems to be ownership. As noted by Bray (1998), this definition of "private" is problematic because of organizations' different combinations of financing, operation, and control. For example, financing may be provided by the government, but operation and control may be nongovernmental, as for the burgeoning "charter" schools in the United States. Or, institutions created and operated by the government may be financed largely by nongovernmental sources, as are many community-based centers that are officially sanctioned and supervised by the government, but supported by community volunteers.

In the recent reviews prepared for the Year 2000 Evaluation of Education for All, most countries reported that a certain percentage of students enrolled in early childhood programs are enrolled in private (i.e., nongovernmental) programs. This percentage varies widely among the countries. For example, in Cuba, early childhood education and development is considered the responsibility of the government, and the percentage of private institutions is reported as zero. In various African countries and parts of the Middle East, however, the government places heavy responsibility for early care and education on families and local community organizations, and enrollment in these "private" initiatives is reported as 100 percent. The data for these countries do not indicate the extent of governmental support to subsidize the programs.

Nevertheless, for educational statistics in general (and data on early education and care in particular), the nongovernmental, administrative definition of private appears to be the definition of choice or of least resistance. Because most statistics do not include the contributions of private, unregistered institutions that are providing care and education, the estimates of private-sector activity may be significantly underreported.

Involving Institutions

Figure 1 distinguishes between business and social organizations, a distinction that corresponds approximately, and respectively, to "for-profit" and "not-for-profit." When using this distinction, discussion of the private sector could be limited to organizations created to make a profit for those who own and operate the institution (i.e., to row A). This definition is derived from an economic decisionmaking framework which relates efficiency and effectiveness to an organization's desire to maximize profits. The definition can be applied to a firm that produces and sells an educational service or product (column 2, row A) and/or to a business that operates in another market (column 1, row A).

Applied narrowly, this economic definition excludes all not-for-profit institutions such as churches, community groups, or voluntary organizations, even if they operate a school or childcare center and charge fees. In figure 1, these not-for-profit organizations are grouped together in a separate, "social" category because their motivation is supposedly social and altruistic (i.e., serving the public good, rather than seeking private gain).

Distinguishing a business sector from a social sector in relation to profit-seeking behavior is problematic because the behavior of profit-seeking and nonprofit organizations may be similar. Many "nonprofit" organizations operate as profit-making, seeking new markets and trying to perform cost-effectively. A not-for-profit educational organization often charges fees and may actually earn profits, but may (or may be required to) distribute or disguise its profits by paying higher salaries or reinvesting them in the organization. In addition, not-for-profit organizations may seek to maximize nonmonetary benefits (such as socialization to a particular religious orientation) that are more private than social. Conversely, a for-profit, noneducational business organization may use its profits (at least partially) altruistically to support nonprofit and public undertakings, including childcare and education programs. Or, for-profit educational institutions may utilize "sliding" fee scales to allow subsidies for some students, an action that is not aimed at maximizing profits.

If private sector is defined only in economic terms, then "privatization" becomes a narrow concept of privately owned and operated organizations seeking greater control of a defined market and motivated by a desire to maximize profits. Social organizations would be excluded.

Although the distinctions between profit and nonprofit blur, the difference is sufficient enough for societies to continue to distinguish them legally. Also, social organizations are expected to more closely represent the public interest, compared with profit-driven businesses, and to have certain operational advantages over government bureaucracies and corporations. These advantages relate, for example, to their organizational structure and their ability to interact with local populations and adjust to cultural differences.

Figure 1 further segregates large organizations from small and medium organizations [e.g., "mom and pop" (mostly "mom" in this case) operations]. When discussing privatization or the role of the private sector, emphasis is usually given to large firms, in the hope of identifying large-scale, rapid, and efficient ways to improve systems. In the developing world, however, most nongovernmental childcare and education programs are operated by small groups, communities, or individuals, with larger social, but usually not business, organizations (e.g., religious groups or international NGOs) sometimes involved. The combination of small, as well as large, enterprises (and particularly, small enterprises delivering a service) constitutes a major category of private-sector organizations involved in the operation of early childcare and education programs.

Figure 1 also segregates social organizations as community groups, NGOs and PVOs, churches, and philanthropies. These categories may overlap (e.g., a community group may be rooted in religious beliefs), and the groups may differ substantially in motivation, ways of becoming involved in care and education, and persons to convince about involvement (e.g., the local priest, mayor, or women's leader). Except for philanthropies, which have funds to provide, many of the other groups, including NGOs and PVOs, must seek funds and/or operate with donations of time and in-kind contributions.

Size, again, is an issue. Although not conveyed in figure 1, involving an international NGO or philanthropy that has an annual budget of US$100 million is different than inviting a local women's group to donate time and money to organize a service.

Involving Individuals and Families

A different perspective of "private" is needed for discussions of involving individuals and families. Their private role may be as immediate providers of childcare and education or as users of, and payers for, these services (see figure 1, column 2). Or, individuals and families may be considered potential sources of support for care and education programs (if they do not have children) (see column 2). In either case, the discussion shifts from the power of private and public producers to the power of private consumers, who may choose to be at-home providers of care and education.

Families and individuals have their own criteria for choosing whether to (or how much and how to) invest in early childcare and education in or outside the home. Their incentive to invest may be a child's development in a center or work-related childcare needs. Their information about options and their knowledge of the possible benefits for the child may be extensive or limited. Their choices will be affected by the characteristics of available services [e.g., cost (in relation to ability to pay), distance, flexibility of hours, quality, and confidence in the program].

Understanding how families make their decisions to invest time and money in early childhood programs, including care and education at home versus nongovernmental or governmental settings outside the home, is important. Their decisions may be affected, for example, by:

- Offering private education at different prices and of different quality
- Offering public subsidies as direct payments, scholarships, tax credits, or vouchers for use in private or public programs as the user chooses
- Extending parental work leaves
- Providing additional information about available programs.

From the perspective of families and individuals, the concept of privatizing education is associated more with increasing the choices for potential users to meet particular needs than with shifting the operational base from governmental to nongovernmental institutions. Choice is viewed as good in and of itself and is linked to a market-based orientation of knowledgeable consumers, high competition, and availability of many options (see Plank and Sykes 1999). These conditions are not currently present in most developing countries.

In the recent dispute at the National Autonomous University of Mexico, a public institution, students demonstrated against privatization, defined as the introduction of modest fees for some students according to their ability to pay. It did not involve a change in the operation and control of the university, which would continue to be a public institution. Although the students won their 9-month fight against privatization, the demand for entrance into higher education shifted, interestingly, toward private institutions, which increased their enrollments and thereby increased privatization of higher education in Mexico.

Along with the notion of improving private choices, the idea of increasing parents' share of the cost of care and education (i.e., making a greater private investment) has also become more popular in recent years. Governments have begun to introduce fees for public programs, a form of privatizing, and to encourage development of privately operated schools for families who can pay for them, leaving the government to serve others. These ways of capturing private funds from families for care and education programs may increase the choices for some families but reduce those for others, and they may create greater inequities if not accompanied by subsidies. These considerations are relevant to discussions of private versus public care and education.

Private Versus Public Care and Education

At least six general concerns "drive" discussions of public versus private financing, operation, and control of social programs, including early care and education. These concerns are:

- Availability of resources and educational opportunity
- Efficiency and cost-effectiveness
- Accountability
- Quality
- Equity
- Diversity and choice.

The relative weight given to each of these concerns, as they are converted into criteria for judging the effects, will set the tone and affect viewpoints of private-sector involvement.

Availability of Resources and Educational Opportunity

The concern that governments simply cannot find sufficient money for adequately financing education programs, including early childhood programs, is widespread. Competing demands for governmental funds lead to underfinancing and "a need to restrain expenditures so as to reduce deficits and debts" (Tooley 1999). This concern is usually linked to the expressed desire to improve access and coverage of programs for children who are "left out" because governmental funds are scarce.

Regardless of whether governments have the ability to increase funds for early childhood programs, the proportion of a government's budget allocated for these programs is minimal—often less than 1 percent of the total education budget in most developing countries, an amount that is virtually invisible in their gross domestic product. Even when health expenditures are included, the allocation is small, and transfers from planned expenditures for defense, security, or even other educational levels are not deemed feasible.

Accordingly, businesses, communities, and other social organizations and individuals are considered the first "alternative" sources of funding to supplement limited government capacity (or willingness to spend) for early childhood (or other care and education) programs. The search for private funding:

- Motivates exploration of additional ways for the corporate and business world (i.e., the noneducational, profit-making part of the private sector) to be convinced to use its resources for the public good by supporting programs
- Provokes interest in programs operated by community groups and voluntary organizations, which can capture new funds or involve individuals in giving their time to provide early child-care and education
- Leads to initiatives that require or entice parents to pay for services offered through private, and sometimes public, programs.

Seeking alternative financing broadly in the private sector may, or may not, reduce the public role in operating and controlling programs. While recognizing that obtaining additional funds from the private sector may be desirable, some critics continue to view the state's role of protector as important and necessary, and they suggest that the search for alternative funding can have undesirable results. For example, the costs of private programs may thwart the participation of low-income families in care and education programs unless the public continues to provide free services or help defray the costs of private services. Private-sector involvement could thus adversely affect equity (see "Equity" below).

Additionally, governments may have an "excuse" not to allocate funds to these programs, leaving their support to the whims of various private groups. One suggested alternative is that governments should strengthen their position by increasing taxes for families that can afford to pay and using these revenues to expand early care and education programs.

Efficiency and Cost-Effectiveness

Another concern is the common complaint that public programs are administered inefficiently and use the scarce resources they can obtain poorly. The bureaucracy is viewed as large and lethargic, and possibly corrupt, not directly accountable to the users of its services, subject to political influence, and having little incentive to improve the administration of its programs. Presumably, programs that are privately operated within a competitive system would need to be accountable to users and therefore seek the most efficient and cost-effective ways of providing early care and education. The emphasis here is more on operation and control than on direct funding, which could come from public sources via vouchers or from users' direct payments.

In a review of a private secondary education, Bray (1998) suggests that more research is needed to confirm the already considerable evidence that private schools are more efficient than public ones. Clearly, circumstances vary widely among different settings depending on the populations served by private or public systems.

While acknowledging that the search for efficiency is legitimate and even necessary, some critics are concerned that the cult of efficiency can distort educational goals and distract operators from their primary task of educating and caring for children. These critics suggest that an organization can be efficient but ineffective, or, perhaps, have a limited standard of effectiveness (e.g., children finish school without repeating grades), while disregarding whether children learn and develop in an integrated way. These critics are concerned about the increasingly common view of children as "products."

Also, in the ECD field, using funds for half-day programs focused on 5-year-olds may be efficient if the primary purpose is to prepare children for school, but this focus de-emphasizes other purposes, for example, meeting the needs of parents who must work longer hours and seek full-day programs for younger, as well as older, preschool children. Similarly, having large numbers of children per caregiver or teacher may be efficient, but the children are then likely to be "herded" rather than helped to learn.

Efficiency must be viewed in terms of outcomes and not simply mechanistic accomplishments (e.g., timely delivery of "inputs," meeting payrolls for teachers, reducing grade repetition). A central question with regard to private versus public funding and operation of programs is whether the definition of outcomes is narrowly organizational and monetary or broader and more humanitarian.

Accountability

Accountability is closely related to efficiency. In this case, it refers more to the delivery of results than to forms used in delivering them. Accountability is the meeting of standards and the responding to users' articulated personal and social desires.

Although national governments spend public monies on education, they are only generally accountable to the public. Bureaucracies are entrenched and most public servants cannot be voted out or replaced by the public. Locally, where school boards and committees interface directly with their constituents, the administrators and teachers in public schools may be held directly accountable for the services delivered. Yet, for the most part, little attention is given to early childcare and education. Moreover, criticizing those who are viewed as experts (in childhood education) is not considered appropriate in many parts of the developing world.

One may assume that accountability will improve if private institutions operate childcare and education centers and/or if parents have to pay fees for a service. However, this assumption may not be accurate in cultures where market values do not dominate and lines of authority and forms of relationships differ from those in the market-oriented developed world. Bray (1998) provides examples of both situations.

Quality

As with accountability, advocates of private-sector education programs argue that these programs, which charge fees, will be of higher quality than public-sector education because the programs have to be responsive to clients within a competitive environment. This argument is not linked primarily to lack of funding, although this issue may be relevant, but to features of private education, such as the ability to clearly define outcomes and expectations, the selection and retention of good teachers (Rothstein, Carnoy, and Benveniste 1999), the use of evaluation, and a greater propensity to innovate (Finn, Manno, and Vanourek 2000). The argument depends on the assumption that users will be able to define, recognize, and monitor quality and that quality will be a primary consideration when they choose among programs.

A contrasting argument suggests that allowing private organizations to operate programs could reduce quality because tangential, but related, factors (market imperfections) may influence users' decisions, interfere with competition, and diminish an organization's responsibility for accountability. For example:

- Low-income parents who must work may need childcare, but they may have little choice among programs because they cannot pay for expensive programs and must avail themselves of low-cost, potentially low-quality private alternatives if higher-quality public programs are not available or accessible or operate during their work hours. In this instance, distance, hours, and cost take precedence over quality.
- Parents may not be aware that they qualify for programs that would provide quality care and education and/or they may not be informed of the potential benefits of a quality program that offers services beyond simple custodial care. Knowledge is not uniformly distributed.

These "imperfections" in the system may allow operators to "cut corners" and reduce quality, for example, by hiring inexperienced caregivers and teachers at low salaries. Operators may offer users acceptable tradeoffs (e.g., longer hours, but reduced quality).

In a study of selected public and private schools in California, Rothstein, Carnoy, and Benveniste (1999) suggested that the location of schools in high- or low-income areas was more important to the clarity of a schools' goals and the teachers attracted to a school than whether the school was public or private. The results of a recent comparative study in Latin America (Casassus and others 1998) showed that the test scores for children in Cuba (an entirely public system) were clearly superior to those for children in Colombia (which has mostly private elementary and secondary schools).

In a recent survey (Myers 2000a) conducted for the Year 2000 Evaluation of Education for All, at least three ECD professionals from different developing world settings mentioned that the number of private organizations providing very-low-quality early childcare and education was expanding rapidly, and they urged institution of government controls. In sum, the availability of private organizations for early childcare and education does not guarantee higher-quality programs and may even result in lower-quality programs, depending on the circumstances.

Equity

Discussions of the role of the private sector become more negative when focusing on equity. In this instance, the private sector is often cast as a villain, a possible source of inequity, rather than social correction. Most private offerings are assumed to be available only to those who can pay for them, a situation that can create (or reinforce) a divided social system. In this case, the elite have access to quality private schooling, while the poor "make do" with an inferior public system, and urban children are favored over rural children.

Tooley (1999) suggests that this assumption may be misconceived because (a) the public provision of services can be inequitable and has hidden costs, and (b) innovative private programs for disadvantaged populations can be identified. Tooley (1999) presents eighteen examples of privately operated programs which demonstrate the potential benefits of private education, mainly at secondary and higher education levels. He highlights operators that established "tutoring" programs which became large-scale, alternative education programs characterized by low fees and results comparable with, if not better than, those of public institutions. However, Tooley does not clarify the meaning of "low cost" or the benefit of these programs to the poor, as distinguished from the lower-middle-class or middle-class population.

Some argue (Sancho 1999) that tapping alternative sources will enable governments to target public subsidies better and to increase the flow of funds to programs for the poor. The unstated assumption is that this flow of funds will reduce inequities because the poor will have greater access to programs. However, if private programs tend to be of better quality than public programs, as is also argued, a two-tiered system will be created, and inequity will be related to quality rather than to access. That is, the public system will provide "second-rate" programs for the poor, and the private system will provide quality programs for those who can pay. Lack of access to quality programs is seldom considered an indicator of continuing inequity.

This view may be exaggerated because, as already noted, high-quality public programs exist, as well as poor-quality private programs. Nevertheless, there are sufficient examples of inequitable, bifurcated systems related to quality. Equating increased access directly with improvements in equity should be questioned.

Diversity and Choice

Discussions of private education also involve questions related to the choices among diverse approaches. The offerings of public education tend to be homogeneous, and large-scale public programs have difficulty responding to parents' demands for specific attention during the school years to cultural and religious differences. Public school systems also have difficulty entertaining alternative curricula, which has led to the growth of private schools operated by religious or cultural groups that are in the minority or are attracted to specific curricula (e.g., Montessori, creative arts) not sanctioned by educational authorities.

These tendencies within public schools may be moderated by decentralized systems with local control of curricula and the hiring of teachers. However, there will still be groups whose desires are not adequately represented in the public school system, and these groups have, historically, developed their own schools as a preferable alternative. The desire to respond to parental desires and to marginalized social groups can be applauded as a celebration of diversity, but may also reinforce social disjunctions and separateness.

Involving the Private Sector

The broad view of the private sector, adopted in this chapter, includes business and social organizations and individuals that are not directly involved in providing early childcare or education, but have resources that could be tapped to benefit young children. Two of the components depicted in figure 1—business organizations and adults without children (column 1, rows A and C)—could become much more involved in early care and education. Potential ways of involving these businesses and individuals are suggested below.

Involving Private Enterprise

Noncare, noneducation businesses may desire to invest in, or support, early childhood programs because of enlightened self-interest, social responsibility, and/or altruism. With regard to their self-interest, businesses may wish to consider three pertinent findings:

- Research suggests that company employees who do not have to worry about the care of their children will be better workers and have less absenteeism.
- The good publicity gained from participating in social programs can help sell products.
- Some forms of contributions can result in tax exemptions.

Improving the quality and productivity of the labor force is advantageous to private companies, for their own self-interest and the general public interest. The growing research literature on ECD links investments in early childhood to better performance in school and enhanced productivity later. Although the fact that healthier, more intelligent children will be more productive workers later in life is intuitively obvious, employers sometimes have difficulty accepting this long chain of causality because it is hard to envision and such investments do not yield immediate payoffs. The connection between education and productivity is more obvious and convincing for programs at secondary and university levels, when the children and youth are older and the direct relationship between training and work can be visualized more easily.

Support can be provided, or is already being provided, to ECD programs by private businesses in several general ways—within companies, outside companies in the broader social arena, and collectively. Possible ways to contribute are suggested below.

Within Companies

One way of supporting early care and education is "at home," focusing on company employees. When government does not require companies to provide childcare or maternity benefits, some firms have taken the initiative to provide these benefits to their own employees. The benefits may include:

- Instituting flexible work hours so that parents can better attend to childcare at home.
- Establishing a childcare or early education center onsite, operated by the firm or under contract with a separate service provider. Whether onsite services will be useful and successful depends somewhat on the distance employees have to travel to work. This approach has not been particularly effective in many developing countries because working mothers do not want their children to endure long trips twice a day on crowded public transportation.
- Providing parents with a cash benefit or voucher to be used for a program that meets certain standards.
- Providing parental education programs for employees.
- Asking employees to contribute to general social programs (e.g., the United Fund in the United States, which usually includes some support for early childhood programs) or to more-specific early childhood programs sponsored by the company or conducted by others.

The suggestions above entail "extra" expenses for a business, which many companies in the developing world are not willing to entertain, particularly when their comparative advantage in the world market depends on maintaining low production costs. Companies are not likely to take these actions unless they see direct benefits to productivity or have a large social conscience. An example is the noncompliance with laws in many developing countries which require businesses with more than a certain number of female employees to provide a childcare center onsite. Even in these situations, most firms do not provide day care, and most governments do not enforce the law. In some settings, the result may be institution of a "cap" on hiring female labor (to keep the numbers low and avoid providing childcare), or female laborers are hired temporarily and rehired periodically (or let go) so that the firm can avoid paying a benefit.

Partly because businesses are reluctant to provide employees with childcare and early education benefits, many governments have included childcare within mandated social security benefits. Other ways governments have helped companies afford these benefits for their employees include allowing companies an exemption from taxes or from paying child-related social security benefits if the companies provide their own services or other benefits.

Outside Companies, the Broader Social Arena

Another approach, which can generate even wider support for ECD, is for firms to provide support for new or ongoing programs operated by governments, private educational firms, organizations in the social sector, or individuals. The business community does, and can, support these efforts in many ways—by paying taxes, supporting philanthropies, contributing to social trust funds, "adopting" schools, and donating products or services. Taxes and philanthropic programs are the two most prominent indirect forms of contributions by private enterprise to ECD for the public good. These forms of contribution are addressed below, as are the other, more direct, ways to contribute to ECD.

Paying Taxes. Tax contributions by private enterprise to support social programs, including programs for young children, are sometimes overlooked, perhaps because they are not always visible to the public and do not involve direct, easily credited actions by companies. Contributions to ECD that are made through general taxation and budget allocations are likely to be small for individual companies and for the entire private sector because tax rates are relatively low, ways may be found not to pay taxes, and a very small proportion of general budgetary allocations are spent on young children.

Sometimes, however, taxes are earmarked. Paying into a social security fund used, in part, to support childcare programs operated by the public sector or an approved agent is one form of earmarking. Mexico and Sweden are two countries that earmark taxes in this way, whereas the United States does not (Myers 2000b). These funding arrangements, which tap private-sector funds, are usually shared with employees, who pay a portion of their salary into the fund, and government, which contributes from general revenues. The earmarked funds also may be used to support maternity and job-leave benefits for parents. Liberal arrangements for maternity support are available in Sweden and most socialist countries. In the developing world, however, they are seldom available or are honored only in special circumstances. And, unless companies are monitored, earmarked taxes may deter some from hiring female employees, because these employees will increase a company's costs.

In Colombia, one variant of this form of contribution is the requirement that each organization, private or public, pay a 3 percent payroll tax designated for early childhood activities of the Colombian Institute for Family Welfare. The program supported is organized and controlled by the government and operated by communities, as is usually the case when private-sector contributions are made through taxes to the government.

Establishing a Philanthropy. Philanthropic giving has expanded greatly across the developed world, but is still in its infancy in most countries of the developing world. Nevertheless, foundations established by major companies operating in the developing world are beginning to gain social importance. A philanthropy established by a business to donate all or part of its funds to ECD may continue to be linked closely to the company or may become totally independent, operating as part of the not-for-profit social sector.

Funds from a philanthropy can be used to support many possible initiatives to improve early child development. For example, they can support centers operated privately or publicly, and they can be used for the full range of complementary strategies in ECD (e.g., centers, parental education, child-centered community programs, training and other forms of capacity building, advocacy).

Recent history indicates a relatively low level of involvement of philanthropies in ECD, although specific data are not available. However, the trend appears to be changing slowly as increased contributions are spurred perhaps by the search for new activities to support, new knowledge about the importance of early childhood, changing social and economic conditions, human rights considerations, and other reasons. The cases described in the next chapter (e.g., the Abrinq Foundation for Children's Rights, the Aga Khan Foundation) illustrate the growing philanthropic involvement of the private sector. However, despite these pioneer and continuing efforts, the shift toward greater support for ECD does not appear to apply yet to the developing world in a significant way.

Establishing and Helping to Operate a Social Trust Fund. Businesses could become more directly involved in ECD by establishing and helping to operate a social trust fund. As a demand-responsive form of involvement, the fund would support programs proposed by care and educational institutions, rather than preset packages of activities. Businesses could operate the fund like a philanthropy or have a much more active and protagonistic role (e.g., providing direct technical or legal support to early childcare and educational institutions, offering loans, becoming involved in advocacy efforts).

A social trust fund is an excellent opportunity for building partnerships across sectors to support ECD, involving governments, private enterprises, and international organizations in contributing to a common fund. All contributors and potential users could be represented on an oversight, governing committee, and an NGO could be established to operate the programs using the fund's resources. The fund could operate nationally, internationally, or within countries in particular geographic or political areas.

A major purpose of the fund would be to help create and strengthen ECD programs. Activities would be focused on helping communities, NGOs, and small entrepreneurs establish and improve programs, and the fund could provide additional support to institutions financed and/or operated by government. Emphasis could be placed on developing strategies of self-sufficiency for institutions serving lower-income groups that cannot afford to pay the full costs of services. Technical assistance could be provided to help eligible institutions develop proposals for funding.

"Adopting" a School. Programs for companies to adopt a school have been established in Costa Rica and Paraguay. The companies offer the school a range of assistance, such as helping with construction; purchasing or donating materials; and providing management advice, scholarships, and food. One example is the Arauco Company in Chile which provides support to various local community schools (UNICEF and Fundación Andes 1994). For privately operated schools, companies may help support a capital fund, sometimes on a matching basis, to provide a guaranteed, ongoing source of financial support from the earnings of the fund.

Donating Products or Services. In the past, private enterprise often has provided in-kind assistance to various parts of the educational system. The most notable example of this assistance is the large-scale donation of new computers. In the United States, for example, a mechanism has been created to recycle computers replaced by businesses. A similar mechanism could be created in developing countries to help communities and NGOs administer and provide early childcare and education. Other in-kind contributions by private enterprise have been mostly for elementary schools and include donations of school supplies (e.g., paper, crayons, books), construction materials, and sometimes food.

Other opportunities for involvement that are less related to immediate needs or expenditures are also available. For example, for community or private schools, industry could donate products that can be resold, and donations could be used to build sustainability by helping local institutions develop their own capital funds. Or, industry could offer management assistance to schools, for most institutions of early education are administered by individuals who have no management experience. Courses could be developed to help directors of early childhood centers, operated by community organizations or NGOs, perform self-diagnoses of the centers' organizational and financial condition.

Some larger private businesses will be able to offer specialized assistance, such as computer support or other examples suggested below:

- Book publishers could provide courses for entrepreneurs in early childcare and education using books and materials they already sell.
- Banks could offer small loans, possibly on favorable terms, to small entrepreneurs in education. Or, credit card arrangements could be made, similar to those used to accumulate "frequent travel" miles, to assign a small percentage of one's purchases to a fund for care and education.
- Communications organizations can help publicize educational options and offer expertise and "air time" to support campaigns for early distance education and to sensitize and inform parents (e.g., CNN's current agreement with UNICEF, the World Health Organization, and others to inform the public about children's rights). Telephone companies could allow messages to be printed on their telephone bills to reach a large number of families.

Collective Involvement

Besides the possibilities for individual companies' involvement in ECD, collective contributions from the private sector are also possible and perhaps more feasible. Examples of collective involvement in education include the Coffee Growers Association in Colombia and the Sugar Growers Association in Guatemala.

Establishing a committee to help monitor whether particular firms are providing the benefits or services that should be provided under law in relation to young children could be one form of collective involvement. A "seal" could be created to identify companies considered to be "child friendly."

Involving Private Citizens

Private citizens who are not parents can play a role as individual philanthropists in support of ECD. Other opportunities have been addressed elsewhere, such as use of vouchers, which privatize education and increase parents' choices for their children's education, and individuals' donation of time to help care for or educate young children, a phenomenon often found in many settings of the developing world, but not the developed world.

Individual Philanthropy

In the developed world, churches, charities, hospitals, and other organizations have long recognized the value of soliciting funds from private individuals, a tradition of microphilanthropy that has developed and perhaps been abused. Large international NGOs (e.g., Save the Children, Christian Children's Fund, Plan International, World Vision) are among the institutions that have used this approach to support programs to improve the condition of children in the developing world. These organizations have been very successful in obtaining funds by establishing programs for individual donors to "sponsor" a child or family in the developing world, drawing their funds mostly from individuals in the developed world. Although some of this philanthropic tradition also exists in the developing world, individual philanthropy is not as strong as in the developed world, partly because the number of middle- and upper-income people who can individually donate funds is much smaller.

Nevertheless, individual involvement in childrearing by nonparents in communities of the developing world may be very high because of extended family and kinship arrangements and traditions of community work. In addition, similar to the developed world, a new approach to involvement is arising as individuals are asked to make financial contributions to social programs. For example, in

Bangladesh, GrameenPhone appeals directly to individuals for financial assistance, and, in Colombia, the Center for International Development and Education is experimenting with an appeal for donations from Colombians living outside Colombia.

The explosion of the Internet greatly expands possibilities for microphilanthropy to a new level. For example, a small European group used the Internet to appeal for assistance after Hurricane Mitch, raising US$200,000 almost overnight. Because of this success, the group is considering developing a mechanism for similar appeals that would include, for potential donors, a "menu" of NGOs in the developing world and short presentations of their programs. The organizations (and appeals) would be screened independently to validate their authenticity, experience, and need. One technology is already available to facilitate such an effort. As reported in *TIME* magazine (Schenker 2000), "… technology industry executives spoke to some of the world's largest banks at the [recent] Davos meeting about using digital certificates so that small amounts of money can be transferred between individuals." Undoubtedly, there are many examples of similar potentially fruitful efforts in the developing world, and documenting them and learning from their successes and failures would be useful.

Conclusion

This chapter has explored possible opportunities for involving components of the private sector in early child development. The main observations are summarized as follows.

1. Involving the private sector is different from privatizing. "Privatization" is a much narrower concept that refers to the shifting of ownership and operation, and sometimes financing, from governmental organizations to nongovernmental organizations or individuals. "Involving the private sector" is a broad notion that refers to the wide participation of all components of the private sector in a full range of activities.

2. For early child development in the developing world, privatization may not be the main issue, as suggested by the very high proportion of private-sector support for early childcare and education programs and the high proportion of early childhood programs operated privately. Rather, the task may be to identify ways for various parts of the private sector to help parents with their child's education, to improve existing childhood programs operated by the private sector, and to partner with government to improve access to, and quality of, programs financed and administered by the government. Attention may need to be given to making early childhood programs more public and involving governments in a field they have been reluctant to enter.

3. The arguments for investing in ECD may be compelling to governments and different social organizations, but may not be convincing to private businesses or individuals that may expect direct, private payoffs, or returns, from their investments, particularly if the businesses or individuals are not already involved in early childcare or education. If the private sector does not assume some responsibility in this area, and governments do not act, ECD programs will be underinvested (i.e., the level of private-sector benefits will not match the level of social benefits ECD programs can provide).

4. The assumption that there are knowledgeable consumers and competitive markets in many settings of the developing world is doubtful. The lack of these ingredients in many settings undercuts existing arguments for privatization, which postulate improved quality, accountability, and efficiency by offering incentives to private providers or funds to consumers for choosing among options.

5. The criteria for evaluating the effects of increased involvement by the private sector or privatization of early childcare and education include changes in levels of funding, access, accountability, efficiency, quality, diversity and choice, and equity. Applying these criteria may lead to contradictory conclusions. For example, the tendency to use the criteria of funding and access

often leads to neglect of equity and differences in quality, or in-equity. Shifting the balance between public and private support affects these criteria in different settings, and researchers have yet to accumulate all the evidence about these effects.

6. The opportunities for involving noneducation and noncare businesses in early childcare and education are many. One promising approach is their participation in establishing and operating social trust funds.

7. Individual microphilanthropy is another promising approach for tapping private-sector resources that has not been promoted or examined widely within the developing world.

Note

In writing this chapter, the author benefited from papers or thoughts by Jeffrey Puryear, Miriam Waiser, Claudio Castro, Henry Levin, Stephen Heyneman, Mark Bray, and Ellen Mangenheim. The responsibility for the contents is solely the author's.

References

Bray, M. 1998. Privatization of Secondary Education: Issues and Policy Implications. In J. Delors, ed., *Education for the Twenty-First Century: Issues and Prospects*. Paris: UNESCO.

Bronfenbrenner, U. 1979. *The Ecology of Human Development*. Cambridge, Mass.: Harvard University Press.

Casassus, J., J.E. Froemel, J.C. Palafox, and S. Cusato. 1998. *Primer Estudio Internacional Comparativo Sobre Lenguaje, Matemática y Factores Asociados en Tercero y Cuarto Grado*. Santiago, Chile: UNESCO, Regional Office for Education in Latin America and the Caribbean (Chile), Latin American Laboratory for Evaluation and Quality of Education.

Finn, C.E., B. Manno, and G. Vanourek. 2000. *Charter Schools in Action: Renewing Public Education*. Princeton: Princeton University Press.

Mangenheim, E. 1999. Preschools and Privatization. Paper presented at the conference on Setting the Agenda for the Center of the Study of Privatization in Education. Columbia University, Teachers' College. Mimeo [Forthcoming from Westview Press in a volume edited by H.M. Levin.]

Myers, R. 1995. *The Twelve Who Survive: Strengthening Programs of Early Childhood Development in the Third World.* Ypsilanti, Mich.: High/Scope Press.

———. 2000a. Early Childhood Care and Development, A Global Review: 1990–1999. Paper for UNICEF and The Education for All Forum, contributed to the Year 2000 Evaluation of Education for All. Paris: The Education For All Forum. [Available on http://www.unesco.org/education/efa]

———. 2000b. Financing Early Childhood Care and Education Services. In M. Neuman, ed., *International Journal of Educational Research* 33:75–93.

Plank, D., and G. Sykes. 1999. How Choice Changes the Education System: A Michigan Case Study. In C. Soudien and P. Kallaway, eds., *Education, Equity and Transformation.* Dordrecht, The Netherlands: Kluwer Academic Publishers, in cooperation with UNESCO Institute for Education.

Rothstein, R., M. Carnoy, and G. Benveniste. 1999. *What Public Schools Can Learn from Private Schools.* Aspen, Col.: Economic Policy Institute.

Sancho, A. 1999. *Sintesis del la Conferencia sobre Oportunidades de Inversión en Educación Privada en Países en Desarrollo.* Washington, D.C.: International Finance Corporation.

Schenker, J.L. 2000. Plans to Dotcom the World. *TIME Europe*, Feb. 14, 40.

Schweinhart, L., H. Barnes, and D. Weikart (with W.S. Barnett and A. Epstein). 1993. *Significant Benefits. The High/Scope Perry Pre-school Study Through Age 27.* Ypsilanti, Mich.: High/Scope Press.

Tooley, J. 1999. *The Global Education Industry. Lessons from Private Education in Developing Countries.* London: Institute of Economic Affairs, in conjunction with International Finance Corporation.

UNICEF (United Nations Children's Fund) and Fundación Andes. 1994. *Aportes de la Empresa Privada al Mejoramiento de la Educación en Chile*. Santiago: UNICEF.

Van der Gaag, J. 1995. *Private and Public Initiatives. Working Together for Health and Education*. Washington, D.C.: The World Bank.

Chapter 11

Communities Can Make a Difference: Five Cases Across Continents

Simone Kirpal

This chapter presents five case studies of community-based early child development (ECD) programs. The cases are examples of good practice, which gives priority to extensive involvement of the local community to create ownership and establish successful, cost-effective, and sustainable programs. The case studies highlight ways the private sector can influence public policy and provide insight on two key issues:

- How do effective ECD programs involve local communities to become culturally and financially sustainable?
- Can private-public partnerships enhance the potential for taking ECD programs to scale?

Both questions are closely related. Knowing how high-quality ECD programs can reach the most vulnerable and poorest children and enhance their life chances without being prohibitively costly is important for providing technical support to governments, advocating for ECD programs, facilitating decisionmaking about these programs, and justifying investments in them. Moving programs to scale and increasing their accessibility by lowering unit costs is one way of reaching out to poor children and to rural areas. Yet, if programs are meant to have a lasting effect on changing and improving the condition of children and society, they must be culturally sustainable and respond to local needs and demands. Only if local communities are involved in programs and take ownership of them will ECD programs persist and continue to have the same positive effects when outside donors cease their funding.

Five Case Studies: Overview

The five cases presented in this chapter share certain commonalities. They all provide direct ECD preschool or center-based services to poor communities. In addition, all programs have developed a training component to train teachers and/or caregivers. They all rely on some form of community support and are struggling with the issue of scaling up to reach more children. The cases, all examples of effective programs, are summarized briefly below and described separately in greater detail later in the chapter.

The *Montessori Preschool Project* in Haiti offers a 9-month teacher training course for scholarship students from poor communities who have relatively low education levels, enabling them to become certified Montessori preschool teachers. On graduation, the teachers are given financial support to return to their community to establish preschools, mostly in poor and rural areas, if the local communities provide the necessary resources for the schools to become financially sustainable after a few years. Since its inception in 1986, the project has trained more than 450 teachers and has supported forty-three preschools spread throughout Haiti, serving approximately 2,000 children each year. Recently, two additional centers for training teachers have been established to increase local capacity for early childhood education.

The *Mother-Child Day Care Center Services (MCDCCS)* in Uganda provides low-cost, high-quality childcare for children ages 0–10 years to help poor working mothers living in slums and rural trading areas become economically self-reliant. The program aims to improve the condition of young children by empowering mothers and supporting their development so that they can better provide for their children. In addition to providing a safe and stimulating environment for children and reliable childcare services, which enables mothers to work, the three MCDCCS centers offer a variety of integrated programs, which include counseling on child health and breastfeeding, family planning, parenting skills, and literacy. Approximately 6,600 children have benefited from the program since the first center opened in 1987.

SERVOL is a nongovernmental organization (NGO) in Trinidad and Tobago that has developed and administers several education programs in disadvantaged and poor areas of the country. The programs include an early childhood care and education (ECCE) effort, a parent outreach program, an alternative school enrichment initiative for secondary school students, a skill training program for adolescents, and a high-technology course for young people ages 20–25 years. All programs, including content and monitoring, are operated entirely by individuals in the community. Initiated in 1971, SERVOL's programs have gradually become sustainable financially and, in 1987, the government of Trinidad and Tobago, through the Ministry of Education, established SERVOL as its agent for nonformal education and assumed payment of salaries for teachers and instructors. Currently, SERVOL administers, manages, and closely monitors 160 public ECCE centers in Trinidad and Tobago.

The Aga Khan Foundation supports two efforts, the *Madrasa Resource Centers* (MRC) in Kenya, Uganda, and Zanzibar, which work with disadvantaged Muslim communities to help establish community-owned and community-managed preschools, and *Improving Pre- and Primary Education* (IPPS) in rural Sindh, Pakistan, which helps local communities establish and manage their own preschools and primary schools. These efforts emphasize the strengthening of local capacity to improve the quality of basic education and often involve partnerships with NGOs and local governments. The IPPS and MRC project teams conduct community awareness and mobilization activities; help develop curricula and leadership skills; identify partners' roles and responsibilities; and train and support communities and school management committees in organizing, establishing, managing, and financing their own ECD activities or primary schools. Special emphasis is given to the education of girls and the empowerment of women by, for example, ensuring that girls constitute at least 50 percent of the total enrollment and selecting and training local women as teachers, heads of schools, and members of school management committees. By early 2000, the MRCs were working with approximately 130 communities across East Africa, and the IPPS project, which began in 1996, was working with 12 communities to establish preschools and primary schools. IPPS plans to expand to another six to eight communities in rural Sindh and to work with mothers and other caregivers, focusing on children under 3 years old and on childrearing practices in the home.

The *Step by Step* program differs from the other four cases in not originating from within a local community in a developing country. Instead, the program was designed originally for former communist countries and implemented initially in Central and Eastern Europe and the Former Soviet Union. Gradually, the program has spread to other parts of the world, including Haiti, Mongolia, and South Africa. Step by Step provides a teaching methodology to guide and support education reform. It includes materials, courses, and training programs, for teachers and caregivers, which introduce child-centered teaching methods and support community and family involvement in preschool and primary education. The aim is to engender democratic ideas and principles within young children and their families by encouraging children to make choices, take responsibility, express their ideas with creativity, and develop critical thinking skills. The institutional reform process is reinforced by training teachers and administrators at preschool and primary school levels, introducing new course content and interactive teaching methods at universities and pedagogical institutes, encouraging cooperation on educational content and policies among different government ministries, and establishing national associations for parents and teachers. In 2000, its sixth year of operation, Step by Step was training 40,000 teachers annually in twenty-eight countries and serving more than 500,000 families and children in preschools and primary schools. The program cooperates with more than 300 institutions which train, and retrain, teachers to implement new practices.

Table 1 summarizes the activities and types and forms of partnerships in the five cases. Following on the framework suggested by Myers in the preceding chapter, the table identifies involvement of the public and/or private sectors; includes community within the private sector; and indicates the role of the community in initiating, contributing to, or participating in the programs.

Table 1. Five Successful ECD Programs: Overview

				Projects			
			Montessori	MCDCCS	SERVOL	MRC/IPPS	Step by Step
Type of program			Preschools, teacher training	Childcare, training, parent education	ECCE centers, teacher training, parent education	Preschools, training, capacity building	Preschools, teacher training, methodology
Private sector	Community involvement	Community initiative	no	✓	✓	✓	no
		Community contribution	✓	✓	✓	✓	✓
		Community participation	no	no	✓	✓	✓
	Support from international donors or foundations		✓	✓	✓	✓	✓
Government support or involvement			no	✓	✓	✓	✓
Financial sustainability			Preschools: ✓ Training: no	no	✓	Preschools: ✓ Training: no	✓ (At country level)

ECD, Early child development; ECCE, early childhood care and education.
✓, Yes.

Features of a Successful ECD Program

Comparison of the five examples of good practice in this chapter suggests several common features that account for their success. The programs give priority to the following essential elements:

- Child-centered approach
- Parental involvement and family support
- Community ownership
- Cultural and financial sustainability
- Training and capacity building
- Integration within a broader framework of development
- Private-public partnerships.

Child-centered Approach

Each of the five programs has adopted a child-centered approach that supports the integral development of each child through services addressing a child's cognitive, motor, psychosocial, and emotional development simultaneously. The teaching methods give priority to the development of individual attributes and social skills, such as self-esteem, confidence, responsibility, problem solving, and critical thinking. This approach distinguishes these programs from the countries' traditional, mainstream educational programs, which feature large classes; rote learning and memorization; a purely academic, no-play orientation; no group activities; and preschools conceived as an extension of primary schools, without accounting for the specific developmental needs of 3–5 year olds. The underlying values of the child-centered approach are particularly important when targeting poor and vulnerable children to enhance their life chances, because these children are often marginalized, stigmatized, and suffer from low self-esteem.

Parental Involvement and Family Support

A variety of adults and family members are integral to a child's daily life. One of the most effective ways of supporting a child's development is to build on the knowledge and skills that these individuals already have and to give them additional resources to enhance their roles as caregivers. Both SERVOL and the MCDCCS programs are supporting families and working directly with parents, particularly mothers. By working with adults and family members, the programs are extending their benefits to caregivers, as well as children.

ECD programs have a much greater effect when activities and patterns of communication and interaction are reinforced consistently between the program setting and the home environment. Also, a child's positive development is more likely to be sustained when ECD activities are integrated into the child's daily life than when provided for only a few hours a day. The effect of any ECD program will be limited if the program is conducted in isolation. When ECD-related activities are replicated at home, by working with parents and modifying their behaviors and parent-child interactions, the program's outreach is extended and benefits other siblings and children in the household. This extension is particularly important for children from poor households because financial constraints often allow families to send only a very limited number of young children from the same household to educational programs such as preschools. By working with parents and achieving these spill-over effects, and thus benefiting children who do not attend any form of early stimulation program, the programs attain a broad outreach at relatively low cost. Parents acquire a better understanding of their child's developmental needs and are encouraged to support their child's educational development later on, thus increasing the chances that a child will continue schooling beyond pre-primary education. Parents' interest in their child's educational achievement is an important factor that affects a child's future school performance positively (Young 1996).

Involving parents in school and classroom activities familiarizes them with the teaching environment and the (child-centered) teaching method used and ultimately increases their acceptance of the entire formal education system. This acceptance is important, because a considerable number of poor families are reluctant to give priority to investing in formal education for their children. In addition, uneducated individuals and members of socially excluded and marginalized groups often have difficulty understanding the education system and interacting with formal institutions. They may be unfamiliar with administrative procedures, feel uncomfortable and discouraged when having to communicate with administrators, and avoid interacting with teachers and school officials. In turn, the education systems in developing countries often tend to discourage parental participation (e.g., in Haiti, parents are not permitted in the classrooms). Nonformal or semiformal ECD programs can bridge this gap by providing a point of entry for parents to participate in children's development and, ultimately, support them in their educational achievements later on.

Community Ownership

In this chapter, "community" refers to the (local) community where an ECD program is anchored. It includes all formal and informal structures, social groups, and individuals. Formal institutionalized structures may include those mentioned by Myers in the preceding chapter (social organizations, community groups, NGOs, private voluntary organizations, religious organizations, business organizations, as well as local government). Generally, community involvement extends across private (for-profit, not-for-profit) and public sectors.

Except for the Montessori Preschool Project (in which all preschools are privately owned by individuals), the cases highlighted in this chapter are founded on extensive community involvement in financially supporting, implementing, and managing ECD programs. The programs have established partnerships with the communities and rely on the communities as local resources for reducing a program's costs and improving a program's quality. Community involvement and ownership are crucial to a program's effectiveness. However, the dynamics of community mobilization, contribution, empowerment, and participation affect programs differently and may, or may not, foster desired outcomes.

Community involvement is a complex process implying a wide range of activities and commitments. "Community contribution" and "community participation" are referred to herein as two different dimensions of community involvement. A local community may become involved in an ECD program by providing different types of contribution, including labor and in-kind support (e.g., to help construct a school building, operate a food canteen, or organize fundraising activities). Parents may also contribute to a program's content and quality by, for example, assisting in the classroom or creating teaching materials. Some authors refer to this type of community involvement, providing "inputs," as "passive participation." Evans, Myers, and Ilfeld (2000, p. 35) describe this participation as "the contribution of each individual to a common endeavor—a contribution of time, or labor, or money, or knowledge, or of several of these." In passive participation, parents and communities have little control or say over what actually happens for their children.

A stronger form of community involvement is the active participation of a local community, beyond mere consultations with community groups and parents to obtain input. Active participation includes shared responsibility by the groups for decisions that are made. Although passive participation is useful and may be necessary (e.g., the presence of parents or community leaders at meetings), a program is more likely to be sustainable if this participation is complemented by a community's active participation in making decisions about the program and sharing responsibilities for implementing it. Active participation requires, and results in, community decisionmaking and community management. When a program is controlled by a community, the community is much more likely to take ownership of it.

Experience shows that community involvement, in general, is effective for reducing a program's costs and creating at least minimal ownership by the community. However, the active participation of a community substantially increases potential effectiveness and long-term sustainability by fostering an extension of services, building local capacity, and empowering communities. The challenge for all ECD programs is to nurture this approach over time and to acknowledge communities as equal, full-fledged partners, rather than mere resources (Rugh and Bossert 1998). Among the cases in this chapter,

SERVOL and the MRC and IPPS projects are two examples that are pursuing this type of partnership approach most effectively.

Cultural and Financial Sustainability

In poor countries where resources and capacities of the public sector are limited, parental and community involvement are prerequisites for achieving long-term sustainability of ECD programs after outside funding has ceased. Long-term sustainability is a key issue for each of the cases presented in this chapter. All of the programs began as small-scale initiatives and have expanded gradually in response to demands from their local communities.

Sustainability has two different aspects: cultural and financial. Cultural sustainability refers to program content and teaching methods that reflect the local community's knowledge and practices of child development and socialization. In general, an ECD program is more likely to be culturally appropriate when initiated from within the local community through a participatory process, from the beginning, for program development and implementation. The SERVOL and MRC and IPPS projects exemplify how long-term sustainability can be achieved through active participation and establishment of a culturally responsive program.

An alternative approach to achieving cultural sustainability is to adapt training and teaching methods to respond to the educational and cultural context of the community and society. The Montessori Preschool Project and Step by Step program have adopted this approach. They offer a relatively flexible didactical framework (Montessori) or a teaching and classroom methodology (Step by Step) that can be adapted and modified to incorporate a community's local language, educational background, and cultural context.

Financial sustainability refers to continued funding and support to maintain and ensure the viability of a program after outside funding has ended. ECD programs designed to serve the poorest and most disadvantaged children in a community cannot exist solely on the contributions of these children's parents. As demonstrated by the cases in this chapter, additional financial or in-kind support from local communities and/or governments is needed to maintain these ECD programs over time. Each program is pursuing a different strategy for achieving financial sustainability, but all rely on local community structures and individuals for cofunding their activities.

For example, SERVOL partners with the government which is responsible for paying the salaries of teachers and instructors. The MRC and IPPS projects, Step by Step, and the Montessori Preschool Project rely on community contributions and support from local groups (e.g., churches, government, foundations), which provide buildings, matching grants, and even long-term subsidies. For both Step by Step and the MRC and IPPS projects, fundraising is important for supporting and promoting the programs. Both programs also have introduced microcredit schemes and use of endowment funds to increase their communities' financial resources, for the benefit of all participants.

The MCDCCS program in Uganda has innovatively combined microcredit schemes and income-generating activities to support children and mothers through the ECD centers. The program specifically aims to increase household incomes, in the belief that all children in a household will benefit if mothers are empowered and supported financially to better provide for them. The MCDCCS centers directly provide childcare services for working mothers; childcare and employment opportunities in small-scale, income-generating projects for unemployed mothers; and microcredit opportunities for all mothers. Throughout the program, the women's ability to pay childcare and health services fees has increased constantly over the years and the children's health and nutritional status has improved significantly.

Training and Capacity Building

In all the cases, the mere provision of childcare or preschool services is complemented by high-quality training for childcare providers or preschool teachers. All the programs have been supplemented gradually by significant capacity-building activities, to increase their local community's capacity to maintain and expand the program over time. Although these training efforts were conceived initially as a tool to facilitate small-scale, local capacity building for the programs, the training components have, in all five cases, evolved into separate, independent entities advocating holistic training approaches or methodologies for ECD. Typically, these training components are accompanied by a series of training manuals and materials. The teaching methodologies used by SERVOL, the MRC and IPPS projects, and Step by Step have expanded far beyond their initial contexts to be adopted, adapted, and further refined by other programs in other countries. This expansion demonstrates that an ECD training program can, in itself, be an important tool for scaling up successful ECD initiatives beyond their country of origin.

Integration Within a Broader Framework of Development

Integrating early interventions within the broader framework of development reinforces and helps sustain ECD programs in the long term. Several of the cases in this chapter have embedded ECD interventions in other projects designed to support parents and local communities. For example, the core ECD programs in the MRC and IPPS projects, MCDCCS, and SERVOL are sustained by a range of complementary programs addressing human, social, and economic development more broadly. Among the cases, the MRC and IPPS projects apply the most structured strategy and approach for mentoring communities, to strengthen local capacity, develop leadership skills, raise awareness, and mobilize the community. Two key principles pervade their activities: (a) empowering local women through support and training and ensuring that women are represented on all management committees, and (b) enabling communities to manage and finance their own schools.

The MCDCCS program is centered on the needs of poor working mothers and empowerment of them by providing childcare and related services. MCDCCS' integrated approach combines childcare services and training of childcare providers with parent education and other services for mothers (e.g., health education and literacy; counseling on breastfeeding, family planning, parenting skills, and

HIV/AIDS; gender equality) and income-generating opportunities for unemployed mothers. All these activities and services are integrated within each center.

SERVOL has taken a different approach, to establish gradually a series of stand-alone, but complementary, programs which include ECCE services, parenting programs, programs for secondary school dropouts and adolescents, and higher training for young men and women. With a life-cycle approach and programs for different age groups, SERVOL aims to break the intergenerational cycle of poverty.

Private-Public Partnerships

Most of the programs highlighted in this chapter began as demand-driven, small-scale projects, with one preschool or center, in response to a community's immediate needs. As the community's demand for ECD services increased, the local initiatives began to seek outside funding from international donors (e.g., private foundations, bilateral and multilateral organizations) to be able to serve more children and improve the quality of the programs.

For example, both the Montessori Preschool Project and the MCDCCS program were established and maintained on a small scale for about 15 years, receiving extensive community support and small grants from international donors. Both programs were well received by their communities, helped mothers and caregivers, benefited the children enrolled, and were financially sustainable locally. However, major investments are now needed to expand the programs to other communities and to broaden the scope of the programs. To secure its viability, the MCDCCS program is seeking to establish new centers and to invest in additional small-scale, income-generating projects. The Montessori Preschool Project is seeking to expand its teacher training program by establishing more training centers and offering continuing professional development for school teachers from all educational levels (preschool to secondary education), particularly primary school teachers.

Although such major investments will help to consolidate a program, expand its outreach, and maintain or even improve its quality, most donors will not continue to fund a program substantially over a long term. Innovative models for private-public partnerships within countries are needed to take ECD programs to scale and to sustain them over time. In general, international donors cease or reduce their funding after 10–15 years. SERVOL is one example. Outside donors are often willing to support local educational initiatives, but are also interested in actively supporting or creating incentives to establish a structure that will enable programs to become viable and self-sustaining over time. Having such a supportive structure is a prerequisite for moving programs to scale and should be developed at different levels—within the community, through capacity building and community support, and regionally and nationally, through generating an enabling environment and legal guidance.

The MRC and IPPS projects have focused on developing this supportive structure at the community level by strengthening the capacities of local project teams to enable communities to develop, implement, and monitor the MRC preschool program on a larger scale and to manage the IPPS preschools and primary schools. The projects also encourage local NGOs to partner with local governments.

The Step by Step program is working locally as well as regionally and nationally, but is giving priority to initiating an institutional reform process that will ultimately be accepted and supported by government institutions. SERVOL is a unique case of a nonformal ECD program moving to scale and becoming financially sustainable through private-public partnership. Although now fully supported by the government, legally and financially, SERVOL has been able to remain truly community-based and community-managed and, yet, is the government's formal agent for delivering nonformal education services and administering 160 public ECCE centers. SERVOL is truly a success story, but the process has taken more than 20 years.

Conclusion

The goal of any community development program should be to enable a process that will be maintained after outside funders leave.

One way to begin this process is to have those who will ultimately be responsible for the program take ownership of it from the beginning. A partnership approach to planning, funding, and implementing a program enables parents and community members to gain the knowledge and skills they will need to continue the initial program (sustainability) and to create additional programs on their own (replicability).

In early child development, parental and community involvement is a particular strength and resource for achieving highly effective programs that are culturally appropriate. In addition, parental involvement will increase the potential that elements of the programs are replicated at home and integrated into children's daily life, thereby also extending the program's benefits to other children in the household.

Because resources at the household level are extremely limited in poor countries, communities become crucial partners in providing financial and in-kind support for ECD programs. In countries that have weak institutional capacities, communities are the greatest asset. But, communities alone cannot establish and maintain large-scale programs. They need support from other stakeholders, including governmental and nongovernmental agencies, local funders, and the private sector. Long-term financial sustainability of ECD programs can only be ensured when both the private and public sectors become equally involved in supporting an ECD initiative and creating an enabling environment for developing the program further. Ultimately, these partners will complement parents' and families' contributions to fund and maintain a program in the long term. The case studies in this chapter demonstrate that new forms of private-public partnership need to be developed and institutionalized to reinforce these processes because support from international donors is usually temporary and limited in taking ECD programs to scale.

Community mobilization and parental participation are relatively easy to achieve in early intervention programs, compared with other educational services, because preschool education and other

ECD services for children ages 0–6 years benefit children, parents, and other household members *directly*. Although Lokshin and Tan (2000) refer to improvements in child outcomes through ECD interventions as "direct" benefits, and Myers (1995) refers to the positive effects of ECD programs on household income levels and well-being as "indirect" (or immediate) benefits, this distinction may not be necessary. "Freeing up" family members for economic activities or attendance at school by providing childcare services can also be interpreted as a direct benefit of ECD programs, and enhanced parenting skills benefit parents, children, and younger siblings equally.

These benefits accrue from all ECD services that provide some form of childcare. The services benefit parents, and particularly mothers, by providing increased opportunity for income-generating activities. They also benefit other family members, especially older siblings, by liberating them from childcare responsibilities, in many cases enabling, especially, girls to continue their education. Programs that also provide counseling on the broader aspects of child development (e.g., health, nutrition, breastfeeding) support parents in their roles as caregivers, enhance their parenting skills, and educate and empower them.

Another factor resulting in a high level of parental support for ECD programs, compared with, for example, sending children to primary or secondary school, may be the relatively low opportunity costs for families as preschool-age children are not expected, in most societies, to help in the household or on the farm and generally are not yet, or only randomly, involved in economic activities.

The unique combination of these features in ECD programs offers great promise for mobilizing families and communities with limited resources in developing countries to invest in young children at an early stage. As exemplified by the five case studies in this chapter, ECD programs that combine these features are most likely to be effective and sustainable and to have the greatest impact on children, families, and communities. Each of the five cases is described in detail below.

1. Haiti: Montessori-Based Teacher Training and Preschools

The Montessori Preschool Project provides high-quality, internationally recognized teacher training. Through a scholarship scheme, individuals with limited economic resources are financially supported to become certified preschool teachers and to open their own preschools. The project was created and is supported by the Peter-Hesse Foundation, Solidarity in Partnership for One World, a non-profit organization registered in Germany and Haiti. Peter Hesse started the foundation in 1981 for the purpose of sustaining small self-help projects for poor people in Haiti. Initially, the foundation focused on 2-day seminars on project management for self-help groups and on alleviation of small financial bottlenecks, mostly for rural initiatives. In 1984, the foundation changed its emphasis to early childhood care and development, which led to creation of the foundation's first teacher training center (in 1986), the Centre Montessori d'Haiti.

Mission

The Montessori Preschool Project aims to influence Haiti's education sector, at public and private levels, by demonstrating that high-quality early childhood education is possible—even with limited resources—if the quality and length of teacher training are adequate. The mission of the Montessori program is to give poor children a better chance to develop themselves early enough through quality teacher training and creation of community-based preschools. The training of qualified teachers translates directly into increased local capacity to provide early stimulation and education programs of good quality to children ages 2.5–5 years.

Cultural Context

Haiti's culture is based heavily on oral communication. Teachers are accustomed to memorizing and reciting teaching material, but have difficulty applying this knowledge in the classroom. To improve application, most of the Montessori training course is presented through oral instruction in Creole, the local language. In addition, the project adapted the curriculum to the needs of student teachers in Haiti, adding substantial practice time to help them transfer theory into practice. The student teachers must complete supervised internships, create didactical material, and be able to adapt everyday objects as teaching tools. Haitian teachers compensate for a shortage of books and materials by developing their own lessons, teaching materials, and visual aids.

Methodology and Approach

Montessori education embraces a child-centered philosophy that emphasizes individuals' learning paths and the capabilities of each child. Children can access different kinds of materials freely and are encouraged to learn at their own pace. The freedom for purposeful activity allows children to develop not only their intellectual faculties, but also their powers of deliberation, intuition, independence, and self-discipline, as well as the social awareness and behavior needed to function in the world. Teachers and children are taught mutual respect and nonaggressive behavior; competition is strictly avoided.

In the Montessori approach, didactical materials present knowledge to children in an orderly way so that their intellect can classify the information into an organized system of thought. This process of working with the material exercises a child's intellect constantly and expands the child's mental abilities. The effectiveness of the material derives from the thoughtfully planned manner of its presentation, which flows from:

- Concepts presented in isolation (which reduces the confusion of receiving too many ideas at once), to
- Appreciation of various difficulties in isolation, from easiest to most difficult (for young children, from concrete to abstract), to
- Use of a graduated series of self-teaching materials suited to the various stages of a child's development, to
- Incorporation of body movement (occupation) for specific purposes (i.e., combining movement and mental concentration).

More than 50 percent of the didactical material for Montessori preschools, including most reading material, is produced locally. Teachers make most of the material at the beginning of the academic year. In addition, one basic set of imported Montessori teaching materials, which costs approximately US$1,000, is provided to each new preschool. Because the Montessori teaching material benefits the child's cognitive development even when a teacher does not fully understand the didactical background, teachers who do not completely comprehend the Montessori pedagogy can become effective teachers. From training in the Montessori teaching method, people from poor communities and with relatively low levels of education have become certified teachers.

Children attending Montessori preschools range in age from 2.5–5 years and, in exceptional cases, 6 years. Classes are not divided by age groups, and children are invited to learn from each other and to interact across ages. Older children learn to take pride in helping weaker and smaller children and, thereby, enhance their social skills.

Implementation

Montessori student teachers complete a 9-month training course, a final examination, and two 6-week internships in an affiliated Montessori school. They can receive three types of diplomas: assistant's diploma, national teacher diploma, and international Montessori directress/director diploma. All student teachers are examined and given their diploma by the Centre Montessori d'Haiti. To obtain the international diploma, students must pass all parts (written, oral demonstration, practical) of the national examination conducted by the Centre Montessori d'Haiti, demonstrate a complete understanding of the Montessori philosophy, and pass a second examination conducted by an outside, internationally recognized specialist. About 20 percent of all Montessori-trained student teachers have obtained the international Montessori directress/director diploma, which certifies them as Montessori teachers entitled to teach and open schools in Haiti and around the world. After teaching for 1 year, they can also become assistant student teacher trainers in one of Haiti's Montessori training centers.

About 50 percent of all Montessori student teachers are scholarship students who sign a contract with the Centre Montessori d'Haiti which obliges them to teach for 3 years in a poor community after they complete their training. Most teachers return to their own locale to establish a school, and most extend their commitment beyond the initial 3-year agreement.

All Montessori project preschools throughout Haiti are strongly linked by their common structures, teaching philosophy, and administrative organization. Each summer break, the teachers gather for a 3-week workshop to share experiences and enrich their teaching skills. During 1996–97, the Centre Montessori d'Haiti interrupted its teacher training courses to strengthen the Montessori preschool structure across Haiti and to conduct evaluations. Also in 1996, seventy-five Haitian Montessori teachers established the Association Montessori d'Haiti (AMOH), a professional teachers group.

Evolution

The Montessori Preschool Project in Haiti began in 1986. Since then, forty-three Montessori preschools have been established, and forty-one are still operating, having persisted in Haiti's turbulent years of political instability. They provide services, in sixty preschool classes, for about 2,000 children each year from poor communities.

Sustainability and increasing local teaching capacity are essential aspects of the project. When it began, one Montessori training center, with a preschool class of twenty-five children, trained twenty teachers in the first 9-month course. Both the center and the class were directed by expatriates. Under the leadership of a London-trained Montessori specialist from Trinidad, the capacity of the center soon grew to an annual average of forty students, mostly women. Recently, two additional training centers were established with financial support from the Peter-Hesse Foundation and are linked closely to the original center. With all three centers, the Montessori project currently has the capacity to train sixty teachers each year.

The forty-one operating Montessori preschools include one for children with human immunodeficiency virus infection, one for deaf children, and two attached to an orphanage. Since the project began, an average of three new preschools open each year. Over the years, only one preschool has ceased operation, and one has returned to Haiti's traditional system of rote learning. Classes remain "small" (thirty children per class), compared with the traditional Haitian classrooms of sixty children. To date, 450 teachers have been trained; 297 have received national teacher diplomas, and 83 have received international teaching diplomas. The increase in local capacity to train qualified teachers translates directly into increased capacity to provide high-quality stimulation and education programs for preschool-aged children. The children stay in the Montessori schools an average of 2 to 3 years. Of the 2,000 children enrolled each year, only about 10 percent drop out. About 660 children graduate each year, and more than 80 percent continue on to primary school. Parents do not seem to favor enrollment of boys over girls at the preschool level, which helps to increase the number of girls going on to primary school.

Financial Support

The average annual financial support for the Montessori Preschool Project has been US$100,000 or less. Often far less has been available, but funding has always been sufficient to support the project. Financing is secured privately by the founder and approximately fifty individual donors per year. The German government occasionally assists with small grants to cover exceptional needs. The United Nations Development Programme (UNDP) and the German Development Service (DED) have financed a U.N. volunteer in past years.

The foundation's funding supports overall project coordination and supervision and scholarship students who later teach in schools for disadvantaged children in poor communities. In addition, each new preschool receives US$3,000–$4,000 in startup funds which are used to purchase a basic set of Montessori teaching material, help with school construction and administrative organization, and procure technical advice. Montessori graduates are encouraged, and financially supported, to open Montessori preschools for children at risk if the local community provides support to enable the school to become sustainable in the long term.

Other financial resources are limited, but sufficient to sustain the preschools and are secured through school fees and community in-kind contributions (e.g., providing a building). The Montessori training centers raise financial contributions from the regular fees paid by student teachers who are not on scholarship. The two recently established training centers are paying back startup funds to the project by providing scholarships for a number of student teachers each year.

Principles of Success

The success of the Montessori Preschool Project can be attributed to the following characteristics.

- *Driven by Demand.* The Montessori Preschool Project started small and has expanded in a sustainable manner.
- *Community-based.* Schools are opened only when requested by a community and when community involvement proves to be reliable.
- *Teacher Ownership.* Teachers privately own the schools and are accountable for financing, student performance, and school reputation.
- *Financially Sustainable.* Schools and training centers become financially independent after approximately 1 year.
- *Culturally Relevant.* The project builds on indigenous cultural patterns, and the teaching methods are adapted to the local language (Creole) and oral culture.
- *Well-defined Selection Criteria.* Selection criteria for student teachers are clearly defined, and scholarship students are screened carefully to ensure their future commitment to rural communities.

- *Low-income Employment Opportunities.* The project provides employment opportunities for low-income individuals. Poor students who have completed secondary education can become qualified and certified teachers and are supported to open their own preschools.
- *Economically Inclusive.* The program brings together teachers and children from different economic backgrounds. The combination of poor and rich students helps the schools become financially sustainable and achieve a good reputation.
- *Successful Teaching Method.* The Montessori approach builds self-esteem, confidence, problem-solving skills, and positive life attitudes.

Outlook

The Montessori Preschool Project is making strides in going to scale, program evaluation, and advocacy and visibility.

Going to Scale

Haiti continues to have a great unsatisfied demand for high-quality preschools. With the two new Montessori training centers, training capacity has increased from twenty to sixty teachers per academic year. This increase is expected to have long-term spill-over effects as new teachers open new preschools in poor communities.

To improve the educational standard in Haiti, better teacher training is needed at all school levels. The Peter-Hesse Foundation proposes to establish a resource center to provide assistance and professional development for teachers of preschool and primary school. To improve their skills in teaching and curriculum development, teachers using the center would be able to participate in continuing education and special-topic seminars with professional education experts. They would have professional assistance to access print and electronic media materials, do research, and review didactical materials for specific classroom needs. To reach working teachers, the center would be available to any teacher from the public or private sector and would remain open during off-work times (e.g., Saturdays, vacation periods).

Program Evaluation

In addition to its own 1996–97 evaluation, the Centre Montessori d'Haiti is pursuing an independent external evaluation of the project's effect on the educational outcomes of poor children and the professional development of proficient preschool teachers.

Advocacy and Visibility

Promoting high-quality early child development and education as a priority in development politics, in Germany and internationally, is an important part of the foundation's activities. For broader visibility, the foundation registered as an NGO and is represented in several childcare networks and at international early child development and U.N. conferences. The foundation's "Three Suggestions for One World Development" was selected as input from NGOs to the U.N. World Summit for Social Development, held in March 1995. The Montessori Preschool Project was also internationally selected for presentation at EXPO 2000 in Hannover, Germany.

2. Uganda: Community-Based Mother-Child Day Care Center Services

Community-Based Mother-Child Day Care Center Services (MCDCCS) provides modern, affordable childcare for working mothers living in the slums and rural trading areas of Uganda. The target group is poor, disheartened, and homeless mothers who cannot afford to pay for regular childcare services and who are not reached, permanently, by national and international programs addressing the needs of women and girls.

Using an integrated approach, MCDCCS offers a variety of programs to help these women, including formal and nonformal education (e.g., literacy courses), counseling on breastfeeding and family planning, promotion of safe motherhood, public health education (e.g., hygiene and nutrition) for children and mothers, assistance with health issues and immunization, promotion of gender equality and girl's education, enforcement of positive childrearing practices, training of childcare workers to the certificate level, and creation of employment opportunities for mothers through income-generating projects and microcredit facilities.

The microcredit facilities from the centers' revolving funds are MCDCCS' most important services. For many women, these facilities offer the only way to borrow money to cover their social, domestic, and business-expansion needs and to pay school fees for their children. Loans are most often used to pay for prompt medical treatment for sick children.

Mission

MCDCCS has adopted the philosophy that "women empowered are children liberated." Its mission is to improve the conditions of young children and end the cycle of poverty, illiteracy, and ignorance, beginning with their mothers. The belief is that, once poor women are freed from constant childcare and are given the chance to become economically active, the future of children will be ensured.

Cultural Context

In many African countries, including Uganda, men strive to show their worth by fathering as many children as possible. This practice is particularly true for unemployed, low-income, working-class men. Uganda's illiteracy rate is high, and studies reveal that the number of educated and self-sufficient women is low, compared with other countries. The majority of women carry the burden of childbearing and childrearing, often with little or no financial support. High illiteracy and birthrates remain a problem that stalls the productivity and potential of many women.

In 1997, the Uganda government introduced Universal Primary Education (UPE), for four children per family initially and with plans to include all Uganda's children in the near future. This proposal was intended to benefit girls; however, their traditional role at home and in the workplace makes their attending school from early ages on, without interruption, almost impossible. Several other government-launched programs directly related to the advancement of women in Uganda do not reach the poorest and most marginalized women and mothers because they are not able to take advantage of these programs.

Methodology and Approach

The MCDCCS program aims to improve the condition of young children by empowering mothers to become economically productive and less ignorant. When women are liberated from constant childcare and become involved in financial activities, the future of their children is safer, healthier, and more productive, and girls are freed from their roles as surrogate mothers caring for younger siblings.

A breakthrough can be made only if women and family issues are addressed together and the specific needs of targeted women are taken into account. When low-cost, high-quality childcare services are provided for infants from a few days old to children more than 10 years old, mothers can become self-reliant economically and provide better for their children's basic needs.

In contrast with traditional Ugandan childcare centers, which are expensive and provide services for children aged 3 and older, the MCDCCS centers focus on children from ages 0–8+ years. MCDCCS' general approach is integrated and holistic, and the program addresses issues such as child health, family planning, gender concerns, and special needs of girls. Besides providing a safe environment for children and educating their mothers, the centers train caregivers and teachers and generate employment opportunities for women through small-scale, income-generating projects and microcredit schemes.

MCDCCS is an important step toward increasing women's independence and helping them attain a position to negotiate greater control over family planning and birthrates, safe motherhood, and the curbing of sexually transmitted diseases, especially HIV/AIDS. An integrated approach also fosters education of women at the grassroots level and supports health initiatives (e.g., immunization campaigns) and the practice of positive public health habits (e.g., proper use of latrines).

Implementation

Three MCDCCS centers are currently operating. Oriented wholly toward serving mothers' needs, they are located near the workplace (i.e., markets) so that mothers can conveniently drop off and pick up their children. The centers operate from 6:30 a.m. to 6:30 p.m. If a child is less than 1 year old, the mother is required to come in periodically to breastfeed. The centers offer hourly drop-off arrangements and after-school care for older children. They also help mothers acquire immunization cards, which are required for all children, and keep track of immunization records.

Over time, the centers have become special places for both mothers and children. They have become focal points for learning, teaching, and relaxing—places where women can openly discuss their major concerns of daily life. The centers also are vital safe havens where battered women and children in crisis can find shelter and counseling. More than 90 percent of battered women who seek refuge come with their children. Trust and understanding, which are nurtured in the centers, build a foundation for broader health and education programs, particularly family planning services. These services are open as well to women who do not have children in the centers.

Basic data on the centers are monitored carefully and regularly. Some important findings are as follows:

- Between 1987 and 1999, more than 900 mothers used MCDCCS services and approximately 6,600 children benefited from the program.
- Children who attend the centers beginning at an early age (i.e., from a few days to 1 year old) perform much better in all aspects of child development and skill learning than children who begin coming to the centers at age 3 or later.

- Infant mortality among MCDCCS children is extremely low (3 out of 6,600 children compared with Uganda's average of 83 per 1,000 live births) .
- The growing demand for family planning services has led to a decreased number of very young children (less than 1 year old) in the centers, from a daily average of twenty-five in 1987 to four in 1999.

As women are liberated from childcare duties, they can engage in economic activities to better provide for their family. A mother's ability to pay the monthly fees for childcare services promptly can be interpreted as a direct indicator of a reduction in poverty. Between 1987 and 1999, the number of MCDCCS mothers who paid promptly increased from 20 percent to 50 percent despite a tenfold increase in fees.

Mothers who attend the centers' programs soon become agents of positive change within their homes, communities, and workplaces. Community-level indicators for evaluating and monitoring the effect of the MCDCCS centers include:

- Increased number of women requesting family planning services
- Improved weight and overall health status of children attending the centers
- Decreased infant and child mortality rates
- Increased immunization coverage
- Increased school readiness and, thus, school attendance, especially for girls
- Increased literacy rate among girls
- Decreased population growth rates
- Decreased rate of sexually transmitted diseases, especially HIV/AIDS
- Improved living conditions for center children diagnosed with HIV/AIDS, as a result of receiving proper care, adequate feeding, and prompt medical treatment

- Better opportunities for center mothers diagnosed with HIV/AIDS, to continue working if they can
- Reduced violations of children's rights (e.g., sexual abuse, child marriage, child mothers)
- Improved parenting skills of women.

Evolution

In 1994, a group of Ugandan women, who were members of the Uganda National Council of Women (now known as the National Association of Women Organizations in Uganda, or NAWOU), initiated a project for underprivileged women. The aim was to give poor women struggling in Ugandan slum areas a chance to become more productive economically, more confident, and better able to care for their children properly.

This group identified the burden of continual childbirth and child-rearing as the greatest handicap to economic productivity of women and increased school enrollment rates for girls. Affordable, high-quality, mother-child day-care centers were proposed as a practical solution to enhance poor children's chances by providing a safe, healthy, and stimulating environment. In addition, these centers provided a setting for gradually introducing related educational and health programs.

After the project was initiated, the mothers began to view the day-care centers as special places where they could ask for advice on almost everything concerned with daily life. Related educational and health programs were introduced gradually and, in time, the centers evolved into sanctuaries where local women and children could learn, teach, and relax.

Financial Support

The MCDCCS strategy combines income-generating efforts with financial support from international donors and assistance from national governmental and nongovernmental agencies. The program generates money by collecting small fees from the mothers for child-care services (as mothers' potential for economic productivity increases, they are expected to pay higher fees for services); engaging in income-generating activities, such as poultry (selling eggs and hens) and pig farms; operating small farms and gardens for subsistence-level production of local fruits and vegetables; charging fees for training services; and renting out the main hall of the centers for special events.

MCDCCS offers employment possibilities for unemployed mothers who use the centers' childcare services. An average of sixty workers per month, mostly mothers, are employed in the three centers and for the income-generating projects.

The Ministry of Education provides technical assistance to maintain the legal and professional status of the centers and a training school. Family planning materials are supplied by the City Council of Kampala, Department of Health. The program also receives major technical and financial support from NAWOU, which promotes MCDCCS locally and helps establish international contacts. In the past, the Swedish International Development Cooperation Agency (SIDA) provided a grant of US$15,000, and the United Nations Educational, Scientific, and Cultural Organization (UNESCO) provided a grant of US$25,000.

At the Development Marketplace 2000, held February 8–9, 2000, in Washington, D.C., MCDCCS received US$90,000. The Development Marketplace provides a forum to identify and nurture innovative ideas in the development community. In a competition open to NGOs, businesses, academia, foundations, and bilateral and multilateral agencies, the Development Marketplace awarded approximately US$5 million in startup funds for project proposals to reduce poverty. MCDCCS committed the new funds to improve and update the three existing centers; expand services by starting three new centers; increase its income-generating potential by producing children's books and teaching material and expanding farm production; increase local capacity—through training, supervision, improved teaching material, performance assessments, and evaluation—to provide high-quality childcare services; introduce new elements, such as music and computer equipment and skills; and launch a major marketing campaign (e.g., using posters, radio, newspaper, and TV announcements) to create awareness of child development issues related to health and education in the early years and the positive role of the family.

Principles of Success

The success of the MCDCCS program can be attributed to the following characteristics.

- *Holistic Approach.* Creatively, MCDCCS combines early child development, parent education, and family planning with job creation and income-generating activities.
- *Targeted Needs.* The program is designed to meet the specific needs of one of the poorest and most marginalized groups in Uganda—illiterate and excluded women in slum areas.
- *Community-based.* The centers are community-based and adjust their programs to meet mothers' needs.
- *Flexible.* The program is flexible in providing education and health programs on demand.
- *Monitoring.* The centers carefully monitor the children's growth and their motor and cognitive development.
- *Linkages.* MCDCCS has wide and various spill-over effects because the centers establish linkages between nonformal education for women, health education, and family planning with other national health and immunization campaigns.
- *Empowerment.* MCDCCS alleviates poverty at the grassroots level through empowerment.

Outlook

The MCDCCS program is planning for long-term sustainability, influencing public policy, and improving literacy among Ugandan women.

Sustainability

With six centers, MCDCCS plans to become financially sustainable by expanding its income-generating activities, providing professional training for teachers and caregivers, and enhancing the ability of mothers to pay higher fees for childcare.

Advocacy

MCDCCS envisions having a broader influence on public policy by raising awareness of the need for mother-child services in communities and eventually achieving a nationwide effect.

Literacy

One center program that has not reached most MCDCCS women is literacy. The mothers' key objective is survival and, beyond that, they rely on the centers to enable them to increase profits from their businesses. They cannot imagine spending precious time studying. The mothers also note that, because they are now able to educate their children, the children can read and write for them if needed. As long as women are poor and struggling to survive, they will not consider literacy a priority. Only by establishing day-care centers on a massive scale will girls be able to begin their education early and in large numbers. These centers, in the long term, will dramatically help reduce the number of illiterate women in Uganda.

3. Trinidad and Tobago: Integrated Education and Early Childhood Program

SERVOL (Service Volunteered for All) is an NGO in Trinidad and Tobago that administers high-quality education programs in disadvantaged areas. The programs include a parent outreach program for parents ages 17–30, an early childhood program for children ages 2.5–5, a nonformal secondary school program for children ages 13–16, a human development and skill training program for adolescents ages 16–20, and a high technology program for young men and women ages 20–25.

All programs are operated entirely, both in content and monitoring, by people from the community. Each of the 160 early childhood centers and 40 adolescent centers operate under the auspices of a village board of education, which hires and fires teachers in consultation with SERVOL. These boards convene monthly meetings to obtain input from parents, and they regularly canvas 4,500 adolescents to obtain their views on the effectiveness of the programs and suggestions for improvement, which are then implemented.

Mission

SERVOL is "igniting the fires of hope." It is an organization of weak, frail, ordinary, imperfect, and yet hope-filled and committed people seeking to help weak, frail, ordinary, imperfect, and hope-drained people become agents of attitudinal and social change in a journey that leads to total human development.

Cultural Context

The Black Power riots, which took place in Trinidad and Tobago in 1970, were interpreted by Fr. Pantin, the founder of SERVOL, as a "cry for help" from the ghetto. As he walked up the hill of Laventille to try to respond, he was confronted by the social problems of the area and its people: unemployment, poverty, and low self-esteem. Fr. Pantin observed that the main cause of these problems was a total breakdown of family life, coupled with inappropriate parenting practices. Not knowing how to respond to the situation, he decided to begin by listening to the people and helping them start their own small projects.

The people first asked SERVOL to establish early childhood programs (focused on day care, not education), and they subsequently challenged SERVOL to give their children access to quality education, computers, and advanced electronics. SERVOL became a people's organization committed to the building of bridges between the ghetto and the world of commerce and industry by offering high-quality programs to low-income families. To ensure that these programs meet international standards, SERVOL's Early Childhood Teachers' Certificate is validated by Oxford University, and its Hi-Technology programs are examined by the firm of Cambridge Information Technology.

Methodology and Approach

SERVOL's pioneers believed that previous efforts to help poor people had been largely unsuccessful because well-meaning "do-gooders" assumed, with cultural arrogance, that they could organize intervention programs without consulting the beneficiaries. SERVOL insists on beginning by asking, "How can we help you?", and then by *listening attentively* to the response, before attempting to organize any projects. SERVOL calls this type of intervening in the lives of people "respectful intervention."

SERVOL's pioneers also observed that many poverty programs attempted to address one or more problems in isolation but that poverty reaches every aspect of life and demands an integrated approach. Although lack of financial resources is clearly an important factor, it is not the most debilitating affliction of poor people. More pernicious is the sense of powerlessness and hopelessness that, for most poor people, makes climbing out of "the pit of poverty" virtually impossible. To meet this challenge, SERVOL embraces the empowerment of individuals, families, and communities through integrated educational programs designed to revive hope.

SERVOL's guiding principle is to use people from the community to develop the community. Ninety percent of the 600 teachers, trainers, and administrative staff are grassroots community members. All programs are truly community-based and parent-oriented. The community boards of education manage the SERVOL centers; employ the teachers and instructors; pay their salaries and their National Insurance and Health Surcharge contributions (from government funds transferred to their accounts by SERVOL); monitor teachers' attendance, punctuality, and performance; and dismiss delinquent teachers in consultation with SERVOL.

Implementation

The aims of SERVOL are implemented through a variety of programs to reach across a range of age groups in the community. Five major programs are described below. These programs have stood the test of time and their current success reflects a sometimes long and difficult development effort.

Parent Outreach Program

Guided by latest research findings in neuroscience and the social sciences, SERVOL established the Parent Outreach Program (POP) to give poor children a good start. Evidence shows that children's growth and development between 0 and 3 years largely determine how they will develop and learn subsequently and that, by the time they reach age 6, they are resistant to change. Waiting for children to enter primary school is too late to begin to attack the effects of poverty. Efforts must begin with pregnant mothers, many of whom are single parents who, because of financial and psychological stress, may neglect or batter their children.

To reach these families, SERVOL has trained twenty-five POP facilitators who visit the remote villages and ghettos of Trinidad and Tobago each day, going from house to house, making friends with parents, and helping them deal with their problems with small children and life in general. The facilitators praise the parents for their accomplishments and counsel them on the importance of proper nutrition, breastfeeding, and alternatives to physical punishment. In subsequent meetings, small groups of parents share common problems and possible solutions. The facilitators also teach the parents income-generating crafts enabling them to earn money while staying home with their children.

An extension of the POP program is Parent Partners. Under this activity, one parent from the village agrees to be trained to work with the POP facilitator, and small day-care facilities, for three or four children, are established in the houses of selected parents who are willing to be trained in day-care skills.

POP facilitators do not project the conventional image of professionals who have all the answers, an approach that may intimidate parents; rather, the facilitators praise the parents for their accomplishments in difficult situations and convince them that they are the primary educators of their children and can solve their own problems with a little help. The POP program has been received enthusiastically by thousands of parents, acknowledging their growth in parenting skills and self-confidence. Many have become successful entrepreneurs in making crafts and other products while staying home to care for their children.

ECCE Program

SERVOL has established and supervises a national ECCE program that involves 160 centers and more than 300 teachers serving almost 5,000 children ages 2.5–5 years. All teachers have been carefully trained, and most have received an Early Childhood Teachers' Certificate validated by Oxford University.

Like POP, this program is guided by SERVOL's belief that "what goes on in the home is more important than what goes on in the school." A high-quality early childhood education that is community-based, parent-oriented, and administered by trained teachers is one of the most important ways to bring about desirable, fundamental change in poverty situations. The ECCE program extends empowerment from the child and parents (emphasized in the POP program) to the community and, importantly, encourages and permits teachers to influence parents' childrearing practices. The program is intended to have a cumulative effect on parental practices over time. The community actively participates in the operation of the centers, which are managed by the village board of education.

Junior Life Center Program

With few exceptions, all children enter primary school in Trinidad and Tobago (ages 5–12). However, only 80 percent of the 30,000 children who attend and complete primary school enter secondary school. The vast majority of this large number of children who drop out come from poverty areas and are so "turned off" by the traditional educational system that special approaches are needed to rekindle their hope. SERVOL's Junior Life Center (JLC) program offers more than 6,000 children ages 13–16 an innovative curriculum designed to restore self-esteem and enable them to rejoin the mainstream educational system.

In this program, classes are small (one teacher for twenty-five students), and each corner of the classroom has a special function, serving as a miniature bank, post office, department store, or supermarket. These "props" are used to teach literacy and mathematics and to demonstrate that learning can be fun. Data show that 70 percent of these children perform very well in the post-primary examination and are able to return to traditional secondary schools.

Adolescent Development Program

Another feature of the educational system is the high number of 16–19 year olds who do not complete school or complete school functionally illiterate and with limited knowledge. Reasons include poverty (resulting in chronic absenteeism), substance abuse, and an overly academic approach to education that is unsuitable for young people seeking vocational training. SERVOL's Adolescent Development Program (ADP) is designed to serve these young people and has graduated more than 40,000 adolescents over the past 30 years.

ADP is a four-stage program. It begins with a 3-month intensive attitudinal component, which transforms hostile adolescents who have battered egos into confident young adults who learn to understand themselves through a variety of courses in, for example, self-awareness, spirituality, literacy, emotional understanding, rap sessions, public speaking, and art analysis—all administered by trained staff. Most importantly, both young men and women are exposed to an Adolescent Parent Program in which they learn about the needs of their future children and interact with babies and toddlers in reinforcing practical sessions held in the centers' day-care units.

In the second, 9-month, stage, the young adults pursue technical training in a skill of their choice from fourteen vocational courses offered. They are then placed with private companies for job training, which is evaluated by the company. At the end of this training period, they graduate from SERVOL and seek employment or apply to

SERVOL's sister organization, FUND-AID, for a small loan to purchase equipment and become micro-entrepreneurs.

SERVOL graduates have a reputation as reliable and hardworking employees, most of whom find a job within a year. A number of surveys reveal that 78 percent of all companies interviewed would give preference to SERVOL graduates because they display a more positive work attitude and a good work ethic, a result that was confirmed in a 1998–99 study. Evaluation studies also show that SERVOL's female graduates tend to postpone childbearing until their mid-20s—a significantly higher age than the norm of 16–18 years. So far, SERVOL has not had any problem with any "delinquent" students taken in at the request of the Ministry of Education. Each year, the Ministry asks SERVOL to accept thirty to forty adolescents who are deemed unmanageable by their school principals; at the end of the 3-month ADP, these young people can return to their original school or pursue a vocational course with SERVOL.

Hi-Tech Program

Five years ago, SERVOL assessed its accomplishments after 25 years. Despite its documented success, dissatisfaction arose with its graduates' lack of access to technology careers. Although SERVOL had successfully trained thousands of carpenters, practical nurses, electricians, and other skilled experts, most of whom had secured employment, SERVOL's graduates had no access to the world of high technology that was sweeping over Trinidad and Tobago. As a consequence, SERVOL explored funding possibilities to provide opportunities for technology careers.

Recently, the Inter-American Development Bank (IDB) agreed to fund SERVOL's Hi-Tech project, offering postgraduate courses in computer technology, digital electronics, and computer control electronics in one of SERVOL's three Hi-Tech centers, which graduate 400 students yearly. Local industry hires many of these graduates immediately. Among the 1998–99 class, 53.0 percent were placed in jobs immediately and 20.7 percent opted for further education. Only 26.3 percent of all graduates could not be placed or contracted.

Evolution

Three months after Fr. Pantin walked into the ghetto of Laventille in 1970, he confessed to a resident, Chaca, that he was "getting nowhere" and was thinking of returning to his teaching post at St. Mary's College. Chaca was vehement in his protest: "You cannot do that! It is true that you have done nothing more than get jobs for a few dozen kids, but what you have really done is to bring hope to the area. Every morning you walk up the hill, those watching you think, maybe tomorrow it will be my turn to get a job. And once people have hope, they will continue the struggle."

Initiated in 1971, SERVOL achieved sustainability in 1987 when the government of Trinidad and Tobago, through the Ministry of Education, established SERVOL as its agent for nonformal education and assumed payment of the salaries of teachers and instructors, which were formerly paid through grants from overseas foundations. In 1992, based on a very special private-public partnership agreement, the Ministry of Education assumed full financial responsibility for SERVOL's programs.

SERVOL still "walks up the hill" every day, but Fr. Pantin and Chaca have been replaced by thousands of adolescents, hundreds of early childhood educators, and scores of outreach workers who visit parents. This growing number of trainees, instructors, and preschool children proclaim silently to people throughout Trinidad and Tobago: "We are SERVOL and we bring with us a message of hope."

Financial Support

1971–86

In this initial period, SERVOL depended heavily on the financial support of overseas foundations. The main contributors were the Bernard van Leer Foundation, The Netherlands (for the ECCE Program); Misereor, Germany (for ADP); Helvetas, Switzerland (for infrastructure development); the Inter-American Foundation, United States (for rural agricultural and development programs); Save the Children, Canada; and Development and Peace, Canada (for training and equipment).

Although SERVOL's programs clearly provided a valuable service to Trinidad and Tobago, the government provided no support initially, except for two contributions for the construction of two adolescent centers. However, the business community and the public provided significant support. Eventually, SERVOL was able to derive some 15 percent of its total income from the production of its adolescent training departments, which accepted construction and maintenance contracts from customers.

1987–91

The new government in 1986 asked SERVOL to expand the ECCE Program and the ADP across Trinidad and Tobago. Unfortunately, the new government had inherited an almost bankrupt economy and had few funds available to support expansion. With support from three foundations that had been providing significant funding over the previous years (the Bernard van Leer Foundation, Misereor, and the Inter-American Foundation), SERVOL was able to negotiate a 5-year contract with the Ministry of Education. Under this contract, SERVOL secured foundation support for the expanded program over the next 5 years (1987–91) on a declining basis, beginning with total funding for 1987 and dwindling to zero funding in 1992; the Ministry of Education provided minimal funding in 1987 and gradually increased its contribution to total support in 1992.

1993–2000

In 1992, the Bernard van Leer Foundation indicated that it would cease funding for SERVOL. This announcement posed a financial challenge because the Ministry of Education funded only salaries of teachers and instructors and SERVOL depended entirely on the foundation for support of administrative and infrastructure expenses.

SERVOL proposed that the foundation help establish an endowment fund to eventually make SERVOL independent of overseas financial support. SERVOL launched a vigorous fundraising campaign, focusing on banks and local business conglomerates, and the foundation matched every dollar SERVOL collected. SERVOL's endowment fund currently has approximately US$3.5 million and SERVOL is almost self-sufficient.

SERVOL and the Ministry of Education currently have a tacit agreement whereby the Ministry officially recognizes SERVOL as its agent for the development and dissemination of early childhood and adolescent programs in Trinidad and Tobago. Since 1990, the government budget includes an annual subvention to SERVOL. SERVOL operates relatively autonomously in implementing its nonformal education programs, with the stipulation that it submit regular reports and annual audited accounts to the Ministry.

The government has entrusted the entire ECCE program to SERVOL, and SERVOL plays an active role in influencing public policy and the funding of ECCE programs. When SERVOL began to develop its own ECCE program in the 1970s, the government of Trinidad and Tobago was not interested in early intervention programs. The only public program consisted of fifty preschools based in community centers and managed and staffed by young women with little or no training. SERVOL embarked on a public education program to alert the population to the importance of the early years of childhood. By 1981, SERVOL had become known throughout the Caribbean as the agency that offered high-quality training for early childhood educators. Over the past 20 years, SERVOL has trained approximately 600 teachers from all over the Caribbean region to certificate level, as validated by Oxford University. As a net effect, the SPICES curriculum developed by SERVOL is now used widely throughout the Caribbean and has been adopted for teacher training programs at the School of Continuing Studies of the University of the West Indies.

Four recent, significant events highlight SERVOL's importance and positive effect on ECCE in Trinidad and Tobago:

- *Maintaining Government Support.* When the new government in 1992 slashed the ECCE budget by 40 percent, SERVOL mobilized the 150 communities operating parent-supported ECCE centers. As a result, the Senate postponed discussion of the national budget until the government guaranteed restoration of the ECCE budget.

- *Securing IDB Funding.* SERVOL had campaigned to increase the salaries paid to the training staff and teachers of its 150 centers. In 1996, the IDB, Ministry of Planning and Development, and SERVOL signed a grant agreement which effectively doubled the salaries and significantly improved the status of teachers. This agreement implies that the Ministry of Education will assume this financial commitment when the IDB grant expires.

- *Expanding POP into the Ministry of Education.* In 1993, the government commissioned a task force to review the entire education system of Trinidad and Tobago, and SERVOL's executive director was asked to chair the ECCE subcommittee. One of the subcommittee's resolutions suggested application for a loan to build and staff fifty new preschools and to augment POP by paying for twenty-five additional parent outreach facilitators. This resolution signaled a breakthrough in educational policy.

- *Establishing an Association for ECCE.* By 1999, enthusiasm for ECCE had increased remarkably, fueled largely by the growing number of trained personnel emerging from SERVOL. A number of these graduates formed an association for ECCE in Trinidad and Tobago which included ECCE personnel from the private and public sectors.

Principles of Success

The success of SERVOL can be attributed to the following characteristics.

- *Idealism.* Idealism permeates the organization, empowering people to transform their own lives every day. SERVOL shows how a person, in contact with small children, adolescents, mentally challenged individuals, parents, and communities, can become a change agent. The SERVOL staff complete each day exhausted, but electrified, because by helping others change, they are themselves transformed in rewarding and satisfying ways.

- *Decentralization.* SERVOL is a decentralized organization and all participants have enough room and autonomy to be creative. As the organization expands, bureaucracy is avoided as much as possible.
- *Constant Training and Retraining of Staff.* As a relatively small organization, SERVOL invests much time and money in continual training of staff and building sustainable capacity in order to be able to rely on its own human resources and to promote staff within the organization. Staff members have risen from instructors and coordinators to the highest levels of administration, and approximately 25 percent of the staff were formerly trainees in the ADP or ECCE program.
- *Tight Fiscal Control.* All of SERVOL's finances are carefully controlled. Vouchers and receipts are required for even minor financial transactions.
- *Fulfillment and Satisfaction.* Most significantly, SERVOL offers everyone an opportunity to contribute to a noble, righteous cause outside of themselves. Many of SERVOL's dedicated staff stay at SERVOL even when apprentices they have trained return and say they are making more money than their instructors.

Outlook

SERVOL is striving to reach out to more children, extend ECCE programs to children ages 0–2.5, and engage private childcare centers in ensuring high-quality standards. SERVOL has also successfully expanded its programs to other countries worldwide.

Going to Scale

SERVOL has established the groundwork for high-quality ECCE in Trinidad and Tobago and seeks to build on this accomplishment by expanding the program so that every child ages 2.5–5 years has access to high-quality services. To reach out to the majority of the poorest children, the number of the current 160 public ECCE centers must be doubled or even tripled.

Extended ECCE

By the time a child enters an ECCE center, inappropriate parenting practices during the first years may have already caused considerable damage. One aim is to extend the current ECCE programs to children between the ages of 0 and 2.5 years to complement the efforts of the POP program. Support of preventive programs is far easier and less expensive than repairing damage that has already occurred.

Improved Private ECCE

In addition to the 160 public ECCE centers that SERVOL closely monitors and regularly evaluates, Trinidad and Tobago has approximately 600 privately operated ECCE centers, most of them lacking supervision and adequate quality standards. More support for private childcare centers and monitoring is needed to improve their operations, train teachers, and ensure that the center structures are adequate.

Expansion to Other Countries

SERVOL has expanded its ADP and ECCE program to almost every country in the English-speaking Caribbean and as far afield as South Africa and Ireland. Expansion to a country begins with an invitation from SERVOL to interested persons to visit a SERVOL project. If the individuals decide that the project is applicable to their country, they are invited to send a senior person to spend time (from 3 months to 1 year) to be trained as a teacher trainer and then return to the home country to initiate the project.

4. East Africa and South Asia: Capacity Building and Innovations in Early Child Development

The Aga Khan Foundation (AKF) is a private, nondenominational development agency created under Swiss law in 1967. It operates in fourteen countries through field offices located in Kenya, Uganda,

Tanzania, India, Bangladesh, Tajikistan, Pakistan, and Mozambique. AKF focuses on four main areas: rural development; health; education and enhancement of NGOs, organizations, and related concerns including community participation; and women and the environment.

AKF currently supports more than 100 projects and programs. Twenty-five of these are related to education, approximately half to the Young Children and the Family (YCF) program and half to the School Improvement Program (SIP). The overall goals of these two programs are to: (a) increase the quality of formal and nonformal educational settings and of early childhood care and development (ECCD) programs, and (b) increase access, completion, and learning achievement rates for disadvantaged groups, especially girls, isolated rural children, and poor urban children.

AKF is part of the wider Aga Khan Development Network, a group of institutions interested in social and economic development and in promoting and supporting culture. The foundation collaborates with governments (e.g., Canada, United States, Switzerland), other donor agencies (e.g., European Commission, World Bank), and foundations (e.g., Ford Foundation, Bernard van Leer Foundation).

Over the past 15 years, AKF has helped to create and strengthen local NGOs and selected government resource bases. Many of the NGOs partner with local governments to improve the quality of basic education. Others primarily help communities and community-based organizations establish, manage, and finance their own ECD activities or primary schools. This assistance usually occurs where alternative education models facilitate increased access to education for disadvantaged communities (e.g., rural areas, ethnic minorities) or for girls.

Two AKF-supported projects are described below: the community preschool program linked to the Madrasa Resource Centers (MRCs) in East Africa, and the preschool and primary community schools project in Sindh, Pakistan, led by Aga Khan Education Services, Pakistan (AKES, P).

Mission

The mission of AKF is to promote creative and effective solutions to problems that impede social development in specific regions of the developing world.

Cultural Context

The MRCs in Kenya, Uganda, and Zanzibar help disadvantaged urban, peri-urban, and rural Muslim communities establish community-owned and community-managed preschools. The curricula and overall ethos of the centers reflect each country's national ECD framework and/or curricula, language, and culture (e.g., the Swahili culture on the coast of Kenya and the Zanzibar islands, the Luganda culture in Uganda) and values and beliefs drawn from Islam.

The project in Sindh, Pakistan, Improving Pre- and Primary Education (IPPS), operates in rural Sindh. The AKES,P team leading the project helps communities establish community-owned and community-managed preschools and primary schools. The team helped develop a preschool curriculum that encourages the integral development of children, drawing on their parents' and communities' cultural backgrounds and values.

Methodology and Approach

Both the MRC and IPPS programs focus especially on: (a) ensuring that girls constitute at least 50 percent of the total enrollment; (b) selecting and training local women (who may not have completed grade 10) to serve as school teachers and administrators; and (c) promoting and ensuring that women are represented on management committees. Many girls and women in the participating communities have limited opportunities outside the home. The directors of the three MRCs and the director of IPPS are women.

The two programs adapt their similar approaches to their particular contexts. Both programs:

- Work closely with communities to build trust and partnership and to encourage dialogue and full participation

- Provide intensive and regular training and mentoring for communities to strengthen local capacity, develop leadership skills, raise awareness, and mobilize the communities
- Promote development and use of low-cost teaching and learning materials
- Introduce activity-based learning and develop appropriate curricula
- Support local women and promote girls' education
- Pursue financial sustainability by strengthening the local communities' capacities to manage and finance their own schools.

Implementation

Various activities are undertaken in the MRC and IPPS programs to build trust and encourage dialogue; train, mentor, and provide support; and monitor and assess progress. Key activities are described below.

Initial Community Work and Establishment of Schools

To build trust and encourage dialogue, the MRC and IPPS teams conduct initial community awareness and mobilization activities for 3 to 12 months, holding discussions with community members on key program components, including partners' roles and responsibilities. The IPPS teams conduct an initial survey of potential school-age children. The MRC teams collaborate with community development officers, who lead the mobilization and train and support school management committees for 2 years.

The AKES,P and the MRCs sign a contract with interested communities outlining the terms and conditions of the partnership and responsibilities, and the communities open bank accounts for their schools. The communities then find suitable premises for the schools. In the MRC program, existing madrasas (traditional Islamic schools usually devoted exclusively to religious education) are used when possible because they are usually vacant during the mornings; otherwise, the communities build their own preschools. In the IPPS project, the communities rent buildings, obtain donations of buildings, or build new schools. The communities also identify local women candidates to be trained by the project teams, and they elect the management committee. In IPPS, local Community-Based Education Societies (CBES), which include parents and community leaders, are formed and registered. The MRCs work with their communities to register their preschools.

Training, Mentoring, and Support

The MRC and IPPS teams provide ongoing training, mentoring, and support for trainees, who will serve as teachers and administrators in communities and schools.

MRCs. The MRCs provide initial orientation training of 1 month to introduce basic concepts of active learning, organization of appropriate learning environments, and ways to develop low-cost classroom materials. Thereafter, teachers receive in-school support once a week for 78 weeks during the 1.5 years of the contract and then two or three times a month for the duration. Teachers also meet weekly in small groups at the MRCs throughout the 2 years for planning and problem solving with MRC trainers.

IPPS. Teacher development consists of an initial 5–6 months of intensive, holistic training provided in Karachi and focused on the women trainees' personal, moral, and professional development, as trainees will have multiple roles on their return to the community (as teachers, women, and extended family and community members). Training emphasizes self-development, responsibility, mutual respect, collegiality, and teamwork. The IPPS team provides additional in-service training and biweekly follow-up support in schools throughout the first 2 years. Training also is provided to the MRC's school management committees and the IPPS' CBES on community mobilization, fundraising, basic accounting skills, and school management and planning. Most of this training occurs in the communities.

Monitoring and Assessment of Progress

Progress is monitored and assessed continually to assure quality, good management, and financial sustainability.

MRCs. Trainers and community development officers visit schools weekly to work with teachers, management committees, and the community. A Madrasa Evaluation Instrument (MEI) is completed by MRC staff and shared with the school management communities every 6 months. The results of this evaluation are discussed and used to plan for the next 6 months. The MEI is adapted from the High/Scope Program Implementation Plan and addresses the projects' main components: quality of teaching and learning, adult-child and child-child interactions, parent and community participation, school management, and appropriate use of local cultural and religious values. The MEI is an important part of the criteria for the school and community's "graduation" from the program, with expected levels of achievement outlined.

IPPS. The IPPS team meets monthly with each CBES to provide training and perform regular audits. IPPS field supervisors offer biweekly support to teachers. In addition, three AKES,P board members, IPPS professional staff, and all CBES chairpersons meet quarterly in workshops to improve management, administrative, and fundraising skills and to share experiences and solve problems across communities.

Evolution

The MRC and IPPS programs began separately and at different times, but have influenced each other as they have developed.

MRCs

The MRC program began in Kenya in the mid-1980s to address communities' concerns about strengthening children's understanding of their local culture and religion and increasing their chances for access to, and success in, formal education. A local, well-respected Muslim woman, trained as a primary teacher, began working with a few communities to develop the curriculum and approach. Over time, interest grew and the AKF helped to establish the first MRC in Mombasa, Kenya, in 1986. AKF established the MRC in Zanzibar in 1990 and the MRC in Uganda in 1993.

In the mid-1990s, AKF staff undertook an internal review of the MRCs and their preschools, which numbered three in Uganda, fifteen in Kenya, and about twenty in Zanzibar. The main issues facing the program at that time included (a) strengthening the MRCs' capacities to develop, implement, and monitor the preschool program on a larger scale; (b) addressing the financial sustainability of the preschools and ensuring that they were community-owned and community-managed and that they provided quality early learning experiences; and (c) achieving sustainability for the MRCs.

By early 2000, the MRCs were working with more than 130 communities across East Africa, each with its own preschool. The MRCs have strengthened their organizational and technical capacity and have improved their community skills. For the future, they are considering continued work with disadvantaged Muslim communities, provision of selected training of trainers and short courses for preschool teachers from a broader range of communities, and "piloting" new activities (e.g., working with parents and other caregivers).

IPPS

The IPPS project began in 1996 and currently involves twelve communities that are establishing preschools and primary schools. The schools begin with preschool classes and add on additional grades each year as the children progress. During initial development, the MRC program shared lessons with its IPPS colleagues in Pakistan. Currently in its second phase, IPPS plans to expand to another six to eight communities in rural Sindh. Additional work with mothers and other caregivers, focusing on children under 3 and childrearing practices at home, is also planned. IPPS hopes to extend its effects by mainstreaming its key lessons and approach to other NGOs working with community schools around Sindh through training trainers and, possibly, attaching these organizations' staff to IPPS for certain periods of time.

Financial Structure

MRCs

The MRCs receive cofunding from AKF and one or more of the following: the Canadian International Development Agency, European Commission, Ford Foundation, Bernard van Leer Foundation, government of Kenya, World Bank, and Rahimtullah Trust (a local philanthropy). Each community receives the equivalent of US$1,000 as an initial seed grant for learning and teaching materials and basic school equipment (e.g., low shelves, mats, outside play equipment). This money is also used as "top-up" funds for refurbishment and low-cost construction of the building. In general, the seed grant is given in small disbursements according to an agreed-upon plan and costs estimated by the community.

To address the continuing vulnerability of the preschools, especially in poorer communities, the AKF and MRCs are piloting the use of community-level mini-endowments pooled within countries and regions. A portion of the returns (5 percent) on the investment would be returned regularly as dividends to the communities to contribute to (but not fully pay) the operating costs of their preschools (including teachers' salaries, a main cost). Communities are expected to continue to ensure that the mutually agreed-upon school fees are paid (or subsidized from elsewhere) and to conduct other fundraising activities to cover any deficits or increase their endowment.

Each mini-endowment consists of a "graduation grant" of US$2,500 given to schools that meet agreed-upon criteria for graduation, which include a quality learning and teaching environment, regular and active participation of the school management committee, and regular payment of teachers' salaries for the previous 6 months. Communities also can add funds to their endowment, and up to US$2,500 would be matched by the program. With this matching program, the community could accumulate an endowment fund of US$7,500. As of April 2000, the average endowment capital per graduated school was $4,701 in Kenya, $3,640 in Zanzibar, and $2,932 in Uganda.

An initial group of thirty-eight schools have "graduated" across the three countries. AKF has held lengthy discussions with the communities about types of investment mechanisms (e.g., mutual funds, treasury bills, fixed income accounts) and with local banks, MRCs, and the national boards about management of the endowments. During 2000, the thirty-eight schools will participate in a piloting of the mini-endowment concept. This pilot effort will be monitored to assess whether the endowment is an effective mechanism for enabling schools to become self-sustaining and to determine factors that enable schools to use the endowment dividends effectively.

IPPS

The IPPS project is funded by AKF and the U.S. Agency for International Development (USAID). Since the beginning of the program, AKES,P has tried to help build long-term sustainability of the community schools and to ensure the quality and relevance of the teaching and learning process. Financially, the IPPS project has adopted a similar approach to the MRCs' mini-endowments. The goal for the community schools is to become financially self-sufficient within 2 years. Approximately ten of the twelve schools initiated during the first 3–4 year phase are currently self-sustaining financially. The following steps are taken to achieve self-sufficiency:

- Each IPPS project covers all operational funds for its schools, including teachers' salaries and operating expenses.
- During the first 2 years, the CBESs collect fees from students and additional donations from local sponsors, which are often used to off-set fees for the poorest students. These funds are deposited into a "collection account" managed jointly by IPPS and the respective CBES. IPPS does not release funds for teachers' salaries until the monthly fees have been obtained, and the CBES account only increases if the fees and donations collected adequately cover the salaries and other operating expenses.
- Money deposited into the account is allowed to grow, in accordance with banking regulations of Pakistan, for 2 years and

then the account becomes an investment fund invested on behalf of the CBES. When the CBES achieves adequate local capacity to manage the securities, the money is transferred entirely to the CBES.

- On transfer of the funds, an account is opened for the CBES to cover the schools' operating expenses. For most CBESs, the fee level is sufficient to cover operating costs and they do not need to draw on their investment funds.
- The IPPS team has developed alternative options to assist poorer communities that have not been able to fully cover their schools' operating expenses. These CBESs are organizing fundraising activities and seeking donations to cover student costs (e.g., for girls from poorer households).

Principles of Success

The success of the MRC and IPPS programs can be attributed to the following characteristics.

- *High Levels of Trust.* Both programs have built high levels of trust with the participating communities. Staff listen and work with the communities on their concerns and ideas for helping their children. The roles and responsibilities of each partner are defined clearly.
- *Community Mobilization and Organization.* An intensive process of mobilization and organization is incorporated within each program. The process includes regular support and monitoring of local management committees, especially during the first 2–3 years, to continually reinforce community ownership and the community's ability to manage ECD activities.
- *Spill-over Effects.* Success with one community can help replicate success and build trust with other communities that observe their neighbors' involvement and the positive effect of the programs on children's learning experiences.
- *Use and Development of Local Resources.* The projects rely on the local material, financial, and in-kind resources available to build

ECD centers. Major investments to develop local human capacity, focusing on women, are a priority.

- *Quality Learning.* The MRC and IPPS programs emphasize quality learning that both builds on local cultural and religious values and uses lessons and knowledge from other ECD efforts.
- *Mentoring and Follow-up.* Both programs provide continual, systematic mentoring and support. The teachers, community leaders, and school management committees benefit by implementation and absorption of ideas that are facilitated and shared through large- and small-group training exercises and continual in-school support.
- *Flexibility.* The programs are flexible and able to address and incorporate needs and issues that emerge as the programs evolve. For example, the MRCs introduced community development officers to strengthen community development efforts; the MRCs established literacy classes for mothers and in-laws; and IPPS organized nonformal classes for older, out-of-school girls.
- *Financial Sustainability.* Sustainability over the long term is the programs' major goal. Both programs achieve sustainability of schools by focusing on capacity building, testing and sharing different strategies on a regular basis, and involving all partners and stakeholders, including donors, from the beginning.

Outlook

Through the MRCs and IPPS project, the AKF is fostering demand for ECD programs; strategies of sustainability; sharing of skills and knowledge; selected research studies and evaluations; and networking among institutions.

Increased Demand

The demand from other communities for community-owned schools and teacher training programs for both programs continues to grow. The MRC and IPPS teams have to assess whether this demand will shorten the time needed to raise awareness and mobilize communities, and thus increase efficiency and reduce costs. They also need to develop new strategies and training programs (e.g., short, "alternative" training courses for interested preschool teachers).

Sustaining Quality and Organizational Inputs

Innovative strategies are needed to sustain the programs after completion of the initial intervention. Communities that have successfully completed the MRC program are developing graduate preschool associations to provide continual support and to foster interaction between schools and quality of learning and teaching. The MRCs also are training lead teachers and local community mobilizers for each school to assume the mentoring and leadership development roles formerly provided by the MRCs. The IPPS is convening regular meetings for head teachers and CBES members and is training locally based supervisors to provide technical advice for small clusters of schools.

Sharing of Skills and Knowledge

A continuing challenge for the programs is to creatively and realistically plan for disseminating the skills, knowledge, and lessons (e.g., through technical assistance, training, mentoring, or dissemination of materials) to help others adapt or replicate their work. The IPPS team does not extend the scale of its operations significantly, but focuses on training teachers and trainers from other community-based organizations instead. The MRCs are responding to other countries (e.g., in West Africa) that are expressing interest in learning about replicating and adapting the MRC program.

Research Studies and Evaluations

In-depth research and evaluation of the impact, effectiveness, and costs of the MRC and IPPS programs are necessary for internal reflection, effective program implementation at the community level, and growth. The studies are also essential to improve assessment and understanding of the effect of community-based ECD programs on children, families, and the broad community.

Capacity Building and Networking

Identifying ways to build and strengthen a variety of institutions and to encourage networking among them is essential for achieving access to quality and culturally appropriate and affordable ECD services for poor children. Nongovernmental and community-based organizations (e.g., women's groups, religious groups, preschool committees) and the private and public sectors are all potential collaborators and partners that need to be able to access expertise on technical issues, organizational development, fundraising, and financial management for long-term sustainability of ECD programs. Their efforts need to be supported by governments, local and international donors, foundations, and others.

5. Central and Eastern Europe, the Former Soviet Union, Mongolia, Haiti, and South Africa: Step by Step—Early Childhood Education Reform

Step by Step is an education reform program for infants and children, 0–10 years, that introduces child-centered teaching methods and supports community and family involvement in preschools and primary schools. The aim of the program is to engender democratic ideas and principles within young children and their families. The methods used encourage children to make choices, take responsibility for their decisions, express their ideas with creativity, help each other, develop critical thinking skills, and practice independent thinking. The program promotes the rights of all children to a quality education, and special teaching materials and training programs are designed to enhance equal access for children of ethnic minorities (e.g., Roma), refugees, children with disabilities, and families living in poverty.

Step by Step offers an innovative and comprehensive approach to institutional reform of early childhood education programs at all levels, by training teachers and administrators at preschool and primary school levels through ongoing professional development; training faculties at universities and pedagogical institutes on the application of new course content and interactive teaching methods; cooperating with education and health ministries on educational content and policies; establishing national associations for parents, teachers, and faculties; and creating an international forum (the International Step by Step Association, or ISSA) for parents, teachers, and faculties to promote open society values in education.

The Open Society Institute (OSI), a private grant-making foundation, launched the Step by Step program in 1994 to address the decline in services for young children in regions affected by the economic upheaval after the fall of communism. OSI seeks to promote the development of open societies by supporting a range of programs dealing with educational, social, and legal reform. Created by George Soros, OSI forms part of the network of Soros foundations, a group of autonomous NGOs operating in 30 countries around the world, including the countries in Central and Eastern Europe and the former Soviet Union, Burma, Haiti, South Africa, Guatemala, and the United States. The foundations support initiatives in education; civil society; independent media; Internet and e-mail communications; publishing; human rights; arts and culture; and social, legal, and economic reform.

Children's Resources International (CRI), a nonprofit organization based in Washington, D.C., serves as OSI's partner and provides international technical assistance to Step by Step. CRI has developed the program's philosophy and core written materials, which include methodologies, courses, and training programs for teachers and caregivers of infants and toddlers and for preschools, early primary grades, and institutions of higher education. CRI works with a network of trainers to provide ongoing support to each country team. The goals of all technical assistance to the program are to transfer expertise to each country and to enable country teams to continue the program in the future using their own resources.

Mission

The mission of the Step by Step program is to create an educational experience that promotes democratic thinking and action. The culture of democracy is taught and modeled day by day. By starting this process with the youngest citizens, the children, the principles of open societies are instilled in the next generation. Child-centered classrooms promote democratic principles and inspire life-long learners who are able to succeed in open societies (Hansen, Kaufmann, and Saifer 1997).

Cultural Context

Step by Step emphasizes change and democratic transformation, based on the experience of countries in transition, and addresses the continuing challenge for all democracies to provide the kinds of educational experiences that ensure continuation of open and free societies. Step by Step's child-centered philosophy is based on the work of international theorists in early childhood education (Erikson, Piaget, Vygotsky, Dewey) and is universally applicable when adapted to local cultural circumstances.

The core program components are family and community partnership, individualization of the learning process, active learning, self-initiative, self-efficacy and empowerment, shared control, freedom of thought and speech, and respect for differences and similarities. These components are especially relevant for the countries where the program is being implemented initially (in Central and Eastern Europe and the former Soviet Union, Mongolia, Haiti, and South Africa). These countries have strong traditions of teacher-centered education and are struggling to make the transition to democratic societies during a time of enthusiasm for educational reforms, tempered by harsh realities. The realities include sharp economic declines regionally; decreased social services (including early childhood programs); reduced state services for training teachers; professional isolation from Western pedagogical trends; closing of preschool facilities, due to lack of financing; and reduced funding for the remaining preschools, resulting in a reduction in national nutrition and health programs, inadequate education materials, a crumbling infrastructure, and delays in paying staff salaries.

Step by Step has sought to build on the strength of previously existing systems by "opening up" their structures to community and family involvement; developing ministry-approved retraining programs within established teacher training systems; and, initially, making contributions to rebuild the preschool infrastructure. The program has focused on developing, in each country, a professionally based (rather than politically, state-based) NGO that can contribute to a plurality of approaches in education and the development of civil society.

Methodology and Approach

As described by OSI and CRI (1998), the Step by Step program:

- Is a program of teaching methods that need to be adapted locally in each country to fit with national educational standards and needs
- Offers an alternative teaching approach to the official curriculum, to give parents choices, but seeks official recognition and support from the ministry of education
- Emphasizes long-term replicability, sustainability, and growth by partnering with the ministry of education and institutions that train and retrain teachers and caregivers
- Collaborates with existing publicly funded institutions (kindergartens, preschools, primary schools, pedagogical institutes, universities, training centers) to create long-lasting change and systemic effect
- Is a child-centered model that emphasizes meeting the individual educational needs of each child in a classroom
- Builds on the principle that parents are the primary educators of their children and should be invited to participate in the schools
- Encourages community involvement from local government and businesses
- Promotes equal opportunities, nondiscrimination, and inclusiveness to integrate into regular classrooms children from diverse backgrounds, ethnic minorities, and those with special needs

- Seeks to produce and purchase all educational furniture and materials in the region, wherever possible, to boost local economies.

Implementation

Each country team has primary responsibility for adapting (translating, publishing) the core written training materials developed by CRI and for refining the implementation strategy to meet the country's specific needs and concerns. Step by Step follows a 5-year developmental cycle in each country. In collaboration with an international network of trainers, CRI, OSI, and ISSA support each country team by:

- Training core project members in child-centered methods, adult training techniques, and educational reform
- Developing educational and training materials
- Providing in-country training and ongoing technical assistance
- Mentoring teams as they develop implementation strategies and plans.

In each country, intensive methodology training is given initially to a team of early childhood experts responsible for adapting the program to the country's context and needs. Model classrooms are implemented in preschools and primary schools and then expanded to new classrooms at low cost, relying on matching funds from communities. Training is also provided for faculties from higher education institutions to ensure inclusion of child-centered methodologies in professional training and retraining programs for teachers. In addition, the country team cooperates with the ministry of education to introduce child-centered policies and programs and establishes an independent Step by Step NGO or association in the country. This organization:

- Provides ongoing professional development for early childhood educators by offering training and sharing experience through professional journals and conferences

- Monitors the quality of the Step by Step program in preschools, primary schools, and teacher training programs
- Advocates greater parental involvement in education and developmentally appropriate education methods nationally
- Promotes child-centered methodologies to schools and communities
- Develops quality programs for marginalized groups, such as Roma and other ethnic minorities and children with disabilities
- Develops standards and evaluates good practice in early childhood education as an independent, nongovernmental voice in the educational community.

By the end of the 5-year developmental period, Step by Step hopes to have established high-quality, self-sustaining training programs that are officially accredited by the ministry of education and are available and affordable to all teachers and schools seeking to learn child-centered methods. The program also aims to be financially sustainable and replicable within each country. (Sustainability refers to the ability of participating schools to continue the Step by Step program after OSI funding ends. Replicability refers to the ability of preschools and primary schools to receive training and implement the program without OSI funding.)

Evolution

George Soros established his first foundation, the Open Society Fund, in New York in 1979 and his first Eastern European foundation in Hungary in 1984. He now funds a network of foundations operating in more than thirty countries throughout the world dedicated to building and maintaining the infrastructure and institutions of an open society.

The Step-by-Step program was initiated originally to address the decline in services for young children in Central and Eastern Europe and the former Soviet Union, caused by the economic upheaval after the fall of communism. In its first year in 1994, the program was established in 200 preschool classrooms in fifteen countries. In its sixth year of operation, the program trained 40,000 teachers annually in twenty-eight countries and territories, serving more than 500,000 families and children in preschools and primary schools. The program cooperates with more than 300 institutions that train and retrain teachers to implement new practices.

Countries have joined the program at different times, and the program is at different stages of development in the participating countries and territories. Currently, these are: Albania, Armenia, Azerbaijan, Belarus, Bosnia-Herzegovina, Bulgaria, Croatia, Czech Republic, Estonia, Georgia, Haiti, Hungary, Kazakhstan, Kosovo, Kyrgyzstan, Latvia, Lithuania, Macedonia, Moldova, Mongolia, Montenegro, Romania, Russia, Slovakia, Slovenia, South Africa, Ukraine, Yugoslavia.

In early 1999, the program formally established ISSA, which is registered in the Netherlands as a nongovernmental membership organization. ISSA serves as an international Step by Step forum for national associations of teachers, parents, and faculties. Among its goals and objectives, ISSA aims to promote the Step by Step program and philosophy internationally; facilitate information sharing among member organizations; provide opportunities for professional development; encourage and disseminate research on child-centered learning; develop international initiatives in early childhood education in partnership with interested organizations; and assist members in fundraising and building partnerships.

Financial Support

OSI provides the initial investment for Step by Step in each participating country. To initiate financial sustainability, the country team undertakes a grassroots effort by approaching potential funding partners after the first year of the program to secure partnership funding to support expansion of the preschool model classrooms. The program provides a catalyst for cofunding by offering matching funds for training and educational materials (to cover capital costs) for preschools that expand their staff by funding additional salaries or creating a volunteer program.

The grassroots effort is targeted to local governments and parents. The team promotes connections with local authorities and communities by inviting them to training sessions and school festivals and by keeping them informed and involved in the development of the program. Despite severe constraints for financial support, local authorities have been able to sustain and replicate Step by Step locally. Parents volunteer as classroom assistants, participate in fundraising to support schools, provide labor to renovate classrooms and playgrounds or to make furniture, and donate equipment or books. The program also encourages partnerships with businesses and other foundations and international organizations, and cofunding and donations have been obtained in several countries.

Principles of Success

The success of the Step by Step program can be attributed to the following characteristics.

- *Private-Public Partnership.* By collaborating with existing publicly funded institutions, Step by Step creates long-lasting change and long-term commitment among all its stakeholders.
- *Culturally Appropriate Methods.* Step by Step accounts for each country's cultural background by encouraging adaptation and modification of the teaching methods and methodology to meet local needs, language, and educational standards.
- *Child-centered Teaching.* The program promotes a child-centered approach and interactive learning method to meet the individual educational needs of each child in a classroom.
- *Community and Parental Involvement.* Step by Step encourages extensive involvement of communities and parents, and parents are invited to participate actively in school activities.
- *Financial Sustainability.* Long-term replicability, sustainability, and growth of the program are achieved in partnership with ministries of education and institutions that train and retrain teachers and caregivers.

- *Nongovernmental Support.* Step by Step supports the continuous development of child-centered early childhood programs and professionals and the development of civil societies by establishing, in each country, an independent, nonpolitical national association or NGO that contributes to plurality in education.

Outlook

Step by Step builds effectively on its program evaluations and is striving for a new teaching approach that is socially inclusive and culturally and financially sustainable.

Studies and Program Evaluation

Multiple evaluations, at national and international levels, have shown that the same or even better educational results can be achieved by using Step by Step's child-centered teaching methods, compared with traditional teacher-centered methods. National studies conducted in cooperation with pedagogical institutes, universities, and ministries have been essential in the acceptance of the program's preschool and primary school methodologies by the ministries of education in the twenty-eight participating countries and territories. Most interestingly, several studies have shown that the Step by Step program supports children's social and emotional development more strongly than traditional programs and that the participating children average higher scores on tests that measure their cooperation, leadership, self-esteem, problem solving, and perseverance.

An independent evaluation of the Step by Step preschool program in four countries (Bulgaria, Kyrgyzstan, Romania, Ukraine) by USAID in 1999 confirmed that Step by Step supports children's democratic behaviors and values, as related to their making choices, taking initiatives, valuing individual expression, and contributing as members of a learning community. Classroom observations showed that these values are embodied in Step by Step classrooms in staff-child interactions and the curriculum and physical environment.

Social Inclusion

There is strong evidence that child-centered approaches enable teachers to respond more effectively to children's individual needs. The USAID evaluation suggests that the Step by Step program is particularly beneficial to children with low academic skills and to disadvantaged children from ethnic minorities. For example, data collected over 3 years on Roma children who attended Step by Step preschools in Yugoslavia show that, in comparison with Roma children who did not attend the preschools, the children had a much higher proficiency level in Serbian, attended primary school more regularly, completed the first grade (100 percent), and scored higher on math and reading tests at the end of first grade. Data also show that participation in Step by Step preschool more than doubles educational outcomes for severely disadvantaged children, supporting the claim that adequate preschool education is an important means of ensuring equity among children.

Step by Step is conducting a pilot project to assess the effect of using Step by Step methods to educate the large number of Roma children placed in schools serving predominantly children who are mentally retarded. In the Czech Republic, for example, as many as 80 percent of Roma children are currently labeled "mentally deficient" and placed in these special schools. The aim of the pilot project is to reintegrate Roma children from these schools by grade 3 or 4. Early results confirm that most of the Roma children are misdiagnosed as having mental deficiencies, unnecessarily reducing their educational potentials.

Special Education

Step by Step hopes to contribute to development of anti-biased adult education programs, objective tests and procedures for child assessments, and educational approaches to meet the specific needs of these children to address this basic human rights issue in the region. Step by Step also is pursuing activities to include children with special needs into regular preschools and primary schools,

through teacher training projects and university courses that prepare teachers.

Sustainability

Between 2003–05, the twenty-eight countries and territories initially
participating in Step by Step will become fully independent of OSI.
Initial studies in four countries indicate that the Step by Step NGOs
established in these countries have the capacity to continue all program activities in the future without outside financial assistance. The
responsibility for regional and international activities and coordination of programs in new countries is shifting to ISSA.

Note

The five case studies have been developed in close collaboration with
the respective projects. The author would like to thank, in particular,
the following individuals for providing valuable information, contributions, and comments:

Carol Guy-James Barratt and Peter Hesse
Peter-Hesse Foundation
Römerstr. 1A
D–41564 Kaarst-Büttgen
Germany
Tel: 49-2131-756.830
Fax: 49-2131-756.831
website: http://www.solidarity.org

Alice Byangwa Mujunga
Mother-Child Day Care Center Services
P.O. Box 1663
Kampala
Uganda
Tel: 256-41-346.597
Fax: 256-41-345.293

Ruth Montrichard
SERVOL Ltd.
91 Frederick Street
Port of Spain
Republic of Trinidad and Tobago
West Indies
Tel: 1-868-623.7009 and 1-868-627.9360
Fax: 1-868-624.1619 and 1-868-622.1043
website: http://community.wow.net/servol

Kathy Bartlett
Aga Khan Foundation
1–3 Ave de la Paix
1202 Geneva
Switzerland
Tel: 41-22-909.7200
Fax: 41-22-909.7291
website: http://www.partnershipwalk.com/akf/index.htm

Elizabeth Lorant and Sarah Klaus
Open Society Institute
International Step by Step Association
400 West 59th Street
New York, NY 10019
U.S.A.
Tel: 1-212-547.6918
Fax: 1-212-548.4610
website: http://www.issa.nl; http://www.soros.org

References

Evans, J.L., R.G. Myers, and E.M. Ilfeld. 2000. Early Childhood Counts. *A Programming Guide on Early Childhood Care for Development.* Washington, D.C.: World Bank.

Hansen, K.A., R.K. Kaufmann, and S. Saifer. 1997. *Education and the Culture of Democracy: Early Childhood Practice.* Washington, D.C.: Children's Resources International, Inc., in Partnership with the Open Society Institute.

Lokshin, M., and T.L. Tan. 2000. Different Countries–Similar Problems: The Effect of Costs of Early Child Development Programs on Household Behavior. Abstract. Preliminary Draft. Washington, D.C.: World Bank.

Myers, R. 1995. *The Twelve Who Survive: Strengthening Programs of Early Child Development in the Third World.* 2nd ed. Ypsilanti, Mich.: High/Scope Press.

OSI (The Open Society Institute) and CRI (Children's Resources International, Inc.). 1998. *Step by Step: A Program for Children from Birth to Ten Years and Their Families.* 1998 Country Report. Washington, D.C.

Rugh, A., and H. Bossert. 1998. *Involving Communities. Participation in the Delivery of Education Programs. Washington,* D.C.: U.S. Agency for International Development.

Young, M.E. 1996. *Early Child Development: Investing in the Future.* Washington, D.C.: World Bank.

Part V

Investing in the Future: Action and Policy

Chapter 12

Narrowing the Gap for Poor Children

Enrique V. Iglesias and Donna E. Shalala

The reasons for investing in early child development are many. Perhaps the most important is ethical, for so many children lack the essential care needed to develop their full human potential. As noted by Amartya Sen (1999), the core of human development is really a question of choice and freedom—which millions of children in the world today still do not have.

Gross underinvestment in children, and their mothers, especially those in the poorest households and with the least education, is one of the most potent "engines" driving the growing inequality within and between nations. Investing in early childhood is essential for nations and regions trying to eradicate mass poverty. Latin America is only one example of a worldwide problem. The issues are the same everywhere. This chapter addresses the underlying basis for the increasing problem of inequality and ways to combat this problem through action and policy.

Intergenerational Poverty

Two of the most dramatic concerns for the global community are the growing number of children in poverty and the vicious circle of poverty—reproduction of poverty and intergenerational poverty. In Latin America, for example, more than four out of ten children under age 9 (or about 43 million children) live on less than US$2.00 per day. These children account for almost 10 percent of the total population (500 million) in Latin America currently. Since 1980, the number of children in poverty has increased by almost two-thirds (from about 26 million) (IDB 1999).

Not only are many of the region's children poor, however; they also face multiple, difficult obstacles related to poverty. Many have not completed primary education, and most live in poverty that is both material and educational. Many suffer from malnutrition, disease, abuse, and neglect, which begins during the critical period from conception through early childhood and impairs their ability and capacity to learn.

In Chile, for example, a study of children's psychomotor development by age 18 months and thereafter showed that 40 percent of the children from poor families were developmentally delayed by age 5, 50 percent were delayed in language development, 30 percent in visual and motor development, and 17 percent in gross motor development (Seguel, Izquierdo, and Edwards 1992). Poor children, such as these, are condemned unnecessarily to illiteracy, low earnings, and few opportunities for a better life.

As adults, children of poverty pass their poverty on to their own children. This "reproduction" of poverty, or intergenerational poverty, is one of the major causes for the persistent poverty, income maldistribution, street children, and increased violence and crime throughout Latin America and other world regions.

This tragic interlinkage develops as follows. Poor parents have many children and larger families, but do not have the means or parenting skills to provide for them or meet their developmental needs. Intellectually and emotionally stunted, the children are less able to learn and often fail in school, repeating grades and eventually dropping out. As unskilled youth with scarce market skills, most have to work in poorly paid "dead-end" jobs and some engage in better-paid illicit activities. When they have children, they replenish, and renew, the vicious circle of poverty.

The new age of information technology will offer many opportunities for Latin Americans born today, but the children of poverty will be left even further behind, unable to effectively acquire the skills needed to participate fully in modern life. Even more so than previously, schooling will determine future job options and earnings. Between 1980 and 1997, the earnings ratio of office workers to manual laborers in Latin America increased 30 percent, from 1:3 to 1:7.

Children who do not complete secondary school are increasingly disadvantaged. Those who are most vulnerable are children in poverty, from indigenous social groups, living in urban shantytowns or rural areas, and malnourished. Any one of these factors decreases their chances of completing secondary school. And, the lives of many of the 43 million children already in poverty in Latin America are affected by more than one of these factors, which is often the case. The overall impact for development in the region is, and will remain, strongly negative until this poverty cycle can be broken.

Breaking the Cycle

Fortunately, the knowledge and the means exist for greatly improving the lives and economic potential of poor children and families. Recent research in Latin America and elsewhere suggests effective ways for breaking the linkages in the cycle of poverty. Six methods are clear:

- Life education and counseling for older children and adolescents, and quality reproductive health services for young women
- Prenatal care and nutrition for mothers, and good nutrition and health care for children in their early years
- Education and training in parenting skills
- Community-based education and training in safety, health, and nutrition
- Childcare to keep children safe and to provide adequate stimulation to foster development and readiness to learn

- Academic and psychological support for disadvantaged children during the initial school years, to increase their chances of success in school and society.

Communities and nations can break the cycle of poverty by intervening in these ways in an urgent and decisive manner. The technical and economic opportunities are available to confront the problem, but tremendous political will and commitment are needed to solve the problem. Government cannot act alone. The resources and talents of government must be matched by other sectors. By joining hands and sharing responsibility, the civil society, private sector (including nongovernmental organizations), and government, supported by international agencies such as the World Bank, the Inter-American Development Bank (IDB), and other regional development banks, can meet this great social challenge of the new millennium and make a difference in many lives.

The IDB, for example, funds and supports many efforts throughout the Americas to improve the lives of disadvantaged children and youth. Some of these efforts are stand-alone projects, and more are part of multifaceted antipoverty programs. The motivation for many activities is the highly visible and troubling problem of street children in large urban areas—a key link in the poverty cycle. In partnership with the World Bank and other organizations, the IDB sponsors seminars and other events to increase and disseminate relevant knowledge and produces policy and program materials related to early child development.

Yet, no institution in government, the private sector, or international development can say today that it is doing enough. International agencies such as the IDB, which would like to do much more, are often constrained by the availability of subsidized funding and the reluctance of some countries to borrow at prevailing terms for child development programs.

Every dollar that is invested in poor children (e.g., in improving childcare, training teachers, building schools, and supporting parents) is a dollar well spent, now and for the future. Even in the

United States, where there is broad consensus that investing in poor and at-risk children early in their lives pays dividends, more can be done. From a business perspective, investment in early child development "works." Building brainpower builds economic power, and building healthy bodies builds healthy nations. The world cannot afford to waste a single future worker.

Intervening Effectively

Even modest investments in community-based child development programs that involve parents, schools, and local health organizations can have broad impact for society, by reducing the reproduction of poverty between generations and lessening related effects (e.g., violence, abuse, criminal behavior, mental illness). Recent data from the United States, for example, demonstrate the effectiveness of prevention programs for children: the number of children who are victims of abuse and neglect declined in this country for the fifth year in a row, and the incidence of maltreatment decreased to 12.9 cases per 1,000 children, the lowest rate in 10 years (United States 2000).

Much more information about early child development is known today than even a decade ago. And, every child, in every corner of the globe, deserves to benefit from this knowledge and from the progress that has been made through programs such as Head Start.

Head Start

In the United States, some of the most important lessons about early child development have come from the Head Start program, which celebrated its thirty-fifth anniversary in 2000. This government program of comprehensive early intervention for low-income preschool children, and their parents, enjoys remarkable political support. The reason is simple: Head Start "works," it is cost effective, and it benefits the country.

Head Start began as part of President Lyndon Johnson's War on Poverty and in response to literature and media coverage during the early 1960s on the extent, and depth, of poverty (e.g., among migrant workers) in the United States. In the face of America's growing wealth at this time, millions of low- and very-low-income families were suffering alone and in the shadows, unprepared to help their preschool children and passing on a life of poverty from one generation to the next. Child development experts in government and academia soon recognized that poor children needed "a hand up" very early in life. Waiting until a poor child entered kindergarten was often too late, and the public schools were incapable of overcoming the losses suffered by poor children in the first years of life. The time for making a national investment in poor children had arrived, and Head Start was created.

Head Start was never intended to focus only on education, but, rather, to help develop socially, emotionally, and physically healthy children. A typical Head Start class has seventeen children, one teacher, one assistant, and one other adult—usually a parent. At least 10 percent of the enrollment opportunities must be available to children with disabilities. The curriculum is of high quality, comprehensive, age-appropriate, and standard across the United States. Much attention is given to cognition and language. But that is only the beginning.

Head Start children also receive comprehensive health services, including immunizations, physical and dental examinations, and nutrition support. They are helped to overcome their fears and they learn to share, cooperate, listen, and take turns. They receive lunch and a snack, and some children receive breakfast. The typical day is a mixture of instruction, creative play inside and outside, and balanced meals.

Head Start also focuses on building families. Parental involvement and learning are extensive, and parents progress toward their own educational, literacy, and employment goals by training and working in Head Start.

Although funding and enrollment have increased dramatically since 1965, Head Start maintains its core mission of developing the whole child and enabling each child to reach his or her full potential.

Head Start has accomplished a great deal. Research on the program shows that children leave Head Start with a wide range of specific skills and knowledge, which they need to succeed in kindergarten. The practical, common-sense achievements that they make lay the groundwork for their future learning and emotional development. Yet, improvements continue to be made in the program. During the past 7 years, administrators have expanded Head Start, strengthened parental involvement and learning, improved quality, and demanded more accountability.

Currently, almost 900,000 children are enrolled in Head Start, and another 45,000 are enrolled in Early Head Start, a complementary program that was created to meet the special needs of children ages 0–3. Recently, Head Start received its largest budget increase ever, and additional funding is being sought.

Although most countries do not have the resources to fund early childhood education at this level, the investment is worth far more than the cost, because every child who enters Head Start is one less child that is on the road to poverty with no "off-ramp." Enrollment in Head Start will not break the cycle of intergenerational poverty for every child, but it does increase the possibility of escaping poverty. As noted earlier, more resources are better than less, and some are better than none.

Lessons Learned

After 3.5 decades of experience with Head Start, six lessons have become clear for maximizing investments in early child development. These could be considered "six lessons for children to grow by." They are as follows.

1. *The earlier intervention begins, the better.* This lesson is perhaps the most important. Research shows that development of the brain in the early years is a pathway that affects physical and mental health, learning, and behavior throughout the life cycle (Carnegie Corporation of New York 1994; Karr-Morse and Wiley 1997; Keating and Hertzmann 1999; Shore 1997). The research

findings, which were presented at the United States' White House Conference on Early Childhood Development and Learning, in April 1997, and elsewhere, provided the impetus for initiating the Early Head Start program.

2. *Quality counts.* In a long-term study of poor children (Campbell and Ramey 1994), one-half of the children were assigned to high-quality day care from infancy to age 5, and the other half received only nutritional supplements and visits from social workers. The group assigned to the high-quality day care were more successful later in life in almost every measurable way.

Money alone is never the answer, however. For this reason, Head Start is imposing new performance standards for all its centers and has allocated 25 percent of all new funding to support higher standards and investments in quality. The performance standards are rigorous, clearly stated, and mandatory. They are being used to evaluate all aspects of the Head Start program, from children's readiness to read and their social development, to the effectiveness of program management. (Tarullo describes the performance standard initiative in an earlier chapter in this volume.)

Excellence has to be the goal. Since 1995, 150 Head Start grantees have been terminated or have relinquished their grants for lack of quality. The program's consistent demand for high quality benefits parents and children. Recently, Head Start received the highest score in customer satisfaction of any government agency or private company in the United States.

3. *Quality early childhood education begins with training.* The turnover rate for Head Start staff is very low—less than 11 percent a year. And, 80 percent of Head Start teachers have 5 or more years of experience. A qualified and committed staff is one of the benefits of providing and supporting professional training. All Head Start teachers are currently required to have a special child development certificate. By 2002, the aim is to achieve a majority

of Head Start teachers with a 2- to 4-year degree in early child-hood education. The government is helping to expand the ca-pacity of colleges and universities to teach early childhood edu-cation and to train childcare staff to work with infants and toddlers. Head Start also is increasing staff salaries and investing in the health and safety of its facilities.

4. *Parents must be involved and accommodated.* One of the reasons that parents express such a high level of satisfaction with Head Start is that Head Start "listens" to them. The program learns from parents and encourages them to remain involved. This emphasis has continued since the earliest days of the program and is the key to its success. In fact, many Head Start parents be-come Head Start teachers.

   Keeping parents engaged and involved is not sufficient, how-ever. Programs also must accommodate their changing needs. For example, when Head Start began, the number of women in the work force and of single-parent families was far fewer than today. As work patterns changed, Head Start had to change. Currently, Head Start is expanding its hours, increasing the flex-ibility of its hours, taking early childhood education programs into the workplace, and encouraging Head Start centers to part-ner with quality programs that provide childcare after Head Start and until parents return home from work.

   Head Start also has learned the importance of keeping par-ents connected to the communities where they live. Programs must be culturally sensitive, involve community leaders, and keep decisionmaking at the local level as much as possible.

5. *Early childhood education must be integrated with other needs.* Poor children do not need one strategy. They need a comprehensive strategy that extends beyond early childhood stimulation and education. Integrated services, especially for infants and tod-dlers, are a prerequisite for success. For example, in Head Start, childhood immunizations were an early priority. Today, at least

90 percent of U.S. children receive the most critical immunization doses by age 2. Immunizations save not only lives, but also resources, by preventing disease before it strikes. This understanding is important even for countries that do not have universal health care coverage (e.g., the United States) or have only limited resources to purchase and distribute vaccines.

For the same reason, the U.S. government is expanding access to health insurance for poor children. Three years ago, the State Children's Health Insurance Program was initiated with the states to ensure that millions more children from low-income working families have health insurance. Programs such as Head Start and childcare centers are effective ways of identifying children who are eligible for health insurance. Integrated services help ensure that nurses talk to teachers, teachers talk to nutritionists, nutritionists talk to staff, and everyone talks to parents.

6. *Government should make early childhood education a national laboratory and catalyst for change.* "If you build it, they will come" is a now-famous phrase from a recent U.S. movie, *Field of Dreams.* An adaptation of this phrase conveys an imperative for early child development: Build it and *change* will come.

Head Start has been a national laboratory and catalyst for change. Since its creation in 1965, Head Start has transformed how people think about, educate, and care for young children in the United States and how quality is measured in all childcare settings. The Early Head Start program is doing the same for infants and toddlers.

When investing in early childhood education, maintaining an active research agenda is important. Because "one size never fits all," continuing efforts are needed to determine which programs are effective for which children under which circumstances and to use this knowledge to build better programs, integrating the best research as quickly as possible.

Conclusion

The most important reason for investing in programs such as Head Start or quality childcare is to "even up the odds" for poor children. The economic benefits are significant, as noted by van der Gaag in this volume.

Yet, there is also a profound moral purpose for investing in early child development. This is a new millennium, a time of high technological achievement when almost no scientific advancement seems impossible. But, millions of children on every continent are struggling to survive. This "disconnect"—between two real, but inconsistent, concepts—is unconscionable for the world today. The time has come to connect, to narrow the gap for poor children, between what can be done and what is being done.

Much has been learned about how to help very young children grow to be smart and healthy. The important step, however, is the next step—to engage families, communities, universities, religious and other organizations, as well as government, to invest in the first and most lasting hope of the new century, the world's children. A 2-year-old in the barrios of Peru, a baby crying for milk in Lagos, a little girl not yet 4 years old in the slums of Calcutta, and a 3-year-old in Head Start in rural North Dakota—these children, all children, are the future.

Note

This chapter is derived from the authors' keynote addresses at the World Bank Conference on Investing in Our Children's Future, held April 10–11, 2000, at the World Bank, Washington, D.C.

References

Campbell, F.A., and C.T. Ramey. 1994. Effects of Early Intervention on Intellectual and Academic Achievement: A Follow-up Study of Children from Low-Income Families. *Child Development* 65:684–98.

Carnegie Corporation of New York. 1994. *Starting Points: Meeting the Needs of Our Youngest Children.* New York.

IDB (Inter-American Development Bank). 1999. Breaking the Poverty Cycle: Investing in Early Childhood. Washington, D.C. [www.iadb.org/sds/soc]

Karr-Morse, R., and M.S. Wiley. 1997. *Ghosts from the Nursery: Tracing the Roots of Violence.* New York: Atlantic Monthly Press.

Keating, D.P., and C. Hertzman, eds., 1999. *Developmental Health and the Wealth of Nations: Social, Biological, and Educational Dynamics.* New York: The Guilford Press.

Seguel, X., T. Izquierdo, and M. Edwards. 1992. Diagnostico Nacional y Elaboración del Plan de Acción para el Decenio en el Area del Desarrollo Infantil y Familiar. Santiago, Chile: United Nations Children's Fund (UNICEF).

Sen, A.K. 1999. Investing in Early Childhood: Its Role in Development. Keynote address presented at a seminar on Breaking the Poverty Cycle: Investing in Early Childhood, Annual Meeting of the Boards of Governors of the Inter-American Development Bank and the Inter-American Investment Corporation, Paris, France, March 14, 1999. [www.iadb.org/sds/soc]

Shore, R. 1997. *Rethinking the Brain — New Insights into Early Development.* Families and Work Institute. New York, N.Y.

United States. Department of Health and Human Services. Administration on Children, Youth and Families. 2000. *Child Maltreatment 1998: Reports from the States to the National Child Abuse and Neglect Data System.* Washington, D.C.: U.S. Government Printing Office.

Chapter 13

The Political Challenge: Commitment and Cooperation

Eduardo A. Doryan, Kul C. Gautam, and William H. Foege

The final question for this volume, and perhaps the first question in early child development, is: Why intervene in the lives of young children? In the previous chapter, Iglesias and Shalala highlight the ethical and moral impetus for early child development (ECD) programs to "narrow the gap" for poor children. Earlier, van der Gaag connects early child development to human development overall.

For children and families, the benefits are clear, as communicated throughout this volume. But, the benefits also must be obvious to the larger society and government because their support is essential for maintaining and sustaining effective programs. To reap the full benefits of the many community-based efforts under way, programs must be taken to scale nationwide. The final challenge, then, is political—to obtain the necessary commitment and cooperation, from all sectors, to realize the full potential of early child development, nationally and globally.

This chapter considers the societal benefits and constraints to investing in early child development and the political challenge for doing so. Some factors, steps, and "rules" are suggested for investing in policies of action that would help bring ECD programs to scale.

Transforming Society Through ECD

Much progress has been made over the past 15 years in bringing early child development to the attention of society and government. Today, nations (e.g., Brazil, Philippines, Namibia, Ghana) are adopting national plans for accelerating early child development, and multinational organizations [e.g., the United Children's Fund (UNICEF), the World Bank) are promoting the well-being of children, women, and vulnerable populations in development efforts that include ECD interventions. These efforts are complemented by, and in some cases, coordinated with, the interests and actions of organizations in the private sector [e.g., foundations, nongovernmental organizations (NGOs)]. Increasingly, early child development is viewed as the best proxy or contributor to economic development and national development.

All these participants deserve to be congratulated for the transformations in society that they have stimulated and underwritten. Their continued support and commitment can be the launching pad for achieving even greater transformations over the next 15 years to fulfill the hopes and expectations of many more children and their families. The long-term benefits of investing in early child development are extraordinary. The consequences of not investing or of neglecting children are equally far-reaching—lifelong deprivation and deficits for many children and major cumulative losses for their families, communities, and nations.

What are society's aspirations for children, and what can ECD programs offer? From a global perspective, four aspirations would be that children grow up to reach their full human potential and that they live in a society where human rights are respected, democracy flourishes, and poverty is not an insurmountable barrier to human progress. Investing in early child development significantly helps to achieve these hopes.

Human Potential

ECD programs are instrumental for achieving human potential—through, for example, the lifelong effects of improved intrauterine growth (resulting from better maternal health and nutrition), psychosocial stimulation in early infancy, and preparedness for school. These and other benefits for enhancing the human potential are well summarized by the other chapters in this volume.

Human Rights

Human rights are often equated with civil and political rights, freedom of speech, freedom of religion, and rule of law. But, human rights also include social and economic rights. The Universal Declaration on Human Rights and the Convention on the Rights of the Child, as well as other human rights covenants, recognize the right to life, survival, health, nutrition, education, and protection. A society that honors these rights must begin with the rights of the youngest children. The very essence of human rights is to protect the weak and vulnerable from the tyranny of the strong and powerful.

Protecting the rights of children who cannot defend themselves, to ensure their survival, growth, and development, is the obligation of all adults and all countries that signed or ratified these human rights instruments. In a very fundamental sense, human rights begin with the rights of children, and a society that does not invest its resources, to the maximum extent possible, for the survival, protection, and development of children fails to honor its human rights obligations, especially those set forth in the Convention on the Rights of the Child.

Participation

Because children do not vote and have no voice in society, some might say they have no stake in democracy. But, the way children are reared and the type of physical and psychosocial environments they grow in have lifelong effects on the development of their values and personality traits. Nurturing children in an atmosphere of mutual respect and compassion and inculcating them, from the earliest stages of life, with the values of sharing and taking responsibility contribute to the creation of caring societies that espouse democratic values.

From an adult's perspective, democracy requires that political and civic leaders be responsive to the protection of rights of all their constituents and that public resources be utilized in the most effective manner to help their constituencies. Democratically oriented leaders and electorates should find that investing in children is the most enlightened and visionary public policy they can promote.

Reduction of Poverty

Poverty has many faces, which include malnutrition, childhood disease, lack of learning and play opportunities, and violence against women and children. These and other facets of poverty undermine the optimal development of young children and diminish their potential for breaking out of the cycle of poverty. As suggested by Iglesias and Shalala in the preceding chapter, early child development is the shortest route of breaking the intergenerational cycle of poverty.

Children who are born healthy, fed well, stimulated in infancy, protected from childhood illnesses, and nurtured in stimulating and affectionate environments will grow up to become healthy adults, involved parents, and productive citizens. Successful child development results from adequate care at home facilitated by basic community services and supportive national and international policies. Women's role is critical. Research shows that children survive and thrive better in communities where women have dignity, access to resources, and political influence. These elements are all essential for reducing poverty and promoting early child development.

Constraints to Investment

For society, knowing the well-established benefits of early child development may not be sufficient for making the decision to invest in ECD programs and to support them fully. Policymakers may ask why there is not more investment in these programs globally if investing in early child development is so important. What are the constraints to investing in ECD? Common constraints for society and government are:

- *Immediate costs versus long-term gains.* The costs of intervening early are immediate, but the investment is long term. Because the observable benefits do not accrue until long after a government or administration has left office, ECD programs tend not to be popular among politicians, who desire more immediate recognition for their achievements. The benefits of constructing a school or clinic or distributing textbooks may not be obvious for years, but they contribute over time to the building of social capital and, hence, economic development.
- *Difficulty delivering integrated services.* Early interventions that address integral needs of young children and families are difficult for society and government to deliver in a coherent and coordinated manner. Government (and donor agencies) tend to be oriented sectorally, and government departments or ministries tend to be organized vertically. Because the needs of children and families (e.g., health, education, social assistance) cross these artificial partitions, they are not easily addressed within the bureaucracies. Comprehensive development frameworks are needed to integrate the vision of policymakers and to coordinate action "on the ground."

In addition, two barriers to good decisionmaking in global health and development are:

- The distance between a decision and an effect
- The time between a decision and an effect.

The greater the distance, or the time, between a decision and an effect, the more difficult it is to make good decisions. The most difficult decisions to make are those that involve both distance and time (e.g., decisions about nuclear or toxic wastes, which have incubation times of hundreds of years and may be disposed of in other countries). Decisions to invest in positive early child development are similar, because society's effects are realized over generations, even centuries, and may be broadly dispersed.

Believing that society can change and that children's future and destiny can be improved is a first step. Once a nation adopts this positive perspective, determining what can be changed and what cannot be changed becomes easier to address. These decisions depend on the science.

The Challenges

Conferences on early child development, such as those held by the World Bank and other multinational organizations, are an important step in publicizing the benefits of early child development and overcoming the constraints expressed by governments and policymakers. These meetings enable researchers, administrators, and politicians to share and interpret research findings, celebrate the creativity and innovation of ECD programs, better understand the role of healthy child development in economic development, and appreciate the importance of investing in early child development for both human and global development.

The chapters in this volume, which emanate from one conference, highlight four challenges for the field of early child development:

- Promoting a balanced view of development that includes ECD programs
- Making explicit the link between the needs of poor children and families and the concerns of politicians
- Developing improved methods for measuring and evaluating the effectiveness of programs
- Achieving sustainable, national programs.

One way to achieve sustainability is to change social norms. Measles, for example, used to be an expected childhood disease, but now a single case in developed countries is newsworthy and causes the public to question the activities of the local health department. The public relates to cause and effect. As Hawkins notes in his book *A Brief History of Time*, the history of science is the gradual realization that things do not happen in an arbitrary fashion (Hawkins 1988). Or, as noted in a New York subway booth and reported in the *New York Times*, "Lots of people confuse bad management with destiny" (Nemy 1999, sec. B, p. 2). The challenge now for early child development is to create better destiny through better management, to apply the science and invest in a better future for every child in every country.

Cause and Effect

History tells us that everything that now exists has a past and that everything that is done now will have ripples in the future. Knowledge about the brain's development—the windows of opportunity in the early years, the effects of learning on later years—supports this concept.

But, some effects are more permanent and some losses can never be recouped. Society cannot, for example, reverse the retardation caused by insufficient iodine intake during a child's first months and years, or return function to the legs of a child crippled by polio, or eliminate a child's trauma from experiencing war. Other causes, such as toxins (e.g., alcohol, tobacco smoke) and abuse, also have lifelong effects.

Recently, the U.S. Centers for Disease Control and Prevention (Felliti and others 1998) published the first scientific study of the health of adults who were abused as children. The study documented, for the first time, that smoking, drinking, drug use, depression, suicide attempts, and overweight all were elevated in adults who had experienced, during childhood, physical, psychological, or sexual abuse; a mother being beaten; or a family member using drugs or going to jail. In 1962, Kempe coined the phrase "the battered child syndrome" (Kempe and others 1962). The causes may be both genetic and environmental. Influences in a child's upbringing have a role in the mental health of the child and, later, the adult. The battered child syndrome causes a battered adult syndrome, and an accumulation of battered adults causes a battered society syndrome, which, in turn, continues to foster battered children. This intergenerational cycle complements, and enhances, the effects of a cycle of poverty.

Inefficiencies

Many of the current approaches to social issues are inefficient. For example, mothers often bear children whom they may feed, nurture, and love for 9 or more months, only to lose them then to measles—this is inefficient. If the child survives measles and continues on to primary school but drops out in the early grades, or thrives in school but then contracts an HIV infection and subsequently develops AIDS in the early 20s—this, again, is inefficient. Rearing children while being depressed and addicted because of being abused as a child also is inefficient. And, allowing children to be retarded because of preventable deficiencies in micronutrient intake is inefficient.

Similarly, not providing health and educational benefits to all children is inefficient, and building prisons to house troubled youth and adults because society "saved" money by not supporting community programs of health and education is inefficient. These approaches are not only inefficient, however, they also have heartrending and society-rending effects. Obviously, these inefficiencies are not rational and do not contribute to acceptable societies.

Nevertheless, inefficiencies persist, partly because of human tendencies to procrastinate, but also because of longstanding and unchallenged social norms. Societies may verbalize the need for prevention, but hesitate to take preventive action. For example, many countries have historically placed greater value on treating lung cancer, rather than helping people stop smoking. This emphasis is only now beginning to change, with the support and action of global organizations, including the World Health Organization (WHO), the World Bank, and UNICEF. And, despite professed interest in children and investments in Head Start, U.S. support for children is far less than that for older persons. In his book *The Virtues of Aging*, President Carter notes that for every US$12 spent on people over age 65, the U.S. Government spends only US$1 for children and youth under age 18 (Carter 1998). These are only two examples of the mismatch between rhetoric and action on prevention.

In the United States, a major change in perspective occurred when the rhetoric of disease prevention was modified to include health promotion. While disease prevention focuses on pathology and reducing the extent of a problem (e.g., mortality and morbidity), health promotion focuses on positive changes in scale. The philosophy, objective, and expectations are different and, when communicated to the public, can help change social norms and values.

Societies' thinking about children has heretofore reflected the pathological approach of waiting until a "disease" is evident before reacting. Leadership is desperately needed, to ask questions such as "what is good for the future?" and "what is good for the world?" Efficient, positive approaches must be promulgated and fostered, for the vast majority of the public that government serves has not yet been born and may be of different nationalities.

Policies for Action

The decision to invest in early child development must be matched by efficient and effective policies to stimulate ECD efforts. Whereas the decision may appear to be noncontroversial, especially with regard to narrowing the gap for poor children, the policies which allocate, or reallocate, resources to health, education, and nutrition for young children are not. Some individuals and groups may support such policies, but many may not. Merely making "pro-poor" policies to focus on more vulnerable segments of a society or improve conditions in a particularly poor region does not guarantee that the policies will be adopted or implemented effectively. The political implications of a policy, including the support or opposition of key stakeholders, often influence adoption of the policy.

Four Considerations

Policymakers who are, or will be, designing and implementing ECD programs will need to address four factors: the stakeholders, or "players," in early child development; the relative power of each stakeholder; the position of each stakeholder; and public perception.

- *Players.* The stakeholders include all individuals and groups who will be affected by the change in policy and who may become involved in influencing its outcome. The players may include government ministries (e.g., health, finance, agriculture, education) and local government; professional groups (e.g., physicians, nurses, preschool teachers); business organizations; religious organizations; consumers of health and education services (e.g., urban and rural, poor and middle-class individuals, families, and communities); and international organizations (e.g., the International Monetary Fund, World Bank, WHO, donors). Each group and subgroup will understand and act on the policies from a different perspective.
- *Power.* Poor people are often poorly organized and politically weak, particularly in rural areas. Children, particularly in their early years, do not have a representative association, and adults are usually more influential, although not necessarily well organized. Additionally, power and influence are exercised differently depending on the political system and the traditions of a country and culture.
- *Position.* The position taken by each stakeholder will reflect their support of, or opposition to, the policy and the intensity of their commitment. When multiple reforms are proposed, each stakeholder may support some policies and oppose others. The various positions taken serve as a basis for negotiation.
- *Perception.* The public's perception and understanding of the issue and the proposed policy may affect which groups become mobilized and their positions on the policy.

For "pro-poor" policies, a coalition of stakeholders (both domestic and international) needs to be developed to achieve sufficient adoption and implementation of the policies to sustain a positive change. As Hsiao and others (2001) suggest, development of this coalition depends, in turn, on the skill and commitment of those who support the policies, the nature of the proposed changes, and the overall country context. Successful implementation of any policy depends on the political skill of its advocates, and not simply political will. This skill must be technically based.

Six Steps for Government

Government has an essential role to play in early child development. By blending good politics (i.e., well-founded proposals) and good techniques (i.e., political skill), government can stimulate public support for ECD policies and programs which will strengthen its position and power to implement the policies and programs and foster cooperation and coordination with other stakeholders and potential funders. Six effective steps for government action are as follows:

1. *Create a political constituency for children.* Include the constituency in a strategic communications plan, which would be a component of the design of ECD programs. Build early child development into a holistic, integrated, comprehensive development framework designed to overcome the cycle of poverty and to foster a balanced view of economic, financial, human, governance, and institutional issues across government sectors. Having a political constituency for ECD programs can strengthen the power of the various stakeholders and change the public's perception of early child development.

2. *Earmark public resources.* This action will ensure the availability of resources for ECD programs, protect the investment in children in times of crisis, and guard against changing political interests. Government should monitor children's growth and development as closely as, or more closely than, it monitors the growth in gross domestic product. Examples of successful ECD efforts that have been sustained by earmarked tax revenues include Colombia's use of a 3 percent payroll tax to support stable financing of day-care programs, even in times of financial

adjustment or political upheaval. Earmarked revenues can serve to create a strong power base for ECD.

3. *Provide incentives for community support of ECD.* Government should encourage initiatives by small community groups, civil society, and local government. The U.S. Head Start program is one example of a federally funded effort founded on community initiatives. By supporting such efforts, government can help create community-based productive and small business sectors, with new stakeholders, that can promote early child development with one voice. Having a "voice" is the first step toward empowerment.

4. *Create demanding consumers.* Government can allow and even encourage private-sector providers (not-for-profit and for-profit) of ECD programs. Government also can provide public subsidies for poor families, to help them access ECD services and make them effective consumers. These actions will further increase the number of stakeholders who are interested in, and supportive of, ECD programs.

5. *Provide information on the choices available.* Government has a role in developing and disseminating information, standards, training materials, and program evaluations to enable consumers to make informed choices about early child development and alternative providers of ECD programs. Government can leverage improvements in the quality of ECD programs based on this information and on pilot studies of funding alternatives. One alternative, for example, is New Zealand's mixed funding model of block grants and subsidies. By enhancing public information, government would foster transparency of ECD programs and potentially enhance the public's perception of these efforts.

6. *Create new providers.* Mothers can be effective ECD providers in home-based programs, such as in Colombia and Bolivia. The women receive training and minimum assistance, on credit, to meet facility standards. They are "accredited" as eligible to provide day-care services. Such efforts enable providers to benefit from public subsidies while also participating in a competitive,

choice-based system of ECD programs. In addition, they benefit parents by increasing the number and type of care options to choose from (e.g., based on convenience, proximity, flexibility of hours). By helping to create new providers locally, government helps consolidate the players, power, position, and perception of early child development, primarily at the local level.

By taking these six steps, government can achieve a "golden triangle" of civil-society participation, market-driven mechanism, and a clear role for government. Government also can launch the necessary political action to foster sustainable ECD programs that can be moved to scale. As noted by Papert (1980, p. 29), "What is happening now is an empirical question. What can happen is a technical question, but what will happen is a political question, depending on social choices." Clearly, early child development is, first and foremost, a political, or social, choice. It is no longer an empirical question, but, rather, an issue for action.

Five Rules for Investing

Before committing a nation's resources to early child development, policymakers should have appropriate guidance from the ECD community. This guidance should be evidence-based and timely. Five general rules for investing in early child development are offered below:

1. *Invest early and invest wisely.* Often, there are no second chances for child development. Each child has only one opportunity, to grow and develop, and this opportunity should not be squandered.
2. *Identify opportunities to contribute to early child development in every development project.* Children are everyone's business and not the exclusive concern of one department, ministry, or sector. Every development project has a place for ECD initiatives. Early child development is integral to human development, as well described by van der Gaag earlier in this volume.

3. *Ensure that all governments and donor agencies honor the 2020 commitment,* that all developing countries will allocate 20 percent of their budgets for basic social services, and that all donors will allocate 20 percent of their official development assistance for these services. This commitment was made at several United Nations conferences and is vital for early childcare and development, a basic social service.

4. *Empower women.* The well-being of children is inextricably linked to the well-being of women.

5. *Make the commitment to children,* beginning with early childcare and development, the foundation for peace, democracy, and human rights in families, communities, nations, and the world.

The love and care for children, and the imperative to invest in early child development, can be the basis for uniting a divided world.

Building a Global Coalition

"Build it and change will come," is an imperative for early child development introduced previously in this volume by Iglesias and Shalala. The time is ripe now for building a global coalition for early child development that will stimulate actions and policies for investing in the future. Similar to the remarkable Global Alliance for Vaccines and Immunization, which was recently organized and funded by a generous gift from the Bill and Melinda Gates Foundation, the coalition for early child development would combine good science with good policies and involve all stakeholders, including local and national groups, governmental agencies, multinational organizations, NGOs, foundations, religious groups, industry, and other public- or private-sector interests.

A deliberate plan to build and fund a coalition would capture local and community enthusiasm for early child development, the political commitment to ECD programs that has already been made by many countries, and the passion of donors who recognize the global need for efforts targeted to children worldwide. The coalition would represent a conscious decision to combine resources, experiences, scientific findings, ingenuity, a sense of community, and new approaches to education for the benefit of generations to come. Building a coalition will make change happen, including perhaps, the designation of ministers of child development.

Conclusion

More information is not needed to act now to support early child development. If appropriate action is taken, future generations will know and be grateful that politicians and economists, based on scientists' teachings, invested adequately in their children. The concept of the "tipping point" applies. That is, there is a drop that causes the glass to finally overflow, there is a moment when a friendship becomes permanent, there is a minute when a vaccine provides protection, and there is a day when the world finally "does right" by its children.

For children to have the positive core elements that offer them a successful life, they need parents who have a capacity to nurture, good mental health, and a network of positive social support. These parents are more likely to be found in societies that are committed to parenthood, equity, economic stability, appropriate childcare, and effective education. Yet, to raise a child takes more than a village—it takes the whole world—and society and government need to identify how to do a better job. Focusing on averages is no longer sufficient; the important measures now are standard deviations, and the children and families represented by these deviations.

The ECD community is an assemblage of individuals with diverse interests, expertise, and talents who are bound together by a shared goal to create a world that honors children by enhancing their positive development. The next step is to build a coalition, an alliance, that will promote, measure, and improve the well-being of children, beginning in the early years. This is now the "tipping point" for early child development, the day when the investment in early childhood moves to a new stage, so that all children henceforth will benefit and progress cannot be reversed.

The beliefs and commitments of others can serve to guide those who continue the effort. As James P. Grant, former head of UNICEF, said in his last speech to the United Nations' General Assembly, "The vital vulnerable years of childhood should be given a first call on societies concerns and capacities....There will always be something more immediate; there will never be anything more important. If we believe that, lets organize to do it. Lets combine authority, resources, and responsibility in a person in every country" (Grant 1994). Gandhi observed that people often become what they believe themselves to be, and children often become what their parents and society believe them to be. And, Jonas Salk noted that evolution will be what we want it to be.

The message is: if we can envision it, we can achieve it. Creating the future starts with the ability to envision the future, and that day is today.

Note

This chapter is derived from two presentations on "What Policymakers Need to Know," by Eduardo Doryan and Kul Gautam, and on William Foege's closing address, "The Political Economy of Investing in Young Children's Early Development," at the World Bank Conference on Investing in Our Children's Future, held April 10–11, 2000, at the World Bank, Washington, D.C.

References

Carter, J. 1998. *The Virtues of Aging.* New York: Ballantine Books, Random House.

Felitti, V.J., R.F. Anda, D.F. Nordenberg, D.F. Williamson, A.M. Spitz, V. Edwards, M.P. Koss, and J.S. Marks. 1998. Relationship of Childhood Abuse and Household Dysfunction to Many of the

Leading Causes of Death in Adults: The Adverse Childhood Experiences (ACE) Study. *American Journal of Preventive Medicine* 14(4):245–58.

Grant, J.P. 1994. Child Rights: A Central Moral Imperative of Our Time. Statement by the Executive Director of UNICEF to the Third Committee of the 49th General Assembly of the United Nations. New York, November 11.

Hawkins, S. 1988. *A Brief History of Time*. New York: Bantam Books.

Hsiao, W., M. Roberts, P. Berman, and M. Reich. 2001. Political Analysis and Political Strategies. In *Getting Health Sector Reform Right*. Background paper for World Bank Institute flagship course on Health Reform and Sustainable Financing. Washington, D.C.: World Bank.

Kempe, C.H., F.N. Silverman, B.F. Steele, W. Droegemueller, and H.K. Silver. 1962. The Battered-Child Syndrome. *Journal of the American Medical Association* 181:17–24.

Nemy, E. 1999. Metropolitan Diary. *The New York Times*, sec. B, p. 2, May 3.

Papert, S. 1980. *Mindstorms*. New York: Basic Books, p. 29.

Authors

Eduardo A. Doryan, Ph.D.
Vice President and Head
Human Development Network
The World Bank
Washington, D.C., U.S.A.
  Currently:
  Special Representative to the United Nations,
    New York
    for The World Bank
  Office of the Special Representative
    to the United Nations
  New York, New York, U.S.A.

Judith L. Evans, Ed.D.
Director
Department of Programme Documentation
  and Communication
Bernard van Leer Foundation
The Hague, The Netherlands

William H. Foege, M.D., M.P.H.
Presidential Distinguished Professor
Rollins School of Public Health
Emory University
Atlanta, Georgia, U.S.A.

Kul C. Gautam, M.P.A.
Deputy Executive Director
United Nations Children's Fund (UNICEF)
New York, New York, U.S.A.

Enrique V. Iglesias, Ph.D.
President
Inter-American Development Bank
Washington, D.C., U.S.A.

Simone Kirpal, M.A.
Social Scientist
Early Child Development Team
Education Sector
Human Development Network
The World Bank
Washington, D.C., U.S.A.
    Currently:
    Staff
    Institute of Technology and Education (ITB)
    Bremen, Germany

John M. Love, Ph.D.
Senior Fellow
Mathematica Policy Research, Inc.
Princeton, New Jersey, U.S.A.

Alicia L. Meckstroth, M.A.
Researcher
Mathematica Policy Research, Inc.
Princeton, New Jersey, U.S.A.

J. Fraser Mustard, M.D., Ph.D.
Founding President
Canadian Institute for Advanced Research,
    The Founders' Network
Toronto, Ontario, Canada

Robert G. Myers, Ph.D.
Independent Consultant
Tlalcoligia, D.F., Mexico

Peter Z. Schochet, Ph.D.
Senior Economist
Mathematica Policy Research, Inc.
Princeton, New Jersey, U.S.A.

Kerida Scott-McDonald, Ph.D.
Early Childhood Development Officer
United Nations Children's Fund (UNICEF), Jamaica
Kingston, Jamaica, West Indies

Donna E. Shalala, Ph.D.
Secretary
U.S. Department of Health and Human Services
Washington, D.C., U.S.A.
    Currently:
    President
    University of Miami
    Coral Gables, Florida, U.S.A.

Louisa B. Tarullo, Ed.D.
Senior Social Science Research Analyst
Administration on Children, Youth, and Families
U.S. Department of Health and Human Services
Washington, D.C., U.S.A.

Jacques van der Gaag, Ph.D.
Dean
Faculty of Economics and Econometrics
University of Amsterdam
The Netherlands

J. Douglas Willms, Ph.D.
Director
Canadian Research Institute for Social Policy
University of New Brunswick
Fredericton, New Brunswick, Canada

Mary Eming Young, M.D., Dr.P.H.
Lead Specialist
Education Sector
Human Development Network
The World Bank
Washington, D.C., U.S.A.

Index

A

Abecedarian (Carolina) project, U.S.
6, 40–42, 125–126, 141, 161
Abrinq Foundation for Children's
Rights 284
Accountability 13, 219, 230, 273,
276, 289, 369
Administration on Children, Youth,
and Families, U.S. 219, 231
Advance Brazil Program 138
Advocacy 215, 248, 251, 284,
315–316, 324
Aga Khan Foundation (AKF) xi, 14,
284, 295, 336–338, 341–344, 346,
359
Aga Khan University 116
Agueda Movement, Portugal 201
Animal studies 8, 24, 26, 28, 30,
32–35, 39, 43–44
Argentina 82, 91–93, 113
Assoçiação de Criança Familia e
Desenvolvimento, Mozambique
199
Association for the Advancement of
the Ethiopian Family and Child,
Israel 199
Atençao à Criança Program, Brazil
138–140
Attributable risk(s) 99–101, 107–109

B

Bangladesh 288, 337
Barriers to good decisionmaking 15,
379
Benefit-cost analysis, benefit:cost ratio
10, 17, 134–136
Benefits and costs 132–135
Benefits, of early child development.
See also Economic benefits, Societal
benefits v, 1, 3, 6–9, 11, 15, 33,
42, 52, 60, 63–64, 67–68, 70–75,
77–78, 124, 132–135, 136, 140–
142, 161, 172, 277–278, 291, 299,
307–308, 311, 367, 370, 373
Bernard van Leer Foundation xi,
195, 202, 217, 235, 331, 332, 337,
343
Biological pathways 3, 4, 8, 24,
26–32, 34, 59
Bolivia 42, 82, 91–93, 113, 386
Brain development, function 4–5, 8,
18–19, 26, 31, 32–33, 36, 41, 46,
49, 54–55, 68, 76
Brain/hormone pathways 26–29
Brazil 6, 10, 82, 91–93, 95, 113, 116,
123–124, 129–142, 376

C

California 153, 168, 170, 277
Canada x, xi, 8, 24, 44, 46–52, 59,
88, 118–121, 331, 337
Canadian Institute for Advanced
Research (CIAR) 51, 54, 118, 120
Canadian International Development
Agency 343
Canadian Research Institute for Social
Policy 87, 121
Capacity building 14, 140, 214–215,
284, 298, 303–304, 306, 336, 346,
348
Caregivers 43, 50, 148, 154, 159,
173, 178–180, 186–187, 191–192,
196, 228, 234–236, 241–242,
245–246, 249–251, 253, 258, 267,
276, 294, 296, 299, 308, 318, 324,
342, 349, 351, 355
Caribbean x, 121, 239, 290, 332–333,
336
Carolina project. See Abecedarian
project

Case studies, community programs
  13, 216, 293–294, 307–308, 358
Catalyst for change 15, 372
Center-based childcare 151–157, 172,
  173–188
Central and Eastern Europe 14, 296,
  348–350, 353
Childcare 10, 12, 15–16, 30, 55, 67,
  73, 123, 136, 145, 258–259
Child-centered approach 14, 298,
  356, 358
Childhood vulnerability 83, 87,
  104–106, 108–109, 111
Children at risk. *See also* Vulnerable
  children 84, 135, 367
Children's Resources International
  (CRI) 349, 351–352, 360
Child–staff ratio 10, 148, 151–152,
  160, 164, 173, 191
Chile 5, 82, 91–93, 95, 113, 121,
  284, 290, 292, 364, 374
Christian Children's Fund xi, 287
Civil society(ies) ix, xi, 85, 199, 349,
  351, 356, 366, 386
Classroom dynamics 10, 147–148,
  151–153, 160–161, 165
Classroom quality 226, 230, 172,
  174, 176–183, 185, 187
Classroom structure 10, 147–148, 160
Cognitive development 19, 39, 47,
  53, 63, 72–73, 125, 127–128, 142,
  152–154, 158, 168, 173, 311, 323
Collective involvement 286–287
Colombia 82, 91–93, 113, 200, 210,
  218, 276, 282–283, 286, 288, 384,
  386
Community 10, 13–14, 51, 86,
  88–89, 115–116, 121, 130, 137,
  150, 162, 195, 197, 199–201, 205,
  207, 209–210, 222–223, 234–238,
  241–242, 244, 246–247, 249–253,
  258, 262–263, 266–270, 274, 282,
  284–286, 293–298, 300–307, 309,
  312, 314, 316, 320, 322–324, 326,
  328, 332–333, 337–348, 350–351,

353, 355–356, 359, 365, 367, 371,
  375, 378, 382, 386
Community-based Family Education,
  Philippines 200
Community-based (programs) 14, 51,
  130, 199–200, 234, 236, 244, 246,
  249–252, 268, 293, 306, 309, 314,
  316, 323, 326, 328, 337, 340,
  347–348, 365, 367, 375, 386
Community-based Rehabilitation
  Program, Jamaica. *See also*
  Dedicated to the Development
  of the Disabled (3D) Organization,
  Jamaica 234, 236–237
Community development 14, 197,
  263, 306, 339, 341, 346
Community involvement 253, 296,
  300–302, 307, 314, 351
Community mobilization 300, 307,
  340, 345
Community ownership 14, 298,
  300–302, 345
Community services 222, 223, 378
Community support 294, 305–306,
  386
Companies, involvement in early
  childhood development 139, 257,
  260–261, 264, 280–283, 285–287,
  329–330
Complementary approaches,
  programs, strategies 253, 263,
  284, 304–305, 369
Comprehensive approaches, programs,
  strategies 10, 74, 129, 137, 196,
  253, 348, 367–368, 371, 379, 385
Consultative Group on Early Child-
  hood Care and Development xii,
  195–197, 217–218
Continuity 10, 147–150, 210, 245
Convention on the Rights of the Child
  (CRC) 234, 252, 259, 377
Corticotropin-releasing hormone
  (CRH) 27–31, 33–34, 38, 43
Costa Rica 82–83, 285
Cost-effectiveness 13, 68, 273–275

Cuba 45, 82, 91–93, 94–95, 100, 112–113, 117, 268, 277, 379

Cultural sustainability 212, 214, 294, 302, 305, 317, 365–366, 378, 382, 385

Cycle of poverty. *See also* Intergenerational poverty v, 2, 12, 14, 233, 252, 365–367

D

Dedicated to the Development of the Disabled (3D) Organization, Jamaica. *See also* Community-based Rehabilitation Program, Jamaica 236–237, 239–242, 244–251

Definitions, early child development 257–259

Development and Peace, Canada 331

Development economics 9, 64–66

Dimensions of quality. *See also* Elements of quality, Quality 151–154, 157–158

Dominican Republic 82, 91–93, 113

E

Early childhood care and education (ECCE) 291, 295, 297, 305–306, 328, 331–336

Early Development Index 51

Early Head Start program, U.S. 6, 14, 369–370, 372

East Africa xi, 296, 336–337, 342

Economic benefits. *See also* Benefits 52, 197, 260, 373

Economic development v, vi, 86, 304, 337, 376, 379–380

Economic productivity 197, 260, 321

Economic returns. *See also* Return(s) to (on) investment 1, 251

Education for All 2, 81, 268, 278, 291

Education pathway 9, 63–64, 66–67, 72–74

Effective childcare and education 10, 145–193

Effectiveness Initiative 11, 195, 197–218

Effective programming 11, 195–218

Elements of quality. *See also* Dimensions of quality, Quality 12, 157, 162, 233–253

Embedded communications, model 209–213

Empowerment 199, 210, 241, 296, 300, 304, 323, 326, 328, 350, 386

Environmental effects 8, 35–38

Equality. *See also* Inequality 2, 9, 52, 63–64, 71–74, 85, 94, 138, 205, 305, 317

Equity 2, 13, 52, 260, 262, 278–279, 291, 296, 348–350, 353

Europe x, 14, 261–262, 291, 296, 348–350, 353

European Commission 337, 343

Evaluation 1, 10–12, 17, 53, 123, 161–167, 196, 200, 217–218, 231, 246, 250–251, 268, 276, 278, 290–291, 312, 315–316, 322, 330, 341, 346–347, 356–357, 386

Examples of good practice 293, 298

Expenditures for early childhood education, Brazil 131–132

Experimental designs 163–165

F

Family and Child Experiences Survey (FACES), Head Start program, U.S. 11–12, 219, 224–231

Family background 88, 95, 104–105, 107–108, 110–111, 113, 117, 156, 163, 169, 178–180, 192

Family-based childcare 10, 157–161, 189–193

Family involvement 296, 348, 351

Family support 14, 16, 126, 139, 222, 235, 238–239, 249, 298–300

Features of a successful program. *See also* Principles of success 14, 298–308

Financial sustainability 14, 298,
302–303, 307, 339–340, 342, 346,
354–355
Financing, of early child development
136, 199, 261, 267–268, 272–274,
288, 291, 296, 313–314, 350, 385,
391
Flexibility, of programs 214, 238,
241–242, 248, 271, 346, 371, 387
Florida Child Care Quality Improvement study 152, 169
Fogel, R.W. 3, 24–25, 65–66
Ford Foundation 82, 337, 343
Formal programs 12, 130, 136, 252
Former Soviet Union 14, 296,
349–350, 353
For-profit organizations 130,
267–269, 284, 300, 386
Foundation support 14, 195, 198,
235, 283–284, 295, 297, 303, 305,
332, 336–337, 343–345, 349,
353–355, 376, 388
Future earning capacity 10, 124,
132–135

G

Gene-environment interactions 4, 8,
32, 33–34
Genetics 24, 35
German Development Service 313
Germany 19, 309, 313, 316, 331, 358
Ghana 376
Global coalition, for ECD initiatives
15, 17, 388–389
Goals for international development
2
Going to scale. *See also* Taking the
programs to scale 315–316, 335,
375
Government, role and support. *See
also* National government, role of
14–15, 16–17, 46, 49, 51, 72, 130,
138, 198, 200, 207, 209, 215, 234–
236, 242, 246–248, 250–251, 260,
262–263, 265–268, 270, 272–273,

278, 281, 283, 285, 288–289, 295–
296, 300, 303, 306, 313, 317–318,
326, 330, 332–334, 337, 343, 351,
366–368, 369–373, 378–379,
382–390
Great Britain 24
Guatemala 286, 346

H

Haiti xi, 14, 294, 296, 300, 308–316,
348–350, 354
Head Start program, U.S. 6, 14,
219–226, 229–331, 367–373, 386
Health and well-being 25, 85–86, 320
Health pathway 9, 64, 67–70, 72–74
Health status 68–69, 86, 320
Helvetas, Switzerland 331
High/Scope Study, U.S. *See also* Perry
Preschool Project (study), U.S. 41,
54, 60, 78, 142, 161, 172, 200,
290–291, 340, 360
Hippocampus 27–28, 31–33, 58
Historical evidence, for prosperity,
health, and child development 8,
24–26
Home-based program(s) 12–13, 197,
233, 235–236, 386
Home visiting models 234–253
Home visiting program(s) 233–253
Honduras 82, 91–93, 113, 201
Human development ix, x, 9, 23, 25,
51–52, 56, 61, 63–78, 84, 116, 118,
142, 171, 290, 324–325, 363, 375,
387
Human potential 15, 363, 376–377
Hypothalamus-pituitary-adrenal (HPA)
pathway 4–5, 26, 27–29, 31,
33–34, 38, 43

I

Immune system, effects 26, 29, 34–35
Improving Pre- and Primary Education
(IPPS), Pakistan 14, 295–297,
302–304, 306, 338–348

India   x, 6, 18, 42, 199, 262, 337

Indicators of effectiveness   196

Individual involvement in ECD efforts   266–267, 271–274, 282, 287–290, 300–302

Inefficiencies, in society   382–383

Inequality. *See also* Equality   3, 10, 19, 61, 64, 75, 77–78, 86, 120–122, 363

Infant Health and Development Program (IHDP)   6, 125–128, 142

Initial Education Project, Mexico   6

In-kind assistance, contribution   248, 270, 285, 301–302, 307, 314, 345

Institute of Applied Economic Research (IPEA)   10, 18, 75, 132, 135, 140–141

Institutionalization   12, 238, 246–247, 251

Integrated approach, programs, services   63, 235, 295, 304, 316, 318, 326, 371, 379

Integrated Child Development Service (ICDS), India   6, 18, 262

Inter-American Development Bank (IDB)   xi, 18, 82, 197, 330, 334, 364, 366, 374

Inter-American Foundation   331–332

Intergenerational poverty   v, 14, 17, 252, 363–365, 369

International Adult Literacy Study (IALS)   94, 116

International Monetary Fund   384

International Step by Step Association (ISSA)   349, 359

Investing in early child development   v, 52, 363, 367, 373, 375–376, 378, 380, 387–388

Ireland   336

Israel   199

J

Jamaica, and government of   12, 39, 56, 76, 233–253

K

Kenya   14, 78, 199, 295, 336, 338, 340–342

Korea   43, 57

L

Laboratorio Latinoamericano de Evaluación de la Calidad de la Educación   82, 118

Language, development of. *See also* Literacy, Verbal skills   3, 11, 31, 44, 51, 60, 82, 90–91 95–96, 100–101, 125, 153–155, 158–160, 168, 170–171, 221, 224, 230, 236, 364, 368

Latin America   x, 9, 45, 81–122, 201, 214, 262, 277, 290, 363–365

Lessons from research   10, 145–193

Lessons learned, to maximize investments in ECD   7, 15, 369–373

Level playing field   2, 16, 71

Lewis, W.A.   65

Literacy. *See also* Language, Verbal skills   3–4, 19, 31, 44–50, 59, 61, 81, 85, 94, 116, 121, 124, 130, 139, 221, 223–224, 226, 240, 244, 250, 295, 304, 316–317, 320, 323–324, 329, 346, 364, 368

Longitudinal designs   151, 163–165, 182–185, 193

Longitudinal studies   3, 24, 35–36, 38–39, 251

M

Madrasa Resource Center (MRC), Kenya, Uganda, Zanzibar   14, 199, 295–297, 302–304, 306, 337–348

Madres Guias, Honduras   201

Malnourished Children's Program, Jamaica   234, 237–238, 240–247, 249–251

Mathematical ability (performance), mathematics   3–4, 18, 41–42, 48, 54, 90, 92, 95, 97, 101, 104, 117

Measuring the early opportunity gap
8, 9, 79–142
Mexico 6, 82, 91–93, 113, 125, 218,
272, 283
Microphilanthropy 287–288, 290
Mongolia 14, 296, 348, 350, 354
Montessori Preschool Project, Haiti
14, 294, 297, 300, 302–303, 305,
309–316
Moral purpose 373
Moral values 259
Mother-Child Day Care Center Ser-
vices (MCDCCS), Uganda 14,
294–295, 297, 299, 303–305,
316–324, 358
Mozambique 199, 337

N

Namibia 376
Narrowing the gap for poor children
7, 14, 363–374, 383
National Day Care Study, U.S. 151,
171
National Education Plan, Brazil
137–138
National government, role of. *See also*
Government, role and support
209, 252, 276, 321
National Institute for Educational
Research, Brazil 116
National Longitudinal Survey of Chil-
dren and Youth, Canada 46–47
Netherlands 201, 331
New Zealand 386
Nonexperimental designs 163, 165
Nonformal program(s) 130, 136, 139,
200, 235, 295, 300, 306, 316,
323–324, 331, 333, 337, 346
Nongovernmental organizations
(NGOs) v, ix, xi, 8, 13, 139, 200,
209, 260, 266–267, 270, 284, 288,
295, 316, 324, 351–352, 356, 366,
376
Not-for-profit organizations 268–269,
284, 300, 386

O

Ontario xi, 19, 46–52, 58, 77
Open Society Institute 349, 359–360
Organization for Economic Cooperation and Development (OECD)
44, 59, 120–121
Orphanages, children in 43
Outcomes 3, 8–12, 25, 42–43, 45, 49,
68, 70, 72, 75, 78, 81–122, 125,
127, 141–142, 147, 149, 151–166,
168, 172–195, 197, 204, 206–207,
209, 216, 219, 222, 224, 226, 230,
233, 238, 265, 275–276, 300, 308,
316, 357
Outcome standard(s) 101–102

P

Pakistan 14, 116, 295, 337–338, 342,
344
Paraguay 82, 91–93, 113, 285
Parental involvement 14, 83, 99,
101–104, 106–109, 112–113, 252,
298–300, 307, 353, 355, 368, 371
Partners for Learning 125, 142
Partnerships 7, 10, 13, 17, 136, 138,
150, 247, 252, 284, 293–294,
297–298, 300, 305–306, 354–355
Pathways, to human development 9,
63–78
Perry Preschool Project (study), U.S.
See also High/Scope Study, U.S. 6,
60, 78, 125, 128–129, 142, 160, 172
Peru 82–83, 91–93, 200, 214, 373
Peter-Hesse Foundation 309, 312,
315, 358
Philanthropy(ies) 13, 266, 270, 282,
283–284, 287–288, 290, 343
Philippines 200, 214, 376
Plan International 287
Play materials 236, 238, 243–244,
250
Policies for action 383–389
Political challenge 15, 375–391
Portugal 201

Poverty   v, vi, 1–2, 10, 12, 14–18, 35, 44, 54, 66, 73–75, 77, 84, 86, 124, 129, 139, 158, 233–234, 236, 244, 247, 252, 305, 317, 320, 322–323, 325–328, 348, 363–366, 368–369, 374, 376, 378, 382, 385

Pre-post design   11, 151–153, 163–165, 178, 186, 192

Preschool interventions, education, effects of   10, 124–129

Primer Estudio Internacional Comparativo (PEIC)   9, 82–83, 89–90, 94, 99–102, 114–117

Principles of success. *See also* Features of a successful program   314–315, 323, 334–335, 345–346, 355–356

Private sector, definitions and dimensions   265–270

Private sector, role of   x-xi, 7–8, 13–14, 17, 49, 53, 110, 130, 138, 255, 257–292, 293, 296–297, 307, 315, 366, 376

Private citizens, involvement in early child development   287–288

Private-public partnership. *See also* Public-private partnership   13–14, 17, 293, 298, 305–307, 331, 355

Private versus public care and education   13, 257, 272

Private voluntary organizations (PVOs)   13, 266, 300

Privatization   262, 266–267, 269–270, 272, 288–291

Program efficacy   260

Program of Indicators of Student Achievement (PISA) study   95

Program performance measures, Head Start program, U.S.   11, 219–225, 230–231

Programa No-formal de Educación Inicial (PRONOEI), Peru   200

Proyecto de Mejoramiento Educativo, de Salud y del Ambiente (PROMESA), Colombia   200, 209–210

Public-private partnership. *See also* Private-public partnership   7, 13, 136, 138

Q

Qualitative research tools, strategies   11, 195, 198, 204–217

Quality   3–5, 8, 10–13, 15–16, 19, 23, 25, 30, 43, 46, 48–52, 55, 61, 66, 81, 85–86, 94, 99, 106, 112, 117, 120–122, 136–138, 145–195, 205, 220, 222, 225–226, 229–231, 233–253, 263, 271, 273, 276–280, 289–290, 293–295, 300–301, 303, 305, 309, 313, 315–318, 321–322, 324–325, 328, 333, 335–337, 340–344, 346–348, 353, 363, 365, 368–373, 386

Quality in Family Child Care and Relative Care study   158–159

R

Rahimtullah Trust   343

Relative risk(s)   100–101, 107–109

Research and evaluation   161–162, 166, 231, 347

Resources   v, vi, 2, 11, 13–15, 17, 57, 76–77, 82, 85, 88, 99, 103, 105, 107–108, 110–115, 117–121, 132, 138–139, 146, 159, 162, 201, 206, 217, 224, 229, 233, 244, 251, 253, 263–265, 267, 273–274, 280, 284, 290, 294, 299–303, 307–309, 314, 326, 335, 345, 349, 360, 366, 369, 372, 377–378, 383, 385, 387, 389–390

Return(s) to (on) investment, *See also* Economic returns   77, 124–125, 129, 134–135

Right Start, U.S.   41–42

Roma children   357

Romania   43, 53, 59, 354, 356

Roving Caregivers Program (RCP), Jamaica   234–236, 239, 241–251

Rural Family Support Organization (RuFamSo), Jamaica 235, 249

S

Samenspel, Netherlands 201
Save the Children xii, 199, 287, 331
School policy and practice 99, 105–107, 110–114, 118, 105
School profiles 83, 89–90, 95–99
School resources 99, 105–107, 110–114, 118
Schultz, T.W. 65
Scientific evidence, of links between early child development and human development 3–5, 66–68
Self-Employed Women's Association, India 199
Self-regulation, of behavior 155–156, 176, 183
Sen, A. 63, 66, 78, 363, 374
Sensory pathways 26, 29–31
Serotonin 34, 54
Service Volunteered for All (SERVOL), Trinidad and Tobago x, xi, 14, 295, 297, 299, 302–306, 324–336, 358–359
Social capital 9, 12, 52, 64, 70–74, 76–78, 86, 119, 121, 234, 379
Social class 4, 36–39, 45–46, 85, 175
Social cohesion 73, 85–86, 120
Social competence 12, 70, 73, 169–170, 184–185, 220, 222
Social equity. *See also* Equity 260
Social policy xi, 85–87, 89, 121
Social trust fund 282, 284, 290
Social values 73, 259
Societal (social) benefits, effects. *See also* Benefits 2, 15, 67, 70–75, 259–261, 289, 367, 375–378, 381–383
Socioeconomic gradients 9, 18, 47, 54, 83–95, 114–115
Socioeconomic status (SES) 35–36, 39, 44–48, 55, 58, 82–84, 86–88, 94, 99, 120, 129, 149, 157, 159, 176, 179, 180, 186

Soros, George xi, 349, 353, 359
South Africa 14, 296, 336, 348–350, 354
South Asia 336
Staff characteristics 10, 147–151, 153
Staff retention 238, 244, 250
Stages of (brain) development 29, 31–32
Stakeholders 15, 195, 198, 202, 205–208, 211, 214–215, 247–248, 252, 307, 346, 355, 382–386, 388
Standards for superior schooling 102–104
Standards of care 9, 81–122
State Children's Health Insurance Program, U.S. 372
Step by Step program 14, 296–297, 302–304, 306, 348–360
Steroid receptors 27
Stress 3–5, 26, 34, 37, 43, 55–56, 58, 60, 65, 150, 162, 167–168, 178, 182, 188, 199, 232, 260, 327
Supports 10, 26, 36, 51, 134, 145, 149–151, 160, 166, 232, 238–239, 242, 247, 249, 252, 295, 298, 313, 319, 337, 348, 356, 366, 381
Sustainability. *See also* Cultural sustainability, Financial sustainability 13–14, 210, 238, 242, 247–248, 251–252, 286, 297–298, 300, 302–303, 307, 312, 323, 331, 339–340, 342, 344, 346, 348, 351, 353–355, 359, 380
Sweden 38, 94, 283
Swedish International Development Cooperation Agency (SIDA) 322
Syracuse Family Development Research Program 161

T

Tajikistan 337
Taking the programs to scale. *See also* Going to scale 7, 13–14, 246, 293
Tanzania 77, 337
Taxes, earmarked for social programs 252–253, 385

Teacher-child interactions   147–149, 152, 160

Teacher's qualifications   153

Teacher training. *See also* Training   15, 103, 105, 107–108, 294, 297, 305, 309, 313, 315, 333, 346, 351, 353, 358

Technology, role of   288, 324, 330, 365

Teenage Mothers Project, Jamaica   235, 249

Third International Mathematics and Science Study (TIMSS)   116

Tinbergen, Jan   64–65

Training   vii, 10, 12, 14–15, 67, 103, 105, 107–108, 112–113, 116, 130, 137, 147, 149–150, 153, 157, 159–160, 168, 181, 186, 188, 192, 196, 199–201, 206, 220, 223, 231, 235–237, 239–240, 243–246, 248–251, 266, 281, 284, 294–298, 302–305, 309, 311–312, 314–315, 317, 322, 324, 329, 331–335, 338–342, 346–335, 358, 365–366, 368, 370, 386

Trinidad and Tobago   xi, 14, 295, 324–325, 327–328, 330–336, 359

Tropical Medicine Research Institute (TMRI), Jamaica   237–238, 243

Turkey   125, 201

2020 Commitment   388

U

Uganda   14, 199, 294–295, 303, 316–318, 321, 323–324, 336, 338, 341–343, 358

United Fund, U.S.   281

United Kingdom   25, 38–39, 55

United Nations Children's Fund (UNICEF)   xi, 67–68, 76, 235, 245, 251, 259, 285–286, 291–292, 374, 376, 382, 390–391

United Nations Development Programme (UNDP)   63, 313

United Nations Educational, Scientific, and Cultural Organization (UNESCO)   xi, 82, 90, 117–118, 121, 290–291, 322

United States   6, 10, 40–42, 44–45, 54, 120–121, 124, 145, 166, 219, 262, 268, 281, 283, 285, 331, 337, 349, 367–368, 370, 372, 374, 383

Universal Declaration on Human Rights   377

University Hospital of the West Indies   237

U.S. Agency for International Development (USAID)   xi, 344, 356–357, 360

U.S. National Education Goals Panel   221, 232

V

Venezuela, Républica Bolivariana de   82, 91–93, 113

Verbal skills. *See also* Language, Literacy   38, 44, 46

Vulnerable children. *See also* Children at risk   9–10, 110–111, 121, 124–129, 298, 365

W

West Africa   347

White House Conference on Early Childhood Development and Learning, U.S.   370

Willingness to pay   135–136

Women's multiple roles   238, 240, 249

World Bank   v, vii, ix–x, 1, 7, 10, 18–19, 42, 44, 52–53, 60–61, 68, 77–78, 82, 85, 116, 118, 130–132, 135, 140–142, 197, 292, 337, 343,359–360, 366, 372–373, 376, 380, 382, 384, 390–391

World Conference on Education for All   81

World Health Organization (WHO)
xi, 67, 69, 78, 286, 382, 384
World Vision   xii, 287

Y

Year 2000 Evaluation of Education for
All   268, 278, 291

Z

Zanzibar   199, 295, 338, 341–343